Water Brings No Harm

NEW AFRICAN HISTORIES

SERIES EDITORS: JEAN ALLMAN, ALLEN ISAACMAN,
AND DEREK R. PETERSON

David William Cohen and E. S. Atieno Odhiambo, *The Risks of Knowledge*

Belinda Bozzoli, *Theatres of Struggle and the End of Apartheid*

Gary Kynoch, *We Are Fighting the World*

Stephanie Newell, *The Forger's Tale*

Jacob A. Tropp, *Natures of Colonial Change*

Jan Bender Shetler, *Imagining Serengeti*

Cheikh Anta Babou, *Fighting the Greater Jihad*

Marc Epprecht, *Heterosexual Africa?*

Marissa J. Moorman, *Intonations*

Karen E. Flint, *Healing Traditions*

Derek R. Peterson and Giacomo Macola, editors, *Recasting the Past*

Moses E. Ochonu, *Colonial Meltdown*

Emily S. Burrill, Richard L. Roberts, and Elizabeth Thornberry, editors, *Domestic Violence and the Law in Colonial and Postcolonial Africa*

Daniel R. Magaziner, *The Law and the Prophets*

Emily Lynn Osborn, *Our New Husbands Are Here*

Robert Trent Vinson, *The Americans Are Coming!*

James R. Brennan, *Taifa*

Benjamin N. Lawrance and Richard L. Roberts, editors, *Trafficking in Slavery's Wake*

David M. Gordon, *Invisible Agents*

Allen F. Isaacman and Barbara S. Isaacman, *Dams, Displacement, and the Delusion of Development*

Stephanie Newell, *The Power to Name*

Gibril R. Cole, *The Krio of West Africa*

Matthew M. Heaton, *Black Skin, White Coats*

Meredith Terretta, *Nation of Outlaws, State of Violence*

Paolo Israel, *In Step with the Times*

Michelle R. Moyd, *Violent Intermediaries*

Abosede A. George, *Making Modern Girls*

Alicia C. Decker, *In Idi Amin's Shadow*

Rachel Jean-Baptiste, *Conjugal Rights*

Shobana Shankar, *Who Shall Enter Paradise?*

Emily S. Burrill, *States of Marriage*

Todd Cleveland, *Diamonds in the Rough*

Carina E. Ray, *Crossing the Color Line*

Sarah Van Beurden, *Authentically African*

Giacomo Macola, *The Gun in Central Africa*

Lynn Schler, *Nation on Board*

Julie MacArthur, *Cartography and the Political Imagination*

Abou B. Bamba, *African Miracle, African Mirage*

Daniel Magaziner, *The Art of Life in South Africa*

Paul Ocobock, *An Uncertain Age*

Keren Weitzberg, *We Do Not Have Borders*

Nuno Domingos, *Football and Colonialism*

Jeffrey S. Ahlman, *Living with Nkrumahism*

Bianca Murillo, *Market Encounters*

Laura Fair, *Reel Pleasures*

Thomas F. McDow, *Buying Time*

Jon Soske, *Internal Frontiers*

Elizabeth W. Giorgis, *Modernist Art in Ethiopia*

Matthew V. Bender, *Water Brings No Harm*

David Morton: *Age of Concrete*

Marissa J. Moorman, *Powerful Frequencies*

Water Brings No Harm

*Management Knowledge and the Struggle
for the Waters of Kilimanjaro*

Matthew V. Bender

OHIO UNIVERSITY PRESS ꙮ ATHENS, OHIO

Ohio University Press, Athens, Ohio 45701
ohioswallow.com
© 2019 by Ohio University Press
All rights reserved

Printed in the United States of America
Ohio University Press books are printed on acid-free paper ∞ ™

29 28 27 26 25 24 23 22 21 20 19 5 4 3 2 1

Library of Congress Cataloging-in-Publication Data

Names: Bender, Matthew V., author.
Title: Water brings no harm : management knowledge and the struggle for
  the waters of Kilimanjaro / Matthew V. Bender.
Other titles: New African histories series.
Description: Athens, Ohio : Ohio University Press, 2019. | Series: New
  African histories
Identifiers: LCCN 2018056337| ISBN 9780821423585 (hc : alk. paper) |
  ISBN 9780821423592 (pb : alk. paper) | ISBN 9780821446782 (pdf)
Subjects: LCSH: Water-supply—Tanzania—Kilimanjaro, Mount—
  Management. | Water security—Tanzania–Kilimanjaro, Mount. | Chaga
  (African people)—Tanzania.
Classification: LCC HD1699.T34 K553 2018 | DDC 333.91150967826—dc23
LC record available at https://lccn.loc.gov/2018056337

For my grandparents,
Helen and Benjamin Bender
and Frances and Clem Farny

Contents

Illustrations

TABLES

Acknowledgments

This book has been a long time in the making, and the thanks I owe are many. First and foremost, I thank my mentors at Johns Hopkins University, where I spent several formative years as a graduate student. Sara Berry is my greatest role model as a scholar. Her courses inspired this project, but her encouragement and compassion inspired me as a person. I cannot thank her enough for her insight and mentorship—and for encouraging me to push the boundaries of my thinking. I owe a debt to Pier Larson, who is among the most generous people I know and who inspired me to think more deeply about the connections between environment and culture. At Hopkins, I was fortunate to be part of a great community of scholars. I am grateful to Randall Packard, Jane Guyer, and Ronald Walters for their support of my work, and I am also grateful to the numerous participants in the Africa Seminar including Claire Breedlove, Kelly Duke-Bryant, Walima Kalusa, Otis Mushonga, Emily Osborn, and Elizabeth Schmidt.

My interest in Africa began while I was an undergraduate at Washington University in Saint Louis. I am thankful to Timothy Parsons, for introducing me to African history, and to Richard Davis and Mungai Mutonya for their mentorship. The late James McLeod, dean of the School of Arts and Sciences, supported my burgeoning interest by buying me my first plane ticket to Africa. One of my greatest regrets is that I never got to express my gratitude to him in person.

This book is based on research that took place on the slopes of Kilimanjaro and in the archives and libraries of Dar es Salaam. I am grateful to the Tanzania Commission of Science and Technology (COSTECH) for granting me permission to conduct my fieldwork. The archivists at the Tanzania National Archives and the librarians at the University of Dar es Salaam's East Africana Collection helped me navigate the wealth of material in their collections. I am especially grateful to the history faculty at the university—Isaria Kimambo, Fred Kaijage, Oswald Masebo, and Yusufu Lawi—for lending their support, expertise, and encouragement to my work.

My research took me beyond Tanzania as well. I would like to thank the archivists and staff at the National Archives (Kew), the Rhodes House Library, and the Oxfam Archives in the UK; the Congrégation du Saint-Esprit Archives in Chevilly-Larue, France; and the Deutsches Historisches Museum in Berlin. I also thank the library staff at Johns Hopkins University, Yale University, and The College of New Jersey for helping me locate materials from around the world.

Numerous organizations have provided funding to my work over the years. I thank the Fulbright-Hays Program and the Boren Fellowship programs for supporting my early fieldwork, as well as the Department of History and the Institute for Global Studies at Johns Hopkins. I had the privilege of spending a year as an Agrarian Studies Fellow at Yale University, under the mentorship of James Scott and Shivi Sivarama-krishnan. Much of this manuscript was written in my time there, and I cannot thank them enough for their skillful guidance. My fellow Agrarian Studies colleagues—Rishab Dhir, Todd Holmes, Janam Mukherjee, Juno Parrenas, and Gabe Rosenberg—lent support and wisdom.

Several communities of scholars have given me a home over the years. My fellow scholars in African studies and Tanzania studies have been a resource as well as an inspiration to me. Special thanks go to Jamie Monson, Jan Shetler, Greg Maddox, and Sheryl McCurdy, who have supported me since my earliest days of fieldwork. I also thank Jesse Bucher, Barbara Cooper, Steven Fabian, James McCann, Wendy Urban-Mead, Fran Vavrus, and Julie Weiskopf, as well as the many others who have attended conference panels and engaged my work. I am part of a growing community of scholars focused on water history, and these individuals have helped me think more critically about water and gain a perspective that extends beyond Africa. I am grateful to Ellen Arnold, Maurits Ertsen, Heather Hoag, Johann Tempelhoff, Terje Tvedt, Terje Oestigaard, Maya Peterson, and many others.

I am fortunate to work at The College of New Jersey, an institution that supports the research passions of its teacher-scholars. I have received financial support from the School of Humanities and Social Sciences, the Support of Scholarly Activity program, and the Gitenstein-Hart Sabbatical Prize. The Mentored Undergraduate

Summer Experience has helped fund undergraduate research collaborators. I thank those in the administration who have supported me, including R. Barbara Gitenstein, Jackie Taylor, Susan Albertine, Ben Rifkin, and Jane Wong. My faculty colleagues have supported me over the years and have contributed to my scholarship in more ways than I can count. I give special thanks to Maggie Benoit, Lynn Gazley, Marla Jaksch, Mindi McMann, Janet Morrison, David Murray, and Amanda Norvell as well as my colleagues in the History Department, particularly Dan Crofts, Celia Chazelle, Chris Fisher, Jo-Ann Gross, Laura Hargreaves, Craig Hollander, Adam Knobler, and Robert McGreevey. Above all, I thank Cynthia Paces, my friend, mentor, and avid proofreader. The College of New Jersey prides itself on student-faculty collaborative research, and my work is all the better for it. I am grateful to all the students who have engaged with my work, particularly those who served as collaborators: Katerina Buchanan, Beatrice Kwok, Taylor Hart-McGonigle, Ryan McClean, Corinne Winters, and Tamra Wroblesky.

Ohio University Press has been an excellent partner in bringing my book to fruition. I am thankful to Gillian Berchowitz for her encouragement and support and to the editors of the New African Histories series—Jean Allman, Allen Isaacman, Derek Peterson—for their careful and caring engagement with my work. Two anonymous readers carefully read my manuscript and provided a wealth of comments. Special thanks go to Nancy Basmajian and Sally Welch, who expertly guided me through editing and production and provided me with excellent advice. Ricky Huard, Samara Rafert, and Beth Pratt helped me with questions related to images, copyrights, and marketing. I thank Alice White and Robert Kern at TIPS Technical Publishing for their help with copyediting and typesetting. Brian Balsley did a skillful job of generating the maps. Alice White also lent her expertise in creating the index.

This book includes excerpts from some of my previously published works: "'For More and Better Water, Choose Pipes!': Building Water and the Nation on Kilimanjaro, 1961–1985," *Journal of Southern African Studies* 34, no. 4 (2008): 841–59; "Millet Is Gone! Considering the Demise of Eleusine Agriculture on Kilimanjaro," *International Journal of African Historical Studies* 44, no. 2 (2011): 191–214; and "Being 'Chagga': Natural Resources, Political Activism, and Identity on Kilimanjaro," *Journal of African History* 54, no. 2 (2013): 199–220. I am thankful to the publishers for their permission to include this material.

My greatest thanks go to the peoples of Kilimanjaro, who shared their stories and memories and welcomed me into their communities. My work would not have been possible without their contributions and encouragement. I thank Efraim Muro for introducing me to the mountain and making me feel at home in Machame. Joachim Mkenda and Monica Lasway assisted me in Mkuu Rombo. Father Aidan Msafiri introduced me to Kilema and challenged me to think deeply about the role of water in everyday life. I am most grateful to Aristarck Stanley Nguma, my research assistant in Kilema and someone I am proud to call a friend.

Lastly, this book would not have been possible without the love and support of my family and friends. I would be nowhere without my mother, Betsy Flynn, my greatest supporter and inspiration. I am grateful to my stepfather, father, sisters, brothers-in-law, and my numerous nieces, nephews, and godchildren. Your belief in me means more than you know. Thanks to my good friends Sarah and Joe Adelman and John and Linda Jusiewicz for their support over the years. Chris Josey has been my best friend and confidante for more than twenty-five years. Thanks to Doc for the afternoon hikes at Baldpate.

I dedicate this book to the memory of my grandparents: Frances and Clem Farny and Benjamin and Helen Bender.

Abbreviations

CMS	Church Missionary Society
DOAG	Deutsch-Ostafrikanische Gesellschaft (German East Africa Company)
IMF	International Monetary Fund
IWRM	Integrated Water Resources Management
KCCU	Kilimanjaro Chagga Citizens Union
KNCU	Kilimanjaro Native Cooperative Union
KNPA	Kilimanjaro Native Planters Association
MAJI	Ministry of Water [Tanzania]
NGO	nongovernmental organization
NWP	National Water Policy [Tanzania]
PBWO	Pangani Basin Water Office
TANESCO	Tanganyika/Tanzania Electric Supply Company
TANU	Tanganyika African National Union
UN	United Nations
WDD	Water Development Department [colonial]
WD&ID	Water Development and Irrigation Department
WUA	water user association

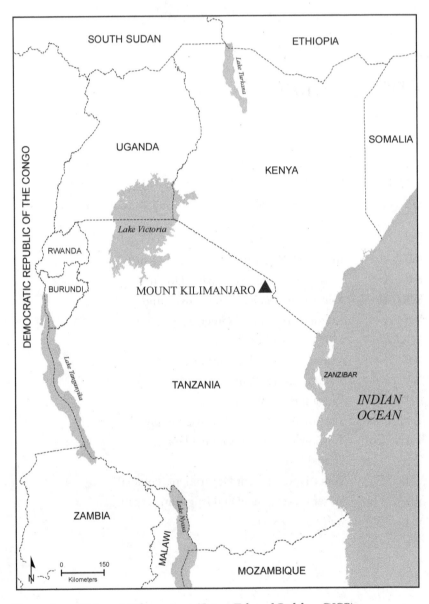

Tanzania and Mount Kilimanjaro (*Brian Edward Balsley, GISP*)

Introduction

IN JULY 1937, several prominent *wamangi* (chiefs) from Mount Kilimanjaro wrote the colonial governor of Tanganyika to express the most pressing problems facing the mountain.[1] The peoples of Kilimanjaro, known to the administration as the Chagga, had recently emerged as a success story, with a thriving economy based on coffee cultivation and a population that was eagerly investing in education, health, agriculture, and infrastructure. Yet these developments sparked their own challenges that the wamangi sought to address. Their memo focuses on two issues they see as crucial: land and water. "The Wachagga are mainly agriculturalists and such work is good and profitable to us all," they state, "but, for this, two things are necessary – room to cultivate and an adequate supply of water to our farms." They thank the government for providing "progressive agricultural methods" that allowed them to "progress beyond our own vision." To ensure future prosperity, they ask the government that their "soil be conserved and, moreso, our water supplies which are the blood in the veins of agriculture. Without water our farms will be as bodies without blood." They conclude by pleading with the government to "consider and apply the best methods of soil and water conservancy."

At first glance, these words seem straightforward. The memo identifies land and water as critical issues on the mountain, and it calls on the government to be more involved in ensuring access to both. A deeper reading of the source, however, indicates the wamangi's carefully constructed rhetorical strategy. While they extol the government for bringing progressive methods, their analogy of water and land as akin to blood and the body emphasizes the importance of irrigation, which the government had criticized for being harmful and wasteful. Further, neither the wamangi nor the colonial administration held effective control over water. Rather, local specialists closely guarded their power over the

1

mountain's rivers, streams, and *mifongo* (irrigation canals or furrows[2]) and vehemently denied attempts by others to engage in water issues. The words of the wamangi were an attempt to usurp power from the specialists by acquiescing to state control. What emerges from the memo is that water is more than a physical necessity for the peoples of the mountain. It is a resource with multiple layers of importance and meaning, and it is a focal point of struggle among competing groups.

Water is a fundamental building block of life, essential to the chemical and biological processes that make all living things possible. At the same time, it is among the most elusive of resources. This can be seen vividly in the steppe plateau of East Africa. Much of the semiarid region is unsuitable for crop agriculture or high-density populations and has historically been home to nomadic peoples such as the Maasai. In the midst of these plains, and in stark contrast to them, rise a number of mountain ranges and freestanding peaks, the most famous of which is Kilimanjaro. These highland areas feature dense forests and generate large amounts of precipitation. This rainfall gives rise to rivers and streams that reach far beyond the physical space of the peak. The combination of ample rainfall and cooler temperatures allows these montane areas to support sedentary living and larger populations.

While it is clear that water is vital for life and livelihood, the importance of water transcends its utility. Peoples in East Africa and elsewhere have long recognized the power of water to give life, and this is reflected in beliefs about human origin, religion, and spirituality. Therefore, water has become a crucial part of cultural practices and rituals including celebrations of birth, initiations into adulthood, and funerary rites. As a scarce resource vital to biological, spiritual, and community life, water has influenced the development of social institutions and power structures. Those who possess specialized knowledge of water management, such as how to produce rain or construct mifongo, wield power within their communities. In addition to its physical utility, water has long had powerful political and social dimensions, generating and sustaining relationships among people and defining and reinforcing hierarchies.

This book is about water. More pointedly, it is about how communities manage water and about the struggles that ensue when differing ideas regarding water management come into conflict. It focuses on the historical experiences of the mountain peoples of Kilimanjaro.

Since the 1850s, these communities have been influenced increasingly by outside groups that include Swahili traders; European explorers, missionaries, and settlers; German and British colonial officials; the independent Tanzanian state; development agencies; and climate scientists. This study explores how these actors have perceived the waters of Kilimanjaro and examines the struggles that transpired as they attempted to impose new forms of water management. In doing so it provides a powerful look at water as a social, cultural, and political construct and shows the multiplicity of ways in which struggles over the resource play out.

This book advances three main arguments. First, water management on Kilimanjaro has long been defined by distinct, interconnected bodies of knowledge: hydrological, technical, cultural, spiritual, and political. The peoples of the mountain depend on water to irrigate farms, form mud blocks, refresh livestock, cook food, brew ritual beer, clean homes, and bathe children. These waters came from a multiplicity of sources: rainfall, streams, springs, waterfalls, rivers, and mifongo. Each of these could vary in volume and clarity seasonally or year to year. Water also figured into numerous spiritual rites and cultural practices. The many uses of water, as well as the multiplicity of sources, meant that numerous people on the mountain possessed knowledge about how to manage it. Therefore, water management consisted of a diverse, dynamic set of practices that were inherently local and politically decentralized. Those who possessed expertise held positions of authority in their communities, and much of their knowledge was bound by social status, gender, and age. This meant that water knowledge shaped local politics as people with different expertise negotiated—and often competed—with one another over whose knowledge was most salient. Rival chiefdoms and clans even fought over control of watercourses, especially during droughts. Though specialists possessed a great deal of water knowledge, everyday users held expertise as well. Most men knew how to clean mifongo, and most women knew how to locate sources and use water for the home. Across Kilimanjaro, communities developed a shared sense of the value of water and its connection to the physical space of the mountain.

Second, water management became a focal point of conflict during the colonial period. The struggles that ensued can best be understood as a clash between conflicting knowledges of water. This did not occur initially, nor was it necessarily inevitable. For seventy years, Europeans considered Kilimanjaro (fig. I.1) to be a place of water abundance, and this led them to embrace local hydrological and technical expertise. This changed in the 1930s amid rising populations, skyrocketing demand, and fears of increasing aridity and soil erosion. In response, colonial actors began to criticize local knowledge as harmful, unscientific, primitive, wasteful, and prodigal. Rather than use overt coercion, they undermined local knowledge by introducing "modern" ideas and practices grounded in "scientific" management. Initially, colonial actors disseminated new water management through political and legal tools and educational efforts. Starting in the 1950s, they employed new technologies such as pipelines and dams. Since the rise of the independent Tanzanian state, the government and development agencies have used all three (political tools, educational efforts, and new technologies) to push for changes in water management, ostensibly to provide people with more and better water. These interventions have promoted two major shifts in thinking about the resource: toward a centralized, technocratic model of management and toward a commodified notion of water as something for which people should pay.

Lastly, this book argues that the peoples of Kilimanjaro have responded in ways that reflect the diversity and dynamism of water-management knowledge. Communities proved adept at negotiating new ideas and practices, allowing them to take advantage of new opportunities and react to new challenges. Yet the introduction of new technologies, along with changing economic and social realities, gradually eroded many aspects of local knowledge, reduced the roles of local experts, and made people dependent on government-controlled water resources. This fractured the interconnected nature of water knowledge, which in turn sped the decline of local control and the shared sense of responsibility. Today, people still believe that water is their divine right, but most are detached from its everyday management. This fracturing of water-management knowledge has led to a situation where many have poorer access to water than their parents or even their ancestors. Government actors have struggled to provide water both because they lack resources and because they pursue inconsistent and contradictory development strategies. They are also hindered by their lack of appreciation for the cultural dimensions of water, their contempt for traditional technologies and customary community-based water management, and their belief that commoditization is essential to building sustainable water systems. Though neoliberal reform speaks of integrating local communities in water management, it offers users little effective power. This neglect of local opinions and knowledge is especially evident in recent discussions over global climate change and its relationship to the recession of the mountain's glaciers.

FIGURE I.1. Kilimanjaro from Moshi Town (*Matthew V. Bender*)

WATER AND SOCIETY IN LITERATURE

In the past decade, water has emerged as a critical topic of study in the social sciences. Most published work has come from scholars and activists concerned with current or impending water scarcity.[3] Works in this genre tend to approach the topic similarly. For one, they almost exclusively discuss water in terms of its physical properties and its necessity for sustaining life, focusing on specific cases in which the available water supply is inadequate due to excessive use, lack of investment, pollution, global water trading, or political manipulation. They also emphasize conflict that will arise from competition over water, the impending "water wars." Many focus on the countries of the Global South that face the greatest challenges to accessing clean water. While such literature draws attention to rising scarcity in many parts of the world, it depicts water in limited terms: water's physical utility and the conflicts over access. Such studies detach water from cultural specificity, suggesting that most people think of water in essentially the same way. A notable exception is Vandana Shiva's *Water Wars*, which shows the spiritual and traditional role of water in communities in India, as well as the importance of culture in ensuring access to water.[4]

Historical scholarship that examines water in the context of social and political development actually predates this literature by decades. One of the earliest studies to examine this intersection was Karl Wittfogel's 1957 book *Oriental Despotism*.[5] In this work, Wittfogel sees the control of water, in particular large-scale irrigation works, as crucial to the rise of despotic power in Eastern societies such as dynastic China. Defining such societies as "hydraulic societies," he argues that the development of waterworks and the bureaucratic structures needed to maintain them was critical to the development of large bureaucracies and despotic state power. *Oriental Despotism* broke ground as one of the first works to analyze the relationship between water management and political power. As such, it has become required reading in the field of water history. The book has inspired fierce criticism from historians concerned with Wittfogel's Marxist interpretation of Asian history and from those who question the extent to which water was a critical factor in the rise of state power. Today, scholars consider the book as a piece that has raised important questions but whose conclusions no longer hold water.

In the years since *Oriental Despotism*, scholars have examined the relationship between water and power in various contexts. Their work has done much to extend the analysis beyond the physical, looking at how water control and management have intersected with broader social, cultural, and political issues. Donald Worster's *Rivers of Empire* examines the centrality of water control to the rise of the American West. In this arid region, the control of water resources by political actors, and its manipulation by engineers, led not only to radically transformed landscapes but also to the economic rise of the region.[6] Richard White's seminal work on the Columbia River, *The Organic Machine*, eloquently shows how human and natural history are intertwined, to the point where one cannot be understood without the other.[7] More recent works such as Paul Gelles's *Water and Power in Highland Peru*,

Stephen Lansing's *Priests and Programmers*, and David Mosse's *The Rule of Water* have gone further, looking at the intersection of politics and culture as related to irrigation works in Peru, Bali, and South India, respectively.[8]

Scholarship on water in African history has developed more slowly than scholarship on water in other regions, which is surprising given the continent's struggles with water scarcity. The continent has, however, been the focus of a wealth of scholarship in the fields of agricultural and environmental history, but while much of this work touches on water issues, it tends to focus on land spaces. James McCann's work on agriculture in Ethiopia, for example, discusses the importance of water by showing how farmers developed techniques specially adapted to the natural cycles of rainfall.[9] Rain is an important factor influencing farmers, but the core unit of analysis is the land. Likewise, the work of scholars of Tanzania such as Chris Conte, James Giblin, Isaria Kimambo, Helge Kjekshus, and Gregory Maddox has shown the importance of water in shaping patterns of settlement, agriculture, and disease control.[10] Scholarship that touches on water has extended beyond agriculture as well. Richard Grove's work has shown the influence of water in forming colonial island "Edens" that shaped early conservationist thinking.[11] Robert Harms's study of the Nunu shows how the Congo River shaped the lives of those living along its banks.[12] Steven Feierman's *Peasant Intellectuals* discusses rainmakers, along with other community intellectuals, in Shambaa society.[13] These works, and others on topics such as drought and boreholes, do not focus on water per se but rather on broader cultural, economic, and political issues that relate to water.[14] Though engaging, they discuss water in a way that obscures its dimensionality and uniqueness.

In recent years, studies have emerged that feature water more centrally. A good example is the scholarship on the development of African rivers. Heather Hoag's *Developing the Rivers of East and West Africa* examines the role of waterways in the continent's economic, social, and political development.[15] Hoag treats water as the "lead actor" in her narrative, which allows her to examine the centrality of watercourses to the lives of those who live near them and to see the broader impact of colonial attempts to harness rivers through damming. Allen and Barbara Isaacman's *Dams, Displacement, and the Delusion of Development* examines the Zambezi in the context of the development of the

Cahora Bassa Dam.[16] By focusing on the river, they demonstrate the disconnect between the rhetoric and the actual political, economic, and environmental impacts of the project. Another area that has featured water centrally is the study of irrigation. John Sutton's work on the Engaruka irrigation system in the Rift Valley of Northern Tanzania is some of the earliest and most noteworthy.[17] More recently, Monica van Beusekom's work on the Office du Niger's irrigation project in Mali has shown the importance of water development in relationships between colonial experts and local farmers.[18] Maurits Ertsen's recent book on irrigation in colonial Sudan focuses a bit more on water itself. He sees irrigation as a process that generated "continuous negotiations" between farmers and the colonial state.[19]

Although these recent works have broken new ground in analyzing the deeper significance of water, many important areas have yet to receive attention. There has been virtually no scholarship on how communities of Africans manage water. Each day, people use water in myriad ways, in their homes and on their farms. Each of these actions reveals much about their understandings of the resource and about broader social and political relationships. Furthermore, much of the existing work examines rivers, dams, or irrigation systems. The focus on single manifestations of water—naturally occurring or human engineered—allows the authors to dissect their political, social, and cultural dimensions and the conflicts that they have generated among users, between specialists and users, and between locals and outside actors. The drawback is that this makes it more difficult to get a holistic perspective as to how people think about water. It assumes that the water system in question is—or is perceived to be—discrete from other forms of water, such as rainfall, clouds, glaciers, wells, or neighboring systems. The question of where such boundaries are drawn is highly relative and culturally contingent. Yet in colonial contexts, such boundaries are often contested.

KILIMANJARO AS WATERSCAPE

This book approaches water in an innovative way. It examines how a community of people—the residents of Kilimanjaro—has managed its water resources amid a changing world and strong external pressures. Rather than focusing on a particular manifestation of water, it uses the concept of waterscapes to analyze multiple water resources in tandem and their intersections with society. What is a waterscape? In short, it is a term that describes how people see water. Many water features, such as rain and rivers, appear naturally. Others, such as irrigation canals and dams, are engineered by people. Most are visible to the eye, while others, such as underground rivers, are not. Water features show tremendous dynamism. Rain and surface water resources move, often covering very large distances. They vary seasonally and with long-term shifts in climate. What people see, therefore, depends on time, place, and perspective. Furthermore, the impression of these watercourses and their relationships with one another are socially and culturally constructed. When people describe places as lush or arid, or employ terms such as abundant or scarce, they are seeing water through their own beliefs, needs, and expectations. All of these change over time as societies use water in new ways and in greater quantities, which in turn influences how people choose to use, manage, and engineer those resources. Waterscapes thus provide a conceptual framework for understanding how water sources intersect with the expectations and needs of those who depend on them.

The term waterscape is relatively recent, and its value and meaning have been subject to debate among scholars. It derives from work looking at landscapes as socially constructed, or "anthropogenic, the result of the interaction between natural processes and human action."[20] However, it brings water, rather than land, to the fore. Some scholars of water have started to embrace this term,[21] while others consider waterscapes to be mere watery landscapes. I see the concept as illuminating the uniqueness of water and its impact on human societies. As noted by Hoag, "whereas *landscape* can evoke stationary images of expanses of dry land, *waterscape* implies fluidity, motion, and dynamism."[22] This is particularly important for places like Kilimanjaro, where water is the defining natural feature. Waterscape also emphasizes the socially constructed nature of water. Geographer Erik Swyngedouw, who has written extensively on water in Spain, sees waterscapes as "hybrid socio-natures" produced by the intersection of people and environment.[23] They are a "liminal landscape . . . [that] is embedded in and interiorizes a series of multiple power relations along ethnic, gender, and class lines." These power relations "operate at a variety of interrelated geographical scale levels, from the scale of the body upward to the political ecology of the city to the global scale of uneven development."[24]

Swyngedouw sees waterscapes as shaping relationships and hierarchies of power from the local to the global.

By centering my analysis on waterscapes, I am able to analyze the multiplicity of water sources on Kilimanjaro based on how different actors saw them over time. This emphasizes the dynamic nature of the resource and the knowledge produced about it, which in turn shows the uniqueness of water compared to other resources. For the peoples of the mountain, water was the defining feature of the space they inhabited. Water features shaped the topography and gave life to flora and fauna, and they defined culture, politics, and belonging. People therefore imagined these water sources in a way that reflected their culture and history. Those who encountered Kilimanjaro from the outside in the nineteenth and twentieth centuries, as colonizers, missionaries, settlers, government officials, and scientists, constructed different visions of the waterscape that reflected their own impression of the water sources as well as their social and cultural contexts. Waterscapes emphasize how people's impressions of water are constructed by their circumstances. The groups of people who have encountered Kilimanjaro since 1850 may have been looking at the same space, but they were not seeing the same thing.

WATER BRINGS NO HARM

Water Brings No Harm draws on waterscapes to examine struggles over water both among the mountain populations of Kilimanjaro and between them and outside groups. These struggles center on competing knowledges of water shaped by different imaginings of the waterscape. Furthermore, the views of these various groups changed over time in response to environmental conditions, consumption patterns, and the availability of new knowledge and technologies. A commonality of these struggles is that they came to be articulated in a language of harm. This book analyzes these struggles and the impact they have had on the peoples of the mountain.

In the late nineteenth century, Chagga-speaking peoples resided in over twenty chiefdoms on the southern and eastern slopes of Kilimanjaro. They drew from the mountain's streams, rivers, and rainfall to establish a thriving agrarian economy, one that exemplifies Sara Berry's observation of African agricultural systems as "fluid, dynamic, and ambiguous."[25] These resources were utilized for irrigating crops such as bananas, yams, and eleusine; for livestock; and for domestic needs such as cooking, bathing, and brewing. To more effectively use water for these purposes, local people developed mifongo to channel water into settlements. In addition to its utility, water was crucial to notions of origin and spirituality. It appeared in numerous adages, proverbs, and fables. It shaped ideas of community belonging and defined social boundaries along clan, gender, and generational lines. Knowledge of the tangible and intangible properties of water empowered a variety of community specialists who managed water systems or performed rituals and offerings.

This book's title, *Water Brings No Harm*, demonstrates the centrality of waterscapes to local thinking. A translation of *mringa uwore mbaka voo*, this adage was common on southeast Kilimanjaro in the years before colonialism. It indicates belief in the inherent purity and goodness of water. It also implies a specific notion of harm as well as practices for managing any harms that relate to the resource. Before the twentieth century, the most common water-related harms were attributed to human action or malevolent spirits. To ensure that water would bring no harm, people in the community actively managed the resource. In the case of a broken mfongo, canal specialists known as *meni mifongo* worked with the society of users to restore the water. This involved not merely fixing the physical canal but also making offerings to the relevant spirits. In cases of drought or excessive rain, those with expertise in rainmaking medicine and spirit divination made offerings to the spirits and the creator god Ruwa to make it rain or make it stop. Though spirits or human action could bring these harms to the water supply, people generally believed that water, in and of itself, was the source of life and brought no harm. Keeping it that way involved careful management that tied together technology, spirituality, and community.

On Kilimanjaro, water was a fluid resource whose significance shifted in response to environmental, political, and social conditions. It often inspired debate between various specialists and between specialists and other community leaders, such as the wamangi and clan heads. After 1890, these debates became more pronounced. Colonial rule introduced new actors to Kilimanjaro who settled on the mountain and made demands on its resources. At first, these individuals believed that water existed abundantly, and they embraced local knowledge of the resource, in particular the mifongo. This persisted until the late 1920s. By that point, the rising population and increasing demand for water from users on the mountain and in the lowlands led Europeans to reimagine the waterscape as scarce. At the same time, they became concerned with dangers such as contamination and soil erosion. The tandem led colonial agents to embrace a discourse that challenged local water management as harmful to the landscape, the water supply, and the people themselves. Colonial scientists, district officers, and wamangi criticized the mifongo as wasteful of water and destructive to the land. Midwives and schoolteachers promoted the idea of water being contaminated with bacteria and therefore harmful to those who consumed it. They joined with the missionaries and Christian converts, who had long criticized diviners and rainmakers for promoting spiritually harmful beliefs and practices. These actors in turn promoted new knowledge of water that was grounded in allegedly modern, science-based thinking. Only by adopting new knowledge, and rejecting the old, could communities save their resource and build a better future. Colonial attempts to influence mountain peoples included the creation of new laws and regulations, the manipulation of chiefly authority, and the educational efforts of European and African colonial officers, clergy, teachers, and midwives. In the 1950s, the government became involved in providing water by constructing pipelines intended to replace the mifongo. These efforts challenged not only a host of social and political relationships on the mountain but also the position of water specialists.

Struggles over water did not ease with independence. In 1967, Tanzania embarked on a program of socialist economic development, Ujamaa, that defined water as a national resource that should be provided by the state as a public good, for free. Ujamaa policies, along with new development projects such as water pipelines, effectively challenged the idea of local water management by considering it to be harmful to the nation. In the mid-1980s, the government switched course again as it abandoned African socialism in favor of structural adjustment. In this era, the national government embraced a new strategy called Integrated Water Resources Management (IWRM), devolved oversight of water to regional basin authorities, and adopted the policy that water should be treated as a commodity and that people should pay for it. In recent years, the most intense conflict over water has involved the shrinking of the mountain's venerable ice cap, which is predicted to vanish entirely by the year 2030. Scientists are heatedly debating about the causation of this phenomenon and its potential linkage to global climate change. This has made Kilimanjaro a visible icon of broader debates over global environmental issues, while ignoring the opinions of the mountain's own peoples.

Water Brings No Harm asks important questions about the relationship between water-management knowledge and political power. Since the 1920s, colonial officers, missionaries, the postcolonial state, development agencies, and scientists have criticized local water management, yet they have rarely used force or heavy-handed policy to make mountain communities alter their practices. Rather, they have used science and technology as political tools, extolling the virtues of modern management and its superiority to traditional or customary management. In most cases, local actors have negotiated these interventions or rejected them outright, demonstrating that the relationship between knowledge, authority, and power is far from linear. Many Africanist scholars have challenged the binaries (traditional versus modern, customary versus scientific) that defined colonial thinking about knowledge, and they have shown the extent to which everyday Africans negotiated these interventions. Paul Richards, in his work on West African agriculture, shows how peasant farmers are adept at producing new knowledge through experimentation and innovation, hallmarks of the scientific method.[26] Locals possess expertise that outsiders do not, and this is due to their long-standing interaction with the land. Likewise, Timothy Mitchell's work on Egypt reveals how modern states rely on discrete categories of knowing—fields such as engineering, chemistry, and economics—that are led by so-called experts.[27] This separation effectively excludes locals from participating in processes for which they are deemed lacking in knowledge. More recently, Helen Tilley's work on science in colonial Africa has shown not only how science-based knowledge has held the power to both coerce and liberate but also that the application of such knowledge can be used by local communities for subversive purposes.[28]

Water Brings No Harm builds on these studies by complicating our understanding of what constitutes expert knowledge of water as well as who can possess that knowledge. For much of its history, management knowledge on Kilimanjaro has consisted of hydrological and technical expertise that was very much scientific, derived from centuries of observation and experimentation. Early colonizers admitted as much by embracing local expertise for nearly seventy years. It was only when their vision of the waterscape shifted that they rejected local knowledge. This study also shows how adept local communities proved to be at negotiating knowledge from the outside, which stemmed in part from their belief that outsiders had little legitimate authority over water. This belief enabled them to negotiate outside actions by embracing elements of knowledge they found useful while rejecting the assertions of power that accompanied that knowledge. Local communities also benefited from the power of geography. By being the most upstream users in the watershed, they had an inherent power to resist outside interventions.

This book also encourages us to think more deeply about the meaning of development in Africa and the Global South. In the 1950s, colonial officials began working with the wamangi to develop new water systems, such as canals and pipelines, for the communities of Kilimanjaro. Though extolled as a way to provide more and better water, these projects also reflected the desire of colonial actors to assert political power over communities and reshape local knowledge of water. This use of development continued largely unaltered into the postcolonial period, with projects promoted by the socialist and neoliberal regimes and a host of development agencies. The relationship between development and state power has been analyzed in depth by scholars such as James Ferguson, James Scott, and Monica van Beusekom. Ferguson, in his study of Lesotho, notes that development "is a machine for reinforcing and expanding the exercise of bureaucratic state power." This can happen almost invisibly because of the attractive nature and seemingly "neutral, technical mission" of the project itself. Development discourses promote "technical solutions to technical problems" in a way that allows the state to ignore or deliberately exclude local communities.[29] There are echoes of this on Kilimanjaro, where development is both implicitly and explicitly linked to attempts to impose state authority. Scott's work on high modernism indicates how the hegemonic nature of large-scale state-sponsored projects contributes to their failure. Such projects fail by dismissing "local knowledge and know-how" in favor of "formal schemes of order."[30] Van Beusekom argues that development became more effective once colonial actors recognized the value of local knowledge. Her work on the Office du

Niger's irrigation project in Mali shows that output and productivity improved once French officials started paying attention to local knowledge, resulting in development that was a hybrid of the colonial, or Western, and the local.[31] Colonial and postcolonial attempts to develop water on Kilimanjaro echo these cases and indicate the drawbacks of top-down, state-driven development.

Water Brings No Harm expands the existing literature in three respects. First, it pushes us to think about development over a longer timeframe. Debates about how to develop water resources, by whom and using what technologies, did not arise with colonial rule. They had preoccupied local experts for centuries, just as they preoccupied colonial scientists and engineers working for the Tanzanian state. Second, it shows that development has involved a larger toolbox than is commonly assumed. Most studies of development center on a case study, and many of these are specific projects, like dams or irrigation schemes. By focusing on developing a resource rather than a technology, this book shows that the toolbox used by development actors has included legal, scientific, and cultural interventions as well as political and technical ones. Lastly, this book shows that development struggles in the absence of social resonance and engagement with local knowledge. Community water management thrived for centuries because the diverse forms of management knowledge linked together to create a shared sense of responsibility and ownership. Though the mifongo may have become antiquated in light of alternative technologies and the changing needs of users, the social networks they engendered could have been embraced to make new technologies more effective and sustainable. Yet colonial and postcolonial development deliberately excluded local communities for decades. In recent years, the Tanzanian government and development agencies have engaged with local communities, but they have done so only in limited ways and under the assumption that local knowledge has little to offer. This book indicates that the key to successful development is not just engaging the local, but incorporating the local in meaningful ways that builds social connectivity and engages local knowledge and expertise.

THE UNIQUENESS OF KILIMANJARO

Mount Kilimanjaro is an illuminating place for this study, in part because of its physical uniqueness. It is the tallest mountain in Africa, the world's fourth tallest in geographic prominence, the tallest of volcanic origin, and the tallest that does not lie in a range. It stretches 95 kilometers from east to west, 65 kilometers from north to south, and is separated by at least 30 kilometers from neighboring peaks.[32] Two volcanic cones define the massif: Mawenzi (5,149 meters) and the glacier-capped Kibo (5,895 meters). Neighboring peaks—Mount Meru to the west, the Taita Hills to the east, and the Pare Mountains to the southeast—all lie beyond its foothills. The semiarid grasslands of the steppe surround the mountain on all sides and average about 800 meters in elevation. A sky island in a sea of aridity, the mountain features its own unique climate zones with large variations in temperature and precipitation.[33] At the highest points of Kibo lie two ice fields that stretch downward from the peak. Beneath these is a region of alpine desert (4,000–5,000 meters) marked by minimal vegetation and animal life. Next is a zone of heathlands and moorlands (2,800–4,000 meters), a transition zone with minimal precipitation and various heathers and small shrubs. Beyond this point are areas of high precipitation. An alpine rainforest lies between 1,800 and 2,800 meters, featuring abundant water and a wealth of vegetation. Further downhill lies the area of focus for this study, the temperate forest, or agroforest zone. Called home by mountain peoples, it lies between 800 and 1,800 meters and features moderate temperatures, rich soils, and annual rainfall between 750 and 2,500 millimeters. Beyond this lies the lowland steppe, which averages less than 500 millimeters of rain per year and has only scrubby vegetation.

Water features define this mountain landscape. The most renowned is the ice cap at the top of Kibo. The upper reaches also receive seasonal snowfall, giving the whole of Kibo a distinctive white layer during periods of the year. The surface waters that flow from the rainforest through the agroforest zone are generated by the precipitation of two rainy seasons. Rainfall in the forests feeds dozens of rivers and streams that run in deep ravines by the time they reach the settled area. The most voluminous of the rivers are (from west to east) the Kikafu, the Weru Weru, the Karanga, the Himo, and the Lumi. All converge into the Pangani River, which flows southeast along the Pare and Usambara Mountains until it reaches the Indian Ocean. The Pangani Basin is today one of the most crucial watersheds in Tanzania, home to more than 2.3 million people and 17 percent of the country's hydroelectric capacity. River and stream flow is seasonally dependent, with high rates of flow during and immediately after the rains and low rates of flow in the dry seasons. Though the mountain possesses ample water in contrast to the surrounding steppe, it experiences drought on average every six to eight years. Kilimanjaro's vast water features, and their juxtaposition to the arid steppe, make the region an important place for studying conflicting knowledge about water.

A second factor is the people who for generations have called it home. The peoples now known as the Chagga first settled the lower slopes more than five hundred years ago.[34] They formed small clan-based communities on the ridges of the agroforest zone, on the south and east sides. These communities shared cultural and economic similarities and spoke related languages, but they did not possess a single identity. The strongest continuity was a form of agriculture defined by the cultivation of bananas, yams, and vegetables on homesteads called *vihamba*. In the nineteenth century, the clans on each ridge began to consolidate politically, and chieftaincy emerged. Yet the mountain remained a diverse place. What outsiders saw as a uniform Chagga society was actually a place of many societies, with strong linguistic diversity and no sense of political unity. The twentieth century witnessed developments including the rise of coffee cultivation, further political consolidation, and the formation of a shared identity. To this day, the Chagga retain cultural pride that is linked to the mountain as a physical space.

What makes these communities unique is the nature of their engagement with water. While all communities in Africa—and the world— depend on water, the peoples of Kilimanjaro developed a unique web of knowledge about the resource that touched nearly every aspect of life. This owed partly to the uniqueness of the mountain, featuring a narrow band of highly fertile soil and ample water wedged between the rainforest and the steppe. As such, waterscapes came to define the identity of mountain peoples and their notions of inclusion and exclusion. Furthermore, the multiplicity of sources enabled many to adopt a multiple-source water economy, in which they gathered water from different locations, at different times of the year, for different purposes. The physical placement of rivers and streams shaped communities, while the importance of water to livelihood shaped social, political, and cultural institutions. Lastly, mountain people have a long history of active water management. The need to control the multiplicity of resources lent power to specialists, but the availability of alternative sources also empowered a wide range of users. As a result, community water management on the mountain was more decentralized than that of most other places.

Lastly, Kilimanjaro has long fascinated outsiders, largely because of its waterscape. The earliest known allusions to a snowcapped mountain by non-Africans date back to antiquity. In the second century CE, Greco-Egyptian geographer Claudius Ptolemy wrote of a Great Snow Mountain near the spring lake that fed the Nile River. Other classical writers, such as Herodotus, speculated about snow mountains that fed the Nile. In the fifteenth century, Spanish traveler Martin Fernández de Enciso wrote in *Summa de geografía* that west of Mombasa stands the "Ethiopian Mount Olympus, which is exceedingly high." These accounts were not verified by firsthand observations until the nineteenth century, when missionary Johannes Rebmann became the first European to see the mountain. With its tremendous size, its isolation from other peaks, its seeming abundance of water amid the steppe, and, most notably, its glaciers, Kilimanjaro became the most renowned geographic feature of sub-Saharan Africa. With the emergence of colonial rule, Africa's Olympus came to be a lucrative piece of territory and a symbol of Europe's desire to dominate Africa. It even became a powerful literary symbol, as we see in Ernest Hemingway's "The Snows of Kilimanjaro." The mountain remains an important symbol to outsiders such as the Tanzanian state, mountain climbers, and scientists concerned with climate change.

The symbolic importance of Kilimanjaro and its waterscape to outsiders makes it a particularly good place for this study. Largely because of its allure, the mountain has attracted an unusually diverse cast of outside actors. As these outsiders have asserted power over the mountain and its people—whether for political domination, economic gain, religious conversion, nation building, alpine conquest, or other goals—the mountain communities have found themselves confronted with new opportunities and challenges. The local population negotiated new ideas about water in everything from religion and politics to health and technology. In the past three decades, numerous scholars have written about aspects of mountain society, including Sally Falk Moore, Emma Hunter, Susan Geiger Rogers, Anza Lema, Robert

Munson, and Ludger Wimmelbücker.[35] Some of this work, notably by Alison Grove, Donald Mosgrove, and Mattias Tagseth, has focused on the mifongo.[36] The last ten years have seen an explosion in scientific discussion of Kilimanjaro, dominated by articles on glacial recession.

By focusing on the intersection of management knowledge and power, this book provides a model for understanding water conflicts not only in Africa, but across much of the Global South. It shows both how local communities produced knowledge about the resource, and what happened when this knowledge confronted new ideas introduced by outsiders. These outsiders attempted to use their "modern" knowledge of water management as a means of attaining power, whether religious, political, or physical, over the resource. In turn, local people negotiated new ideas about water, often rejecting the accompanying power plays by outside actors. In some cases, new knowledge was even used as a tool to refute outside control. This richer understanding of the history of Kilimanjaro and East Africa also provides insights that are relevant to other regions where local communities encountered powerful actors from outside their boundaries. Our understandings of these problems are incomplete if we look at water strictly as a physical commodity to be controlled, divided, and consumed. I aim for this work to encourage those involved in water issues to think more deeply and broadly about the resource, as well as the importance of engaging local communities.

SOURCES AND METHOD

Analyzing the history of community water management on Kilimanjaro presents some distinct challenges. On the one hand, water is a resource that affects everyone and influences a range of thoughts, institutions, and relationships. On the other, everyday management can be routine and mundane, and the knowledge involved in certain practices can be concealed from public view. This means that some issues, like those that garnered the attention of government officials and agencies, are well represented in historical records, while others are scarcely mentioned. The temporal breadth of this book introduces another challenge. Over the 160 years covered, dozens of stakeholders have been important players in managing the waters of the mountain. Though textual sources have become more numerous over time, they do not represent the multiplicity of actors. I therefore draw on a wide range of sources including government and missionary archival records from Tanzania, Germany, Britain, and France; published reports from government agencies and nongovernmental organizations (NGOs); scientific articles; newspapers; historical linguistics; photographs; survey data and GPS measurements; and travelogues and memoirs. I also conducted oral history interviews on the mountain over three periods between 2002 and 2012. By layering these sources, I have pieced together a comprehensive account of water management that encompasses a wide range of voices.

Interpreting these sources requires careful attention to both context and each author's biases. For the early decades of the book, I rely on travelogues, diaries, and letters written by European explorers and adventurers between the 1850s and the 1930s. These writings reflect how outsiders' personal biases, objectives, and literary goals skewed their narratives of the mountain. Despite such challenges, these sources provide rich descriptions of the mountain and its waterscapes, and they are highly effective at showing how each author's presumptions and experiences intersect and also what features and experiences most preoccupy them. As published volumes, the works also give a sense of the knowledge that made its way back to Europe.

In the early twentieth century, several colonial officials and missionaries published ethnohistorical studies of mountain society. The most prominent authors were Lutheran missionary Bruno Gutmann, Catholic missionary Alexandre Le Roy, and the district officer for Kilimanjaro in the early 1920s, Charles Dundas.[37] These individuals lived and worked in close proximity to local communities, and their writings provide a wealth of detail concerning daily life, political and cultural practices, and understandings of history and descent. Gutmann was by far the most prolific. He wrote more than five hundred works during his time as a missionary, dozens of which pertain specifically to Chagga history and cultural practice.[38] Water management was a particular point of fascination for these authors, so these practices are well documented. Their works provide a view into mountain life and a tool for reconstructing life in earlier times, yet they require care in interpretation. Marcia Wright, who refers to these kinds of writers as "intimate outsiders," warns that their work "often verges on fiction in that it enters imaginatively into the life circumstances of Africans . . . and transgresses boundaries between observer and the observed."[39] These works interpret local life through the eyes and expectations of the writer, which can lead to distortions. For example, most writers homogenize the experiences of the people, assuming them to be part of the same "tribe," the Chagga. This assumption of ethnic unity was far from reality, as people identified with clans and chiefdoms and shunned any sense of panmontane identity. These writings also privilege the southeast chiefdoms, in particular Marangu, which had been most receptive to European colonialism and missionary work. The eastern slopes, known as Rombo, are described as resource-poor and impoverished—a reflection of recent environmental conditions and stereotypes held by people in the southeast—despite evidence that they had been prosperous in earlier centuries. If these sources are read alongside others, and with a careful eye to their biases, they can offer a window into late precolonial and early colonial life.

For the colonial and early postcolonial periods, I draw on government archival documents and published reports from government ministries. Most are housed at the Tanzania National Archives in Dar es Salaam, with some additional holdings in Germany and Britain. The archives' holdings include collections from the German period and the British period: district books, the Secretariat Series, the records of the Moshi District and Northern Province offices (and their successors), and the files of the Ministry of Agriculture, Ministry of Health, and Ministry of Lands, Settlement, and Water Development, among others. These contain annual reports, correspondence, and memoranda, which feature useful information about issues of colonial concern. They tell us less about local communities, as they selectively incorporate the perspectives of the governed. Prominent actors such as the wamangi frequently appear, but they are hardly representative of the views of their subjects, and women's voices are almost entirely absent. Despite these deficiencies, these documents provide a wealth of detail about policies, laws, and actions that had real effects on community water management, and they reveal the concerns and motivations of the government administrations. We can also get a sense of local perspective by reading these sources against the grain. Numerous documents, for example, reflect on how local communities responded to new policies and procedures. The descriptions of the responses provide useful information, even if the author's interpretation may be biased. We can then layer these with other sources such as oral narratives to tease out the meanings and motivations behind the responses.

In addition to government documents, there is a wealth of records from the missionary orders, including correspondence between the mission stations and with the head offices, collections of letters from clergy, and serial publications. The richest of these are the journals kept by the mission stations. These provide a daily account of the affairs of the mission, covering issues from baptisms and conversions to interactions with wamangi, elders, and government officials. They also offer detailed observations of the waterscape, including the earliest rainfall data and written accounts of drought in the region. These sources offer different perspectives from those of the government sources, perspectives that are more familiar with local life. Yet despite the fact that many European clergy lived on the mountain for years, even decades, they are still intimate outsiders who interpreted events through a desire to transform. These works need to be read with a careful eye to the objectives of the clergy, but they do offer a tremendous amount of detail and our earliest quantitative data on the waterscape.

Given the limited availability of archival materials for the post-independence period, published works are important for the more recent decades covered by this book. Reports and studies by the Tanzanian government, international agencies, and NGOs provide a wealth of material about water management on Kilimanjaro, in the Pangani Basin, and elsewhere in Tanzania. They document concerns about the water supply, the competing interests in management, and the shift in water policy since the 1960s. The scientific community has likewise published numerous studies, particularly about the glaciers. Some of these date to the nineteenth century, but most come from the past thirty years. These sources provide information for understanding hydrology, the impacts of climate change, and the shifting nature of water management since the colonial era. However, they provide little voice to local communities and either discount or ignore local knowledge.

A common problem with the textual records is that they do not provide a voice to the peoples of the mountain in the past or the present. To tease out these perspectives, I conducted oral history interviews across Kilimanjaro over a period of ten years. When I began this project, I focused my work in two communities: Kilema and Mkuu Rombo. The former is located on the southeast corner of the mountain and the latter on the east side (see map I.1). Both were marginal places, politically speaking, in the decades before colonial rule, but they rose

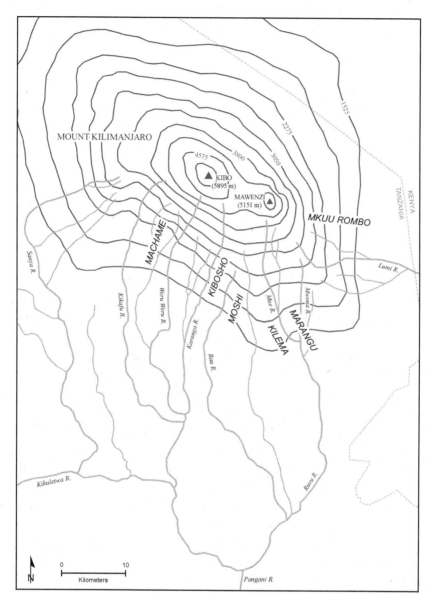

MAP I.1. Prominent chiefdoms and rivers *(Brian Edward Balsley, GISP)*

to prominence in the twentieth century due to the presence of Catholic missions. I spent six months in these two areas conducting interviews with a wide range of individuals. I selected many because of their social position or expertise in water management. I also spoke with men and women from a broad range of occupations, ages, and social standings, people who had an understanding of the nuances of everyday water management and use. In later research trips, I expanded my geographic scope by interviewing in Kibosho, Machame, Kirua Vunjo, Uru, and Moshi Town.

In reflecting the voices of people in local communities, oral narratives have the power to fill the lacuna created by the textual sources. Yet their collection and use has been a point of debate among Africanist scholars since Jan Vansina's pioneering work in the 1950s.[40] One challenge of my work stemmed from my position as an interviewer. I asked people about water management in their daily lives, in the past and the present, with questions that often asked about knowledge considered to be protected or intimate. I did so as an outsider in multiple respects: my race, nationality, ethnic heritage, sex, age, education level, and native language. Any of these could have influenced the willingness of my interviewees to share information or have affected the kinds of information they provided or the way they presented it. This is especially true given the long history of outsiders' meddling in water issues and bringing undesired outcomes. Another challenge related to the nature of the information I sought. Just as knowledge can be intimate and protected, it can also be routine. While people often have vivid memories of specific moments, their memories are less reliable when it comes to more mundane aspects of water use, such as changing consumption patterns or irrigation practices. This presents a particular issue for exploring past practices that continue today, since memories are filtered through the lens of contemporary society. Lastly, interviewees were understandably reluctant to discuss issues that are controversial or relate to underground activities such as water stealing or sabotage.

I took several steps to address these issues. I relied on research assistants who were either from those communities or had connections through family or work. Three were men (two in their sixties, one in his thirties), and the other was a woman in her thirties. These individuals had broad knowledge of the area and a firm understanding of local social and political relationships. They not only introduced me to people and assisted with language, but they also acted as intermediaries, explaining my purpose and the nature of my research. This helped facilitate interviews that would otherwise have not been successful, such as those with women that included questions about domestic issues. I conducted all the interviews by opening with greetings in Kichagga, then switching to Kiswahili or English as appropriate. This helped establish a comfort level with my interviewees and showed my familiarity with the area. Lastly, I developed my question sets with an eye to how they would be perceived by interviewees, relying on the expertise of my research assistants. In my questioning, I worked from the present toward the past, as this helped my interviewees become comfortable with me and think more deeply about water issues.

Another challenge with oral histories lies in interpretation, a question that has informed much of the debate about their value. Some scholars, such as Vansina, hold that oral narratives contain essential truth that can be extracted, allowing them to be reliable historical documents if sufficient care is taken with interpretation. Others, such as Luise White, Stephan Miescher, and David William Cohen, emphasize that oral sources are dynamic and malleable and that they convey discourse and sentiment, allowing us to understand historical viewpoints that may not necessarily be based in truth.[41] Emily Osborn's recent work on statecraft in the Milo River Valley illustrates the potential of employing both interpretive lenses.[42] My approach is similar to Osborn's in that my interpretation depends largely on the moment to which my interviewees are referring. Questions about current and recent topics tend to be answered accurately, except those pertaining to active water disputes or underground activity. I am able to verify this information by comparing interviews and noting outliers and also by layering the oral sources with textual ones. Questions that probe further back in time, asking about history beyond the lifespan of the interviewee, tend to be less objectively verifiable but no less revealing. For these, I am most concerned with how people choose to remember and speak about the past. The way these stories are told demonstrates a remembering that speaks as much about the present as the past, often coming across in vivid language and phrases such as "water brings no harm." As such, these narratives provide an indispensable tool for seeing how people have constructed waterscapes over time and how these notions have clashed with those held by outsiders. Most of all, they provide voices that are missing from the textual records, ones that illuminate the breadth and depth of water knowledge that these communities have long produced.

Lastly, given the environmental approach of this book, I utilize a number of sources that enable me to read the waterscape. These include studies of mountain hydrology, surveys of land and water resources, and photographs. I also used a handheld GPS to mark places of significance, calculate changes in altitude between points, and measure distances between locations. These sources enable me to see, at various points in history, the land and water features as they would have been seen by people at that time. They therefore provide additional data points that I compare with the impressions of officials, missionaries, and mountain peoples that appear in other sources. By examining them comparatively, I am able to see the dynamic nature of these features over time.

THE FLOW OF THE BOOK

Water Brings No Harm examines water management by focusing on moments in time when struggles over water became especially pressing. It looks at how actors responded by producing new knowledge and attempting to influence both policy and practice. The first two chapters examine how different groups—mountainside populations, and traders and explorers—developed impressions of the mountain's waters in the nineteenth century. The subsequent chapters flow chronologically, each examining a moment when local knowledge was challenged or shaped by interactions with outside actors. Altogether, the chapters provide a compelling glance into an array of struggles over water that have shaped the modern history of Kilimanjaro.

Chapter 1 establishes 1850 as the chronological starting point for the book. It examines the origins of the agrarian communities on Kilimanjaro and shows how people developed an impression of the waterscape that embodied the dynamism and diversity of the water sources as well as the sources' importance to people's livelihood. The management of these sources became a defining attribute of these communities, shaping social, political, and cultural institutions and relationships. Water provided for an array of physical needs such as cooking, brewing, and irrigation. Just as important, it was a fundamental part of how people understood their surroundings, their identities, their positions in society, and their spirituality. Those with specialized knowledge of water—a diverse group ranging from rainmakers to mifongo managers—held positions of power and esteem. Yet knowledge of water was not limited to elites. Nearly everyone held responsibility for managing water, from young men who performed irrigation maintenance to women and children charged with procuring water for domestic uses. People also recognized that water could be dangerously scarce. These resources, therefore, required many forms of management, from the spiritual to the technical, which could often be in competition. The chapter illuminates the highly dynamic nature of water management and the extent to which that knowledge was decentralized. Though linguistically diverse and politically disparate, people on the mountain shared a common vision of the waterscape, which defined water as their divine right.

Chapter 2 turns to how those from beyond Kilimanjaro viewed its waterscape. From the 1850s, mountain communities came into increasing contact with Swahili traders and European explorers arriving from the coast. These traders and explorers developed very different perceptions of mountain waterscapes from those held by locals. Europeans perceived Kilimanjaro as an Eden in the heart of Africa. This chapter shows how these notions arose from the experience of encountering the lush mountain after arduous journeys across the steppe and also from the contrast of this encounter with prevailing archetypes of the continent as a whole. While the mountain's tremendous size made it distinctive, it was the waterscape—the white cap and the abundance of rivers and streams—that most captured European imaginations. Kilimanjaro, a place of magical snows, endless water abundance, and favorable climate, emerged as the most known and symbolic geographic feature in sub-Saharan Africa. The mountain's waterscape features placed it centrally into European missionary, scientific, and colonial objectives for the continent. Yet the impression these actors developed, based on visual observations and little data, was a far cry from that of locals. Through centuries of observation and experimentation, they knew all too well that water could be scarce and that these resources required careful management.

Presumptions of Kilimanjaro as a place of water abundance are what informed European thinking into the early decades of colonial rule, as we see in chapter 3. The onset of colonial rule led to the arrival of German colonial administrators, Catholic and Lutheran missionaries, and settlers from Germany, Greece, and elsewhere. In the way these new arrivals imagined the waterscape, they were more like the explorers who preceded them than like their African counterparts, and so they were surprised by the dynamic nature of the resource and the need for careful management. They largely embraced local management knowledge, and they depended on wamangi for access to water and specialists to construct canals to their farms and missions. This relationship, which defies accepted notions of relations between Europeans and Africans in the colonial period, stemmed from factors including the small number of settlers, their lack of hydrological expertise, the economy of earthen canals, and the limited time they had before the disruption of the First World War. Reliance on local expertise gave communities a tool with which to manage their relationships with colonial actors. Despite evidence to the contrary, including a devastating drought in 1907–8, Europeans persisted in their assumption that the waterscape was abundant.

Water-abundant visions of Kilimanjaro persisted until the early years of British rule. Chapter 4 looks at how this belief dried up in the 1920s and 1930s. Along with settlers and missionaries, colonial officials of the newly renamed Tanganyika Territory began to conclude that the waters of the mountain were not in fact abundant but instead scarce and in need of careful management. This rethinking stemmed from an increasing demand for water on the mountain as well as new demand from beyond it, such as hydroelectric power and sisal cultivation in the Pangani Valley. Supply-side reconsiderations arose as well, including fear of increasing aridity, erosion, and wasteful use. These concerns targeted mountain communities, whose once "ingenious" water practices came to be considered prodigal and harmful. The administration and the wamangi responded with a series of initiatives to gain control of the region's waters. These included commissioning colonial scientists to produce studies of mountain hydrology and the problems facing the water supply, and they also included creating laws, policies, and structures to regulate water use and restrict the mifongo. Local communities vehemently resisted these new initiatives. Their perception of the waterscape had always involved volatility and the need for careful management, so these new concerns had little resonance. They also rejected the notion that users beyond the mountain had rightful claim to its waters.

This chapter marks a distinct shift in thinking about the waterscape of Kilimanjaro and also marks the start of struggles that persist to the present day. Seeing the mountain as water scarce, colonial actors felt compelled to transform management practices they considered harmful. To this end, they embraced new knowledge of water produced by scientists and politicians and rejected that held by local experts. Local knowledge came to be viewed as unscientific, superstitious, and dangerous. In the process, colonial actors conflated hydrological and technical knowledge, essentially saying that local expertise was no longer useful because the technology of the canals was outdated. Technocratic management significantly narrowed the field of people who could be experts and thus encouraged the government to develop more centralized planning of the resource. This shift threatened the local control of water and the roles of many specialists.

Even as mountain communities resisted the notion of scarcity and the idea that their long-held management practices were suddenly harmful, they began to adapt new water knowledge. Chapter 5 examines how new forms of water knowledge were incorporated in the areas of health, spirituality, and cultivation. It focuses on the discourse of harm, the tool with which outsiders lobbied for change in local practices. Between 1930 and 1960, numerous actors—missionaries, schoolteachers, colonial officers, coffee co-op employees, midwives, and others—worked in mountain communities to disseminate new knowledge and practices. They cited waterborne disease, non-Christian spirituality, and irrigation of eleusine (linked to erosion and excess beer consumption) as harms that could be rectified by managing water in modern ways. Over time, changes in everyday water use began to materialize, but these must be understood in the context of the dynamic nature of knowledge production. Mountain communities selectivity adapted new ideas in response to conditions on the ground, such as outbreaks of waterborne disease and localized scarcity. In turn, this empowered people to act as specialists in new ways. It consequently contributed to the decline of older forms of water knowledge and the status of those who possessed them.

Despite the adaptation of new water knowledge, the trend toward scientific, centralized management began to impact mountain communities. Chapter 6 examines this in the context of the Chagga and Tanzanian nationalisms that emerged in the 1950s and 1960s. These movements used water development to encourage people to embrace new political identities. In 1952, mountain communities elected the first paramount chief for Kilimanjaro, Thomas Marealle. He promoted a shared sense of ethnicity across the chiefdoms, inventing traditions, ceremonies, and a shared notion of history. Water development lay at the center of his initiatives. He promised to help those facing acute land and water scarcity by investing in new technologies such as pipelines. In doing so, he promoted a state-centered model for water development that embraced high modernism and defied the mountain's long-held tradition of local management. In the early 1960s, Tanganyika emerged from colonial rule as an independent nation, and by 1967 the new Tanzanian state had entered the era of socialist nation-building known as Ujamaa. In this period, the government in Dar es Salaam defined water as a national resource, to be provided to people for free. It invested in large-scale projects such as pipelines and the Nyumba ya Mungu Dam. These projects challenged two tenets of local water knowledge: that the waters of the mountain belonged to its people exclusively and that water should be managed locally. The projects that accompanied Ujamaa, ostensibly about providing more and better water, served as nation-building tools that consolidated government authority over the resource. People in the foothills accepted water pipes and taps when those helped ease scarcity, and people in the upper areas incorporated them into their existing mix of water resources. They therefore tried to embrace the new technologies while rejecting the underlying political objectives.

Mountain communities nonetheless became increasingly dependent on the new systems. In the highlands, an aging population found itself without the labor to maintain the mifongo or traverse long distances for water. In the foothills and lowlands, people had no alternative but to rely on government-built systems. By the 1970s, communities depended on water systems over which they had little control and in which they took little ownership. Local knowledge that was related to water quality and provision became less important in the upper areas and resented by those in the lower areas who viewed it as contrary to their interests. Specialists disappeared as elders passed away and children did not assume their roles. These changes reshaped how people made sense of the waterscape. Rather than one in which most people assumed an active role in management, it became one where people used resources passively.

By the late 1970s, Tanzania had fallen into steep economic decline. Facing economic collapse, the country abandoned Ujamaa and accepted a program of structural adjustment designed by the International

Monetary Fund (IMF). Chapter 7 looks at how neoliberal economic reforms transformed water management. The Tanzanian government, with the aid of international development agencies, embraced Integrated Water Resources Management (IWRM). This called for two major changes: the devolution of control from the central government to basin-level authorities and local user associations, and the introduction of cost recovery to fund projects and maintenance. Communities on Kilimanjaro have responded in highly nuanced and varied ways. Most vehemently reject the notion that they should pay for water, seeing this as an affront to their cultural norms and their pocketbooks. They also generally realize that despite the devolution rhetoric, they are denied any real power over water. Whereas people in the highlands have been most resistant to new water user associations—seeing them as shadows of the real thing—people in lower areas are more accepting, partly out of necessity and also because they have less interest in maintaining traditional forms of management.

The rise of neoliberal water management indicates the extent to which people's impressions of the waterscape have changed, as well as how they have remained the same. The physical water features of the mountain, natural and man-made, are very different from how they were in 1850. Many more people draw on these resources and use them in many more ways. While some forms of local management persevere, especially in the domestic and spiritual spheres, technical and hydrological management has diminished because of a dependency on government-managed pipelines and the decline of the mifongo. There is a substantial difference in thinking between people living in the highlands, who still practice a multiple-source water economy, and those in the foothills and lowlands, who depend solely on pipes. The former tend to look more favorably on older forms of water management, while the latter reject them as counterproductive and antiquated.

The final chapter returns to the most symbolic feature of the waterscape, the snows atop Kibo. For nearly one hundred years, the mountain's glaciers have been shrinking, and scientists predict that they will disappear completely within the next twenty years. Some claim that it is the direct result of human-induced climate change, while others see it as the product of regional factors such as increasing aridity and mountainside deforestation. The debate has spilled over into the political realm, where the snows of Kilimanjaro are used to promote or rebuke policy changes related to greenhouse gas emissions. The political and scholarly discourses of glacial recession ignore the perspective of mountain people and the knowledge they have produced about the glaciers and their place in the waterscape. This chapter shows how local communities are producing knowledge to explain the changes to the glaciers, the likelihood of the glaciers' demise, and how they can manage the implications. This enables them to acknowledge the scale of the problem while retaining a sense of agency. Their desire to interpret glacial recession in terms of both local and global factors reflects the broader historical trend shown throughout this book. Interestingly, scientists have pivoted in this direction over the past few years. Recent studies have shown that deforestation is largely causing the decline in water supplies on the mountain, and the studies cite local resource-management practices as essential to reversing the trend.

⤳

Though this is a historical study, it analyzes one of today's biggest resource dilemmas. Millions around the world, particularly in Africa, face chronic water scarcity. Population growth and climate change will only exacerbate this crisis. This study indicates the importance of examining how communities develop knowledge of water resources and how this knowledge in turn motivates action. The concept of waterscapes enables us to see how water resources are socially constructed and how conflicting views of resources result in struggles between users. Most of all, it shows that the social dimensions of water management—particularly a sense of ownership and responsibility—are essential to the success or failure of any project. The key to water development is building local capacity in a meaningful, engaged manner. My hope is that this work will inspire those involved in water development to think of the social and cultural dimensions of water as more than just adjunct and rather as key elements to developing sustainable water solutions.

1 ◡ The Giver of Abundance and Peace

Water and Society on the Slopes of Kilimanjaro

There once lived two neighbors in the forest. They used to love and help each other. They were both girls and they did not want to get married. Their names were Kibo and Mawenzi.

One day, Mawenzi wanted to prepare a dish of bananas, but she found no fire in her hearth. She went to ask for some live embers from her neighbor because it was getting too late to go to the shop and buy a matchbox.

When she was near Kibo's hut, she could smell something nice being cooked there. "Hodi?" she asked, meaning "May I come in?" Then her friend said, "Karibu." That means "Welcome." After greetings, Mawenzi asked for some fire. Before she was given it, Kibo gave her some of the sweet food she was pounding. This was dried bananas well cooked and mixed with some milk. Then Mawenzi left for her home.

On the way, she thought to herself how to get more of that food, and an idea came to her head. She put out the fire, went back to Kibo's hut, and said the fire went out because of the cold weather. So Kibo gave her more of her food and some fire.

Mawenzi did the same thing again for a third time. But Kibo didn't take the time to listen to her. They started to quarrel, and at the end, Kibo took the pestle she was using to pound her food and started to beat Mawenzi very hard on the head several times.

Mawenzi ran back home crying and started to nurse her wounds, which she still does today.[1]

THIS LEGEND of Kibo and Mawenzi, recited to me in Kilema in 2004, has been told in various forms across Kilimanjaro for centuries.[2] In the story, the neighbors represent the peaks of the mountain: Kibo, the white-capped peak that dominates the landscape, and Mawenzi, the lesser peak to its east. The purpose of the story is to explain their difference in stature and the latter's jagged appearance. Kibo is depicted as bountiful, generous, and wise, while Mawenzi is eager to take advantage of her neighbor's good fortune. The legend reveals much about how people define themselves in relation to their surroundings. For them, Kibo is more than the highest peak of the mountain; it is the source of life, a symbol of vitality, and the embodiment of all that sustains them.

The term "Kilimanjaro," which we now use to refer to the entire massif, comes not from the mountain itself but rather from outsiders. The peoples of the mountain inhabited not a singular space, but rather a diverse one defined by numerous valleys and ridges. Kibo, visible from all parts of the mountain, served as the geographic focal point. With its distinctive white cap and frequent cloud coverage, it came to be considered the source of water and, therefore, of life itself. For generations people have revered it, made offerings to it, washed themselves while looking in its direction, and buried their relatives so that they face it. Its centrality to local life can be seen in proverbs and adages such as "Endure like Kibo" and "As Kibo moves not, so may life not be removed from you."[3] As Charles Dundas described in his 1924 study of Chagga culture, Kibo is the "Giver of Abundance and Peace."[4]

This chapter discusses the mountain communities of Kilimanjaro and the centrality of the waterscape to their development up to the mid-nineteenth century. It does so by examining what it meant to "manage" water and how water management in turn shaped the development of social, political, and cultural institutions and relationships. Water was clearly a necessary resource, essential to agriculture as well as a multitude of other human needs, from brewing to bathing. Water management involved numerous kinds of sources—streams, springs, waterfalls, mifongo—each with different properties, uses, and seasonal variations. Because of the diversity of sources, the organization of communities on mountain ridges, and the persistent threat of drought, water management empowered a wide range of people. These included the societies that managed mifongo, the wamangi and elders who possessed rainmaking skills, the women responsible for procuring domestic water, and even children who were entrusted with protecting watercourses. Yet as reverence for Kibo indicates, the significance of water extended well beyond its physical uses. The resource held deep religious significance; it was key to beliefs about creation, the actions of the spirit world, and Kibo as the source of all life. It also held tremendous cultural power, defining notions of inclusion and exclusion based on categories such as status, education, gender, and generation. The need to manage water in its physical, cultural, and spiritual dimensions engendered a wide range of social interactions and empowered many different actors. Because of this, Kilimanjaro was not a hydraulic society—one where, as Wittfogel imagined, the need to control water led to centralization of power.[5] Rather, the dynamic nature of the waterscape led to a diverse yet interconnected body of knowledge that promoted decentralized control.

THE WATERSCAPES OF KILIMANJARO

Mount Kilimanjaro has long stood among the continent's most notable geographic features. Though impressive in its stature, the mountain has been of greatest value to human societies because of its water features. The humid zones of the mountain—the temperate and tropical woodlands—are most pronounced on its south and east sides. The moisture that gives rise to them originates from monsoon winds that come off the Indian Ocean. As these winds confront the mountain from the southeast, they rise along its slopes and generate precipitation as the atmospheric pressure drops. The north and west sides of the mountain, blocked from these winds, lie in rain shadows. Most precipitation falls in two periods: a long rainy season from March to June known as the *kisiye,* and a shorter period in October and November called the *fuli*.[6] Most of this water flows down the mountain in rivers and streams—some of which flow year-round and others only during the rains—while a lesser amount seeps into the ground and reemerges as springs. Smaller watercourses converge into larger ones as they flow southward, eventually forming the Pangani River more than 40 kilometers beyond the mountain.

The mountain's renowned ice cap lies on the upper reaches of Kibo. What appears as a single layer is actually three separate ice fields situated around and inside the volcanic caldera.[7] Within these fields are sixteen glaciers, most bearing the names of German mountaineers. The glaciers have been mapped only since 1912, which creates some uncertainty as to their size in earlier times. Glaciologists estimate that in the early nineteenth century, they covered about 20 square kilometers of Kibo's surface, compared with 2.5 square kilometers today.[8] This indicates that the white cap used to be more prominent. Though the ice represents a substantial holding of fresh water, it contributes little to the downhill water supply. Studies indicate that the glaciers are not large enough to act as reservoirs or contribute to downstream water flow.[9] Furthermore, the chemical composition of glacial melt differs from downstream springs and rivers.[10] As much as 96 percent of the surface water that flows through mountain settlements originates as precipitation in the rainforest and temperate woodlands.[11] Aside from the permanent ice, Kibo and Mawenzi also receive around 100 millimeters of seasonal snowfall annually.

Though little water from the glaciers makes it to the lowlands, those who first settled the mountain's slopes viewed Kibo as the heart of the waterscape. According to Dundas, people believed "that it is the water from this ice that feeds the forest springs which waters their gardens."[12] This perceived connection between the peak and surface water made sense, given that seasonal rainfall and high river volume coincided with seasonal snowfall. As the white cap grew, rivers and streams filled with water, and as it shrank, the dry periods emerged. Though people understood Kibo to be the source of water, they did not know until the twentieth century that ice and snow accounted for its white appearance. Dundas asserts that most people believed the white cap to be formed by hail, which fell periodically in the settled regions of the mountain.

In terms of settlement, the most important zone is the temperate woodland, or agroforest belt. These highland areas are where the ancestors of the current populations chose to settle when they arrived at the mountain more than five hundred years ago. Approximately 100 kilometers in length but only 12 kilometers in width, the agroforest belt wraps around the mountain's south and east sides. It features fertile volcanic soils, thick vegetation, moderate temperatures, ample rain, and widespread surface water. The topography slopes downhill gradually, with alternating valleys and ridges that emerge in a radial pattern from the upper reaches of the mountain. These valleys, carved over millennia by swiftly flowing water, run deep by the point they reach the agroforest belt. The ridges afforded early communities protection from hostile neighbors as well as wild animals. The richness and diversity of the region are difficult to overstate. In general, temperatures fall and precipitation rises as one approaches the peaks, meaning that the highland areas receive considerably more rainfall than the foothills. Precipitation also decreases as one moves eastward along the southern slopes; it decreases even more as one turns northward along the eastern side of the mountain. Within each mountain ridge, one finds even more variation, with microclimate conditions generated by elevation, sun and wind exposure, and other factors.

One way to conceptualize the diverse conditions of the agroforest belt is to distinguish between three geographic regions: the southwest, the southeast, and the east. The southwest, known since the twentieth century as Hai, features gradual slopes, broad ridges, and a series of deep ravines formed by the mountain's most voluminous rivers: the Sanya, the Karanga, the Kikafu, and the Weru Weru.[13] It has the most surface water of any region of the mountain as well as high rates of annual rainfall, its middle-altitude areas averaging 1,500 millimeters and upper areas exceeding 2,000.[14] The southeast, known as Vunjo, is more rugged and steep than Hai. It features narrower ridges with more sharply descending ravines. Its main rivers—the Mue, the Mwona, and the Himo—are less voluminous than those of Hai and lie in shallower valleys. Rainfall is similar, however, averaging 1,500 millimeters per year in middle elevations. The east is referred to as Rombo. Lying on a broad, gradual incline, it is the most distinct of the three in terms of geology and hydrology. The terrain slopes like Hai but with much shallower ravines. Annual rainfall averages are lower than the other areas, reaching around 1,000 millimeters in middle elevations and 1,400 millimeters in upper ones. The most significant difference is the relative dearth of surface water. Rombo contains only one year-round river, the Lumi. While there are a number of rivers that appear seasonally, there are fewer watercourses in Rombo than in either Hai or Vunjo. This contributes to a landscape that is lush compared with the plains but substantially less verdant than the south side of the mountain.

Another factor to consider when thinking about the lands and waters of Kilimanjaro is timing. The bimodal rainfall pattern determines growing seasons, as temperature is largely consistent year-round. During periods of normal weather, precipitation can be highly variable, falling unevenly and causing localized shortages or flooding. The mountain also experiences periodic drought conditions, which has a tremendous impact on surface water. Rivers, streams, and springs that are normally permanent experience reduced flow, while seasonal ones dry up entirely. In his study of nineteenth-century Kilimanjaro, Wimmelbücker shows that prolonged droughts often resulted in famine, leading to political destabilization and warfare between rival chiefdoms. Famines were so common that they were often named in reference to the impacts they had. In the mid-1930s, for example, a severe drought afflicted much of Kilimanjaro. In Machame, it came to be known as *njaa ya mowishi*, or "the famine in which people had to eat raw whatever they came across."[15] Those who settled the mountain thus came to realize that though Kilimanjaro was a place of relative water abundance, this abundance was by no means absolute. The often-unpredictable nature of rainfall is reflected in adages and fables, the most notable being *kipfilepfile kirundu kechiwa mvuo kilawe*. Translated as "a little rainy cloud that never became rain," it reminds people that they should not trust that rain is inevitable, and that they should be prepared for conditions of scarcity.[16]

Kilimanjaro is a landscape defined by juxtaposition. It is an area of high altitude surrounded by flat grassland, an island of water abundance in a sea of aridity. The waters of the mountain generate a rich, green expanse of vegetation absent from the brown grasslands. The altitude moderates temperatures, creating an area of relative coolness in stark contrast to the intense heat of the steppe. The mountain even sets itself apart in terms of safety; its sharp slopes and cool temperatures discourage dangerous foes such as lions, leopards, tsetse flies, and mosquitoes. The hospitable conditions of the mountain have long been attractive to human communities. Given the presence of water in a region that is largely arid, it is likely that hunter-gatherer and pastoral communities had visited the mountain's foothills for thousands of years. Around five hundred to six hundred years ago, the ancestors of the mountain's current peoples began to settle the agroforest belt. Drawing on the resources of the mountain, they developed a highly sophisticated agrarian society.

The agrarian peoples that have come to be known as the Chagga are of Bantu descent, closely related to other Northeast Bantu peoples such as the Taita and Meru, and more distantly to the Swahili.[17] Throughout much of the nineteenth and twentieth centuries, outsiders considered the peoples of the mountain to be a singular group who shared a common origin and spoke similar dialects of the same language. In the past thirty years, however, historical linguists such as Derek Nurse, Gérard Philippson, and J. Christoph Winter have shown that the dialects of Chagga language are distinct enough to be considered individual languages.[18] The linguistic evidence paints a more complex picture of Chagga origins than had been assumed, giving the possibility of multiple migrations over a period of more than two hundred years. These migrants settled on the ridges of the agroforest belt on the southern and eastern slopes. Within each ridge, people spoke the same language, but across the mountain, dozens of different "Chagga languages" came into being. Together they formed a dialect continuum in which people on neighboring ridges could understand their immediate neighbors, but not those living further away. The linguistic diversity of the mountain is exemplified by the numerous terms for water. In 1955, J. E. Goldthorpe noted more than five "Chagga" terms for water—*moha, murra, mudha, mringa,* and *mota*—as one passed from west to east, likely a smaller number than had existed in previous centuries.[19] This shows how the rivers that carved the mountain's valleys over millennia have influenced the linguistic landscape as well.

These migrants settled the highlands of the agroforest belt because of its moderate temperatures, its fertile soils, the security provided by the rugged landscape, and the prevalence of water. By the sixteenth century, a consistent pattern of agriculture had emerged, focusing on small homesteads known as vihamba (sing. kihamba). These were 2–4 hectares in size and contained dwellings, granaries, burial plots, stalls for livestock, and gardens for cultivating crops.[20] Kihamba gardens featured mixed cultivation of food crops and fodder grasses under the shade of canopy trees (fig. 1.1). For families that practiced polygamy—indicating high status in the clan—each wife possessed a separate dwelling in the kihamba and her own areas of cultivation. Families grew a wide range of crops, bananas being the most prominent. Well suited to the humid conditions of the agroforest belt, high in calories, and low in labor need, they emerged as the dominant food on the mountain. Bananas were so central to local diet that people came to identify themselves as *wandu wa mbdeny*, "people of the banana groves."[21] As many as twenty-one different species were grown, with varieties for cooking, brewing, and eating raw.[22] They also provided shade for the other crops of the vihamba. By the nineteenth century, common staples intercropped with bananas included yams, cassava, beans, taro, sugar cane, sweet potatoes, maize, pumpkins, and papaya.[23] Most homesteads also featured dracaena (*masale*), a spiritually significant shrub used to mark boundaries and notable locations. Across the mountain, people considered vihamba to be the permanent property of the families that resided on them. Fathers provided elder sons with a homestead at the time of marriage, each containing at least a piece of the original estate. The youngest son inherited the remainder of the original homestead, including the original buildings and the most centrally located gardens. Yet women performed the bulk of the labor in these gardens; men assisted by clearing land and irrigating.[24]

Some families also developed secondary fields known as *shamba* in the foothills at the edge of the agroforest zone. On these plots, they cultivated grains such as maize and eleusine (*Eleusine coracana*, or finger millet). The practice of cultivation in the foothills differed markedly from cultivation in the vihamba in that crops were usually grown in monoculture. The most important shamba crop was eleusine, used primarily for producing an alcoholic brew called *mbege*. In times of drought, it could also be used as a famine food. For eleusine, planting took place just after the kisiye, and the crop grew to maturity during the dry period with irrigation. The cultivation of this crop during the dry season as opposed to the rainy season has been explained as a defense against vagrant animals. Dundas notes a story in his writings that attributes the practice to the misfortune of a farmer named Salia. One day Salia tried to scare off elephants that were ravaging his eleusine.[25] Because of the rains, his gunpowder was damp, and he was unable to load his weapon to shoot at them. As he tried to dry his powder, he caused an explosion that killed himself and thirty-nine other people. Learning a lesson from this misfortune, people then refused to plant eleusine in the rainy season, instead planting it after the rains so that it would ripen in the dry period. Despite the prevalence of this story, it is more likely that the practice started because eleusine ripens better with the direct

FIGURE 1.1. A kihamba (*Matthew V. Bender*)

sunlight of the dry period. It may also reflect that eleusine was a prestige crop. Because men performed the bulk of labor related to the crop, the practice helped distribute labor more evenly over the course of the year.

Social development centered on the vihamba and agricultural life. According to Moore, mountainside society initially consisted of "many small, fairly autonomous settlements, most composed of several localized patrilineages [*kishari*, pl. *vishari*], a few consisting of one very large patrilineage."[26] These were led by the most senior men. Settlements tended to be located at the highest points of the ridges where land was flattest. Over time, neighboring communities developed greater connections with one another. Moore notes, for example, that the practice of developing age-sets (*rika*) cut across the settlements.[27] On Kilimanjaro, age-sets were corporate social groups that served as units for organizing corvée labor and warfare.[28] Each initiation class formed a division, or *ilumbo*, within the age-set. These units provided an important means of organizing much of the cooperative work of the mountain. It is important to note that water management remained outside the age-set system, and age-sets were never mobilized for irrigation projects. Given the topography of the mountain, the increasing cooperation among neighboring groups made sense as a means of facilitating access to resources. Settlements closer to the forest had prime access to timber and water, while those closer to the plains had better access to goods procured from beyond the mountain, notably iron ore and pottery. Mifongo, originating above areas of settlement and used as far downhill as the shamba lands, acted as connecting arteries through the mountain ridges, encouraging cooperation throughout any given ridge. Thus, water influenced the development of these communities by being a divisive force, separating communities onto different ridges while also fostering partnership between those uphill and downhill on the same ridge.

Political centralization followed these lines as well. The institution of chieftaincy developed gradually as dominant families on each ridge asserted increased authority over others. In most cases, these families were located farthest uphill, in the areas of greatest water abundance. By the early nineteenth century, cooperating settlements on the same ridges had coalesced into around forty chieftaincies, each led by a chief (*mangi*). The largest of these from west to east were Siha, Machame, Kibosho, Uru, Moshi, Kirua, Kilema, Marangu, Mamba, Mwika, and Mkuu. Wamangi governed in partnership with councils of lineage heads, called *njamaa*, and their main claim to power was likely their control of the warrior age classes.[29] Each chiefdom consisted of districts called *mitaa* (sing. *mtaa*), administered by district heads called *wachili* (sing. *mchili*), who were appointed by their mangi.[30] Over the nineteenth century, the power of the wamangi grew alongside the rise in regional trade and an increase in warfare among groups on the mountain. It is important to note that their role did not include control of land, surface water, or irrigation.

The ability to control rain proved crucial to the wamangi and clan heads' claim to authority. Rainmaking knowledge tended to be held by ranking members of clans and by professional spirit diviners (*wamasya*, sing. *mmasya*). In times of drought or flooding, these individuals made offerings to spirits deemed important to the water supply. These powers could be used for the benefit of the people, or to further one's political interests. Wimmelbücker notes the example of Mashina, a chieftainess who ruled Mamba at the beginning of the nineteenth century.[31] According to oral narratives, she turned against her own people and ordered her rainmaker, Kisolyi, to hold back the rains in order to bring famine and punish her people. She was later ousted from power. This story illustrates the power of a mangi to command control of rainfall, as well as the power of the people to depose leaders who mismanaged the resource. Another example Wimmelbücker provides is Makimende, a mmasya who became renowned for his rainmaking skills during the drought of 1897–99.[32] He traveled throughout the southern chiefdoms, and he became a close confidant of Mangi Marealle. A few years later, his medicines proved ineffective, and Marealle sentenced him to a punishment of fifty lashes and having his cattle taken away. These two examples indicate how one group of specialists did not have a monopoly on rainmaking. Rather, rainmaking knowledge could be exercised by elders, wachili, wamangi, and wamasya, often in competition with one another.

In addition to their economic practices and social structures, the peoples of the mountain shared common rituals and forms of spiritual expression. Initiation, midwifery, burial rites, and worship practices developed very consistently. A collective notion of spirituality, based on the mountain's geography, lay at the heart of these. It framed the mountain as having four regions of spiritual significance: the vihamba, the homeland of the living; the rainforest, the home of the spirits (*waruma*, sing. *mruma*); Kibo, the dwelling place of the creator Ruwa; and the lowlands, the surrounding plains devoid of life and full of dangers and evils. Most daily worship centered on reverence to the waruma.[33] Though they dwelt primarily in the rainforest, they frequented forest groves, waterfalls, banana groves, and dracaena plots, and they possessed the power to intervene in everyday events. If people lived in harmony with the spirits, then the spirits would ensure abundance and peace. If people did not, then harmful outcomes would ensue. This was especially important for water, as many springs were thought to be controlled by waruma who would cut the water flow if they became agitated.[34] To retain good relations with the spirits, the living made offerings and included them in rites and rituals. Professional diviners, the wamasya, could be called upon in dire situations, as could other ranking members of the clan deemed to have knowledge of the spirit realm. People also developed the notion of a supreme spirit known as Ruwa.[35] They considered him to be the creator of the mountain, the one who shaped vitality out of the desolation of the plains. Linked to notions of life, fertility, protection, and goodness, he nurtured his peoples by providing the fertile soils of the vihamba and the waters that filled streams and rivers. According to Anza Lema, people regarded Ruwa as the giver of rain, and they "delighted in the sound and feel of the rain, sensing its promise for a good season in which they harvested plenty and prospered."[36] They also considered rain to be Ruwa's spittle or saliva, a symbol of health, happiness, prosperity, well-being, and favor.[37] Reverence to Ruwa took the form of veneration and spitting in the direction of Kibo as well as ritual offerings of animals and mbege made in watercourses.

Despite the presence of numerous shared cultural, economic, and religious practices, the peoples of the mountain held no sense of shared political identity. The most salient forms of identity were local, based on family, clan, and age-set. Chiefdom identities became more important throughout the nineteenth century, though these proved fluid as chiefdoms merged, separated, and asserted authority over one another. Though mountain people did have some sense of community with one another, a shared geography, and a common belief that people from outside the mountain were different and lesser, they did not see themselves as part of the same polity or ethnicity.

MANAGING WATER RESOURCES

The key factor that facilitated the development of these societies was the prevalence of water. Ample rainfall and an abundance of surface water sources—streams, rivers, springs, and waterfalls—shaped the landscape and gave the agroforest belt its vitality. These were essential to the intensive agriculture of the vihamba and the high-density settlements that formed on the mountain's ridges. Over centuries, people developed intricate ways of managing their resources. They also came to understand the natural patterns of rainfall and stream flow, as well as the challenges of periodic drought. People did not utilize water passively; they actively managed it.

The mountain offered many natural sources of water, including rainfall (see table 1.1), springs, streams, rivers, and waterfalls, as well as man-made irrigation works. These sources each had different characteristics that mattered to users: proximity to the homestead, ease of access, seasonal availability, turbidity, taste, spiritual significance, and claims of ownership. Therefore, most people practiced a multiple-source water economy, in which they procured water from different sources, at different times of year, and for different tasks. Rain was the one source of water utilized by all, as it nourished the crops of the vihamba. Surface water sources could supplement rainfall during the dry months or prolonged periods of drought, but more often they were used for domestic purposes such as cooking, brewing, watering livestock, cleaning, and manufacturing mud blocks used for construction. Decisions about where to collect water were highly localized and dynamic. Patterns of water usage were as unique as the people themselves, varying from homestead to homestead and over time. Though individuals could make claims on naturally occurring water sources, this did not imply ownership, as it was forbidden to charge people or accept payment for water from these sources.[38]

Perhaps the most notable surface water feature was the extensive system of man-made irrigation canals known as mifongo (sing. mfongo).[39] These were excavated ditches designed to divert water from rivers and channel it, using the power of gravity, directly into areas of settlement, where it could then be used for irrigating vihamba and shamba as well as for domestic uses. Mifongo came into use between two hundred and four hundred years ago. The technology was likely imported from neighboring areas with histories of irrigation development,[40] and it developed into the most extensive system of mountainside irrigation in Africa. It is difficult to know the number of canals that existed in 1850, considering the lack of data and the challenge of counting a system that was by its nature dynamic; canals were built, abandoned, and resurrected in response to need. In the 1920s, Gutmann estimated that as many as one thousand canals lined the slopes of the mountain.[41]

Mifongo across Kilimanjaro (fig. 1.2) shared common design characteristics. Each began with a dump (nduwa), a swell within a river

TABLE 1.1

Mean monthly rainfall in millimeters for selected locations (minimum 10 years of recorded data)

Location	Alt (m)	Exposure	Jan	Feb	Mar	Apr	May	Jun	Jul	Aug	Sep	Oct	Nov	Dec	Yearly Average
Kibongoto	1,250	West	58	57	102	349	250	37	21	12	13	27	100	88	1,112
Machame	1,520	South	83	66	96	564	560	161	130	53	29	30	85	71	1,929
Lyamungu	1,250	South	44	65	109	537	456	112	60	35	31	37	97	80	1,663
Kibosho	1,460	South	76	72	159	594	643	204	117	55	39	41	95	91	2,184
Moshi Town	820	South	40	44	117	290	158	30	12	12	13	34	55	48	852
(Old) Moshi	1,650	South	83	97	177	567	411	132	100	53	38	84	171	123	2,033
Kirua Vunjo	1,680	South	89	128	328	617	342	92	119	73	42	164	300	168	2,460
Marangu	1,430	Southeast	70	86	195	391	263	67	65	65	49	88	174	144	1,625
Mkuu Rombo	1,430	East	81	93	224	277	115	30	23	43	38	86	271	202	1,484

Data from Paul Maro, *Population Growth and Agricultural Change in Kilimanjaro*, 1920–1970, research paper no. 40 (Dar es Salaam: University of Dar es Salaam Bureau of Resource Assessment and Land Use Planning, December 1975).

FIGURE 1.2. An mfongo (*Matthew V. Bender*)

that would provide a consistent supply of water. From here, an intake (*kiwamaenyi*) constructed from banana trunk diverted the water into a main canal, which turned away from the river and toward its destination. From this point, the waters flowed downhill at a gradual slope. Once they reached their destination, they were again diverted, this time into secondary canals leading directly into the vihamba. Floodgates made of banana trunks and leaves prevented water from flowing into the secondary canals until the appropriate time. Water from canals could be gathered into a wooden container, gourd, or clay pot for domestic purposes, but most often it was used for flood irrigation of crops. Beyond these general design characteristics, canals had a number of variations. Some canals that drew from small rivers featured multiple intakes to maximize the water supply. Many had culverts or aqueducts to lead water over other streams or under heavily traveled paths. Some had reservoirs that stored the overnight flow and increased the amount of water available during daylight hours. The biggest variables were length and number of branch canals. Mifongo could be as short as a quarter of a kilometer or as long as several kilometers, with only a handful of branch canals or dozens.

The development of new mifongo was a highly ritualized process limited to men in the community. Custom expressly prohibited women and children from tasks related to constructing or maintaining them.[42] The process of creating a new canal began with a group of men's determination that a new one was needed. They designated a leader, or founder, who took the lead in organizing labor and designing a plan for the canal. All men who planned to use the water aided in its construction and ongoing maintenance. Once the labor had been assembled, the founder began the process of surveying of the route.[43] For areas with clearly defined slopes, he determined the path by eyesight alone. Where the slope was less clear, he could survey the land by placing a banana leaf on the ground, pouring water from a calabash, and seeing what way that water flowed. Alternately, he could study the walking paths of fire ants to determine the slope.[44] After determining the path and slope, the founder commanded the men to excavate the primary canal to the desired depth and width. Once they completed that, they constructed the canal intake by excavating an appropriately sized opening from the source river and building the weir using banana trunks. Lastly, each man excavated his own branch canal from the main one. Once the project was complete, the founder became the first *meni mfongo* (canal headman), who held responsibility for its continuing management. Although most mifongo were designed by one of the users, some were constructed on others' behalf by professionals who served as experts in irrigation management. Those who designed successful mifongo gained a reputation, and this translated into a powerful social status. In Kilema, the names of the most esteemed canal founders in history—Anjelini, Maleto, Matanda, Mchau, Mtenga, Mlikamburu, Reu—are remembered to the present day.[45]

Considering the richness of the landscape and the relative abundance of water, one may ask why people went to the trouble of constructing such an immense network of canals. One reason is that mifongo allowed for more flexibility in cultivation. Relying on rainfall alone, farmers were limited to two growing seasons—during and following the kisiye and fuli—in all areas of the agroforest belt except those of highest altitudes. With irrigation, they created a year-round agricultural calendar and maximized their land and labor resources; eleusine cultivation is a great example of this flexibility. A second factor was the challenging placement of natural watercourses relative to areas of settlement. Many of the principal rivers lay in deep ravines as they passed by the vihamba. Women and children, responsible for procuring domestic water, had to descend a steep slope, fill a clay pot with water, and then ascend with the pot atop their head. These inclines were difficult to climb and were often on borderlands. Harry Johnston recalled hearing stories about women who were kidnapped while gathering water from rivers and then forced to become junior wives of their captors.[46] Animals such as leopards and lions also frequented these areas. By providing a reliable supply of water directly into areas of settlement, the mifongo not only reduced the risks associated with procuring water but also eased the labor burden. Lastly, mifongo provided a safeguard against drought. Though men irrigated vihamba regularly, they did so with increasing frequency in times of drought to compensate for insufficient rainfall.

Once water had been procured, it was used for a wide range of purposes. Within the domestic sphere, women used water most often to prepare food. Boiling was the most common method, with bananas and yams prepared into stews. People also drank water, but much of this occurred away from the kihamba and did not figure into the household allocation. Other domestic uses included washing and cleaning. According to Abbott, the peoples of Kilimanjaro were "comparatively clean, actually washing themselves occasionally. The wives are compelled to perform their ablutions daily and soap is in great demand."[47] Raum observed that mothers usually washed babies daily.[48] While most washing took place in rivers, some also took place at home using water from pots. It is difficult to estimate the quantity of domestic water that a family consumed daily in the late nineteenth century, as it differed depending on location, proximity to sources, and time of year. Using interview data from Kilema, I estimate that an average family consumed two to three pots (roughly 40–80 liters) per day when water was readily available.[49] Based on the patterns of water use inherent in the canals, it is safe to assume that rates of consumption were similar in other areas of the south and were lower in Rombo.

Procurement of domestic water was considered the work of women and children (fig. 1.3), and the process of collecting it could be arduous and time-consuming. In Rombo, the longer distances to water sources made the rigors especially trying. For both safety and companionship, women often traveled in groups. While doing so, they conversed and sometimes sang songs to help pass the time. One woman remembered a song that she sang frequently with friends:

> We have been back from taking water. (x2)
>
> Here we are our husbands we are pleased to arrive safely.
>
> Here is the water our husbands, now we have water for cooking, and bathing.
>
> Let me enter to my home my husband.
>
> I come very tired my husband. (x2)
>
> Don't punish me please if I am late because I bring water to our family and our animals.
>
> I am tired, I am tired.[50]

Water was also important in constructing buildings and enclosures. The basic form of house architecture was a conic structure constructed of thatched banana stems, bound together by horizontal stays of wattle and reaching as high and wide as 7–8 meters.[51] People used water from

FIGURE 1.3. Women collecting water from a river (*Arch.photo.cssp*)

nearby canals and streams to produce mud blocks and adhesive for these as well as other types of enclosures. Water was also necessary to bless newly constructed homes. As Dundas notes, on completion of a hut, the father of the one who built it would boil grass and banana stems—symbols of nourishment to people and animals—and all those present would wash their hands in the warm water, saying "May this house give warmth."[52] Thus water served a key role in preparing the home and ensuring good fortune for those who occupied it.

Another use of domestic water was for brewing mbege. This alcoholic beverage, made from bananas, eleusine, the bark of *msesewe* trees (which contains quinine and acts as a bittering agent), and water, served a number of purposes. As a ritual brew, it was an integral element of virtually all ceremonies, from celebrating the birth of children and sending the deceased into the spirit world to marriage rites and initiation into adulthood.[53] Here it served as a means of offering tribute to the spirits, Ruwa, the wamangi, and elders. The brew could be used as a currency to pay fines or bridewealth, as a proxy for corvée labor, or as an offering for the use of canal water. In the early twentieth century, a market for nonritual brew developed as well. Either men or women could prepare mbege, depending on its intended purpose. Knowledge of how to brew was carefully controlled within the household and only given to children after they had achieved maturity.[54] For mbege meant for ritual consumption, brewers procured ingredients from places of significance to the clan, the water coming from springs considered to be favored by the spirits. Brewing required on average 25 percent more liquid than what would become brew.[55] If a family needed to produce two pots of beer to celebrate an initiation, two and a half pots of water were required.

Agriculture required the biggest volume of water. Some of this water was needed for tending livestock: goats, cows, and later chickens. Since families kept their animals in stalls, this water had to be carried to the kihamba in pots. Water could also be used to kill rodents that threatened crops. If an area of the kihamba showed signs of rodent activity, men flooded the area using water from a canal or using stream water carried by pots. Of all agricultural uses, irrigation was the largest for most families. Men irrigated their crops in the kihamba and shamba by opening up a branch of a canal and flooding their field for a specified amount of time. Irrigation patterns depended on the location and the time of year. During the rains, men irrigated only if necessary. During the dry seasons, and especially during droughts, men applied water frequently in support of kihamba crops. For shamba, irrigation enabled dry-season cultivation of eleusine and other grains.

Mifongo were managed on a day-to-day basis by the meni mfongo and a society comprising all the men who held the right to use its waters. By the nineteenth century, the position of meni mfongo had become a position for life, either passed from father to son or selected by the committee of users.[56] They held responsibility for organizing all the management tasks including routine maintenance, emergency repairs, the setting of irrigation schedules, policing the canal to prevent pollution or misuse, and leading the rituals necessary to appease the spirits. The committee supported the meni mfongo by providing labor for the canal in exchange for the right to use water.

Successful management of mifongo depended on the completion of numerous tasks. Some of the most vital related to the spirit realm. People believed that the waters originated as a gift from Ruwa and that the spirits, particularly that of the founder, continued to influence the workings of the canal. The continued success of the canal depended on not only maintaining it physically but also maintaining the favor of the spirit. The meni mfongo held responsibility for organizing these offerings. Periodically, he would call together the committee and key elders to hold a ceremony near the canal intake. The ceremony began with an invocation to the spirit of the founder, such as the following: "Owner of this canal, I come to you because it is you who gave me this canal. I therefore beg you to give me water from this canal. May Ruwa bless us."[57] Those gathered then slaughtered a goat and threw the skin and intestines into the river.[58] They took the meat back to the vihamba and then roasted and ate it. The ceremony served to pacify the founder and bring prosperity to the canal, while reinforcing the position of the meni mfongo and the importance of the knowledge he possessed.

Another key responsibility of the meni mfongo was organizing routine and emergency maintenance of the canal. Because of mifongo's earthen construction and use of natural materials, they could be damaged by the increased water flows of the rainy seasons. These waters also deposited silt that filled the intake and the primary canal. These problems demanded that all users mobilize, sometimes with very little notice. Routine maintenance took place at the end of the kisiye and fuli.[59] Once the rivers had crested, the meni mfongo organized the users to perform maintenance. Each family with rights to the canal provided at least one man for labor. Households that could not manage this, such as widowed women, made an offer of mbege instead.[60] Older men often accepted this responsibility, however, leaving younger men to more physically demanding work such as clearing forests or participating in warfare. The first step was to remove grasses and eroded soil from the primary canal, restoring its width and depth. The group performed this work with the intake closed so that running water would not interfere. This stage of maintenance required the most time, and it took place in the mornings over the course of a few days. Next, the workers restored the canal's intake. This involved removing the excess silt built up from the rains, reconstructing the weir, and ensuring that an adequate amount of water again flowed into the canal. Rehabilitating the intake took less time and effort than cleaning the primary channel, and only a few men participated. At the conclusion of these efforts, the men gathered at the home of the meni mfongo and celebrated with a meal and mbege.

Emergency maintenance had to be carried out much more quickly. Once the meni mfongo had been notified of a break or blockage, he sounded a call to the men using a horn. Those who heard the sound of the horn knew to assemble at his home the next day prepared to carry out whatever maintenance was necessary. The meni mfongo then organized those who came, proceeded to the location of the problem, and supervised repair of the canal. This work was likely much less pleasant than routine maintenance as it most often took place during the rains, when temperatures were cooler, the rivers higher, and the terrain muddier.

Another important management task of the meni mfongo was his setting a timetable for use of the canal: who could use it and when, and how much water could be used at a given time. Guidelines varied widely across Kilimanjaro, as they reflected local circumstances such as the size of the canal and the number of users. In most cases, meni mifongo allowed users to draw as much water as they needed for domestic purposes but required it be taken in the mornings, when the water was usually clearest, most clean, and thought to possess healing powers. This allowed women, the primary collectors of domestic water, to complete this work in the mornings and dedicate their afternoons to cultivation. For irrigation, meni mifongo granted each user a specific period of time in which he could open his branch canal and irrigate his lands. This reflected how time, rather than volume, was the standard for water measurement before the twentieth century. In some areas, a turn lasted half a day, so one user could irrigate from sunup to midday and another from midday to dusk. Irrigation rarely took place at night. The criteria by which the meni mifongo set the timetable reflected the individual politics of each canal. Gutmann noticed that in Marangu, irrigation began with the users who were farthest downhill on the right side of the mfongo. "Then follows the one who lives higher up, and so forth to about the middle of the country. Then the sequence shifts to the left side, again beginning with the one living farthest down. If the left lower half is finished, the upper half follows the same sequence until every user had had a chance to water. Then the series starts all over again."[61] This pattern could be flexible depending on the availability of water. Two or more users could share a turn if the canal had sufficient flow. If one user's crops began to wither, the meni mfongo could require that the "person who has the water . . . must turn the water over to the man with the dry field."[62] The meni mifongo reserved special privileges and the right to alter the timetable at any time. For many canals, they claimed complete rights to the water on every third day.[63] Since irrigation for a whole day was rarely necessary, they would then grant those who needed more water part of this day in exchange for vegetables, eleusine, or mbege.

In addition to a timetable, most canals had bylaws covering issues ranging from access to cleanliness. These functioned as a legal code for the canals, enforced by the meni mifongo and backed by possible punishments. The following are bylaws enforced for canals in Kilema:[64]

- One is not permitted to break the timetable.
- One must close one's own canal after irrigating so that others may use the waters.
- One must attend all activities of the canal, such as maintenance.
- One must not deliberately dirty the canal.
- One must not accidentally dirty it by washing clothes or eleusine in or near it.
- One must not bathe in the canal.
- One must obtain cooking water in the mornings.
- One must dig a pit for the disposal of dirty water so that it will not flow back into the canal.

Violation of these bylaws by anyone, including women and children, resulted in punishment. The most common was a fine; if one violated a bylaw, the entire family would be banned from the canal until one or more barrels of mbege were delivered to the meni mfongo.[65] For severe transgressions, the violator and his or her family could be banished from the mfongo entirely. Children were taught from a very early age to respect the bylaws of the canals, and if they were caught urinating in them, playing in them, or in any way fouling them, they could be punished by whipping. Furthermore, special prohibitions existed for pregnant women. Aside from the normal restrictions against women's performing any labor on canals, expectant mothers were prohibited from crossing canals or approaching their intakes.[66]

While conflict among the users of a canal fell to the jurisdiction of the meni mfongo, the mangi played a role in conflicts among users of different canals within a chiefdom. For example, if a canal drew too much water from a river, leaving downstream canals dry, the mangi could set limits on the upstream canal or order that the intake be reconstructed to reduce flows. These sorts of conflicts were more prominent in the dry months, when the rivers were lower and farmers needed to irrigate eleusine. Disputes over a water source between chiefdoms could be adjudicated through negotiation or warfare. By the nineteenth century, wars stemming from control of mifongo became increasingly common, the victorious chiefdom winning the right to claim as much water as it wished.[67] The wamangi had little direct involvement in water management, aside from these limited roles, until the twentieth century. Rather, these duties remained in the hands of local specialists and societies of users.

SPIRITUAL AND CULTURAL MANAGEMENT

While physical management of water resources was extremely important, this was not the only way in which these resources were managed. Given the centrality of water to cultural and spiritual practices, we must think of water management and of those who manage it in much broader terms. By looking in depth at the spiritual and cultural dimensions of water, and how these properties were managed, we see that management of water resources on Kilimanjaro encompassed a wide range of actors and therefore was inherently local and decentralized.

Managing the spiritual properties of water was vital in these communities. It was the abundant streams, rivers, and rainfall that allowed people to grow bananas, brew beer, and construct mud houses. Water, more than anything else, distinguished the vihamba from the foothills and the lowlands. Lack of water meant death. Knowledge of water's importance had brought the people to Kilimanjaro and, in their minds, separated them from dryland peoples such as the Maasai. In popular imagination, the mere idea of leaving the mountain for the plains generated tremendous anxiety. Charles Dundas observed:

> Not only is the magnificence of the mountain such as [to] compel attachment, but as soon as the mountain dwellers leave it, life becomes intolerable for them. The plain affords them neither their accustomed food nor abundance of water, down there they become the victims of malaria, a prey for the ferocious lion, the blundering rhinoceros and the crafty buffalo, or the loathsome crocodile, all of which are unknown on the mountain, and finally they are exposed to the burning heat. Nothing affrights the mountain dweller more than the threat of being sent to a dry country.[68]

The association of the mountain with all that was good and the plains with evil and danger was so powerful that it persisted into the twentieth century.

The association of water with life and lack of water with death fostered other dichotomies, including the mountain versus the plains, civilized versus uncivilized, and pure versus impure. The most powerful of these was good versus evil. Mountain peoples believed not only that water was inherently good, but also that it had the power to eliminate evil by purifying both the landscape and its people. According to accounts from elders, Ruwa created the mountain itself as a way to distinguish good from evil and reward those peoples he considered to be good.[69] He also used the powers of water to keep evil from reclaiming the mountain. One example, recorded by Dundas, is a fable very similar in style to that of the great flood in the Bible's book of Genesis.[70] It involves a great man, Mkechuwa, who died and left behind much wealth to his children. They showed little sympathy for the poor. Ruwa, angered by this, sent his minister to the community disguised as a man with boils all over his body. The man went to the people and begged for food, as well as fat to anoint his boils. Most turned their backs on him, saying, "Have you no shame?" At last he came to a man of mercy, who offered him food, washed his whole body, and anointed him with fat for his boils. At this time, the minister revealed himself to be the minister of Ruwa. He told the man to bring people of his clan, his family, and his friends to live at his home, for "events are at hand." He then warned the man by saying, "If you hear a noise as of a great water running fiercely, hold fast to the supports of the hut. And on hearing this noise, remain in silence. For Ruwa shall pass among men in his strength." Eight nights later, Ruwa brought a great flood from the forest:

> The water carried away the evil people and all others, and their huts and their food and all their possessions. And the merciful man when he heard this noise, did everything as he had been commanded. And they were saved, all who were with him. The water by its force carried all those people with their cattle, sheep and goats far into the plain. And those people Ruwa turned into elephants. And their cattle became buffalos and eland and their like. And their sheep became pigs and porcupines. And their dogs became leopards and hyenas and their like.[71]

When the man of mercy awoke, he found the whole country empty. He and his people then set out to repopulate the mountain and build a great society. This fable aligns the powers of water with those of Ruwa. Through Ruwa's actions, water acts as an agent with the power to cleanse, reward, and punish. As water flows from the forest to the plains, evil is washed away and the landscape is recreated for the benefit of the virtuous, thus reestablishing the dichotomy of the mountain as good and the surrounding lands as evil.

The cleansing power of water arises in relation to the body as well as the landscape. Several cultural and religious practices involved using water to purify the body when it was harmed. On Kilimanjaro, wrongdoings were considered to be the actions of spirits, and as such they were not merely temporal concerns. Rather, they implied a continuing evil influence on the victim of the transgression, one that could only be eliminated with a rite of purification. Dundas notes numerous examples of grievances subject to rites of purification. Victims included a man bitten by a woman, a man struck by his wife with a cooking pot, a man greeted while carrying a carcass on his head, a man wounded by a leopard, a man who pronounced a curse, a betrothed girl who became pregnant by another man, a woman who bore twins, any goat that bore twins in its first delivery, and any sheep or cow that bore twins at any time.[72] In order to right these wrongs, the victim needed to undergo purification. These rites were the responsibility of specialists, members of a particular clan who possessed knowledge to placate the spirits. In many chiefdoms, certain clans developed a reputation for their purification skills, such as the Wako-Mariwa of Marangu.[73]

The following is an example of a cleansing ceremony recorded by Dundas.[74] In the first step, the unclean person gathers the necessary ingredients: the skin, dung, and stomach contents of a hyrax, the skin and blood of a monkey, the shell and blood of a snail, certain herbs, the tail of a lizard, the skin of a gazelle, the blood of a female sheep, rainwater taken from a hollow tree in the forest, fresh water drawn from a spring in the early morning, two black sugarcane stalks, and fresh mbege. Then the specialist arrives, along with other members of the clan and family. The specialist digs a hollow in which to mix the ingredients and then makes two gateways of sugar cane. As the people gathered pass through the gateways, the specialist dips his gnu tail into the mixture, brushes the people, and says while facing Kibo, "The evil and uncleanness become gentile as these that you will not be tormented again." He then sprinkles the liquid over their heads to imitate rain. The specialist repeats this the next four days, in both the morning and evening. Following the last performance, everyone gathers the remaining liquid and casts it into a river while saying, "The evil and sin and uncleanness which comes from us go with this river. The water of this river carry it to the plain."[75]

This purification ceremony illustrates the significance of water in these types of rituals. The unclean person gathers two distinctly pure forms of water, one from the forest (the home of the spirits) and another from a spring in the early morning. The water serves as the base of a medicine used first to anoint the person and his or her family, second to simulate rainfall (which implies the bringing of new life), and third to carry the evil from the vihamba to the plains. Water therefore assumes several functions: it cleanses the individual of evil, it brings that person life or rebirth, and it extracts evil to its rightful domain, the plains. The properties of water inherent in ceremonies such as purification appear in various adages, further demonstrating the significance of spiritual knowledge of water in daily life. One of these is *mringa uwore mbaka voo*, "water brings no harm." The adage implies that if a destructive event such as a flood occurs, it is the product of either intervention by a malevolent spirit or desire by Ruwa to purify the landscape. As a gift from Ruwa, water itself can bring only good unless it is tampered with.

The management of water also figured centrally in education and initiation practices. These were social rituals that defined people in relation to those around them, conferring upon them social status and community membership. Through its placement in these rites, water marked various stages of transition for individuals as they progressed to adulthood. Its cleansing and curative properties contributed to the rebirth of the person at various stages in life. In his 1940 study of childhood on Kilimanjaro, Otto Raum defined education as "the relationship between members of successive generations."[76] In the era before mission schools, children received education by listening to and learning from their elders, following elders' instructions and examples. These interactions took place in many different contexts (within the home, at the home of an elder or specialist, on the grounds of the kihamba, in the forests, etc.) and could involve one-on-one instruction, group instruction, or hands-on training in everything from speaking and cooking to religion and farming.[77]

As a vital resource, water was a prominent theme in childhood education. From an early age, children learned the nature and significance of the water sources around them from their parents and elders. They were taught to respect the physical sources as well as the spiritual forces that gave them vitality and continuity with their ancestors. As children entered adolescence, they learned the processes associated with procurement and distribution. Girls learned from their mothers how to collect water, from where, and when, while boys learned how to irrigate, as well as the responsibilities of canal construction and maintenance. The adolescents also came to understand much about the world around them, politically and socially, through the concept of water. These lessons together created adults who would continue this physical and social system well after the death of their elders.

The lessons taught to children about the importance of water began at an early age. As soon as they could walk, they heard stories, fables, and tales designed to instill proper behavior and respect. Leoni Motesha, from Mkuu Rombo, recalled such a fable from her childhood involving a wolf and a goat:

> The two were the best of friends, until the goat had two children. Then the wolf began to use every trick possible to eat one of them. Near their homes was a small pool that most animals used for taking water. One day the wolf went to Mr. Lion, the chairman of the animals, and told him that the goat children were spoiling the water by swimming in it. The lion decided to charge the wolf with standing guard over the water. One evening the two goat children came to the pool to take some water. The wolf ran to them, caught one, and ate him. The other child went home and told her mother that the wolf had eaten her brother. The mother goat went to the lion and told him to arrest the wolf because he had killed one of her children. The lion responded by saying that it was her punishment because her children had spoiled the water. The mother goat returned home, crying all the way, and from that day the goat and the wolf became enemies.[78]

Stories such as these drew on the power of negative reinforcement. By showing the misfortune of one family caused by children swimming in a water source, this story intends to frighten small children away from unacceptable conduct. Wilhelm Maunga, also from Mkuu, recalled a similar story that also involved animals:

> There once was a pool for all the animals. That is, except for the hare, because he refused to give his labor when they constructed it. The hare always came and took water and then spoiled the rest by swimming in it. The wild animals chose the monkey to guard the water. The hare used a trick and took a bottle of honey and asked the monkey to let him have some water in exchange for some honey. The monkey agreed, so the hare gave him honey. The monkey tasted it and said, "It is very sweet, give me another one." The hare told him that he would if he could tie the monkey's legs together. The monkey agreed, and the hare tied his legs. But the hare didn't give him any honey. Instead he filled his pot and spoiled the water. The next morning the other animals came to the pool. They were very annoyed to find the monkey's legs all tied up and the water spoiled. The animals punished the monkey and never let him guard the pool again.[79]

This story draws on imagery similar to that of the first, but its moral is different. The antagonist is the hare, who commits a number of transgressions: not participating in the construction of the pool, stealing water, and fouling the watercourse. Yet the monkey, who is susceptible to the trickery of the hare, is blamed. The moral is that children should strive to be like neither. In other words, they should keep the waters clean while being vigilant and smart in protecting water from the actions of others. Fables and stories of these sort were common across the mountain. In Kilema, for example, a common fable threatened children by telling them that if they urinated in a watercourse, their mothers would be swept away with the waters to the plains, never to be seen or heard from again.[80]

As children grew older, they became more interested in water management because of its association with adulthood. Young boys mimicked the work of elders, using sticks to create small channels to drain water from puddles. Raum noted the following example of boys creating their own miniature mifongo:

> One sees boys come out after a heavy shower and look for a pool. Squatting down at its edge they begin to challenge one another: "Who can make a canal that would drain the pool?" Every boy begins to dig a canal. The unskillful is laughed at and called a woman. If all are equally successful, they shout with glee: "Who isn't a man?"[81]

Children gained more responsibilities with water as they approached adolescence. Girls learned from their mothers the skill of procuring water for the household. This required teaching about the sources available at various times of year and about how to choose the best water for a given purpose. As girls took over responsibility for collecting water for the home, they freed up their mothers to perform other labor such as tending crops and brewing. Boys began to learn more about the importance of the canals. Elders taught young boys that the canals were part of their heritage left by their ancestors. In his book on Chagga education, R. Sambuli Mosha noted the following riddle:

> Riddle: Father left me a bowl from which I have been eating ever since.
>
> Answer: The irrigation canal.[82]

Riddles and sayings such as this reminded the youth of the importance of the canals as well as the hard work their fathers and ancestors put into developing them. When boys neared the age of fifteen, they were given the task of irrigating the kihamba.[83] Fathers taught their sons how to spread out the water from the canal by using many small canals and banana sheaths. This ensured that they brought water to the plants as a gentle trickle rather than a quick flow that would wash away soil and manure.

Teaching of mfongo design and management began as boys neared initiation. On the mountain, initiation involved a series of teachings, rituals, and ceremonies that marked the transition into adulthood.[84] Initiation rites for both girls and boys involved division into age-sets, followed by group education in the proper ways of being an adult. This

culminated in circumcision, a physical act that symbolized the rebirth into adulthood that had taken place. Water played a crucial role
throughout this process. First, boys had to be taught the workings of the
system and the responsibilities of being a member of a canal society.
Gutmann writes of a canal cleaning ceremony that took place during an
initiation in Marangu.[85] The boys were gathered together and sent to a
canal to learn the art of cleaning it from a teaching elder. They removed
their clothes and had their heads shaved. The elder then called on them
to enter a dry canal on their hands and knees and begin removing the
grasses that had grown inside it. As they did this he sang a song:

Aleh, my novices, my helper.

Awaken the train of male novices. Lelele hm . . .

Aleh, my novices, I have put my arm in here.

May the juice plant and the mossy fern spring up.

Hoh heh haja ja ja ja ja!

Aleh, my novices, may it prosper, you men, my comrades!

Hah ja ja ja hm . . .

Aleh, my novices, may it rise in billows, up and down, ei you men!

Hah ja ja ja hm . . .

Hei you men, comrades, I am beginning the procession, I am beginning the march.

Hoh heh hm . . . hm . . .

Now I relinquish it to the helper of the child.

He must tell it to his younger brother who comes after him.

Hoh heh hm . . . hm . . .

Aleh, my young brother.

What is it billowing up and down here?

Like the juice plant and the mossy fern!

Hoh heh hm . . . hm . . .

Which springs up there like the sprouting grass.

Hoh heh hm . . . hm . . .

The word *lelele* was onomatopoetic, referring to the sound made by the rushing of water into an empty canal. The elders repeated the song as the boys cleaned the length of the canal. Gutmann concluded that the sound signified the rebirth experienced by the boys through initiation.

After the boys had cleaned the canal, the teacher opened the weir and released water back into the canal. He then instructed the boys to live life as the grasses. As the boys had sent the grasses out from the canal, so must they send out shoots that would flourish in their home-steads.[86] The cleaning of the canal, therefore, was symbolic as well as practical. The boys learned an important skill, while the ceremony itself symbolized their transformation. Just as the grasses were removed from the canal and given new life outside it, so the initiates were pulled from the nurtured state of childhood and released into adulthood.

Circumcision, the culminating step in the initiation process, drew heavily on the perceived powers of water. The cleansing properties of water helped wash initiates of the impurities of childhood and prepare them for adult life. In his book, Dundas describes a circumcision cer-emony for girls and provides a vivid description of the role of water.[87] After much preparation, the girl and her female relatives gathered. The women all came with a gift of eleusine. Before the actual operation, the relatives took the girl to a canal to be washed by one of the senior women. The elder sprinkled only the toes of her right foot, saying, "We wash you of all the uncleanness of heretofore, now we cleanse you of the uncleanness of childhood that you may follow a new path to your death." They then led the girl to a hut to be anointed and then to the hut of an elder, who performed the operation. Afterward, the elder tested the girl for her virginity, and if she passed, much celebration and mbege drinking ensued. After three days, the elder returned to wash the girl, and they began a period of instruction in the domestic duties of womanhood. Water thus served as an agent that purified the girl of the uncleanness accumulated during childhood and that fostered her rebirth as a woman.

The education and initiation of children illustrate water's impor-tance in an array of social and cultural transactions. Especially impor-tant is the way in which water arose as a form of knowledge. For the youngest children, they were taught basic knowledge of water sources at an early age as a way of protecting these communal resources from children's immaturity and inexperience. Initiation represented the time when adolescents were granted deeper knowledge of water and became privy to its cleansing and life-giving powers. The ceremonies themselves were also significant in that they reproduced the power and authority of the knowledge holders, in this case elders and ritual specialists.

~

Analyzing the water-management practices that developed on Kilimanjaro, one clearly sees how people's impressions of the waterscape shaped a web of linkages between water and society. Mountain communities developed a highly nuanced understanding of the dynamism and diversity of the water supply as well as a broad understanding of the knowledge needed to manage it. People needed water to nurture crops and cook bananas, but they also valued it for its power to cleanse people and generate new life. Water could be known in many ways, and people at various levels of the social strata had differential access to this knowledge. Children were denied knowledge of water until they reached initiation and were considered adults. Women were denied knowledge of procuring, controlling, and managing water resources, while they often knew more about water quality, the day-to-day tribulations of finding water, and methods of carrying, storing, and using water. Meni mifongo held knowledge of canal management that made their services and expertise tremendously important to the whole of the mountain.

By the nineteenth century, the peoples of Kilimanjaro had developed a highly successful system of intensive agriculture, one that enabled them to prosper and grow significantly in size. Around 100,000 people lived on the slopes of the mountain by 1850, spread across more than forty mountain ridges. The period brought many changes to the mountain. It experienced a dramatic rise in trade with peoples from beyond the mountain, particularly Swahili long-distance traders. The growing importance of this trade fueled the rise of chieftaincy and the increasingly assertive power of the wamangi. It also led to a rise in warfare on the mountain, pitting rival chieftaincies against one another and forcing weaker chiefdoms on the mountain to either forge alliances or accept subordination.

Despite this trend toward political centralization, the management of water remained decentralized. Wamangi asserted little authority over water until the colonial period. This reflects the mountain's multiple-source water economy, in which people relied on a diversity of water resources rather than a single one that could be easily monopolized. It also indicates the extent to which water management empowered a wide range of people in the community, from rainmakers to canal specialists, from men to women, from elders to children. Management of the resource was widely distributed, and widely shared, relying on a web of intersecting knowledge. At the heart of this knowledge was a shared heritage among the people and the belief that the mountain was the source of life.

2 ⟿ The Mountains of Jagga

Encountering Africa's Olympus
in the Nineteenth Century

ON MAY 11, 1848, Johannes Rebmann of the Church Missionary Society became the first European to see Kilimanjaro. A mere two weeks earlier, most Westerners had regarded the mountain as a legend, a supposed Ethiopian Olympus, a white-capped mountain of gold and silver reaching beyond the clouds. Inspired by tales of this fabled place, Rebmann set out from Mombasa with a guide and a small caravan across the harsh terrain of the steppe. In his journal, he described the radically shifting landscape as they approached the peak:

> We crossed the river Lumi at seven in the morning. The nearer we approached the mountains of Jagga the richer was the vegetation; here and there we met with large and magnificent trees, such as I had not seen since I left the coast, till at last we entered a noble valley, thickly grown over with grass which reached up to our middle. Abundant pasture-land for thousands of cattle! Oh, what a noble country has God reserved for his people![1]

In the eyes of Rebmann, the mountain seemed a God-given place, a Garden of Eden lying in stark contrast to its surroundings. Especially surprising to him was the peak's white layer:

> I fancied I saw the summit of one of them covered with a dazzling white cloud. My guide called the white which I saw, merely "Beredi," cold; it was perfectly clear to me, however, that it could be nothing else but snow.

Rebmann's discoveries, shared through his published letters and journal excerpts, generated curiosity and skepticism throughout Britain.[2] Many dismissed his sightings as fantasy, hallucinations resulting from tropical fever. Nonetheless, they brought the mysterious African peak into the Western consciousness and inspired a generation of adventurers to conquer it for themselves.

Rebmann's expedition reflected a period when the communities of Kilimanjaro came into increasing contact with peoples from beyond the mountain. Never an isolated island, the mountain had long been tied to other parts of the region, and trade between mountain peoples and neighboring societies was a regular occurrence. In the nineteenth century, new players emerged on the scene: traders from more distant parts of the steppe, Swahili caravans from the coast, and European missionaries and adventurers. These outsiders brought new opportunities for trade as well as their own perspectives of the mountain and its waterscapes. Though in many ways different from one another, they shared the common experience of encountering the mountain as an oasis. They defined it as a singular space in opposition to its surroundings, an island of lushness in a sea of aridity. In turn, they considered the inhabitants of this singular space as a singular people. While the massive size of the mountain marked the physical space, it was water (the mysterious snows and the abundance of rivers, streams, and vegetation) that came to define it.

The outsiders who encountered Kilimanjaro in the nineteenth century developed impressions of the waterscape that were very different from those held by the local populations. This owes much to the nature of encounter. Most traders and explorers came to the mountain using the same routes and traveling at the same times of year. These journeys were often arduous; hardships ranged from disease and wild animals to lack of water. The mountain, with its green hills and numerous rivers and streams, emerged as an oasis amid the steppe. African traders saw the mountain as a distinctive place, important in trade and possessing spiritual or mystical significance, but nothing radically out of the ordinary. Europeans, however, developed highly romanticized, idealized visions of Kilimanjaro. At first a fabled Ethiopian Mount Olympus, it was later described as an otherworldly space, an Eden in the heart of Africa. The core of such imageries was water, which gave the place a fecundity and lushness that was absent in the rest of East

Africa and comparable to European locales such as the Swiss Alps and Devonshire.

The way in which Europeans imagined Kilimanjaro indicates not only the importance of the oasis encounter, but also the broader cultural constructs that informed European expectations of Africa. Scholars such as Edward Said and Benedict Anderson have shown the importance of "imagined geographies" in shaping how Europeans have made sense of non-Western spaces and peoples.[3] With Kilimanjaro, we see a physical space that was imagined through the intersection of two elements: culturally produced archetypes and intense experiences of encounter. The first written accounts of the mountain to circulate in Europe created an image that was the product of the initial explorers' culturally ingrained expectations of Africa encountering a space that defied these expectations. The mountain, standing in stark contrast to both its immediate surroundings and prevailing archetypes, became viewed as miraculous and symbolic, described in romanticized terms. The waterscape defined the essence of the region's presumed other-worldliness. With abundant water and mysterious snows, the mountain could service a number of agendas: religious, scientific, and colonial. The waterscapes these explorers produced lacked the nuance of that held by locals, who knew all too well that the waters could be precarious and needed careful management. This occurred because the explorers encountered the mountain as a snapshot, seeing only small parts for limited durations at only certain times of the year. They missed out on the political and environmental dynamism at play. Images of an Edenesque Kilimanjaro, a waterscape of unending abundance, proved resilient despite clear evidence to the contrary, and they shaped the initial period of colonization.

KILIMANJARO AND ITS NEIGHBORS

Though often represented as an "island," Kilimanjaro has a long history of connectivity with neighboring areas. A dearth of surviving sources from Africa's early history has made this difficult to document in specific terms. Nonetheless, we can trace ties between the mountain and neighboring areas using historical linguistics, oral narratives, and archeology. After 1850, documentary sources become more widely available, particularly the writings of European explorers. From these records, it is possible to piece together the relationship between the communities of Kilimanjaro and their neighbors, and how these out-siders made sense of the mountain and its waterscapes.

The clearest linkages can be found with the peoples residing on the other "islands" of the region: Mount Meru, the Taita Hills, and the Pare Mountains. These highland areas are closer to Kilimanjaro than the far reaches of mountain settlement—Siha and Rombo—are to one another. The peoples of these areas—the Meru, the Dwaida, the Gweno, the Pare, and others—shared close common descent with the peoples of Kilimanjaro.[4] They also shared many living patterns. All resided on well-watered lands at similar altitudes, were primarily agricultural, grew similar crops in home gardens, and kept livestock in stalls. They also held similar forms of social organization, living in clusters of homesteads along ridges and identifying with the clan. The Meru, Taita, and Pare even constructed irrigation canals, though on a smaller scale than on Kilimanjaro.[5] By the nineteenth century, many of these communities had ties to Kilimanjaro through trade. It is likely, for example, that much of the raw iron used by blacksmiths on the mountain came from Pare.[6]

How might these groups have viewed the waters of Kilimanjaro? Given their shared descent, common experience of mountainside liv-ing, and deep cultural similarities with the peoples of Kilimanjaro, these communities—particularly North Pare, the closest highland community—likely found the region's features familiar. Michael Sheridan's work on the Usangi area of North Pare shows not only how its water management bears striking similarity to that of Kilimanjaro, but also how irrigation networks shared symbolic similarities with the human body and human fertility, similar to the dichotomy of water as blood and land as body, discussed in chapter 1.[7] Thus, neighboring mountain peoples would have seen Kilimanjaro as a lived space very similar to their own, and its significance would have been understood in terms of cultural connectivity and trade ties. It also seems likely that these groups would have acknowledged the diversity of the mountain's physical space as well as its population.

Aside from mountain farmers, the Kilimanjaro region has also long been home to seminomadic peoples who have resided on the steppe. The earliest were Khoisan hunter-gatherers, followed by Cushitic and Nilotic pastoralists.[8] Most are no longer in existence, having either migrated away or assimilated into other groups, and very little is known of them. By the 1850s, the Maasai had emerged as the largest community in the steppe. In many ways, they could hardly be more different from the peoples of Kilimanjaro. They were Nilotic speakers, they practiced pastoralism and limited crop cultivation, and they organized themselves into bands rather than clans. Most of all, they lived in the lowlands, known for its absence of water. As Wimmelbücker notes, by the nineteenth century, those on the mountain considered the Maasai as "prototypes of the foe."[9] This stemmed in part from their frequent incursions on the mountain aimed at seizing cattle and other goods. Yet as he and others have noted, the relationship was considerably more nuanced. Maasai peacefully frequented mountain markets to exchange goods including salt, milk, and meat for wood, bananas, yams, honey, and other foodstuffs. People also passed between the two, such as prisoners taken in fighting and women of marrying age. It is likely that some social and cultural practices, such as age-sets, passed into mountain society from the Maasai. In the words of Nurse, the relationship was more akin to love-hate than strictly negative.[10]

As seminomadic peoples, Maasai depended on surface water to support themselves and their cattle, and those living near Kilimanjaro recognized the mountain as the source of the rivers and streams on which they depended. These water sources not only provided a needed resource but also served as pathways guiding them to the mountain's chiefdoms. Maasai may have considered the mountain's white peak to be its distinguishing feature. Rebmann claims that those he encountered called it Ol Donyo Eibor, meaning "White Mountain" in the Maa language.[11] Maasai had no familiarity with ice in the 1850s and therefore would only have recognized the peak as distinctive by its coloration. It is also possible that "white" refers to the cloud patterns that leave the peak obscured for much of day. In either case, the white peak clearly would have marked the mountain as different from others in the steppe. Some have also speculated that Maa is the source of the term "Kilimanjaro." In his 1893 memoir, Catholic missionary Alexandre Le Roy claimed that several children in Taveta told him that the Maa word for water is *ngaro* and that they refer to the mountain as the "Mountain of Water" because all the rivers rise from it.[12] However, this is questionable given that there is no word in Maa approximating "Kilima."

These surrounding communities, though distinct from one another, all had a long-standing connection with the peoples of Kilimanjaro through cultural ties, trade, and warfare. The Bantu communities came from similar alpine spaces and did not endure especially long journeys en route. The Maasai dwelt in the lowlands, the very space that mountain peoples deemed harmful, and thus would not have seen the mountain as a superior space but as only different in its features. Though not encountered as an oasis, Kilimanjaro did serve as a focal point for communities living in its shadows.

African communities from farther afield came into contact with Kilimanjaro as well. Given its tremendous size and its abundance of water, it has been part of regional trade networks for centuries. At the start of the nineteenth century, Kilimanjaro emerged as a center of regional trade, largely because of the rising value of ivory. Between the 1820s and the 1890s, prices for ivory at Zanzibar increased by roughly sixfold.[13] This precipitated a massive growth in ivory trading that eventually connected areas of the interior as far inland as central Kenya and the Great Lakes with the coastal ports of Mombasa and Pangani as well as Zanzibar. Initially, most traders that reached Kilimanjaro were from groups such as the Giryama, the Digo, the Shambaa, and the Kamba.[14] For them the mountain served two purposes: a place to secure water and provisions for the continued journey and a place to purchase ivory from local hunters.

European travelogues provide some insight into how these groups viewed the waters of Kilimanjaro. Rebmann, for example, notes an encounter in 1849 with a Kamba chief who calls the mountain Kima ja Jeu, or "Mount of Whiteness."[15] This indicates that the defining feature of the mountain was the white cap. The nature of the ivory trade and the availability of resources lead to other deductions as well. The journeys made by these groups to Kilimanjaro were much longer in duration than those of neighboring mountain peoples and involved passage through the arid interior highlands and days of travel without reliable surface water. The mountain provided a needed source of water and food to the caravans, and thus it would have stood as an oasis in stark contrast to its surroundings. Also, the mountain's streams and rivers attracted large numbers of elephants, particularly during the dry seasons. This made the mountain a destination for traders, either to engage in hunting or to trade with local hunters. Lastly, the mountain offered reprieve from threats of the open steppe such as wild animal attacks and raids by the Maasai.

By midcentury, East African caravan trading began to shift in several ways that would affect Kilimanjaro. Slaves displaced ivory as the most lucrative commodity of the region, a change sparked by declining elephant populations and the rise of plantation agriculture on the coast and Zanzibar.[16] European traders also became a greater presence on the coast, which led to an influx of capital and increasingly profitable trade. The most significant change was the development of caravan routes by the Swahili that connected Kilimanjaro directly with the coast.[17] By midcentury, two primary routes had arisen: one connecting the mountain to Mombasa via the Taita Hills and the other reaching Tanga and Pangani via the Pare and Usambara Mountains (see map 2.1). From Kilimanjaro, two routes continued into the interior, one to central Kenya and the other past Mount Meru to the south shore of Lake Victoria. This placed Kilimanjaro at the heart of a long-distance network extending across much of Eastern Africa. Sally Falk Moore notes that the mountain was in a "strategic position, both as to location and capacity."[18] The chiefdoms provided caravans with a place to purchase ivory, slaves, and provisions.

Swahili porters and traders experienced the waterscape of Kilimanjaro much differently from the groups living close to the mountain. This owes to the nature of the encounter, which came after the rigors of the journey. The journey on foot from the coast took anywhere from a few weeks to a month depending on the route, weather, and stops made. Both main routes passed through difficult terrains: the coastal mangrove swamps, the region of scrubland known as the *nyika*, and for much of the journey, the semiarid steppe. Caravans faced potential attacks from wild animals as well as raids from hostile groups. They also dealt with a range of potential illnesses: heat exhaustion, typhoid, dysentery, malaria, and yellow fever. But the most pressing concern was access to water. On the Mombasa route, water became scarce once the caravans reached the nyika, within a day or so from the start. Caravans could hardly afford to carry lots of water with them, so the journey involved hopping from one water source to another. An unexpectedly dry source could bring deadly consequences. Amid the rigors of this journey arose Kilimanjaro, a massive, green, water-abundant oasis in stark contrast to its surroundings.

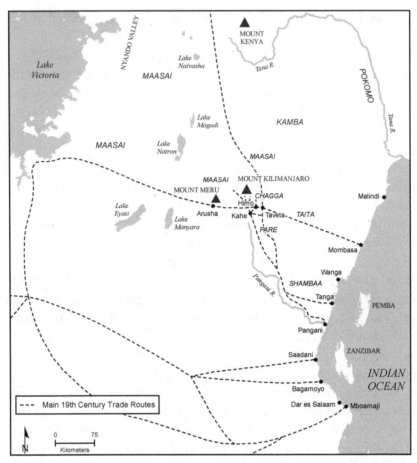

MAP 2.1. Nineteenth-century trading routes (*Brian Edward Balsley, GISP. Based on map in Moore and Puritt,* The Chagga and Meru of Tanzania)

Because the merchants who organized caravans did not keep descriptive travelogues, we can draw on the writings of missionaries who used Swahili guides to understand how the caravans imagined the mountain. Rebmann reputed that the Swahili referred to the mountain as Jagga, a term that referred to both the physical space and the people who lived there, as well as Kilima Ndscharo, which he translates as "Mountain of the Caravans."[19] Interestingly, this is one of the few explanations for the mountain's name that does not involve the white peak. There is evidence, however, that this feature was well known on the coast and had even taken on mystical proportions. Rebmann claims that some Swahili believed its white cap to be composed of silver, while others associated it with evil spirits.[20] In his travelogue, he quotes the governor of Mombasa warning him that he "must not ascend the mountain because it is full of evil spirits . . . people who have ascended the mountain have been slain by the spirits, their feet and hands have been stiffened."[21] The nature of this warning, referring to the symptoms of frostbite, indicates that his views may have been based on actual firsthand accounts. Aside from such tales, it appears that the Swahili thought of Kilimanjaro as an important link in caravan networks but not necessarily an unusual place.

Little water knowledge seems to have passed from the Swahili to mountain communities in the nineteenth century. Yet the caravans had a profound impact on the mountain that would, in future decades, influence the control and management of water. The expansion of long-distance trade with the coast proved to be an economic boon to many areas of the mountain, particularly the southeast chiefdoms. As slavery displaced ivory, the trade resulted in widespread violence and turmoil as stronger chiefdoms engaged in warfare to capture human cargo from weaker ones. By the 1880s, the region had become known for its political instability as well as its natural features.

THE ERA OF EUROPEAN EXPLORATION

Europeans had speculated about the existence of a snowcapped mountain in Africa since antiquity. Yet like many of Africa's other renowned features, such as the source of the Nile River, its existence was not widely accepted until the nineteenth century. Though close in proximity, the African continent had remained largely unexplored by Europeans for centuries because of its difficult terrain (steppe, desert, and rainforest), its lack of navigable waterways into the interior, threats from hostile communities, and the prevalence of diseases such as trypanosomiasis, yellow fever, and malaria. These made treks to the interior highly risky and, consequently, very rare. The risks associated with African exploration and the consequent lack of knowledge of the continent outside its coastlines, the Nile Valley, and South Africa led to an enduring image of the continent as mysterious, dark, and dangerous, and its peoples as savage, childlike, and uncivilized. A notable example of such thought is the work of German philosopher Hegel. In his *Lectures on the Philosophy of History* (1821–31), he wrote:

> Africa proper, as far as History goes back, has remained—for all purposes of connection with the rest of the World—shut up. . . .

It is the Gold-land compressed within itself—the land of child-hood, which lying beyond the day of history, is enveloped in the dark mantle of Night. Its isolated character originates, not merely in its tropical nature, but essentially in its geographical condition.[22]

Hegel describes Africa as a continent isolated, lying beyond the bounds of history. This is in part due to the lack of actual knowledge of its interior and also due to his assertion that Africans were not rational beings and thus could not see themselves historically.

In the second half of the century, explorers trickled into the continent, eager to "discover" its secrets. Among these, the fabled snow mountain emerged as one of the most eagerly sought. Hans Meyer, the famed German mountaineer, estimated that by the 1880s, no fewer than forty-nine Europeans had visited the mountain, making it the most visited place in the continent's interior.[23] These adventurers represented a wide range of backgrounds (cultural, occupational, and religious) and came to the mountain with different purposes in mind. What is striking is the consistency of the knowledge they developed about the mountain and its waterscape. Like the Swahili, the Europeans approached the mountain having undertaken arduous journeys through difficult territory, even using the same routes and guides. For Europeans, however, this encounter took on deeper meaning. They began to imagine Kilimanjaro as otherworldly, distinct from the rest of the continent, and described it in an idealized language with terms such as "Ethiopian Olympus" and "African Eden." In turn, it emerged as a symbol of European aspirations for the continent as a whole.

Why did European explorers imagine Kilimanjaro in such a way? The answer lies at the intersection of the prevailing imagined geography of Africa and the actual encounters of those who reached the mountain. In the eyes of explorers, the mountain stood in stark contrast not only to its surroundings, but also to prevailing culturally constructed notions of the African continent. While the size of the mountain certainly drew explorers' attention, it was the waterscape they found most alluring, the abundance of streams and rivers and the mysterious white cap. These features seemed to be, by the standards of contemporary science, impossibilities for a place so close to the equator. Furthermore, the mild climate attributed to the snows made the locale more akin to parts of Europe than to the rest of Africa. Kiliman-jaro was not merely an oasis in the steppe, but an island of civility that could serve as a springboard for future European endeavors such as missionary work, scientific research, and colonization. Therefore, they produced knowledge of the waterscape in ways that grossly overstated abundance and prevalence, showing considerably less nuance than their African counterparts.

Rebmann's 1848 expedition was the first organized by a European to reach Kilimanjaro. After arriving in Mombasa in 1846, he worked with fellow missionary J. Ludwig Krapf to establish a Church Mission-ary Society presence. They met with limited success, and Rebmann lost both his wife and young daughter to malaria. In his writings, he expresses clear disdain for the coast in both environmental and human terms. He saw the region as unfit for a permanent presence given its climate and the prevalence of disease, and he viewed the Swahili as morally bankrupt because of their Muslim faith and the prevalence of slavery. The two missionaries set their sights on exploring and map-ping the interior, with a mind to assessing sites for missionary work. On hearing tales of a massive, white-capped mountain lying 100 leagues into the interior, Rebmann became intrigued, and in April 1848, he organized an expedition to see it firsthand. He hired a small group of men to serve as his caravan and employed an experienced Swahili guide he refers to as Bwana Kheri. They set out on April 28, 1848, dur-ing the rains and followed the established route into the interior.

Rebmann described the journey as one of tremendous hardship. Once past the nyika, they spent seven days passing through "great wastes . . . wilderness, for the most part perfectly level."[24] They experi-enced reprieve once reaching Kadiaro and Bugada, in the Taita Hills, but then found themselves in a "thick and thorny jungle." From May 3 to 6, the caravan endured a period of constant rain as well as an illness (described as a fever, likely malaria) among one of the porters. They continued through more jungle and, by May 10, passed through a grass field full of "pointed leaves and burs" as well as "wild beasts." With the exception of only one day, Rebmann described the journey as a scourge. Much of this owed to his decision to depart during the rains. While water scarcity was not a problem, the route was muddy, filled with brush, and barely passible. His observations changed dramati-cally on May 11, thirteen days into the trek. In the early morning, he encountered the "mountains of Jagga" for the first time. In his journal, he noted the moment by reading Psalm 111:6, "He hath shewed his people the power of his works, that he may give them the heritage of the heathen."[25] He then noted the sight in sublime detail. He pointed out that there were two separate peaks, referring to the tallest as "the lofty Mount Kilimanjaro with its perpetual snow." The next day he eloquently described the changing scenery. The flat, monotonous wilderness laced with jungle, thorns, and burs gave way to a fecund, varied terrain featuring rich vegetation, trees, and pastureland. At the heart of this "noble country" stood the great snow mountain.

The most striking aspect of Rebmann's account of the mountain is his description of the waterscape. He encountered the oasis at the very moment he crossed the Lumi River. Later that day he reached the Mwona, which he described as "beautiful and sparkling."[26] He was so taken by the sight that he bathed in the river. Noting that the water was cold, he assumed that its source "[could] only be in the snow mountain." Rebmann saw the white cap as the heart of this waterscape. He held no doubt that it was snow, seeing it as "perpetual" and thus the source of the abundant rivers and streams. These watercourses, in turn, made possible the abundant fertility of the mountain slopes. While the mountain's sheer size led him to call it the "king of the mountains of Eastern Africa," it was the silver-colored ice that gave it a crown.[27]

Though Rebmann encountered Kilimanjaro in a way very similar to that of numerous Swahili traders and porters, he interpreted his encounter very differently. Rather than just a place to get provisions and trade goods, he saw it as a miraculous, divinely inspired place. This partly reflected Rebmann's own background. Being from the rolling hills of southern Germany near the Alps, he felt a sense of comfort with a region that reminded him of his homeland. The mountain's existence also defied prevailing scientific notions and general stereotypes about the continent. He was not merely comparing the mountain to its surroundings; he was comparing it to the journey, to the coast, to Zanzibar, and to Europe. Likewise, he compared the people of the mountain, whom he considered to be polite, curious, and possibly intelligent, with the people of the coast and steppe, whom he considered dangerous and heathen. In his opinion, this lush, healthy, "noble mountain" was a perfect place to base missionary work. He emphasized this when on his last day in the region, he prayed "from the depths of my heart, as regards all the populations around,—'Thy kingdom come.'"[28]

Despite Rebmann's enthusiasm, Kilimanjaro did not receive a flood of missionaries. The next one to visit was Charles New, whose expeditions took place nearly twenty-three years later in 1871. A missionary with the United Methodist Free Churches, New came to East Africa in 1863, joining Thomas Wakefield at his mission at Ribe, near Mombasa. Like Rebmann, New became interested in Kilimanjaro in part from his hatred of the coast. In his memoir he wrote:

> The novelty gone, a feeling of inexpressible desolation creeps over you. A feeling of exile; country, home, friends, social intercourse, religion, civilization, are all left behind, and you have nothing in return but a dreary wilderness, strange suspicious people, unpleasant broodings over contrasts, barbarism everywhere, and nothing to look upon but scenes of degradation and depravity.[29]

His biggest concern was the climate and its effects on health. He noted that before real missionary work could begin, the "climate has to be grappled with and conquered. No man can live long in the jungles of East Africa without being attacked by the 'mkunguru,' the fever of the country." He noted that Ribe is "sadly marred by the presence and constant recurrence of fever." His memoir suggests that he became obsessed with malaria, which he linked to the heat and to the dirtiness of the water sources. He likewise criticized the moral condition of the coast. He called Zanzibar "scarcely superior to Sodom," and he spoke only slightly more positively of Ribe, whose people were "a poor, degraded race" but at least "amenable to gospel influences."[30]

Eight years into his stay at Ribe, New assembled an expedition to Kilimanjaro. In his memoir, he explains his curiosity in the "great Equatorial Snow Mountain" in terms of its implications for health:

> If Africa . . . is to take a position with other nations in the march of progress, she will have to be put in motion; an impetus will have to be given her by some more civilized people—by westerns, and probably by the English. But there is her deadly climate, that is sadly against her. If Europeans are to do her some

good, some of them must reside upon her shores, yet to do so is death. However, what about this snow mountain? May there not be found there a more healthy climate? If so, what an immense advantage to the country it may become![31]

New assembled a caravan and set out on July 13, 1871, proceeding westerly on the same route used by Rebmann. Unlike Rebmann, he timed his journey to coincide with the dry season rather than with the rains. Five days in, the caravan reached the steppe, New noting that "gradually the grass became less green, until scarcely any greenness remained, all becoming as dry as desert . . . scenery remarkable only for its want of the attractive and picturesque."[32] As the group began to experience water scarcity, New describes his porters searching, often unsuccessfully, for water to fill their calabashes. On July 19, they unexpectedly stumbled across water emanating from a tree, such a rarity that one of the porters shouted "Bisan!" ("Water!"), and New saw fit to describe how cool and sweet it tasted.[33]

Passing through the Taita Hills, the caravan stopped at Taveta, a place that New describes in largely positive terms. They neared Kilimanjaro around August 5. As in Rebmann's account, this moment marked a distinct shift in how New presented the landscape. The vegetation became greener, and rivers and streams more abundant. Because of cloud cover, he could not see the mountain until after his arrival at Moshi. As the clouds cleared, the white cap drew his attention. He notes, "It *is* snow. It was unmistakable. It was truly a magnificent sight."[34] He surveyed the massif, noting the "hills covered with the most luxuriant vegetation; extensive growths of plantains . . . mountains of dark forest," culminating in the "region of perpetual snow." He summarizes his appraisal by writing that "this prodigious mountain is one of unparalleled grandeur, sublimity, majesty, and glory. It is doubtful if there be another such sight in this wide world." A few days later, New took a stroll by himself and again described his surroundings, this time making a direct comparison with the steppe. He remarks, "How beautifully green everything looked! And what a contrast to the desert below! Here everything seemed to grow spontaneously, and to revel in its growth; there all was barrenness and death. Chaga is a garden."[35]

Like Rebmann, New see this vitality in terms of the waterscape. He speaks frequently of the mystery of the white cap, presuming that the rivers and streams found everywhere must have their source there. He also expresses fascination with the mifongo:

> The watercourses traverse the sides of the hills everywhere, and I now understand what I had been told upon the coast . . . that the Wachagga make the water in their country run up hill! The almost level run of the watercourses, viewed in connection with the sharp descending outlines of the hill tops and the natural course of the stream below, deceives the eye.[36]

This reference to the ingenuity of the canals shows that New saw locals as actively engaging the waters, rather than effortlessly benefiting from them. New's expedition also confirmed for the first time that the white cap is composed of snow. Ten days after arriving, he organized an expedition to the snow line. He departed on August 15 but met with failure. He tried again on the 26th, and that time he reached the snow line. He noted, "My heart sank, but before I had time fairly to scan the position my eyes rested upon snow at my very feet! There it lay upon the rocks below me in shining masses . . . I cannot describe the sensations that thrilled my heart at that moment."[37] He also observed with some amusement the responses of his guide and porters, none of whom had experienced snow before. One of the porters mistook the ice for stones. Another crushed some ice in his teeth and then exclaimed, "Mringa! Mringa!" ("Water! Water!").

New's impressions of Kilimanjaro bear similarities to those of Rebmann, though the two expeditions took place decades apart. Both men saw the mountain as abundant and fertile. They described its potential in terms of water features: the snows, the rivers and streams, and the vegetation fed by those watercourses. Both even described the promise of the mountain's people in terms of water features, as their most impressive characteristic was their ability to create irrigation works. For New and Rebmann, the mountain was more than an oasis or a natural wonder. It became a hope for the continent as a whole to be transformed by Christian missionary work.

The 1880s marked a period of change with the onset of the Scramble for Africa. Kilimanjaro found itself in the heart of it as Britain, Germany, and Zanzibar all strove to claim sovereignty over the great snow mountain. Expeditions in this period reflected a desire not only to explore the region and document its features but also to establish physical claims to the land. Harry Johnston's expedition is a good example of this. In 1884, two prominent organizations—the Royal Geographic Society and the British Association—approached him about leading an expedition to Kilimanjaro, the ostensible purpose being to ascertain whether or not the great height and snowcap of the mountain had created unique features in its flora and fauna.[38] Given Johnston's lack of training as a naturalist and his association with Henry Morton Stanley, it is likely that his charge was to complete treaties with local chiefs and stake British claims to the region.

Johnston began his journey similarly to Rebmann and New, traveling from London to Zanzibar and then onward to Mombasa. He likewise shared their opinion that the coast was unfit for Europeans, being hot and diseased and full of "liars, cowards, thieves, and drunkards."[39] In planning the journey, he even selected the same route. In the middle of May 1884, his caravan of 120 men set out from Mombasa. Though normally this would have been just after the long rains, it had been a year of prolonged drought and most of the region was even drier than usual. Within a few days, water scarcity became a problem of crisis proportions. Johnston notes the difficulties faced by his porters: "You will experience the greater difficulty in preventing your men dropping and dying of thirst . . . they will wring your heart with the sight of their sufferings, and stagger along the dusty path with dry, swollen tongues, parched lips, and blood-shot eyes."[40] They experienced reprieve at Mwatate in the Taita Hills, but once past they entered what Johnston describes as a "waterless wilderness." It was here that he made the following observation: "The fact is, in African travel, it is not easy to combine the accomplishment of twenty or thirty miles walked every day on foot . . . especially when haunted by the knowledge that every minute's delay that separates you from your water-supply is dangerous."[41] Not shy to name his heroics, Johnston describes numerous other challenges of the journey—fever, blistered feet, wild animals, the Maasai, the hot sun—but the one he describes in by far the greatest detail is water.

Perhaps because of his experiences in the steppe, Johnston's descriptions of Kilimanjaro as water abundant are especially striking. Around 50 kilometers from the mountain, he describes "a change of an agreeable character" as the lands change from brown to green.[42] He then reached the River Lumi, which he assumed was fed by the mountain snows. On seeing the mountain for the first time, he describes it as "completely severed in appearance from the earth below" and relates it to the fictional flying island of Laputa from *Gulliver's Travels*. Like Rebmann and New, he describes the slopes as green, lush, and water abundant, an area of "perpetual moisture" that was a "happy contrast to [the] dreary velt."[43] His description of the white cap is vivid. He describes how one's eyes rest "irresistibly on the splendid snowy dome of Kibo, absolute in whiteness," and he held no doubt that "the perpetually melting snow is the cause of the many streams."[44] He also had high praise for the mifongo, noting that

> in each ravine there is a rivulet, and along the cress . . . meanders an artificially-trained stream, diverted from the rivulet at some higher fountain or waterfall, and carried in a gentle descent along the brow of the hill. This, of course, is the handiwork of man, but so industrious have been the Bantu inhabitants of Kilima-njaro, that there is scarcely a spur descending from the southern base of the mountain that is unprovided with the irrigating channel . . . keeping its terraced gardens supplied with water.[45]

Like New, Johnston describes the people positively because of their ingenuity with water. The whole scene he compares not only with the surrounding steppe, but also with various points in Europe. At one point, he refers to Kilimanjaro as "African Switzerland." At another, he goes into length about the mountain having a "mild, equable, and moist . . . climate resembling a Devonshire summer."[46]

Johnston was unique among his contemporaries in that he remained on the mountain for an extended period, almost six months in total. He spent most of his time in Moshi, where he constructed a small farm at a place he called Kitimbiuru (fig. 2.1), on a ridge with an excellent view of Kibo and Mawenzi.[47] According to his descriptions, it featured an expansive garden, several houses constructed of poles and banana fibers, and an irrigation canal that provided "water at [his] very door." In his garden he planted several varieties of seed brought with him from England—mustard, cress, radishes, turnips, carrots, onions, tomatoes, borage, sage, cucumbers, and melons—and claimed that within a week he was already eating a salad of his own growing. This

FIGURE 2.1. Sketch of Harry Johnston's homestead in Moshi (*H. H. Johnston*, The Kilima-Njaro Expedition)

homestead served as the base for his excursions to examine and gather samples of the mountain's flora and fauna. He remained for several months, then moved to nearby Marangu, partly because it had easier access to the higher reaches of the mountain and partly because of his deteriorating relationship with the mangi of Moshi. On his return to Britain he briefly visited Rombo, which he described as unattractive and water poor.

Johnston described the mountain as a largely singular space, and likewise he considered the people to be all the same "tribe." He referred to local fighting between chiefdoms not as conflict between different groups but rather as "internecine wars."[48] Although his work was affected by the fighting, he still considered the people of the mountain to be curious and industrious, and "not savages." His depiction of them as a singular people was especially important in his side business of treaty making. In addition to his official work, Johnston completed treaties of "friendship" with the wamangi of Moshi and Marangu.[49] He handed these over to the British East Africa Company to help establish claims to the mountain and to refute competing claims from Germany and Zanzibar. As a self-described naturalist, but with imperial aspirations, Johnston saw Kilimanjaro with a different eye from either New or Rebmann. His interest lay in appropriating the mountain not for God's kingdom in Africa, but rather for Britain's. He notes that the region should be the "center of operations for commercial activity in East Africa," because of its favorable climate and ample water, and that it was a possible "future sanatorium" for people working on the coast.[50]

By 1889, Kilimanjaro's fate in the Scramble for Africa had been settled. Despite Johnston's efforts, the mountain fell into the colonizing hands of Germany. This led to a flood of new people eager to discover the secrets of the snowcapped peak. Hans Meyer, the first known person to reach the summit, was among the most important. He first arrived on the continent in late 1886, shortly after Germany began consolidating control of its new colonies. It was around this time that he set the goal of being the first person to reach the summit of the "Ethiopian Mount Olympus."[51] In his 1890 memoir, he expresses this interest as twofold. As a scientist, he desired to explore the geography of the mountain in order to discern "the causes of the prevailing climatic conditions [and] the nature of the snow and ice," while as a German he saw it as "almost a national duty" to conquer the summit. Meyer made several trips to Kilimanjaro aimed at reaching the summit. His first attempt in 1887 took him to nearly 5,500 meters, while a second attempt in 1888 had to be cancelled because of the Abushiri revolt. His expedition in 1889 was the first to meet with success, though he would return several times in the 1890s to complete his mapping of the snows.

Though his expedition took place nearly forty-one years after Rebmann's, Meyer encountered the mountain in much the same way. He followed the route from Mombasa via the Taita Hills and chose to travel during the dry season. His impressions of the terrain were generally favorable, and he even took time to note how the steppe plants had adapted to avoid evaporation from their leaves.[52] His first sighting of the mountain inspired a sense of spectacle and majesty. He writes, "All of a sudden the veil of mist was rent apart, and to our admiring gaze was revealed the snowy peak of Kilimanjaro, grand, majestic, more than earthly in the silver light of the morning."[53] The whole scene is marked by contrast with the steppe, "a picture full of contrasts—here the swelling heat of the Equator, the naked negro, and the palm-trees of Taveta—yonder, arctic snow and ice, and an atmosphere of god-like repose." He attributes the vitality of the mountain to its water features, remarking that "Kilimanjaro is plentifully supplied with water throughout the year."[54] He also notes the ingenuity of the mifongo, noting that "the art of constructing these irrigation canals . . . is among the most wonderful to be found among tribes like the Wa-jagga." Like earlier explorers, Meyer saw the mountain as a singular space in stark contrast to the plains, and he viewed the people as a singular "tribe." He concludes that "Jagga is a splendid country . . . one vast garden."[55] He notes that it was a "little mountain paradise in the unending waste of barren, almost uninhabited steppe, savannah, and bush."

Meyer's 1889 expedition is notable in that it provides the first scientific observations of the white cap. He was the first to distinguish between two different aspects, seasonal snowfall and permanent glacial ice.[56] Up to this point, explorers had tended to use vague terms such as "snows" or "whiteness." Meyer noted that the mountain received a significant amount of snowfall during the rainy seasons but that it disappeared during the dry periods. The permanent white cap, on the other hand, was a set of massive glaciers. One lay inside the mountain's volcanic crater, while the others were composed of two massive ice fields, one on the north side of the peak and the other on the south. Each of the ice fields contained several connected glaciers that reached downward from the peak and gradually dissipated. Meyer argued that glacial melt was a crucial part of the water supply for the lower reaches of the mountain, noting that "the extent of the rainfall and the distribution of the ice naturally determine the distribution of the springs, streams, and rivers."[57]

Like his predecessors, Meyer appropriated the mountain for his greater cause. While Rebmann and New saw the mountain as part of God's kingdom, and Johnston tried to secure it for Britain's empire, Meyer claimed it in the names of Germany and scientific discovery. He did so by planting a small German flag at the peak and naming aspects of the peak that he "discovered." This included naming Kibo after Kaiser Wilhelm (Kaiser-Wilhelm-Spitze) and naming the first glacier he encountered the Ratzel Glacier after F. Ratzel, his professor of geography at the University of Leipzig.[58] In doing so, Meyer established the precedent of naming prominent features of the mountain after outsiders.

AFRICA'S EDEN IN EUROPE

The writings of explorers such as Rebmann, New, Johnston, and Meyer circulated widely in the Western world, through newspaper and magazine articles as well as book-length memoirs. Africa's mysterious snowcapped mountain soon gained a popular following, and Kilimanjaro went from being a largely unknown place to being the most recognized natural feature of sub-Saharan Africa. The encounters of the explorers, as most people's only access to information about the mountain, shaped how Europeans generally imagined it. Africa's Olympus came to be identified by its massive size, its mysterious white cap, and the abundance it provided to its surroundings. Most of all, it became thought of as distinct from its surroundings, an island of plenty in the Dark Continent.

Kilimanjaro's celebrity also owed to a public controversy that erupted in Britain soon after Rebmann's 1848 expedition. His observation that the mountain had a snowy white cap provoked a debate involving scientific personalities of the day. Prominent members of the Royal Geographic Society, including renowned expert of East African geography William Desborough Cooley, challenged the notion that a mountain near the equator could have ice. In the May 19, 1849, issue of the literary magazine *The Athenaeum*, the contributors claimed that such a phenomenon was simply impossible. Debate emerged in subsequent issues of this magazine as well as in the *Church Missionary Intelligencer* and the *Proceedings of the Royal Geographical Society*. The most scathing critique came from Cooley. In his 1852 book entitled *Inner Africa Laid Open*, he dedicated nearly thirty pages to rebuking the observations of Rebmann and Krapf. He claimed that Rebmann's discovery of snow "rests more on a delightful mental recognition, than on the evidence of the senses."[59] In other words, the snow was simply a hallucination. Cooley chastised the two's descriptions as "betraying weak power of observation, strong fancy, an eager craving for wonders and childish reasoning." These were strong words, considering that Cooley himself had never stepped foot in East Africa.

Krapf issued a rebuttal to Cooley and other critics in his 1860 travelogue. Since neither he nor Rebmann had actually touched the snow, he first reiterated the nature of their visual observations of the white cap as well as the explanations provided by the local people. His best reasoned justification, however, was the abundance of surface water on the mountain:

> Perennial snow is proved by the multitude of rivers. . . . Of these Mr. Rebmann has counted more than twenty flowing from the heights of Mount Kilimanjaro, and among them two considerable ones, the Mwona and the Lumi, forming the main streams of the river Ruvu, or Pangani. How are we to explain the phenomenon of such a multiplicity of rivers . . . unless we are to admit the existence of snow? Snow existing in considerable masses . . . can alone explain this hypothesis in a satisfactory manner.[60]

Despite Krapf's reply, geographers remained skeptical of the idea that permanent snow could be present so close to the equator. This remained the case until 1861, when the expedition of German explorer Baron Karl Klaus von der Decken and English geologist Richard Thornton reconfirmed the presence of snow.[61] For his part, Cooley refused to acknowledge the presence of ice to his death in 1883, and the debacle cast a shadow over his otherwise brilliant career.

The proliferation of written accounts about Kilimanjaro and the public debate about its white cap helped bring the mountain into popular discourse. By the turn of the century, it had even emerged as a literary motif. Six years after Rebmann's first journey, American poet Bayard Taylor published a poem entitled "Kilima-Njaro."[62] A lengthy piece at 254 words, it provides a vivid window into the image of the mountain that was finding its way into the popular imagination. Taylor begins with what reads like an invocation:

> Hail to thee, monarch of African mountains!
>
> Remote, inaccessible, silent, and lone—
>
> Who from the heart of the tropical fervours
>
> Liftest to heaven thine alien snows

Taylor clearly sees the mountain as a distinctive, otherworldly place. His reference to the snows as "alien" and being lifted "to heaven" allude that this distinctiveness is divinely inspired. In the next stanza, he refers to the snows as the source of other water features:

> I see thee supreme in the midst of thy co-mates,
> Standing alone, 'twixt the earth and the heavens.
>
> . . . .
>
> Zone above zone, to thy snow-crested summits
> The climates of Earth are displayed, as an index,
> Giving the scope of the Book of Creation.
> There, in the gorges that widen, descending
> From cloud and from cold into summer eternal,
> Gather the threads of the ice-gendered fountains—
> Gather to riotous torrents of crystal

Here he cites the mountain's environmental zones as indicating the range of God's creation. The waters that flow from the snows to the plains tie them all together, beginning as "ice-gendered fountains" and becoming "riotous torrents of crystal." The remaining stanzas further emphasize the mountain's grandeur. The overall image of Kilimanjaro is a lush, abundant, divinely inspired place distinct from the rest of Africa. Over the course of the twentieth century, Kilimanjaro figured in numerous other pieces of literature, the most famous being Hemingway's "The Snows of Kilimanjaro."

⌒

The first two chapters of this book have examined how various groups of people made sense of Kilimanjaro and its waterscapes in the nineteenth century. Chapter 1 focused on the mountain's resident populations, the people who would later be referred to as the Chagga. For them, the mountain was a diverse, lived space, heavily symbolic in the extent to which it shaped local culture and identity. Water features shaped the development of local society in numerous ways: sustaining agriculture, defining political and social units, shaping distinctions of age and gender, and influencing notions of the afterlife. A key tenet of local water knowledge was the belief that the water supply was tenuous and required careful management.

Outsiders to the mountain—neighboring mountain and steppe peoples, caravan traders, and European explorers—imagined the waterscape in different ways. Those approaching Kilimanjaro via the caravan routes associated it with water abundance, because of its stark contrast with the plains. European explorers developed highly idealized, romanticized, unrealistic impressions of the mountain. In their eyes, Kilimanjaro was otherworldly—if not an Eden, then at the very least a little Switzerland or Devonshire in the heart of the Dark Continent. It was an oasis not merely from the harsh steppe, but also from deeper-held presumptions of the continent's "darkness": its harsh climate, the harms it posed to health, and the savagery of its peoples. This in turn led Europeans to claim the region—for God, for empire, for science—in ways that their African counterparts did not. The notion of Kilimanjaro as a supernatural place of abundance in the heart of Africa reverberated tremendously. It not only contributed to the mountain's becoming the most famous physical feature of sub-Saharan Africa to people outside the continent, but it also influenced those who made their way to the region as part of colonial rule.

3 ⇔ Do Not Believe That Every Cloud Will Bring Rain

Water Cooperation in the Era of German Colonialism, 1885–1918

IN THE last decade of the nineteenth century, Kilimanjaro came under the colonial control of the German Empire. A renowned tale of this era details how the mountain ended up in the hands of Germany instead of Britain. Richard Baker, a British colonial forester, tells one version in his 1945 memoir *Africa Drums*. He recalls a dialogue between two British Foreign Office officials and the general secretary of the Church Missionary Society, Dr. Eugene Stock, that took place around 1890.[1] In the course of discussion, one of the men asks Stock if he knows of Kilimanjaro. Stock replies, "Yes, of course. That is the Switzerland of Africa. That is where we send our missionaries from the coast to recuperate when they get run down with fever." Both men reply that it is a pity. Confused, Stock asks why they should say such a thing, given the mountain's healthful properties. One of them answers, "We said 'what a pity' because we have just given it to Germany." He explains further, "You see, Kaiser Wilhelm said to Queen Victoria, 'I'd very much like to have the tallest mountain of Africa on my side of the boundary,' and the Foreign Office, speaking for Her Majesty, have replied, 'You shall.' This they have done without knowing anything about it." In Baker's account, the boundary between the Kenya Colony and German East Africa was shaped not by colonial geopolitics or military conquest but rather by Queen Victoria's choice to give the African Olympus to her grandson, the German emperor.

This sentimental tale became widespread in the early years of European colonial rule in Africa. Variations appeared in other writings, notably Karen Blixen's 1937 novel *Out of Africa*.[2] The notion of Kilimanjaro as a gift from grandmother to grandson, however, has no grounding. The mountain's location within German East Africa resulted from negotiations involving claims from Lake Victoria to Mombasa that culminated in the Anglo-German Agreement of 1886. Politics—along with a map, a pen, and a ruler—set the border as it is. Despite the story's inaccuracy, it provides a vivid window into perceptions of the mountain in the early years of colonial rule. Kilimanjaro, a symbol of European colonialism, held powerful allure to the imaginations of outsiders. Those who arrived in this period—colonial officials, missionaries, and settlers—expected to find a Kilimanjaro that was water abundant, healthy, and otherworldly. Many soon realized, as their African neighbors long had, that not every cloud would bring rain.

Those who came to Kilimanjaro before the First World War largely embraced local water knowledge, technologies, management practices, and even power structures. They adapted the mfongo technology they saw in use around them to provide water to their homes, farms, and churches. By 1914, Europeans relied on canals as their primary source of water for domestic uses and for irrigation. The new canals were technically similar to existing ones, and many had even been developed by local specialists. Most tapped into rivers above the chiefdoms, and some were shared with local communities, in which case the Europeans were the users farthest downstream. New canals differed from existing ones in terms of cultural and spiritual management. The choice of Europeans to rely on local water expertise stemmed from several factors, including the German administration's inconsistent policy toward settlers, the short period between colonization and the First World War, the shoestring budgets faced by the missions and settlers, and limited access to materials from abroad. The "indigenous marvel" of the mifongo provided a cheap and effective answer to the question of water management.

For the peoples of Kilimanjaro, European reliance on their water knowledge served as a tool with which they could negotiate relationships with these new neighbors. The Germans, believing that abundance was a defining feature of the waterscape, took few steps to regulate their own water management until after a drought in 1907. Even then, the colony never had formal water law. In the absence of a legal framework, informal arrangements between African and European users defined water management. Scholars who have examined aspects of German colonialism, such as Juhani Koponen, Philippa Söldenwagner, and Thaddeus Sunseri, have remarked on the highly inconsistent nature of its policies toward colonial development before the First World War.[3] Söldenwagner, focusing on settlement, contends that the administration's lack of consistent policy resulted in interactions between Africans and Europeans that were closer than in other colonies. Though a racial hierarchy developed, "spaces of negotiation" also formed in which Africans held power. Water management is an excellent example. European canals frequently drew from intakes located within the chiefdoms. This gave power brokers in the chiefdoms some leverage over their new neighbors in terms of both technology and geography, which they could parlay into other areas of the colonial encounter. This primarily benefitted the wamangi, who served as negotiators and conflict resolvers, as well as the meni mifongo, who developed the new waterworks. This dynamic lasted until the 1920s, when the onset of British colonial rule and coffee cultivation made these tenuous arrangements difficult to sustain.

GERMAN COLONIALISM

The colonization of Kilimanjaro began in earnest in the 1880s. For decades, the mountain had garnered interest from Germany as well as Britain and Omani-ruled Zanzibar. Agents representing these three states, such as Carl Peters of the German East Africa Company (Deutsch-Ostafrikanische Gesellschaft, DOAG), worked feverishly to complete treaties with prominent wamangi establishing protectorates over parts of the mountain. Treaties such as these were, in the words of British Consul-General to Zanzibar John Kirk, "deliberately concocted" instruments designed to legitimize external claims to African territory.[4] Though completed with the signees unaware of the implications, these documents became legal instruments for asserting and refuting claims to territory. The plethora of conflicting claims to Kilimanjaro were largely resolved by the Anglo-German Treaty of 1886, which drew the boundary between British and German territory in East Africa and placed the mountain in the newly formed colony of Deutsch-Ostafrika (German East Africa).[5]

At the time, these conference-table claims resonated little on the mountain. The negotiations that shaped colonial boundaries took place without the knowledge or consent of mountain communities.

A formal German presence took shape after 1885 with the arrival of DOAG expeditions from the coast. The DOAG aimed to control the colony by transforming chiefs and other African leaders into low-level bureaucrats, who would report to DOAG personnel. On Kilimanjaro, the DOAG found a willing partner in Mangi Rindi of Moshi. Eager to strengthen his position against other chiefs, particularly his rival Sina of Kibosho, Rindi welcomed his visitors, and he even sent emissaries to Berlin in 1889 to present an elephant tusk to the kaiser.[6] The DOAG created its first permanent settlement and trading station at Moshi, and from there it approached other wamangi to gain their loyalty. It soon encountered resistance from Sina, who had engaged in a struggle with Rindi to influence the chiefly succession in Machame. Seeing the DOAG as allied with Rindi, Sina rejected their overtures, took down the German flag he had raised, and replaced it with the flag of the sultan of Zanzibar. In February 1891, the DOAG dispatched a military expedition to Kibosho under the leadership of Major Hermann von Wissmann.[7] The expedition of three hundred Sudanese and Zulu mercenaries joined with four hundred auxiliaries provided by Rindi in the attack against Kibosho. In a swift two-day campaign, the German-led forces routed Sina, destroying his stone fort, killing more than two hundred people, and seizing thousands of livestock. Hoping to retain his position, Sina surrendered to the Germans.[8] Other wamangi followed suit and raised the German flag as well.

The fall of Kibosho did not spell an end to resistance. In response to unrest, the German Reich took direct control of the colony in 1891. It created a colonial army, the *Schutztruppe*, consisting of German officers and locally recruited soldiers known as *askari*.[9] These forces were soon deployed on the mountain. In October, they built a new military station at Marangu, leaving only a small contingent in Moshi. The following month, Rindi died, and his son Meli succeeded him. As Meli proved less than cooperative, the Germans found an enthusiastic partner in Marealle, the mangi of Marangu. In early 1892, Meli attacked and routed the German forces, seized control of Marangu, and attempted to coerce the other wamangi into submitting to him.[10] Three months later, the Germans retook Marangu and reestablished authority over most of the chiefdoms, with the notable exception of Moshi. On August 12, 1893, a Schutztruppe expedition led by Colonel Friedrich von Schele joined with forces from Kibosho and Marangu and attacked Moshi. They captured Meli's fortress, routed his army, and effectively subordinated the last independent chiefdom. This gave the Germans effective control over the mountain, though periodic resistance persisted for another decade. For the duration of the decade, a series of commanders administered the region from Moshi Town, a new settlement at the foot of the mountain. In 1906, the mountain became a single district administered by a district officer, who was a civilian. The chiefdoms remained in the hands of the wamangi, who became low-level administrators ruling on behalf of the government. By the turn of the century, the mountain had thirty-seven chiefdoms, each governed by a mangi accountable to the district officer.

For the peoples of Kilimanjaro, the shift to German rule altered many aspects of local governance. Despite the Germans' decision to retain the wamangi, their roles shifted dramatically. Though they lost the ability to monopolize external trade and to organize warfare, the two practices at the heart of their nineteenth-century emergence, they gained several new forms of power. They managed tax collection and organized corvée labor, through the existing system of wachili.[11] They also gained control over the distribution of land, a power formerly held by clan heads.[12] To support these new roles, the government provided the wamangi with military backing. Marealle, who had proved his loyalty in 1893, became the Germans' right-hand man on the mountain, leading punitive expeditions against belligerent wamangi and establishing virtual dominion over Rombo for more than a decade.[13] These developments effectively shifted the nature of chiefly authority. As Moore notes, "chiefly enrichment no longer came from the outside, from war booty and exchange, but from the ever-increasing levels of taxes and labour contributions."[14] Wealth became extracted internally and authority backed externally, an inverse state of affairs to what had existed in the nineteenth century. These changes bolstered the power of the wamangi over other local leaders, notably the wachili.

Colonial rule brought economic changes as well. The German administration aimed to transform the colony into a profitable venture. To that end, it engaged in what Koponen describes as a "development imperative."[15] This consisted of projects and policies aimed at developing the "physical, economic, and social infrastructure" to support an economy based on exporting cash crops. The administration saw Kilimanjaro as one of the most favorable areas for development. Between the 1890s and 1914, it pursued two different strategies. Until 1908, it focused on settler agriculture and cultivation of cash crops such as coffee, sugar, sisal, and cotton. To support these activities, it developed a network of roads and a railway from Moshi to the port town of Tanga, completed in 1912. In 1906, following the Maji Maji uprising, the administration concluded that settlers alone could not develop the colony to its potential. Under the leadership of Governor Albrecht von Rechenberg, the colony shifted to a "dual-mode" of economic development, emphasizing both European plantations and African commercial agriculture.[16] While the administration would continue to support settlers, the focus of the economy would be small-scale production on Africans' own farms.

To get the people to participate in these ventures, the Germans relied on coercion from the wamangi. In 1898, the administration implemented hut and poll taxes across the mountain.[17] These taxes, collected by the wamangi, had to be paid in cash. The need to pay taxes forced people to participate in economic activities that generated currency, such as selling cash crops at markets or working on missionary or settler farms. In the same year, the government mandated that all men work in a paid trade for a certain number of days each year or perform uncompensated compulsory work.[18] This started out as a few days per month but grew to ninety days per year after 1912.[19] The district office kept track of men's work through a labor-card system, by which employers confirmed the days that the cardholder worked. If men did not pay taxes, or if they refused to work as required, they could be arrested and placed in forced labor camps.[20] In addition to encouraging wage labor, the government also required wamangi to organize corvée labor for government-managed construction projects.

Though colonial rule brought many changes to various aspects of life, one area that witnessed few was water management. The German administration imagined Kilimanjaro as an abundant waterscape. Consequently, it did not rush to implement new water laws and regulations, and local officers involved themselves little in water issues. In fact, the main law that applied to water in the period was the Crown Land Ordinance of 1895, which in addition to granting the state ownership of land, specifically excluded navigable streams and rivers from transfers of ownership.[21] Though the administration did not seem concerned about water management, it took an active interest in protecting forest watersheds. On Kilimanjaro, the administration first designated areas of alpine forest as protected in 1889.[22] These activities intensified in April 1907 with the creation of a forest district (*Forstbezirk*). Between 1909 and 1913, professional foresters from Germany surveyed the mountain forests and marked the boundaries for an area that would be declared crown land.[23] The Kilimanjaro Forest Reserve, as it came to be known, consisted of the entirety of the mountain above the settled area, the boundary being the line between the agroforest zone and the rainforest. The desire to protect these areas, as noted by Robert Munson, reflected the prominence of German *Forstwissenschaft* (forestry science) at the turn of the century.[24]

The German administration's desire to protect forests stemmed in part from a desire to protect the mountain's water supply. As early as 1895, it speculated that cutting down trees in the colony had produced a "conspicuous climate change" that if unchecked, would render viable habitats into "steppes and deserts."[25] On the creation of the reserve in 1907, the first forester assigned to the area, Georg Rohrbeck, noted its importance in protecting the water supply.[26] His successor, Theodor Siebenlist, explained the connection in detail:

> The forests of our colonies represent huge financial objects, the value of which will increase with their development. At the same time cultural functions which are of no less importance devolve from them. Principally they are as follows: the preservation of sources and springs and by that the conservation of the fertility of the soil, which would soon resemble a desert without the animating water; a protection against the erosion of fertile soil on the slopes and mountain ridges, hence conservation of the arable land and pastures for the mountain people and a guarantee that they do not drift away; a safeguard for native settlements and European plantations at the foot of the mountains against disastrous floods, and many more.[27]

The value of protecting forests lay, in part, in preserving water supplies and preventing erosion and flooding. Though alpine forests were of primary concern, the Germans also took steps to preserve riverine forests, such as the Rau Forest just south of Kilimanjaro.

Though colonial rule brought major changes to the political and economic landscape of Kilimanjaro, it did so with relatively few

European personnel. Colonial officers and Schutztruppe relied upon African intermediaries, namely the wamangi and the askari, to maintain control and implement policies. Most encounters that mountain populations had with Europeans were with missionaries and settlers. These groups came to Kilimanjaro in higher numbers than did government agents, and they inhabited areas closer to the chiefdoms. Missionaries and settlers came with objectives that differed from the colonial administration's, but they were just as instrumental to developing the colony.

THE ARRIVAL OF CHRISTIAN MISSIONARIES

The first Europeans to create permanent settlements on Kilimanjaro in the era of German colonization were Catholic and Protestant missionaries. Since Rebmann's 1848 expedition, missionary organizations had aspired to claim Africa's tallest peak and bring Christianity to its peoples. A lack of financing and personnel delayed these initiatives for decades, as did the challenges of supporting inland settlements far from the coast. In 1886, missionaries A. E. Fitch and J. A. Wray of the Church Missionary Society (CMS) became the first to establish a permanent mission on Kilimanjaro, at Moshi.[28] Mangi Rindi initially greeted them with open arms, but soon the relationship soured. In 1887, a missionary boxed the ears of a local man who had tried to steal some matches. Rindi, furious that an outsider had disciplined one of his subjects, responded by cutting off the mission's canal.[29] This act denied the mission water, and it also served as a demonstration of sovereignty by the mangi. Over the next few years, several setbacks affected the mission, including an 1892 scandal in which the German administration accused the mission's director Albert Steggall of providing arms to Mangi Meli.[30] With little support from the administration or success in gaining converts, the CMS abandoned its mission in 1893.

The Holy Ghost Fathers (*Les Pères du Saint-Esprit*), a French Catholic order, arrived on Kilimanjaro a few years after the CMS did.[31] In 1890, Bishop Jean-Marie de Courmont and Fathers Alexandre Le Roy and Auguste Gommenginger led an expedition from Zanzibar.[32] They arrived at Kilema on August 16, in what was intended to be a short stop en route to Moshi. However, Mangi Fumba received them warmly and offered them land just west of his royal compound. Hearing of the troubles in Moshi, they remained in Kilema.[33] Father Gommenginger took charge of the fledgling mission, and in 1892 he and his fellow priests constructed a chapel and schoolhouse (fig. 3.1). Over the next few years, the Holy Ghost Fathers expanded their presence on the mountain, opening stations at Kibosho in 1893, Mkuu Rombo in 1899, Mashati Rombo in 1912, and Uru in 1913.[34]

The Evangelical Lutheran Mission of Leipzig (*Evangelische-Lutherische Mission zu Leipzig*), better known as the Leipzig Mission, followed in 1893.[35] A newcomer to missionary work in Africa, it sent a small contingent of missionaries—Reverends Gerhard Althaus, Robert Fassmann, Emil Müller, and Albin Böhme—to the mountain in 1893. They hoped to use the abandoned CMS station at Moshi, but because of the ongoing conflict they went instead to Machame, where the mangi greeted them warmly and offered land and access to water. They opened their mother mission there in 1894. Over the next few years, the Leipzig Mission expanded its presence eastward, opening stations at Moshi and Marangu in 1896 and Mwika in 1901.[36]

Although the German administration had failed to support the CMS, it welcomed the Holy Ghost Fathers and the Leipzig Mission. Mission stations, located in the heart of the chiefdoms, provided a colonizing presence that assisted in maintaining stability and encouraging locals to engage with the colonial economy. The decision to embrace two missions was a practical matter. The Leipzig mission lacked

FIGURE 3.1. Kilema Parish (*Arch.photo.cssp*)

sufficient financing and manpower to cover the whole mountain, while the Holy Ghost Fathers were well funded. The French were not rivals in the region, so the Catholic mission did not generate the same level of suspicion as the CMS. Also, more than one-quarter of the Holy Ghost Fathers—including Gommenginger—were German speakers from Alsace-Lorraine.[37] The administration divided up the chiefdoms between the two, giving them exclusive areas for evangelization to prevent a rivalry.[38] Because of this policy, nearly all the chiefdoms had a mission by 1910.

Both missionary orders aimed to transform the chiefdoms into Christian societies, and this process consisted of several steps. First, the people needed to have their eyes opened to the Christian Gospel, and they needed to accept it by both renouncing existing forms of religious expression and becoming full, baptized members of the Church. This involved evangelizing the adult population and building schools for children. Second, the people needed to adopt a Christian lifestyle. As scholars such as John and Jean Comaroff have noted, this consisted of promoting change in everyday practices, from bathing and clothing to child-rearing and diet.[39] On Kilimanjaro, the Catholics and Lutherans encouraged these changes by offering training in health and sanitation, childcare, and technical skills such as carpentry, masonry, and agriculture.[40] Though the missionary projects of both orders involved much similarity, there were also some important differences in doctrine and practice. For example, the Lutherans strongly discouraged brewing and drinking mbege, while the Catholics tended to be more sympathetic to these practices.

The projects of social transformation necessitated the development of infrastructure. Missions required churches, schools, and dispensaries, and farmland for producing food and income. These projects demanded clean and reliable sources of water. Missions tended to be located in the heart of the agroforest belt and therefore shared the same problem of geography as the chiefdoms: rivers and streams running in deep ravines. The Kilema mission, for example, occupied nearly 60 hectares, with a secondary plot of over 532 hectares. Yet the nearest river, the Mue, lay in a ravine nearly 100 meters below.[41] As a solution, missionaries tapped into the mifongo. They did so by first approaching the wamangi for permission to construct canals from nearby watercourses. The wamangi then arranged for meni mifongo to help design and build the canal and also provided laborers to help excavate the channels and build the intakes and other needed structures.

The development of a new canal at the Kilema mission in 1907 and 1908 provides a good example of this process.[42] After constructing the new church, Father Gommenginger determined that the mission required another canal. The need became even more imperative with the onset of drought in 1907. He assigned Brother Cereus (Cere) Spiekermann, a former carpenter who had earned a reputation as an expert handyman, to the task. In late 1908, they sought the permission of Mangi Kirita, who gave his blessing, arranged for workers, and offered the services of a specialist named Matonga.[43] Over several weeks, Cere and Matonga designed and built the canal. They sited an intake (fig. 3.2) at the Mwona River uphill of the mission, where it would have sufficient water year-round. Then they laid out and excavated a canal, routing it around the vihamba and directly to the mission grounds. Men assigned by Kirita performed the labor and received between eight and sixteen rupees for their work.[44] The canal opened on February 5, 1909. The mission celebrated by holding a ceremony in which Gommenginger named the canal Mtakatifu, "Holy Spirit" in Kiswahili.[45] He then led a prayer before allowing water to flow into the canal. The mangi offered a cow, which the priests blessed, killed, and roasted in celebration of the event.[46]

FIGURE 3.2. Intake for Mtakatifu canal (*Matthew V. Bender*)

The development of Mtakatifu indicates key similarities and differences between the canals built for the missionaries and the existing canals. The new ones were virtually identical in design, structure, and function, since in most cases they were designed by meni mifongo and built by locals. However, there were important differences in terms of usage and maintenance. The only people who had permission to use the new canals were those who worked for the mission or had riparian kihamba and asked for permission to draw water.[47] Paid workers, rather than communities of users, maintained and repaired the canals on behalf of the clergy. But the biggest differences related to spiritual and political significance. The missions dedicated their canals not to the waruma or Ruwa, but rather to the Holy Spirit, the Blessed Virgin, or patron saints. They also appropriated existing rituals and practices, essentially creating Christianized versions of them. In the case of Mtakatifu, Gommenginger held a prayer service and offered a cow, but he invoked God rather than a local spirit and named the canal after the Holy Spirit. Lastly, by asking the wamangi for assistance, the missionaries introduced a new political dynamic to the mifongo system. Though the new canals relied on the expertise of local experts (meni mifongo and experienced users), the wamangi gained a new role in water management.

Practical considerations influenced the missions' decision to integrate themselves into the mifongo system. They were few in number and lacked the skills to do the work on their own, so it made sense to adopt techniques that were cheap and effective. This gave the wamangi leverage over them, especially in the early years when the missions had little community support. For example, in early 1894, Father Rohmer worked with Mangi Sina to construct a canal to the new Catholic mission station in Kibosho.[48] The two soon disagreed about how to divide the waters. A month later, Sina ordered that the canal be blocked. Rohmer had little choice but to agree to Sina's terms.[49] A similar situation occurred in Rombo in 1899. The Catholic mission at Mkuu partnered with Mangi Senguo and a specialist named Humipian to construct a canal nearly 8 kilometers long from the Motale River.[50] During the drought of 1907–8, this canal was the only one in the area with water.[51] Senguo requested access to the water for irrigation, since his own canal had run dry. Father Rudler, the head of the mission, had no choice but to grant Senguo's wishes, knowing that the mangi had the power to cut off the water anyhow.

Though the canals initially gave the wamangi leverage over the missionaries, a mitigating factor soon introduced itself: coffee (fig. 3.3). The missionaries, hoping to make their missions financially self-sufficient,

FIGURE 3.3. Child picking coffee (*Arch.photo.cssp*)

experimented with a number of potential cash crops. The Holy Ghost Fathers cultivated a range of crops including "coconuts, vanilla, cotton, rubber, and cloves."[52] Coffee emerged as having the most potential. In the late 1890s, the missionaries introduced small plots of arabica coffee trees into their missions.[53] They found that coffee grew well in the fertile, well-watered mountain soils. In 1912, the Catholic missions generated nearly five thousand francs in revenue from coffee sales.[54] Though only a fraction of their total expenditures for that year (more than sixty thousand francs), this income gave the missionaries hope that they could become financially self-sufficient.[55] Over the next several years, they moved hundreds of additional hectares into coffee cultivation.

News of the Fathers' success with the new crop spread quickly. The Lutherans began growing the crop at their own stations, as did the settlers on their farms. The wamangi also expressed interest. In 1901, Mangi Fumba went to the Kilema mission and asked Father Gommenginger to provide him with seedlings to start his own coffee farm.[56] The mission granted his request and taught him how to best plant his trees. Over the next decade, others followed his example, notably Marealle, who by 1920 had well over 40 hectares of land in mixed coffee and banana cultivation. Coffee even spread to the general population, as men who worked on the mission estates planted seeds in their own vihamba. By the start of the First World War, coffee trees dotted much of the countryside.

The spread of coffee had an impact on the relationship between the missions and their local communities. The wamangi, in particular, desired access to seedlings and cultivation expertise, as well as pulping machines for processing raw coffee. This made them less likely to use canals as leverage over the missions. In fact, the journals of the Catholic stations show no record of water being cut off after 1910, an indicator that the wamangi became more accommodating. Coffee also piqued the interest of everyday people regarding the missions. In the late nineteenth century, membership of the missions consisted almost exclusively of freed slaves and disassociated individuals.[57] Most people were reluctant to express too much interest in them for fear of alienating themselves from their clans. In July 1902, for example, the Kilema mission hosted a celebration and invited the surrounding community. Father Gommenginger mentions in the Kilema mission journal that it was poorly attended. When he asked several people why they did not come, they replied that the meni mifongo had threatened to cut off their access to water if they did so.[58] Losing water access would have implied a rejection of their membership in the water community and the life of the clan. Ten years later, however, the allure of coffee warmed many people's hearts to the missions. Attendance at mission schools rose substantially after 1910, as did attendance at weekly services. Even so, missions remained on the social periphery until the 1930s.

THE DEVELOPMENT OF SETTLER SOCIETIES

European settlers began to arrive a few years after the missions. While missionaries came to Kilimanjaro desiring to create Christian societies, settlers came desiring profit, wanting to transform the mountain into a haven for cash crop agriculture. As early as the 1890s, German supporters of empire called for emigration to the colonies to build what industrialist and Reichstag vice-president Hermann Paasche referred to as a "Neu-Deutschland."[59] To these individuals, empire provided the opportunity not only for territorial conquest and economic gain, but also for the extension of the German nation. The highland areas of German East Africa—Kilimanjaro, Mount Meru, the Usambara Mountains, and the southern highlands—seemed the logical home for permanent settlements because of their fertile soils, ample waters, and overall healthy characteristics. Söldenwagner notes that proponents of empire wrote about these spaces in a way that stressed their similarity with Germany rather than their strangeness or exoticism.[60] They also wrote about them as if they were uninhabited, just waiting to be seized and settled. The government set the groundwork for a settler population with the Crown Land Ordinance, which established mechanisms to redistribute crown lands.[61] In 1901 and 1903, colonial officers completed surveys of the mountain, which enabled the sale and lease of tracts. Though some settlers acquired land by negotiating with the wamangi as the missionaries had, most did so through the colonial state.

Despite the mountain's seeming potential, few settlers made their way there before 1906. The earliest settlers—small numbers of Germans, Greeks, Afrikaners, and German-speaking Russians—possessed little farming skills or financial backing, and they struggled to negotiate the poor infrastructure of the colony and minimal support of the administration. The most successful were the Greeks. Among the first to arrive, they found success by acquiring lands close to the chiefdoms and cultivating coffee. The main wave of settlement took place between 1907 and 1911, just after Maji Maji. In this period, several thousand settlers arrived in the colony, despite the administration's shift toward a dual emphasis on settler and African production. This influx can be attributed to the changing economic situation in the colony, the extension of railways—the nearly completed line from Moshi to Tanga and the line in Kenya from Mombasa to Taveta—and the emergence of coffee.[62] This made the colony more attractive to upper- and middle-class settlers. Those who arrived bought or leased land on the south side of Kilimanjaro, acquiring open plots from either the colonial state or wamangi who were willing to sell land in their chiefdoms. The rate of immigration increased swiftly. By 1912, nearly 5,000 people of European descent were living in the colony, most of whom were settlers.[63] The population of Europeans on Kilimanjaro totaled 831; among them were 192 adult women and 236 children, and only 55 were missionaries or colonial officials. There were 432 from Germany, but substantial numbers had also come from the British Empire (234), Britain (46), Greece (44), Russia (33), Italy (22), the Balkans (11), and France (3). This represented greater diversity than the pro-immigration groups had envisioned, a far cry from Neu-Deutschland. As of 1914, settlers controlled eighty-six settlements stretching from the far west slopes of the mountain to Marangu.[64]

Though a fraction of the size of the mountain's Chagga population—estimated at 96,834 in 1913—settlers radically transformed the landscape.[65] By 1913 nearly "200 square kilometers of arable land and 567 of pasture land had been alienated" through lease or sale. This compared with the estimated 468 square kilometers of arable land left to local farmers in the agroforest belt.[66] Most of the alienated pasture land lay on the sparsely populated western slopes (see map 3.1), while the arable lands were concentrated on the south side where water tended to be more available. The alienation of prime land—for both settlers and the missions—led to localized land scarcity in chiefdoms such as Kibosho, Uru, and Marangu. Blocked from free access to downhill lands, many in these chiefdoms had no choice but to become peasant farmers on settler or mission estates. District commissioners of the region, such as Johannes Abel and Wilhelm Methner, noticed this dilemma and feared that rebellion might ensue if land continued to be taken away. On August 16, 1911, Governor Rechenberg issued a ban on further land alienation until a formal survey had been completed and a reservation created for the mountain population.[67] This action may have been a few years too late. By that point, an "iron ring" of settlement existed in many areas of south Kilimanjaro that effectively blocked chiefdoms from expanding their territory.[68] As populations grew over the next few decades, land became a key area of contention between African populations and the colonial state.

Relations between African and European farmers on Kilimanjaro, and indeed elsewhere on the continent, have usually been conceptualized as antagonistic. While it is true that these groups quarreled over land, cultivation rights, and labor relations, they also had reasons to cooperate. New settlers quickly discovered that water could be surprisingly elusive in their African Eden. With the German government's fickle support of settlement, settlers realized that their survival depended on positive relationships with wamangi and meni mifongo. Most settler estates

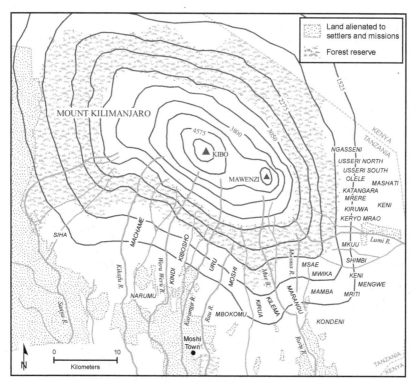

MAP 3.1. Land alienation, 1914 (*Brian Edward Balsley, GISP. Based on data from Wimmelbücker,* Kilimanjaro: A Regional History)

were located in the foothills and lowlands, areas that averaged substantially less rainfall than the highland vihamba. While Kibosho received an average of 2,184 millimeters of rain per year, Moshi Town—less than 6 kilometers further downhill—averaged only 852.[69] Arusha Chini, another 6 kilometers south and the site of a sugar plantation constructed in the 1930s, received only 465.[70] Not only was the rain seasonal, but it could also be unreliable, as settlers learned in the drought of 1907–8. In addition, warmer temperatures in these areas meant that the soil held less moisture. Rainfall patterns thus posed a barrier to settlers wishing to grow crops such as coffee, sugar, cotton, and maize.

The solution for the settlers was to develop irrigation systems that would provide water year-round to their crops. With the administration in a fledgling state and no legal framework for water, most gained access to water by cooperating with their African neighbors. How this occurred is poorly documented, as there are few records that discuss the construction of settler canals before 1923.[71] They likely followed the example of the missionaries, seeking assistance from wamangi and asking for permission and assistance to build canals. As with land transactions, settlers gained this by making payment in the form of cash money, livestock, or supplies such as seed (or a combination thereof).[72] The mangi would then send a specialist and a group of men to perform the necessary work. In some cases, settlers convinced the mangi to allow a project by pitching it as a mutually beneficial endeavor. This led to the development of canals used jointly by Africans and Europeans.

Sometimes, partnership enabled both sides to overcome barriers and better access water. For example, consider a canal constructed jointly by British settler Vincent Humplick and the small, marginalized Kombo chiefdom. Humplick arrived on Kilimanjaro in the late 1910s and attained a concession of land on the western border of Kibosho. His land was bordered on the east and west by the Nsere and Lonzo Rivers and to the north by several Kombo vihamba. In his first three years on the estate, he faced constant problems with his water supply:

> Longer than 3 years I [have strived] hard for obtaining a water canal sufficient for my plantation, till now in vain. In 1922 [and] 1923 every time 70–80% of [my] planted coffee trees [died]; in 1924 [the rains were] more favorable, also . . . the people of Kombo supplied me as possible with water. In 1922, I . . . [asked]

the people of Kombo [to] dig a water canal in common with me, but Mangi Ngilisho of Kibosho prevented it.[73]

To irrigate and process coffee, Humplick needed a reliable source of water. To this end, several barriers presented themselves, one being the challenging terrain around the estate. Though bordered by two rivers, the estate had only limited access to surface water because of the ravines. A canal running into the estate therefore needed to tap one of the rivers at a higher elevation. Given the terrain and the volume of the surrounding rivers, the nearest viable point of extraction was several kilometers to the north of Kombo, in land held by Machame and Kibosho. Negotiations needed to be made with not one chiefdom but two.

Humplick proposed to the mangi of Kombo that they jointly construct a canal with an intake at the Lonzo River in Kibosho and route it through Kombo and into his estate. They would share in the labor and costs and benefit from better access to water.[74] Problems arose in negotiations with Kibosho. In the late nineteenth century at the peak of its strength, Kibosho had annexed many of its smaller neighbors, including Kombo. After the arrival of the Germans, Kombo reestablished its autonomy. In retaliation, Sina's successor Ngilisho denied Kombo permission to use water or construct canals within its boundaries. In response to Humplick's proposal, Ngilisho simply said no.

In response to Ngilisho's refusal, Humplick and the Kombo found an alternative solution. They approached Mangi Marai Shangali of Machame about constructing a canal with an intake in his land. On January 7, 1925, the parties reached an agreement:

> Whereas Mangi Marai agrees to dig a canal with his labor from the River Lonzo to the Northern boundary between farm 225 belonging to Mr. Humplick and the Kombo country, Mr. Vincent Humplick agrees to incur the expense of blasting and removing about 50 yards of rock close to the said River Lonzo, he paying for the labour, fundis, and implements required. Furthermore Mr. Humplick agrees to build a concrete culvert at the place where the canal crosses the Machame–Kibosho Road.
>
> On conclusion of these works, both parties agree to share equally the water deriving from this canal for the mutual benefit of Mr. Vincent Humplick and the Natives.[75]

In this arrangement, the three groups collaborated on a canal that would benefit them all. This example reveals much about the nature of cooperative canal development. Permission for construction and the contribution of labor came from the chiefdom or chiefdoms involved, while the settler contributed payment and inputs such as explosives and concrete. It also implies the presence of local expertise in distinguishing between "labour" and "fundis" (or *mafundi*, sing. *fundi*). The term *fundi* in Kiswahili refers to a skilled craftsman and, in this context, implies specialists in canal construction. Labor, on the other hand, consisted of men brought in to excavate the canal. The agreement thus shows how the canal's development synthesized African and European knowledge, technique, and expectations.

Cooperative efforts were common in the early years of settler agriculture, when both the settlers and the administration were fledgling. In such cases, it made sense to share both the bounty and the burden of new canals. Cooperation could also create potent grounds for conflict. Agreements could be struck for a new canal, only for disagreement to surface later as to how the water should be shared. Conflicts also arose as other projects deemed necessary by the settlers, such as roads, encroached upon canals. The degree to which these neighbors liked or merely tolerated one another varied widely. Today, many elders on Kilimanjaro recall settlers fondly and note that relations were generally cordial, while others recall despising them.[76] What is most important is that they had reason to remain on friendly terms. For Europeans, good relations with neighboring Africans could ensure access to water, while conflict could result in one's canal being blocked with little recourse. Relations between settlers and their African neighbors in the German period were therefore much more complex than has been acknowledged. As new settlers developed a more nuanced view of the waterscape and realized that not every cloud will bring rain, they built partnerships with local communities to ensure access to water. By constructing new canals, they acknowledged the benefits of local techniques, the power of the wamangi, and the knowledge of canal design held by specialists.

CONFRONTING DROUGHT AND SCARCITY

Most Europeans who came to Kilimanjaro in the German period held an initial impression of the mountain as a place of water abundance.

This view of the waterscape came from their own observations and from the image of Kilimanjaro created by nineteenth-century explorers and sustained by pro-settlement organizations.[77] However, between 1895 and the First World War, the mountain experienced lower-than-average rainfall in four periods: 1888–90, 1898–1900, 1907–8, and 1913–15. As noted in chapter 1, these periods presented varying degrees of hardship for mountain communities. For settlers who resided in the foothills and lowlands, even minor droughts threatened their crops. The onset of drought challenged European impressions of the mountain as water abundant and threatened their acceptance of the mifongo and their arrangements with the chiefdoms.

The drought of 1907–8 provides an example of the reaching impacts of water scarcity. It was among the first to be documented by the German administration and missionaries, as well as the first to occur during the wave of settlement. The drought began with the failure of the fuli in 1906, intensified with the failure of the kisiye in 1907, and persisted through lackluster rainfall until after the kisiye in 1909. Seasonal rivers, streams, and canals dried up entirely, and larger rivers such as the Kikafu and the Mwona suffered greatly reduced volume. The peoples of Rombo felt the impacts most severely. According to the journal of the Catholic mission in Mkuu, women and children spent most of their days procuring small amounts of water from remote sources near the forest line.[78] Facing widespread crop failures, some families sought refuge in the missions or fled Rombo altogether.[79] Many men sought work on the settler and mission farms. The journal noted that in July 1908, famine conditions had started to materialize: "Famine is felt moreover in this country. At the mission we do not know how to find food for the children. There are no longer any bananas, nor beans, nor millet in the country and our small harvest of maize will soon be exhausted. Oh when will the famine end?"[80] The mission's canal remained dry throughout the period, leaving no water for irrigating crops. The toll was staggering. According to the Mkuu mission records, famine killed at least one thousand people there by the end of 1909. Wimmelbücker notes that the period became known in the southeastern chiefdoms as njaa ya Mtsimbii, or "hunger of the people of Rombo," because of the large number of Rombo refugees who ended up in those areas.[81] In northeast Kilimanjaro, it became known as njaa ya kangama, or "famine of the morning," reflecting that it caught people unprepared. On the southern slopes, conflicts erupted within local communities as users fought over access to the scarce water. Tensions also flared with the settlers.

The German administration began to recognize the impending crisis. In a September 1907 meeting of the Moshi District Council (*Bezirksrat*), five settlers came forward to describe the water shortages affecting their farms.[82] They discussed how the failure of the rains had left much of their lands unsuitable for agriculture, and they feared that if the rains did not return, they would have to abandon their farms. Their concerns extended beyond the immediate drought. As District Officer Methner summarized in a memo to the Colonial Office in Dar es Salaam on September 11, the settlers claimed that "the wealth of water of Kilimanjaro (in visible watercourses) is not as big as generally assumed." Methner's memo called on the government to provide money for digging wells. Three months later, he followed with another memo providing a more descriptive account. He feared an impending "water calamity" caused by "everybody (either native or colonist) taking as much water as possible out of the most comfortably situated stream, without any regard to people living downward."[83] He ominously predicted, "if the long rains of 1908 will be insufficient again . . . there will be some bloody heads." He called not just for more financial support, but also for some laws to regulate canal construction and irrigation.

Drought conditions began to ease in 1909. As they did, water returned to rivers, streams, and canals, and famine subsided soon thereafter. For most people in the chiefdoms, who were well familiar with cycles of drought, these conditions had been more extreme than normal, but they did not challenge fundamental understandings of the waterscape. Some Europeans began to think more carefully about the nature of the waterscape and the challenges it posed to settlers. In his 1907 tract *Wie wandere ich nach Deutschen Kolonien aus?* (How do I migrate to German colonies?), Dr. Oscar Bongard warns against ill-suited settlers with unrealistic expectations of colonial living.[84] He notes, "Our colonies are certainly not a fairy land. Thus, one who wants to emigrate should carefully check to see what the situation there is." This advice had limited impact. Most European settlers flooded into the colony after the drought, between 1907 and 1911, and they seemed oblivious to the devastation it had wrought. They instead saw a Kilimanjaro that seemed majestic and water abundant, a land in stark contrast to its surroundings, and a place of tremendous potential. The works of German artist Walter von Ruckteschell embody this view. Just before the outbreak of war in 1914, he completed a set of paintings and sketches of the mountain (see fig. 3.4). Featuring Kibo and Mawenzi

FIGURE 3.4. *Ansicht eines Kilimandscharo* (*View of Kilimanjaro*) (*Walter von Ruckteschell, Deutsches Historisches Museum, Berlin. Inv.-Nr: 1990/36.369*)

standing proudly over fields of lush, green banana groves, they very much sold the image of Kilimanjaro as a majestic and verdant space. His work, and the flood of settlers, indicates the extent to which realities did little to shatter the image of Kilimanjaro as an African Eden.

The German administration, however, began to formalize water control with the aim of avoiding shortages and alleviating conflict among users. Wimmelbücker notes that from 1910, the district office issued regulations and quotas in an "attempt to avoid European protest against the squandering of water higher up as well as African protest against the arbitrary measures depriving them of proper allotments."[85] In 1914, it issued regulations calling on any European who intended to create a new canal to apply for permission in advance.[86] The colonial administration issued a draft of its first territory-wide water law that same year, though a final version was never approved.[87] These steps brought few actual changes. They came after land alienation on Kilimanjaro had largely ended and most canals had been constructed, and they were not retroactive. And with the onset of war in July 1914, attempts to create a legal foundation for water all but ceased.

WAR, THE BRITISH, AND THE MAKING OF TANGANYIKA

Colonial rule faced severe disruption with the outbreak of war in Europe. Within weeks of the onset of hostilities, the East African colonies emerged as a theater in the war, with German East Africa pitted against Britain's Kenya Colony, Britain's Uganda Protectorate, and the Belgian Congo. Wedged between the British and German empires and possessing economic and symbolic value, Kilimanjaro emerged as a focal point of the fighting. The first skirmish near the mountain took place on August 15, 1914, when two field companies of askari based in Moshi Town, around 300 men in total, crossed the border just east of town and seized Taveta. Possessing little in the way of defense, the British officers in the town fired a token shot and surrendered. This event embodied the German strategy for war devised by Schutztruppe commander Lieutenant Colonel Paul von Lettow-Vorbeck. As noted by Michelle Moyd, Lettow-Vorbeck aimed to force the Allies to commit resources to East Africa so that they could not be used in Europe.[88] Given his numbers and the unlikelihood of his receiving reinforcements, he engaged the British with small-scale attacks and guerilla warfare, followed by quick retreats to evade capture. For the next year or so, much of the fighting near Kilimanjaro followed this pattern, the German forces launching small-scale attacks against their numerically superior British counterparts, then retreating into the mountain's densely forested hills.

In response to their frustrated efforts to take the colony, the British flooded the region with troops in late 1915 and appointed South African general Jan Smuts to command them. By early 1916, he had 73,330 men at his disposal: 27,575 British and South African troops, 14,300 Indians, 14,000 Africans from the Belgian Congo's Force Publique, 10,000 men from Mozambique, 6,875 troops from the King's African Rifles (KAR), and 580 Europeans.[89] In early March, he advanced his troops toward Kilimanjaro, flanking the mountain. As they reached Moshi Town, they found that the Germans had already withdrawn toward the south. Smuts's officers occupied the town, seized control of the German boma, and effectively took control of the mountain. Though German resistance persisted in the colony for two more years, Kilimanjaro was effectively under British control from this point forward.

The onset of war and the British conquest of Kilimanjaro radically altered life for the region's European populations. They found themselves economically isolated from Europe, which made it difficult to access imported goods and export markets. They also faced social disruption, as many settlers volunteered for military service, joining together to form armed regiments to augment the askari. Once the British seized Kilimanjaro in 1916, the transitional leadership headed by Sir Horace Byatt expelled everyone holding German citizenship.[90] Between 1916 and 1922, his government deported half the mountain's settlers, numerous Holy Ghost Fathers, and nearly the entire Leipzig Mission. This left many farms unoccupied and canals abandoned, and it crippled what little momentum the settler economy had. The Catholic missions filled vacancies by bringing in missionaries from France but left many posts staffed by converts until after the war ended. The Leipzig Mission had little choice but to abandon its missions. In 1922, it handed over its stations to the American Augustana Lutheran order, which managed them until the Leipzig order received permission to return in 1927.

For African populations on the mountain, the transition to British control brought fewer changes. Though the war disrupted the local economy, it had minimal impact on the chiefdoms since they were less dependent on exports and foreign inputs. Some people benefitted by squatting on lands abandoned by settlers. After the hostilities ceased in 1916, the new political order largely resembled its German predecessor. The wamangi governed as they had before the war, and tax collection remained mostly continuous. The missionaries who remained, along with converts working as catechists and teachers, kept many of the churches and schools open. Perhaps most importantly, local farmers kept growing coffee and expanding their holdings. In fact, the large number of coffee trees kept the new administration from implementing restrictions on African coffee cultivation as it had in Kenya.

In 1919, the Treaty of Versailles broke up the former German East Africa, most of the remaining territory becoming part of the British Empire under the authority of the newly formed League of Nations. After much discussion—and even the possibility of naming it "Kilimanjaro"—the Colonial Office in London decided to name it the Tanganyika Territory.[91] In July 1922, the League formalized its legal status as a mandate territory. Under the conditions of the mandate, Tanganyika was to be administered in a way that "promoted the material and moral well-being" of its native populations.[92] With the territory's legal status settled, the British administration embarked on administrative reforms designed to give the colony a structure more akin to that of other British possessions. They divided it into a series of provinces and districts, placing Kilimanjaro in the Moshi District of the Northern Province. Within the districts, chiefs remained the subordinates of district officers, but through a more structured system of indirect rule. The Native Authority Ordinance of 1921 divided the territory into a series of "tribal" areas, each administered by its own Native Authority per local law and custom.[93] It also called on Native Authorities to enforce rules made by colonial administrators as appropriate. For Kilimanjaro, the administration grouped the chiefdoms together into a single Chagga Native Authority. By 1929, it had also created a Chagga Council comprising all the wamangi, as well as a Chagga Court and a central treasury. In the language of the colonial state, the people residing on Kilimanjaro were Chagga, even if they never used the term to describe themselves. The administration held that Kilimanjaro was a singular space, the home of a singular tribe, whether the people acknowledged it or not.

The transition to British rule marked the end of a colonial era for Kilimanjaro in several ways. As this chapter has shown, the German administration often lacked consistency in policy, as is clear in economic development, the role of settlers, and the management of water resources. Except for protecting forest reserves, German policy toward water was practically nonexistent until 1910, and thereafter it consisted of reactive policies meant to deal with localized issues rather than formal laws or administrative structures. This reflected the prevailing view of the mountain's waterscapes. Settlers, missionaries, and administrators—like the explorers who preceded them—accepted that the mountain was a place of water abundance. Working relationships centered on water access arose from the need for irrigation amid the lack of formal structures. Settlers and missionaries embraced the water-management knowledge and expertise of their new neighbors, and they widely adopted mfongo water technology. This in turn gave mountain farmers a tool with which to negotiate their broader relationships with these actors.

British rule brought a much more structured form of colonial governance, one that eliminated many spaces of negotiation that had formed in the German period. Yet a striking continuity between the two periods was how people viewed the waterscape. Like the Germans before them, the British believed Kilimanjaro to be a place of nearly endless waters and considered local water-management knowledge to be ingenious. These views persisted until the late 1920s, when changing circumstances led the British to rethink the waterscape's abundance and the value of local experts' knowledge.

4 ～ From Abundance to Scarcity

Rethinking the Waterscape and
Local Knowledge, 1923–48

IN 1921, Charles Dundas became commissioner of the Moshi District, the first to be appointed after the war and under the new British administration. An employee of the colonial service since 1908 and the son of a consular officer, Dundas had spent much of his life away from his homeland. His four-year assignment on Kilimanjaro proved especially formative. He became an avid enthusiast of the mountain's societies, and in 1924 he published a book entitled *Kilimanjaro and Its People*. The first of its kind published in English, it provides an in-depth discussion of history, law, and custom on the mountain. Several aspects of this book provide a useful view into British attitudes toward Kilimanjaro in the early 1920s. It refers to the people of the mountain as belonging to a singular tribe—the Wachagga—and describes their history as a natural coalescing of peoples destined to be unified. In terms of cultural and social development, they are characterized as unusually sophisticated for Africans due to the combination of "nature and humanity" fostered by the mountain.[1] He sees the mountain as otherworldly, a place of "luxuriant fertility" due to its lush waterscape.[2] The prosperity of Chagga society came from harnessing this abundance through the "innumerable canals conducting water to the fields and groves." In a style that mirrors that of nineteenth-century explorers, the book imagines the mountain as Edenesque and local water management as ingenious.

For more than fifty years, Europeans had thought of Kilimanjaro as a miracle in the heart of Africa, a place of ample waters and permanent ice amid the harsh steppe. The idea of the mountain as a place of abundance is clear in Dundas's account. Its uniqueness made it a symbol of numerous objectives—colonial, missionary, economic—during the period of colonial conquest. As settlers, missionaries, and German colonial officials entered the region at the turn of the century, many discovered that these perceptions were unrealistic imaginings. Yet the idea of the mountain as a place of abundance persevered. By the end of the 1920s, however, visions of Kilimanjaro as water abundant started to fade, replaced by fear that the mountain's waters were dangerously limited. Local management came to be considered the biggest threat to the mountain's waters. Mifongo were not ingenious but harmful to the landscape and contributed to prodigal water use. If steps were not taken, the vitality of the mountain would be lost forever. Suddenly, it seemed that Kilimanjaro could be Eden in another sense, a paradise lost.

This chapter analyzes the radical rethinking of the waterscape that took place in the first three decades of British rule and the impact it had on the production of management knowledge. Factors including population growth, rising consumption, new types of use, and environmental concerns led many Europeans to reconsider the nature of Kilimanjaro's water supply. Local practices that had once been extolled were chastised as harmful to the long-term future of the mountain. The British administration responded by sponsoring scientific studies to generate data about the water situation and then creating a new legal framework for water management using their findings. As scholars such as Richards, Tilley, and van Beusekom have shown, colonial states frequently described the knowledge they produced in terms of binaries—traditional versus modern, customary versus scientific—that dismissed the value of local expertise.[3] This is evident on Kilimanjaro, where state actors promoted scientific knowledge as a modern alternative to traditional water-management practices. Only by embracing scientific management could the mountain's waters be conserved and maximized, and the waterscape saved from devastation. The proposed changes promoted a more centralized, technocratic, and commodified understanding of water.

The colonial administration's attempts to gain control of the water situation revealed tensions between scientists, colonial officials, the wamangi, and local populations, and showed the state to be a terrain of struggle between competing interests. Colonial officials, attempting to reconcile water management with indirect rule, created a water regime defined by distinct yet overlapping spheres of authority. The Moshi Water Board held responsibility for regulating water use by European populations or any new systems, while the Chagga Native Authority—composed of the mountain's wamangi—oversaw water use in the chiefdoms. This was a far cry from the holistic approach advocated by colonial scientists, and it did not reflect the fact that nearly all the mountain's waters passed through the chiefdoms en route to downstream users. Furthermore, the government assumed that it could encourage reforms in local management by funneling new policies through the wamangi. Wamangi embraced the government's plans, as they promised to bolster their authority at a time when rival institutions, such as the Christian missions and the Kilimanjaro Native Planters Association, a coffee cooperative, were gaining influence. The government's strategy ignored the influence of meni mifongo and the canal societies, and therefore it failed almost entirely. These groups resisted new restrictions on canal use and development and, in doing so, stopped a realignment of power over water that was not in their interest.

RETHINKING EDEN

This rethinking of the waterscape can be attributed to several factors. For starters, the British administration encountered two major droughts (1922–24 and 1929–30) in its first decade. Because of the disruptions of the war and the deportation of settlers and missionaries, little memory of drought among the European populations remained. People such as Dundas assumed that the environmental conditions they saw when they arrived on Kilimanjaro were always present. The onset of drought forced the administration to confront the challenges posed by periodic water scarcity. In January 1928, amid drought conditions, the commissioner of the Northern Province wrote a memo to the administration in Dar es Salaam, noting that "difficulties and disputes are increasing." He feared these conditions could pose long-term problems, particularly for more-arid areas in the foothills and lowlands. In his mind, these regions' development depended "to a large extent upon the water available; . . . continuance of existing methods [would] prejudice that development severely."[4]

This rethinking of the mountain's water supply came at a time of tremendous increase in demand. Much of this stemmed from changing demographics. By the late 1920s, a growing number of people depended on the mountain's water resources. The first official population count in 1913 put the African population of the mountain at 96,834.[5] In 1921, the first census in the British period calculated it at 158,185.[6] The following decades witnessed a boom in population growth (see table 4.1), a pattern mirrored across East Africa.[7] By 1948, the government estimated a population of 230,665, representing a growth rate greater than 100 percent over a span of less than thirty years, approximately 3.5 percent per annum.[8] By 1967, it had reached 476,467 and, by 1988, nearly doubled to 743,548.[9] Several factors explain the phenomenal rise: the end of warfare among the chiefdoms and with the Maasai; better nutrition and improved fertility; better sanitation practices and lower rates of disease; and the decline of practices such as breastfeeding beyond age one, birth control, and abortion.[10] The populations of the chiefdoms rose at the same time that the European population rebounded. By 1927, the figure for settlers on Kilimanjaro had reached 534, and the number of missionaries had nearly returned to prewar levels.[11]

The steep rise in population had a tremendous impact on water demand. Assuming flat per capita use, overall mountain consumption would have nearly tripled between 1913 and 1948 from population growth alone. However, per capita rates of consumption rose substantially in the early twentieth century. By the 1930s, African populations were using water more extensively than they had previously, as much as double per capita as in 1900.[12] The spread of Christianity was one factor in this trend. Both the Catholics and the Lutherans promoted forms

---

TABLE 4.1

Population growth in Moshi District (excluding Moshi Town)

Year	Male	Female	Total
1921	59,944	68,499	128,443
1928	66,207	76,806	143,013
1931	73,054	82,288	155,337
1948	107,529	123,138	230,665
1957	179,011	180,083	339,094
1967	231,447	245,020	476,467

Data from Paul Maro, *Population Growth and Agricultural Change in Kilimanjaro, 1920–1970*, research paper no. 40 (Dar es Salaam: University of Dar es Salaam Bureau of Resource Assessment and Land Use Planning, December 1975).

---

of hygiene, such as regular bathing and washing clothes, that necessitated more water consumption. These practices were required for children attending mission schools. Given the prohibition against bathing in open watercourses, water for bathing had to be procured by women or children and brought to vihamba in pots.[13] If each household drew an additional two pots (36–72 liters) of water per day for bathing, the overall rate of water consumption would have increased by 25 percent. The European populations also contributed to rising consumption. The British administration estimated that they consumed at least three times as much domestic water per person as their African counterparts.[14] For irrigation, the difference was much greater. Settler and mission estates were larger, were located in drier areas, and practiced monoculture, all of which required more irrigation water than the vihamba. Furthermore, the crops chosen by Europeans—coffee, cotton, sugar—demanded more water than local varietals such as eleusine.

The single biggest contributor to increasing water consumption was coffee cultivation. In the 1920s, coffee emerged as the mountain's premier cash crop, largely because of Dundas's efforts.[15] In his term as district officer, he actively promoted the industry. Seeing native production as the future of the region's economy, he used district office resources to provide seedlings and technical assistance to local farmers. The industry received a further boost in 1925, when a group of farmers formed the Kilimanjaro Native Planters Association, a cooperative society aimed at marketing the crop and providing technical support. Production in the chiefdoms rose rapidly (see table 4.2). Whereas in 1922 there were 592 coffee growers in the chiefdoms, two years later they numbered 3,320.[16] Farmers also began growing much larger numbers of trees. In the middle of the war, there were an estimated 37,153 coffee trees in the chiefdoms. By 1924, there were 144,138. By 1932, there were as many as 6 million.

Coffee cultivation required farmers to use water in new ways. Newly planted seeds and immature saplings needed irrigation in the dry seasons and in case of drought. This required the meni mifongo and canal societies to enlarge canals to provide more water. Moreover, unlike other crops, coffee required large amounts of water for processing. Raw coffee cherries picked from trees needed to be processed before the beans could be sold. This involved a process called pulping, in which the cherries were soaked in water to loosen the surrounding skins from

TABLE 4.2

Growth of coffee production

Season (July–June)	Growers (Approx.)	Acreage (Approx.)	Green Coffee (tons)	Crop Value (£)	Value per Ton (£)
1923–24	3,300	1,200	32	n/a	n/a
1924–25	4,400	1,500	48	n/a	n/a
1925–26	5,500	2,000	64	n/a	n/a
1926–27	6,600	2,800	80	n/a	n/a
1927–28	7,900	3,500	264	n/a	n/a
1928–29	9,000	4,000	308	n/a	n/a
1929–30	10,000	4,300	416	n/a	n/a
1930–31	11,000	4,600	672	n/a	n/a
1931–32	11,800	4,900	740	n/a	n/a
1932–33	12,530	5,160	867	44,575	51
1933–34	16,800	6,700	716	46,259	65
1934–35	18,550	7,560	1,275	44,728	35
1935–36	21,740	9,380	1,475	45,941	31
1936–37	24,280	12,450	722	25,561	35
1937–38	25,230	14,790	1,177	41,032	35
1938–39	25,730	14,400	1,566	69,762	45
1939–40	26,270	15,170	2,141	85,842	40
1940–41	26,890	16,180	3,250	101,802	31
1941–42	27,330	16,660	1,558	59,457	38
1942–43	27,572	16,860	2,482	163,221	66
1943–44	27,970	16,340	1,691	167,737	99
1944–45	29,310	16,980	3,275	343,474	105
1945–46	29,600	16,830	2,512	256,449	102
1946–47	30,450	17,380	1,834	203,543	111
1947–48	31,670	22,460	3,384	439,573	130
1948–49	32,050	22,400	2,623	373,803	143
1949–50	31,590	23,540	3,359	954,713	284
1950–51	32,030	23,010	5,049	1,214,634	241
1951–52	34,390	23,620	5,670	1,396,310	246
1952–53	35,280	25,100	1,949	685,620	352
1953–54	36,880	27,660	6,304	3,724,184	591
1954–55	36,200	27,150	4,361	1,907,084	437
1955–56	37,600	28,200	6,577	3,078,955	468
1956–57	40,420	30,320	5,522	2,285,695	414
1957–58	44,140	33,100	5,596	2,191,941	392
1958–59	44,320	33,260	5,821	1,851,932	318
1959–60	45,130	33,850	6,798	2,142,143	315
1960–61	45,000	34,000	8,739	2,499,892	286

Michael von Clemm, "Agricultural Productivity and Sentiment on Kilimanjaro," *Economic Botany* 18, no. 2 (1964): 112.

the beans. The beans were then washed with clean water to remove any remaining residue. The need to irrigate and process coffee thus resulted in a large net increase in water consumption for agricultural purposes.

The growth of the coffee industry effectively ended the era of water partnerships between settlers and the chiefdoms. Alarmed by the swift growth of African coffee cultivation, settlers formed the Kilimanjaro Planters Association in 1923. It lobbied the government to institute a total ban on cultivation in the chiefdoms, similar to that in the central highlands of Kenya.[17] Settlers feared that their neighbors would outcompete them and that this success would make it harder to procure labor for their own farms. In public discourse, however, they complained that African coffee "spread disease, devalued [their] product, and encouraged theft."[18] Much of their angst took the form of complaints to the district office. For example, on September 7, 1922, a settler named D. Ghikas accused people in Machame and Kibosho of diverting water from his canal.[19] He claimed that the shortage of water to his pulper had ruined five bags of coffee, costing him more than two hundred shillings. Another example involved Edgar Beech, who wrote a letter on November 15, 1923, complaining that a man named Jowli had been diverting water from a canal just above his coffee washing box.[20] In a scathing critique, he criticized Jowli for causing "trouble with practically every other European in this district by his continual effort to annoy, both in German time and since. He is practically ostracized by all other natives here due to his conduct." District records show a dramatic increase in complaints made by settlers against mountain farmers in the 1920s. This reflected the rise in competition between the two groups over coffee and access to water for irrigation and processing.

Increasing population and usage on the mountain represented only part of the rising demand. New agricultural and industrial interests were also being developed along the Pangani River between Kilimanjaro and the Indian Ocean. At the foot of the mountain, just south of Moshi Town, the Tanganyika Planting Company opened a 30,000-hectare sugar plantation in 1930. To grow and process the water-intensive crop, the company developed an expansive network of irrigation canals that tapped the Rau River. Further down the watershed, sisal emerged as the colony's number one export. By 1910, sisal exports had reached

7,000 tons per year, the bulk coming from a series of large estates lining the middle and lower reaches of the Pangani.[21] Four years later, production had tripled. The industry suffered through the First World War, but production rebounded to 50,000 tons by 1930. During the Second World War, Tanganyika emerged as one of the world's premier producers, yielding 112,000 tons in 1945. The development of sisal production in the Pangani Basin created the first large-scale demand for the waters of Kilimanjaro beyond the mountain. While sisal is a hardy crop that does not require irrigation, it does require water to turn its leaves into usable fibers, a process called decortication. In his 1958 study of the sisal industry, Claude Guillebaud estimated that 8,000 gallons of water per hour were required to process sisal at these factories.[22]

Another industry to arise in the Pangani Basin was hydroelectric power. In 1936, the Tanganyika Electric Supply Company (TANESCO) opened a power station at the Pangani Falls, 65 kilometers upstream from Pangani Town. It initially had a capacity of 5,000 kilowatts, most of which was destined for sisal factories and the port of Tanga.[23] Over the next three decades, TANESCO expanded the capacity to 12,500 kilowatts and constructed two additional power stations on the river: Hale in 1964 (21,000 kilowatts) and Nyumba ya Mungu in 1966 (8,000 kilowatts).[24] Hydroelectric power introduced a new way of thinking about water use. Rather than consuming it directly, the turbines depended on the power of the water's flow, demanding a constant volume and rate (measured in cubic feet of water per second, or cusecs). This presented a challenge for a river system subject to great seasonal variability.

A year before opening the Pangani Falls station, TANESCO became concerned about falling flow rates in the river. In a letter to the Chief Secretary in Dar es Salaam, the company's director pointed out that rates had plummeted from 800 cusecs in 1933 to as low as 450 cusecs.[25] Such a drop caused concern, since inadequate flow would keep the station from reaching its generating capacity. The director noted the presence of drought but instead attributed the problem to a "process of gradual denudation" of the watershed caused by excessive upstream use. He asked the government to take "steps to ensure that an undue quantity of water is not diverted from the river for irrigation purposes in the upper reaches, and if possible to conserve the natural water resources in the area from which the river draws its supply." The director's plea represented the first call for the colonial administration to think of water management in terms of the needs of an entire watershed, rather than merely part of it. It also initiated a struggle between upstream and downstream users in the Pangani watershed that persists to the present day.

The last factor contributing to scarcity discourse was rising concern over the mountain's natural resources. As Grove has observed, tropical Edens have long stimulated conservationist sentiment among colonial actors.[26] The seemingly precarious nature of these spaces led early scientists and officials to implement environmental-management programs, hoping to sustain their vitality. For the first several decades of colonial rule, forest management had been the primary environmental concern of Kilimanjaro's German and British colonial officers. In the 1930s, desiccation and soil erosion emerged as the most pressing concerns. Colonial officers feared that East Africa was becoming progressively more arid, a process exacerbated by poor land management. This promised not only to leave less land suitable for farming, but also to make it more susceptible to erosion. These fears became pervasive in the wake of the Dust Bowl of 1930–36. As Anderson has noted, the massive devastation of the American Great Plains transformed soil erosion into the "first global environmental problem."[27] Images of the event, portrayed in publications such as Jacks and Whyte's 1939 book *Rape of the Earth*, generated concern throughout East Africa that if cultivation and land management practices were not improved, the lush highlands of the country would be transformed into barren wastelands.[28]

As the most symbolic and lucrative agricultural region in the colony, Kilimanjaro drew much attention from agricultural officers concerned about desiccation and erosion. With its steeply sloping contours, fast-running rivers, and intense, seasonal rainfall, the region seemed especially susceptible.[29] These conditions, they figured, were compounded by the region's reliance on traditional water management, particularly the mifongo. Once an "indigenous wonder," mifongo became considered wasteful of water (because of seepage and evaporation) and prone to erosion because of their dirt construction. One of the first critiques of the canals came from A. J. Wakefield, senior agricultural officer for Kilimanjaro. On January 26, 1931, he sent a memo to the director for agriculture in Dar es Salaam citing his fear for the "future fertility" of the mountain. He referred to the mifongo as "a very primitive and wasteful system of irrigation" that was literally washing the wealth of the mountain into the plains.[30] The inherent problems of the mifongo were exacerbated by the rising number of them—due to population growth and coffee expansion—as well as the creation of higher-volume canals reaching the settler farms and Tanganyika Planting Company.

The problem lay not just with the canals themselves, but also with how they were being used. Mifongo had been designed to supply domestic water and to flood irrigate vihamba and shamba, neither of which had been located in arid or steeply sloping areas. By the 1920s, what had originally been a technology adapted to intensive farming was being used extensively with little terracing of land to prevent soil wash. Though Africans and Europeans both practiced flood irrigation and the practices of settlers were arguably the most destructive, the focus of government criticism was the practice of growing eleusine under irrigation during the dry season. By the 1930s, eleusine generated ire among colonial officials who believed it was wasteful, destructive, and detrimental to economic development, as well as among missionaries who believed it contributed to alcohol abuse. In 1941, the government summarized its position by saying that "the growing of eleusine under the conditions at present prevailing in the upper slopes of Kilimanjaro have been largely the cause of the shortage of water in the lower reaches of the rivers during the dry seasons, and of soil erosion with all its attendant evils."[31]

The factors of drought, population growth, increasing consumption, rising demand from beyond the mountain, and concern over natural resources contributed to Europeans' changing perceptions of Kilimanjaro's waterscape. By the 1930s, people began to think of water as scarce. These fears tended to be strongest among settlers on the foothills and among the industrial interests along the Pangani River. Fear of scarcity, in turn, led to more conflicts between users, calls for government regulation, and scathing criticism of the mifongo. Colonial officials no longer spoke of Kilimanjaro as a "Garden of Eden," but rather as a place they hoped to prevent from "developing into a second Kalahari."[32] The mountain's African populations, for the most part, did not echo these concerns. For one, they possessed a much more nuanced view of the water supply, cultivated by centuries of experience and the development of expertise. They also benefitted from being upstream in the watershed. European users felt scarcity more acutely because of their position downstream of this growing population. Perhaps most importantly, mountain peoples viewed the waters as belonging to them. They did not consider those from beyond the mountain as having a rightful claim to the resource, and therefore the outsiders' issues of scarcity were barely acknowledged.

CREATING A LEGAL FOUNDATION FOR WATER

The first step that the British administration took was to develop a water law for the territory, the Natural Water Supply Regulation Ordinance of January 1923.[33] One of the first laws implemented in the British period, it placed legal authority for water in the hands of the colonial government in Dar es Salaam. It empowered the governor to establish water boards responsible for controlling and regulating water supplies within specified regions. The boards, composed of a chairman and individuals chosen by the governor, were responsible for the following:

a. Prohibiting, restricting, or regulating the diversion, taking, storage, pollution, distribution, and use of water from any natural water supply

b. Prohibiting, restricting, or regulating the construction, maintenance, and use of irrigation works

c. Empowering any person to construct, maintain, and use irrigation works . . . on his own land or on public land, or on the land of another person subject to the payment of compensation

d. Empowering any person to use irrigation works or any such works as foresaid in common with the owner subject to payment of such contribution towards the cost of construction and maintenance . . .

e. Requiring licenses to be obtained from the board for anything by which this Ordinance a board is empowered . . . to do

f. As to any other matter or thing, whether similar to those before enumerated or not, in connection with the supply, conservation, distribution, and use of water

The ordinance made regional water boards the primary agents for water management, and it embodied them with the power to adjudicate disputes within their jurisdictions. Those refusing to adhere to the decisions of their respective board could be fined or imprisoned.

A notable aspect of the ordinance is that it created a dual legal system governing the management of water.[34] While water boards held control over water within crown lands—those held by the government, settlers, and other European agents—the ordinance called for the boards to delegate authority over water in African areas to the appropriate Native Authority. Each board's powers would be assigned to the appropriate headman, who would then regulate water management by his subjects per native law and custom.[35] This created separate spheres of authority over water, one under the control of Europeans under common law, the other under the control of dozens of Native Authorities, each managing water through customary law. The law did not recognize the degree to which these spheres overlapped or the extent to which water use in one locality could impact people in another. It also assumed that chiefs actually held power over water in their jurisdictions.

On Kilimanjaro, the ordinance laid the groundwork for the Moshi District Water Board, the first regional government institution dedicated to managing water. Organized just months after the passing of the ordinance, the board consisted of the district officer, acting as chairman, and two appointees.[36] Throughout the 1920s and 1930s, it was responsible for regulating water abstractions, monitoring the construction of new canals, and adjudicating disputes for watercourses used by Europeans. These included canals used solely by settlers and missions and canals shared with Africans. The board asserted control through a system of water rights. Non-Africans who owned canals had to register them with the board, providing detailed information on each canal's construction and water usage. Based on this information, the board then granted a legal right to the applicant to use the water as prescribed. Individuals wishing to construct new canals or modify existing ones had to file for a new water right, a process that involved providing usage data, detailed sketches, and proof that the new canal would not hinder any existing claims. The board then held a public hearing. If all information was in order and there were no complaints, it issued a new right. In calling for water to be conceptualized quantitatively, the water-right system represented the first step toward commoditized water management on Kilimanjaro.

The water board promised to bring order to mountainside water management, but in practice it found itself outmatched by the complex nature of the mountain's waters and a myriad of conflicts among settlers and between settlers and Africans. The board had no actual data on the mountain's water supplies, which made the process of managing them haphazard. It also had no list of the informal rights held by settlers from the German period, which were protected by the ordinance, nor did it have a list of the African canals considered to be customary and thus protected by the Native Authority Ordinance. Without any data to work with, the board was flying blind. A good example of this is a complaint filed by E. Meimarides, a Greek settler who operated a coffee estate in Mweka. In September 1927, he accused five men living above his estate of blocking his canal from the Kitsina River and thus interfering with the water right granted to him by the board.[37] The board investigated the dispute and summoned responses from several individuals, including Mangi Ngilisho of Kibosho. The mangi claimed that the canal had been constructed jointly by his people and a prior settler and thus was subject to a sharing agreement.[38] The board agreed and, in October, issued a decision that the five men should be granted full use of the canal four days each week, and Meimarides the remaining three.[39]

As time passed, the government and users alike criticized water boards for being vague, unscientific, and ineffective. Few board members held any qualifications, and members were often political appointees. Settlers, frustrated with decisions that appeared arbitrary, accused board members of siding with African users or with their personal friends. Searing criticism came from Governor Harold Mac-Michael in 1936:

> The Water Boards have very little data upon which to base their decisions. They have no expert knowledge. They have no means of carrying out many of the responsible duties laid upon them. There is no adequate water law to guide them in their consideration of the important duties which fall to them to perform. They are quasi-judicial bodies with executive functions, with the result that policy becomes confused with interpretation of rights, and the extraordinary result is seen in appeals to the High Court against an executive order rather than for interpretation of an existing right.[40]

Criticism of the boards highlighted the core weaknesses of the 1923 ordinance. It provided little legal context and no specific guidelines for how boards should be run. It also conceived of water management as a local issue, providing no guidelines for planning water on a regional scale. The biggest weakness was that it ignored the conflict between the three categories of water rights—British period, German period, and customary—by allowing existing rights to be grandfathered and native water use to be administered separately. Distinguishing a natural resource by the category of its users proved to be problematic; doing so ignored the geography of places such as Kilimanjaro, where virtually all water used by settlers passed through African lands.

PRODUCING SCIENTIFIC KNOWLEDGE OF WATER

A key criticism of the 1923 ordinance was that policymakers lacked knowledge to make good decisions. To create a new water order that would address increasing scarcity, they needed to better understand the nature of the problem: how much water there actually was, how it was being used (or misused), and the specific nature of water conflicts. In their opinion, scientific knowledge of the water supply was necessary. In the 1930s, the colonial government sponsored a series of studies that analyzed the region's pressing water problems. The most important of these was the *Report on the Investigation of the Proper Control of Water in the Northern Province of Tanganyika Territory*.[41] The report, authored by preeminent colonial scientists Edmund Teale and Clement Gillman in 1934, aimed to "review the problem [of water supplies] in all its geographical and technical inter-relationships with the aim . . . to provide a guide for establishing a suitable controlling organization and a basis on which to adapt the law and regulations to the local conditions." The Teale-Gillman report embodied the trend toward creating new water knowledge based on scientific observations. The first half summarized the geographic and hydrologic features of the mountain, providing statistical data on rainfall distribution, drainage patterns, and users. It then situated these data relative to questions about the control, distribution, and use of water.

The most pressing question for Teale and Gillman was how the waters of the mountain could be managed more efficiently. Based on interviews and analysis of river flows and soil conditions, they concluded that across Kilimanjaro there existed "a very widespread haphazard use of the water."[42] They suggested prioritizing water uses, giving domestic uses the highest priority, followed by industrial uses, irrigation, and hydropower.[43] They also advocated more regulation of the design and construction of water canals. The biggest problem, they claimed, was wastage and erosion caused by inefficient location (in porous rock), poor construction (resulting in excessive erosion or evaporation), or inadequate maintenance.[44] The solution was to relocate and reconstruct wasteful canals using modern measurement tools, taking account of soil conditions, and drawing on advancements such as concrete intakes and the use of reservoirs to store water during the rainy seasons. Finally, they stressed the importance of the rainforest zone as the main source of surface water and advocated a reforestation program.

Teale and Gillman assigned blame to African farmers for several practices they saw as contributing to the problems, including irrigating without the use of terracing and dry-season flooding of eleusine fields. In their critique, however, they held European farmers equally responsible. In his diary, Gillman expresses his view that Europeans, particularly settlers, were the origin of the problems. He writes that local people "knew the art of water engineering long before we super clever whites brought 'civilization' to them and disturbed their equilibrium with Nature."[45] He claims that European settlement disrupted the natural balance the mountain people had with their surroundings, which in turn caused the mifongo system's inefficiency.

As an immediate step, Teale and Gillman called for the government to prevent practices detrimental to the "continued guaranteed water supply."[46] They did not specify any permanent reforms, but rather proposed two programs of research to generate data. The first of these was a topo-hydrographic survey to measure the total amount of water available on the mountain. Over the next several years, Gillman conducted the survey through two separate projects: an aerial photographic survey of watercourses and a ground survey of the hydrologic conditions of the mountain itself. By its conclusion in 1941, the survey had provided the first scientific data on mountain hydrology and the first quantitative measures of water. The second program proposed by Teale and Gillman was a series of agricultural experiments aimed at calculating the irrigation needs of the various users of the mountain's waters. Gillman felt that the question of whether or not irrigation was necessary could not be answered without considering local circumstances: soil conditions, tree cover, crop choice, temperature, precipitation, and surface water resources. His term for this was "duty of water," the specific quantity needed to irrigate crops in given conditions: "Foremost in urgency among these is a very comprehensive series of observations and controlled experiments throughout the area, in order to decide, from place to place, whether or not irrigation is beneficial at all and if so when, how and in what amount it should be applied. In other words the so-called 'duty of water' should be determined in relation to local conditions."[47] The Ministry of Agriculture responded to this proposal by developing a series of irrigation experiments across the mountain. Many of these took place at Lyamungu, a coffee research station and demonstration center opened in 1934 that consisted of over 100 hectares of farmland and laboratories.

In addition to this work, the government also commissioned a follow-up study, the *Report on the Control of the Natural Waters of Tanganyika*. Completed in 1936 by Francis Kanthack, the report intended to complement the Teale-Gillman report and focused on legal challenges related to the mountain's waters. Kanthack, a water engineer with experience in India and South Africa, noted that several factors complicated the government's attempts to control water, most notably that all surface water passed through lands held by Africans. This created a challenge for both the policy of indirect rule and the common law principle of riparian rights. Indirect rule held that Native Authorities should control all resources utilized by Africans, which meant in theory that the government could not intervene with water management in the chiefdoms. Common law held that any person whose lands were "riparian to a public stream could have the right of reasonable use, subject to the reasonable requirements of other riparian owners being satisfied."[48] The problem was that most users of canals did not possess riparian rights to the streams or rivers from which they drew and thus had no common law rights. Kanthack therefore concluded that common law was an unsuitable basis on which to design legal code for the region.

He proposed an alternative: to create a single water law for all users and make all rights dependent on a permit from the government rather than inherent to land occupancy.[49] Permits would specify a type of abstraction, a volume of water to be allocated for use, and the way that water could be used. Exemptions could be granted to users who could claim rights that existed before 1923, including ones granted under customary law or under the German administration. The most interesting aspect of the proposal was that it granted the administration control over all management, including that of Africans' water. By suggesting that government take control of all water, the report proposed undermining the power held by the mountain's water specialists. Kanthack held no qualms about this. He chastised "Chagga" water practices as "primitive, wasteful, and inefficient."[50] While he acknowledged that they had prescriptive rights to water through native law and custom, this did not preclude the government from implementing a permit system: "In the case of natives, therefore, it appears to me that after a comprehensive survey of native irrigation areas the Government itself will have to take over the task of regularizing the canal systems and of framing *pro forma* applications for permits. The whole position would, of course, have to be explained to the canal owners and native chief concerned and their collaboration secured as far as possible." Only by taking direct control of the canals could the government create a sensible water order. He did make a concession by stating that canals, once registered, should remain under local control beyond the point of abstraction. Nonetheless, his proposal constituted a radical rethinking of the relationship between customary law and water management.

After nearly two decades of research and criticism, the government created a new water law for the colony. The Water Ordinance of 1948 was a more comprehensive piece of legislation than its predecessor and addressed many of its problems. It called for creating water boards to control water regionally, but it carefully prescribed their functions and duties, limited their powers, delineated specific procedures, provided grounds for the disqualification of board members, and limited the fees that they could charge. The ordinance called for a set of water courts to be established independently of the boards; these would handle all judicial functions and mediate disputes. It also provided a basic legal context for water by defining concepts such as rights and easements and by placing the ultimate control of water in the hands of the colonial governor.

The new law did not implement any major changes to customary water rights, ignoring the recommendations of the Teale-Gillman and Kanthack reports: "Subject to the vesting of ownership of water in the Governor under the provisions of the next succeeding section, nothing in this Ordinance shall apply to any diversion, obstruction, abstraction, or use of water in the lawful exercise of any rights which is conferred—by native law and custom."[51] The 1948 ordinance actually went further than its 1923 predecessor in this respect. It did not leave the question of native water use to the water boards; it specifically prohibited them from becoming involved at all. It thus left control of all mountainside water use and all mifongo in existence before 1923—and therefore considered customary—in the hands of the Native Authority. Management of new canals beyond the point of abstraction also remained under local control. The government claimed legal authority over all new abstractions and could require farmers to apply for permits and submit designs, surveys, usage estimates, and fees for all new canals, but it remained without any authority to intervene with existing ones.

TRIUMPH OF THE "SPECIALISTS"

Why did the new law do little about an aspect of colonial water management so heartily criticized by the two studies? The answer is not that the government failed to act. Rather, it is that the government acted in a different way from what the scientists proposed. A crucial tenet of indirect rule was that native leaders were the base form of governance, subservient to the district officers under which they served. The administration faced the question of how to disseminate scientific water management to the general population. Rather than take direct control of local systems, it chose to use its existing agents, the wamangi, as well as other forms of soft power to bring change. This strategy ended up failing. It overestimated the influence of the wamangi in local life and underestimated the autonomy of the meni mifongo and the canal societies. What resulted was resistance to most new policies, and the triumph of the water specialists' interests over the wamangi's.

The Water Ordinance of 1948 divided the waters of Kilimanjaro into three spheres of control: urban (Moshi Town), rural (settler estates and missions), and African (vihamba and shamba). Water in the latter sphere was placed under the control of the Chagga Native Authority and included customary canals—those constructed before 1923—and any water sources that originated *and* ended within Chagga lands. All matters of control, maintenance, and usage of the canals remained under the jurisdiction of so-called customary institutions. But if any person decided to construct an entirely new canal, they had to request that their mangi file for a permit from the Moshi District Water Board on their behalf, submit designs and specifications for the new canal, and upon approval operate, manage, and maintain the canal under the permit's conditions.

The strategy of the colonial administration was to maintain local management while also controlling all future abstractions. In the eyes of the administration, this provided the most realistic prospect for ameliorating the water situation while avoiding the hassle of becoming directly involved in the water affairs of the chiefdoms. Direct involvement was also considered unnecessary. Since the beginning of the century, the wamangi had become cooperative agents of the state. They had taken control of many aspects of society formerly held by clan heads, particularly land management. Furthermore, the mountain population as a whole had flourished. Profits from the coffee industry had made them one of the most economically successful communities in Tanganyika. These profits had been invested back into the industry, as well as the development of schools, training facilities, churches, and seminaries.[52] The prevailing wisdom was that one should not change such a successful model. As stated in a memorandum in 1939, "The policy will be to interfere, as little as possible, with indigenous methods."[53]

To bring about needed changes, the government called on the wamangi to implement reforms through the Chagga Native Authority, cloaking them in the guise of customary law and practice. A good example is the "50 Paces Tangazo" ordinance implemented in 1931:[54]

> All persons are absolutely forbidden to fell trees or to plant any crop other than bananas within 50 paces of any stream or spring.
> If any clearing exists within 50 paces of any stream or spring those persons responsible for such clearing must plant European trees or bananas, nothing else in such clearing.
> Any person failing to carry out this order shall be liable to a fine of [50 shillings] or one month's imprisonment.
> Objectives: a. Water conservation for the future.
> b. A first step in education against soil erosion.
> c. Slight control of excessive cultivation of eleusine.

This order aimed to halt the clearing of marginal lands near rivers or on steep ridges, a practice deemed harmful for contributing to soil erosion and eliminating tree cover that controlled the evaporation of surface water. The wamangi implemented other orders of this type before the 1950s, addressing issues such as water pollution, soil erosion, and protection of the Kilimanjaro Forest Reserve.[55]

The government did remain directly involved in adjudicating conflicts between chiefdoms. Disputes over access to rivers, streams, and mifongo lying on the borders of neighboring chiefdoms were on the rise, because of the booming population and because people were forced to settle on lands previously considered marginal. In no place was this more pronounced than on the border of Marangu and Mamba, where a long-standing feud over rights to a water canal led to an outbreak of violence in 1916. Colonial officials eased tensions temporarily with a water-sharing agreement, but increasing settlement along the border revived tensions a decade later. By 1931, the situation had become critical, forcing the Chagga Council and the district officer to become involved.[56] The council unanimously found in favor of Mamba and required Marangu to share the canal on a fifty-fifty basis. After Marangu continued to monopolize the canal, the mangi of Mamba appealed to the district and provincial officers. Both found in agreement with Mamba and the Chagga Council, and they pressured Marangu to honor the water-sharing agreement.

The government also intervened by using agricultural officers to encourage "modern" cultivation practices. As the next chapter will discuss, government agricultural officers were sent into the chiefdoms starting in the 1920s to assist with cultivating cash crops such as coffee and maize. Over time, their duties expanded to include advising farmers about the dangers of soil erosion and the effects of overirrigating crops, the benefits of terracing, and above all, the benefits of replacing eleusine with alternative crops such as maize. The agricultural officers also initiated a project to register the canals on Kilimanjaro.[57] Nonetheless, they remained reluctant to intervene in any way that would undermine the wamangi or the existing system of water distribution past the point of extraction.

Government officials in Moshi Town felt that the mountain population would quickly accept the new water-control initiatives, since they left in place much of the existing apparatus (e.g., the authority of wamangi and meni mifongo, the idea of customary control of existing mifongo). Moreover, officials felt that the benefits were self-evident and would quickly prove themselves to a populace that was educated and investing in cash-crop cultivation. The wamangi and the Chagga Council, as might be expected, were receptive to the government's efforts, as noted in the anecdote that opens this book. In addition to giving its verbal support, the council implemented restrictions on cultivation near watercourses and the forest line and prohibitions on polluting rivers and streams. Several wamangi even restricted water use within their own chiefdoms. The influential Petro Marealle, for example, prohibited irrigation in the highest areas of Marangu and the growing of eleusine during the dry season.[58]

The wamangi also enforced the requirement that new canals and abstractions be built with the permission of the Moshi Water Board. This directly benefitted them, since the board required that all native permit applications be sponsored by a mangi. By the 1930s, many wamangi used this power to circumvent the specialists and organize construction of canals on their own. These mifongo, designed to carry water to new settlements in the foothills, were longer and deeper than existing ones. One example of such a project was the rightly named Mangi's canal, constructed by Mangi Kirita of Kilema to bring water to newly settled areas of the foothills.[59] This immense canal was nearly 16 kilometers long and served dozens of users in an area where, because of the aridity, maize had become the crop of choice. Wamangi had to seek permission from the water board using the new, more scientific language of water. They described their projects in terms of total users, the type of use (irrigation, domestic, construction, or otherwise), the specific measured location of the intake, the dimensions of the canal in feet or miles, and the specific quantity to be abstracted in cusecs.[60] The need to describe water using this new, commodified language of water favored the wamangi as well as the rising educated class, but at the expense of older water elites such as the meni mifongo, who lacked access to such knowledge.

The wamangi had strong incentive to support the administration's water initiatives. Their subjects, however, largely resisted. Throughout the 1930s and 1940s, government officials expressed frustration at the lack of compliance with water policies, the spread of "illegal" canals, and rising suspicion within communities. The most fervent resistance resulted from the government's most direct intervention: its restriction on new canals without a permit. Meni mifongo and the canal communities easily found ways to circumvent the new rule. The most common was to expand existing mifongo by building larger intakes and increasing their width and depth. Since the ordinance only targeted new abstractions and not modifications, this practice was technically not illegal. Given the government's lack of a comprehensive list of mifongo, it was also difficult to prove. Another technique was for a meni mfongo to construct a new canal but claim that it was an ancient canal being brought back into use. Colonial officials wised up to the problem but had difficulty addressing it. In 1947, hydrographic surveyor M. T. Avery noted the continuing impact of illegal canals on flow rates in the Pangani: "In fact I am confident that on several occasions during the past seasons the flow has been less than the guaranteed minimum, this is due both to a succession of bad rainfall years and to increased irrigation, mostly, I admit, by illegal native canals."[61] The water board estimated the number of illegal water extractions to be as high as 50 percent of the total number of authorized ones.[62] Nonetheless, the spread of illegal canals continued well into the 1960s.

The colonial administration also faced a lack of cooperation with its plans to register the customary canals. Originally, the government hoped to have them recorded by the end of the 1920s. This deadline was extended into the 1930s, then eventually pushed back to the end of the war. By 1960, the task had yet to be accomplished, as noted in the annual report of the colonial water office: "There remains the problem of the recording and control of very large numbers of canals constructed under [Native] Law and Custom, the problem of which is becoming increasingly important as the knowledge of the benefit of irrigation spreads among the African farmers which, in many areas, means that too many people want to use the too little water available at the same time."[63] One problem with obtaining an accurate list of mifongo stemmed from belief among colonial officials that they could record comprehensive data at a single point in time. In other words, they believed that canals in use at a moment in time were the only canals ever in operation. This neglected the dynamism of the mifongo system. Mifongo were frequently opened and closed at different points in time depending on environmental conditions. Some could even be closed for years, only to be opened in extended dry periods.

The widespread resistance to these initiatives reflects how mountain farmers responded to what they saw as a threat to their water-management practices. The government assumed it could bring about change by the using wamangi as intermediaries. While people accepted some minor changes, such as the ban on cultivation near watercourses, they rejected the most significant ones, such as the registration of canals and the permit process for developing new ones. This makes sense given the social and cultural importance of the mifongo and the roles of meni mifongo and canal societies. Water management fostered community participation and a sense of ownership. People considered the involvement of the wamangi to be unnecessary and inappropriate. They responded by ignoring the wamangi and by taking advantage of loopholes in the system that allowed them to develop new and existing canals with little chance of being caught. The main exception to this was the growing number of people settling in the foothills of the chiefdoms. These individuals tended to be less committed to the older norms of water management and more open to the role of the wamangi.

Why did the wamangi not do more to crack down on illegal canals? They likely found themselves in a precarious situation, pressured by the government to control illegal canals yet fearful that direct intervention would erode their authority. Their fears were well founded. The rise of coffee cultivation had created a new generation of wealthy men in the chiefdoms, many of whom resented the power held by traditional authority figures such as the wamangi. The Kilimanjaro Native Planters Association (KNPA) is a good example of this. The leaders of the organization tended to be educated Christians who were not members of powerful clans or chiefly lineages. By 1928, the government had come to think of the KNPA as a political threat to chieftaincy and accused its leadership of corruption and mismanagement.[64] In response to this threat, coffee farmers successfully lobbied the government to leave the KNPA intact and allow it to run outside the auspices of the Chagga Native Authority. This effectively dealt the wamangi a blow to their power and prestige. Given their experience with the KNPA, it seems likely that the wamangi's lack of response to widespread water-rule violations stemmed from fear of losing popular support.

Resistance also indicated a growing suspicion of colonial motives more generally. The growth of population, the alienation of land, and increasing tensions with the settlers contributed to fear that the government wanted to take more resources from mountain communities. The presence of agricultural officers in the chiefdoms, conducting interviews and surveying watercourses, only intensified these suspicions. Government officials tried to address the problem by appealing directly to the people. In July 1937, the governor made a speech in which he tried to clarify several recent happenings:

> I have heard that it is said that the Government have sent men with measuring instruments over this Mountain in order that Government may take away your land and give it to the Europeans. Now that is an absolute lie. These men have come on to the Mountain to measure the waters of the Mountain . . . the waters of the Ruvu and other rivers which run to the sea and to measure how much water is coming down from this country.
>
> Later on you will see aeroplanes flying over the Mountain . . . and when they have finished their work the Council of Chiefs and their elders and those who control the canals will be able to see what is happening to their water today—whether they are preventing soil erosion, or giving water to the man who does not want so much water, and less to the man who needs more. The Government will give them the information and they will have to decide how to use it.[65]

Despite these overtures, people remained suspicious that changes in water management were the first step toward a far-reaching grab for their resources. Considering what had happened with the KNPA, as well as plans underway to redistribute land to settlers on Mount Meru, these fears were legitimate.

꙳

The 1920s marked the beginning of a shift in attitude toward water management on Kilimanjaro. Periodic drought, rising population, soaring demand, environmental concerns, and heightened tensions over water between European and African users led to the decline of the popular notion that water was abundant. The optimism of abundance quickly faded into fear of scarcity. Mountain communities, long extolled as exemplars of water management, came to be considered the biggest threat to the future vitality of the mountain. Colonial officers and scientists believed that unless they gained control of water management and also stopped the prodigal, wasteful, harmful practices of mountain farmers, the natural wealth of the region would be lost. Starting in 1923, the government developed a legal framework for water control and promoted scientific research into the nature of both water supply and demand. In doing so, it created a dual legal system for water with separate administrative structures for Europeans and Africans. For the latter, it emphasized the role of wamangi in promoting change in water management, neglecting the important role played by other community leaders.

Water reforms on Kilimanjaro in this period reflected competing agendas within the colonial administration. While the direct intervention advocated by colonial scientists held the potential to solve a host of problems, it threatened to undermine indirect rule and alienate a population increasingly viewed as exemplary—prosperous, educated, and Christian. The colonial government, believing in the power of chiefs as intermediaries, avoided any attempts to take direct control of water away from the chiefdoms. Water law and scientific knowledge also exposed growing political and social divisions on the mountain. For most mountain farmers, the new knowledge of water promoted by colonial actors held little appeal. After all, periodic scarcity had long been a fact of life, and local specialists had developed techniques to deal with such contingencies. Their unwillingness to obey restrictions on water signified a lack of belief in the new knowledge. It also indicated the weakness of chiefly authority and desire among the people for local specialists to retain control over water. The reforms advocated by the government and the wamangi held the potential to shift power away from the populace and into the hands of colonial agents. Resistance to registering mifongo, filing permits for new abstractions, and curtailing irrigation served to defend local interests.

5 ⤚ Water Brings Harm

Transformations in Household Water
Management, 1930–50

IN 1947, Mangi Petro Marealle of Marangu published a book entitled *Maisha ya Mchagga hapa duniani na ahera* (The life of a Chagga here on earth and after death).[1] The Kiswahili-language monograph, the only one ever written by a Kilimanjaro chief, presents a detailed history of traditional Chagga cultural practices. It contains chapters detailing beliefs related to birth, marriage, and death, focusing specifically on religious beliefs and practices and various folk tales. The book follows Dundas's *Kilimanjaro and Its People* by twenty-four years, and it is notable in several ways. It depicts Kilimanjaro as one homogeneous Chagga society, an idea that was promoted for decades by colonial officials but that resonated little with the people. His use of the term indicates its growing utility to the wamangi. The book also represents Marealle's belief that "old traditions, customs, and beliefs [were] rapidly passing away" and, for the sake of posterity, needed to be documented.[2] His work appeared at a time of unprecedented social, cultural, political, and economic change. The onset of colonialism had led to new challenges and opportunities, not only political and economic but also social and cultural, from membership in Christian churches to school education and health care. In turn, many long-held cultural practices were declining, and notions of status, wealth, and the balance of power were beginning to change. Marealle's book is a reflection on the profound transformations that accompanied colonial rule and an expression of lament that much was being lost in the process.

This chapter examines, in the context of water management, the social and cultural changes of which Marealle speaks. Compared with the last chapter, which focused on struggles over political and technological issues, this one focuses on household management. The work of colonial agents such as missionaries, agricultural officers, and health officers often challenged intimate aspects of the lived experience, from the birthing and raising of children to beliefs about spirituality, gender, identity, and belonging. Water provides a revealing glimpse into the nature of these changes. This chapter examines three major changes that took place in household management: the handling of domestic water, the spiritual nature of water, and the cultivation of eleusine. Though seemingly disparate, they share several commonalities. They relate to intimate aspects of water management, taking place within the vihamba and often away from public view. Because of this, I rely on oral narratives to illuminate these changes. They also involve practices that colonial actors considered harmful to the people and the mountain itself. The discourse of harm became a chosen instrument to communicate the deficiencies of existing practices and the virtues of new ones.

Numerous scholars have examined the nature of social and cultural change during the colonial period, asking how and why such changes took place. Early work tended to discuss such change in terms of a dichotomy between traditional and modern. As Africans gained access to modern knowledge, they adopted new beliefs and practices and rejected existing ones. Recent scholarly work has challenged this linear narrative by showing the degree of agency Africans held in negotiating new knowledge. Some examples include John and Jean Comaroff's work on religious conversion, Timothy Burke's work on cleanliness, and the work of Sara Berry and others on agricultural change.[3] Other scholars, such as Derek Peterson, have focused on the role of African intermediaries in relaying new knowledge.[4] These individuals, employed by the colonial state, often translated colonial knowledge to local communities and, in turn, shaped its implementation.

By focusing on health, spirituality, and cultivation, this chapter allows us to see how the peoples of Kilimanjaro negotiated new water knowledge that challenged not just individual practices, but their very impression of the waterscape. Rather than accept outside knowledge uncritically, communities selectively incorporated new ideas, using them to produce new knowledge that made sense given their changing realities. Thus, in practice we see a great deal of continuity amid change. Furthermore, changes did not occur everywhere, or for everyone, at the same time. To this day, many people pray to their ancestors during droughts and refuse to boil their drinking water. This illustrates the dynamic process whereby people shaped their understandings of water on their own accord, in response to the opportunities and challenges around them. The chapter also reveals how this reshaping challenged existing notions about those who possessed relevant knowledge. This empowered some individuals—teachers, clergy, and women in the home—while eroding the authority of others, mainly spiritual figures such as rainmakers, wachili, and wamasya. By midcentury, many of these long-standing social roles ceased to exist, at least in public. Their decline did not mean an end to the spiritual significance of water, but it did weaken the links between spirituality and certain activities, such as maintaining the mifongo. This had long-term implications for community water management.

WATER BRINGS HARM

One set of changes that took place in water management affected how people used and cared for domestic water. As noted in the last chapter, people began using more water for household tasks such as cooking, drinking, bathing, and brewing. In 1948, the Moshi District Water Board estimated an average use of 38 liters per capita of domestic water per day.[5] This figure soared to 76 liters by 1960. This exceeded the consumption of most urban areas of the colony, including Dar es Salaam at just under 45 liters per day.[6] In addition to using more water, people also were collecting and using domestic water differently. Women came to rely on springs and rivers rather than canals for water used in the home. Many people started to boil and filter water used for drinking, cooking, and washing infants.[7] Although these changes began gradually, they were commonplace by the 1970s.

These changes in domestic water management—in terms of quantity, sourcing, and care—reflect Timothy Burke's observation that "Western ideals of cleanliness, appearance, and bodily behavior became increasingly powerful within African communities, even among non-elites, during the 1930s."[8] On Kilimanjaro, changes in the handling of domestic water resulted largely from the spread of knowledge about bacteria and disease. People today recall learning about these harms and their prevention—proper procurement and boiling—from teachers, clergy, and midwives. Leoni Motesha, a retired teacher from Rombo, remembered first learning of bacteria while in primary school.[9] "Pupils were taught in school about what is needed for one to be healthy," he recalled. "They were taught how to keep water from being dirty. Secondly, they were taught proper usage of water and to boil it in order to get rid of unwanted bodies. Teachers explained the importance by telling us the danger of water that is not boiled. We were told about diseases: dysentery, bilharzia, and others. Through this people have become aware of the importance of boiling water." James Mbuya, a student at St. James Seminary in Kilema at that time, recalled that teachers "showed us how to boil water in schools. They told us that unboiled water contained bacteria that were harmful to human beings."[10] Augustina August remembered learning about bacteria in school and from clergy who announced disease outbreaks during church services.[11] Liberati Mbando, a former teacher at Kilema Primary School, provided a compelling answer to why these changes had taken place.[12] He cited the proverb *mringa uwore mbaka voo*, "water brings no harm," and said that people had come to realize that it was not true and that proper steps needed to be taken to ensure the safety of water. He was not alone in his thinking; in other interviews, people described the changes as acknowledgement that water could bring harm.

Mbando's comments provide a window into a deeper understanding of changes in water management and the relation of these changes to broader social transformations. These new methods of sourcing and handling domestic water resulted not merely from accepting new knowledge about bacteria, but rather from reshaping the popular conception of harm and the social institutions necessary for addressing it. The rejection of "water brings no harm" indicates a rich process of integrating new knowledge into existing ways of thinking. This becomes clear when one deconstructs the layers of meaning behind "water brings no harm." As with many African adages, its meaning transcends its literal interpretation. People on Kilimanjaro considered water to be their divine right and intrinsically lacking in capacity to bring harm. Yet they faced all sorts of risks related to the water supply. This contradiction can be explained by the fact that people considered water-related harm to be not inherent to the resource, but rather the result of tampering. In many cases, this could be attributed to deliberate human action, such as dirtying a canal, stealing water, or sabotage. Natural or incidental harms, such as floods, droughts, and animal attacks near watercourses, were attributed to malevolent waruma. Few believed that bad things happened to water strictly by chance.

"Water brings no harm" did not mean that harm could not result from water, but rather that water held inherent purity that could be distorted by the actions of the spiteful or careless. It implied a specific notion of harm, as well as actors and actions for alleviating it. Numerous community specialists—meni mifongo, wamasya, wachili, and others—possessed knowledge to alleviate harms afflicting the water supply. Their actions were spiritual and social as well as technical. Martin Mosha, a meni mfongo, recalled an invocation that he used to help restore water to broken canals. "People believe that the spirits have the power of bringing water, and when they are angered they can prevent water from coming out. There are certain words that [the meni mifongo] uttered at the intake in order to make water come out. These are 'Owners of this canal, I come to you because it is you who gave me this canal. I therefore beg you to give me water from this canal.'"[13] According to Mosha, the process of healing a broken mfongo involved not merely fixing the physical system, but also appeasing the waruma who had kept the waters from flowing. Only meni mfongo, or in some cases other community leaders, possessed the knowledge to appease them and restore health to the mfongo.

Additionally, under the control of certain specialists, water had the power to cleanse people and protect them from harm. As noted in chapter 1, people believed the waters of the mountain to be a gift bestowed by Ruwa. Mountain waters provided life to people, animals, and the vihamba while protecting them from the desolation of the plains. In agriculture, people considered water to be analogous to blood running through the body, providing vital life to crops.[14] These life-giving powers were apparent in a variety of cultural and religious practices. In initiation rites, water served as a cleansing agent, washing away the impurities of childhood and transforming youths into adults. Control over these properties rested in the hands of specialists such as clan elders and circumcision operators.

Thus, "water brings no harm" was a rich idiom that invoked a set of socially accepted notions of water, harm, human action, and control of relevant knowledge. Many of these ideas were challenged, starting in the 1930s, with the rising influence of teachers, midwives, clergy, and colonial health officers, most of whom were school-educated Africans.

Of these, teachers had the most intimate contact with everyday people. In the interwar years, educational institutions became numerous and prominent on Kilimanjaro.[15] By 1934, there were 214 primary schools just in the Catholic areas, with daily attendance of 14,740.[16] Two decades later, there were over 500, giving the mountain the highest ratio of schools to population and the highest percentage of children in school in Tanganyika.

Primary schools taught several subjects that challenged the prevailing wisdom regarding water and harm. In the health curriculum, teachers taught students that they should assume water was contaminated with bacteria and unsafe for drinking.[17] Mbando recalled one lesson he used to teach his students. "We used to teach them that water is never safe unless it is boiled. So they had to boil it before drinking it. Formerly people believed that if water was clear then it was safe, for they did not know about bacteria. They used to drink water right from the canal so long as it was clear. They believed that water could do no harm."[18] He remembered that teachers taught children specifically about the dangers of bacteria and the ways in which bacteria could contaminate water supplies (through human and animal wastes).[19] They prohibited students from frolicking or urinating in canals and rivers, explaining to them that these actions could bring disease outbreaks. To be safe, they needed to gather water from springs, boil it for five minutes, filter it using a clean cloth, and store it in a covered container. Though taught to children, the colonial administration intended for these lessons to migrate into the vihamba. Anza Lema, in his study of the Leipzig mission, asserts that teachers "hoped that the new skills and knowledge gained at school in . . . housebuilding, hygiene, and medical care would be passed on to other people through their example and by their instruction."[20] They hoped that schools would facilitate wider transformations in thinking and practice, not only by educating future generations but also by having children educate their parents.

Midwives also introduced knowledge about water and harm. The institution of midwifery has a long history on Kilimanjaro, as it does in other areas of Africa.[21] In the 1930s and 1940s, however, the government reinvented midwifery as a profession for a select group of educated women, grounded in the newest "modern" techniques of child-rearing and notions of health, hygiene, and sanitation. This mirrored a broader trend in Europe and across the West. On Kilimanjaro, the Moshi District health officer, the Chagga Native Authority, and the missions began training women in midwifery at the hospitals in Machame and Kilema in 1927. Their lessons included basic anatomy and health science, as well as hands-on instruction in child delivery, prenatal and postnatal childcare, general child health, home visiting, and village hygiene.[22] Once trained, these women went from homestead to homestead delivering babies and teaching women how to care for their families.

The teachings of midwives proposed new ways of thinking about water.[23] They taught women that bacteria, an invisible agent, could harm their whole families, especially newborn babies. These bacteria lived not only in water, but also on everyday objects in the home. Midwives instructed women to avoid these harms by gathering water from springs and purifying it through boiling and filtering. They encouraged women to sterilize utensils, bowls, and other objects by immersing them in boiling water. These ideas, like those taught by schoolteachers, proposed a very different notion of harm. Child mortality could now be attributed to a disease vector caused by incidental action rather than the deliberate action of the waruma. Midwives instructed women to wash their infant children daily using clean, boiled water gathered from springs rather than once every few days using mfongo water. They encouraged special attention to washing the teeth, ears, hair, and bowels, which were the sites of common ailments.[24] These washing practices were an attempt to both modify practices and reshape the underlying idea of disease causation.

While teachers and midwives were among those with the most regular contact with everyday people on the mountain, other agents shared new ideas about water, harm, and disease as well. The Moshi District health officer sent assistants into the chiefdoms to encourage people to construct and utilize pit latrines.[25] Clergy announced outbreaks of disease at church services and encouraged people to take precautions to avoid becoming ill.[26] Though focusing on different sets of activities, these groups emphasized bacteria as a source of harm and water as an agent capable both of carrying and removing bacteria; they also stressed the need to reform local practices to prevent disease outbreaks.

Since the 1950s, these new practices became increasingly common. Spring water, long preferred for cooking and brewing, became the water of choice for domestic tasks because of its perceived cleanliness.

Boiling and filtering also became popular, especially for those still dependent on canal water. Meanwhile, the overall consumption of domestic water increased dramatically, a reflection of more-frequent bathing and clothes washing as well as the greater availability of *debe*, 18-liter tin cans that made carrying water much easier.[27] Elders attribute these changes to the knowledge of bacteria they gained from teachers, midwives, and others.[28] From interviews, it seems that fear of bacteria was the primary impetus for many of these changes. The choice of people to articulate these changes through rejecting "water brings no harm" is significant. It indicates that accepting the concept of bacteria and its role in causing illnesses generated change in the practice not only of water but also of expressing the nature of harm. Bacteria were a source of harm that functioned differently from existing ones. Waruma acted on their own accord, as did the living, and their harmful actions could not for the most part be anticipated or prevented. Only specialists who possessed relevant knowledge could address the harm they caused. Bacterial contamination, however, resulted to some degree from incidental activity. Human action, such as urinating near watercourses or watering livestock in rivers, accounted for most cases of bacteria in the water supply. By accepting bacteria as an agent, people were changing how they perceived both harm to the water supply and the role of specialists. This in turn made everyday people greater participants in securing the safety of the water supply.

Why did people accept the idea of bacteria? One factor is that disease outbreaks occurred with increasing frequency in the mid-twentieth century. Journals for the Catholic missions at Kilema and Rombo Mkuu indicate that outbreaks of typhoid, cholera, and diarrhea became more prevalent as time passed.[29] The concept of bacterial contamination allowed people to make sense of these new phenomena as a by-product of increasing population density. Another factor is that schools and missions pressured people to modify their daily practices. This was especially true for bathing and washing clothes, as schools considered these essential for enrollment. As communities became more tied to the schools and missions, these practices carried increasing amounts of social currency. Boiling water and bathing daily became markers of education and social standing. People adopted them not necessarily because of their perceived efficacy, but rather to indicate their place in the changing social order. Lastly, belief in bacteria, as opposed to the spirits, as a cause of harm reduced reliance on the specialists. For centuries, specialists such as healers and diviners had managed the destructive and curative health-related powers of water. The need to protect families from bacteria effectively empowered women to manage properties of water that had previously been managed by others.

Knowledge of bacterial causation of harm did not displace spirit causation entirely. Even today, it is common—though not necessarily acceptable—to make offerings at watercourses during droughts.[30] But this new knowledge did diminish the role of spiritual figures in managing domestic water quality. In light of these changes, it becomes apparent just how ambiguous the phrases "water brings no harm" and "water brings harm" were. Rather than an about-face, they demonstrate a process of negotiating ideas and fitting them into existing frameworks for dealing with problems on a community-wide scale.

WATER COMES FROM GOD

Another change in water management centered more wholly on spirituality. Since the 1930s, new language about the relationship between water and the divine emerged on Kilimanjaro. Many began to assert that the Christian God, rather than Ruwa, was the creator of the waterscape and the source of all water in streams, rivers, and canals. People also started taking advantage of new possibilities in the causation of harm to the water supply, arguing for factors other than and in addition to the spirits. Cultural practices in which water played a vital role were also changing. Initiation, long a marker of membership in the community, fell into decline, and in its place, people were choosing to be baptized. Ceremonies and ritual sacrifices at watercourses likewise became less common. These changes took place at a time when the missions emerged at the mainstream of society. After spending three decades struggling to sustain membership, both the Roman Catholic Holy Ghost Fathers and the Leipzig Lutherans experienced tremendous growth in the interwar period. In 1933, the Catholics claimed to have 29,085 baptized members.[31] This figure rose to 92,505 in 1953 and to 175,340 by 1961. The Lutheran missions claimed similar growth in membership, though slightly fewer total members because of their location in less populated areas. By the late 1960s, an estimated 80–90 percent of the whole mountain's population were Christians.[32]

Given the growth of the Christian missions and their presence in local affairs, one might assume that changes in thinking about water and the divine resulted from the adoption of Christianized ideas about the nature of God and his role in the affairs of the natural world. Yet as scholars such as Paul Landau have argued, changes in religious beliefs and related practices often had multiple levels of significance and were tied to many aspects of local culture and society.[33] While it is true that people joined churches in large numbers during this period, changes in spiritual water management were not a foregone conclusion of conversion, nor did they necessarily indicate a radical transformation in thinking about the resource.

The most significant change was that people began to speak of the Christian God, not Ruwa, as the provider of the waterscape. As stated in chapter 1, the peoples of Kilimanjaro had long believed Ruwa to be the progenitor of water in all its forms: rainfall, streams, rivers, and springs. This water brought life and vitality to the vihamba, and it held the power to cleanse and purify the people. In thanks for Ruwa's gift of life, his overall favor, and his intervention in the affairs of the spirits, people regularly made offerings of animals or mbege while facing toward Kibo. To the Catholic and Lutheran missionaries, this concept of God was problematic. While they considered it good that people professed belief in a kind of supreme deity, most missionaries derided these religious expressions as superstitious and animistic.[34] They encouraged people to instead accept the Christian concept of God, abandon their ways of worshipping Ruwa, and worship God instead through prayer, rituals, services, and above all, baptism and membership in the church.

As people sought membership in Christian communities, the language used to express the origins of water began to change. Instead of claiming that Ruwa provided people with rainfall or ample canal water, many began to say that it was the Christian God who did these things.[35] Public sacrifices to Ruwa declined as people began to pray and make offerings in churches.[36] These changes were by no means quick or universal. Many resisted membership in the missions and chose instead to carry out rituals in secrecy.[37] Others chose to carry out both sets of practices, believing that they not mutually exclusive.

These changes in language and practice could be perceived as an indication of people's rejection of previous spiritual thinking. Yet they do not represent as much of a transition as one might think. First, there was great similarity in the characteristics of the Christian God and Ruwa. Both were characterized as creators, universally good, providers of life, and deserving of praise and worship. And both had created the world for the benefit of humankind.[38] The book of Genesis, for example, describes God as creating the heavens and the earth, then separating the waters from the land, and finally bringing life from the waters.[39] Thus in both the Christian and pre-Christian narratives, the supreme deity is the provider of water, and water has the power to cleanse, give life, and purify. Second, in the language of elders today, the Kiswahili term Mungu is often used to refer both to Ruwa and to the Christian God.[40] One must rely on context to know which is being referred to. It is likely that many people substituted one for the other, adopting a new, more socially acceptable set of practices for worshiping while retaining the same essential understanding of the deity.

Water also demonstrates how people shaped the new faith to fit the specificity of Kilimanjaro. In the Christian narrative, God is a deity who presides over everything, not one who resides at the top of a mountain in Africa. Christian converts and clergy continued to describe the mountain as having a special place in creation, illustrated by its life-giving water.[41] Mzee Mwasha, a Lutheran minister from Machame, recalled one way in which the creation story was shaped: "When God created the world, He made water splendid on the surface of the earth. Water got into His canals, and as the years got on these got deeper and deeper in the valleys."[42] His words provide an elegant, biblical explanation for the ample water of the mountain and the presence of deep valleys. The vitality of the mountain was not coincidence, but the specific intent of the creator. Expressions such as these indicate that in turning to Christianity, many people drew heavily on concepts from existing spiritual practices and beliefs, using these to shape new forms of religious expression.

Another change in this period was that people began to seek explanations for natural events such as droughts through Christian institutions rather than through existing practices of spirit worship. Of all the harms attributed to spirits, drought stood as the most significant. During times of drought and famine, people sought the help of specialists who knew the rites and rituals necessary to appease the spirits and bring the waters back. For example, during the drought of 1897–99, renowned mmasya Makimende traveled the southeast chiefdoms and built a reputation for having powerful rainmaking medicine.[43] Catholic and Lutheran clergy considered these practices unacceptable, as they involved sacrifices in the name of Ruwa or another spirit. In response, the clergy offered their own explanations and remedies for the anomaly while deriding the solutions offered by elders and specialists. A good example of how the Catholics addressed this can be seen in their response to the drought of 1907–8.[44] As noted in chapter 3, this period brought a devastating famine and social upheaval, especially in Rombo.[45] Elders and advisors to the mangi of Mkuu Rombo explained the lack of rainfall as the action of a malevolent spirit. Some insisted that the public participate in a series of rituals to placate the spirit they thought responsible, while others distributed medicines they claimed would make people invincible to the effects of water shortages.[46] Father Rudler, the head priest at the Mkuu mission, criticized the elders for offering ineffective and unchristian solutions, and he called on everyone to come to the mission and the schools and pray to God for rain.[47] In Kilema, Father Gommenginger not only welcomed people for masses, but also organized prayer services and novenas at watercourses and invited people to come to church to light votive candles and pray the rosary.[48]

The clergy responded to the drought by rebuking local specialists and offering their own explanations and solutions, a move meant to establish the missions as brokers of knowledge about the natural world as well as the spiritual. They initially found little success. Attendance at Sunday services dropped in this period, and in Rombo, average daily school attendance slipped from 3,000 to 1,800 because of the longer treks needed to procure water as well as migration to the southern chiefdoms.[49] By midcentury, however, people began to seek understandings of such events through the churches. Today, many elders claim not to remember sacrifices ever being made to spirits at watercourses, while others imply that such practices still happen, but at night and out of public sight.[50] It is likely that the increasing presence of the missions both encouraged people to seek church remedies and drove other practices out of the mainstream.

A third change was the decline of initiation practices and the rise of baptism. As mentioned in chapter 1, initiation in mountain communities involved a lengthy set of rituals, instruction, and rites that culminated in the spiritual and physical transformation of children into adults. It was a good example of how religious and spiritual ideas were embedded within larger cultural and social frameworks.[51] Initiation not only transformed the individual but also conferred membership in the age-set and the adult life of the clan. It opened the door to a new world of knowledge, rights, and privileges. Water contributed to this process in several ways, as elders taught initiates new knowledge of water as part of their education. Water also facilitated the actual process of transformation, cleansing initiates of the dirtiness of youth and giving them life as full members of the community.

Clergy saw initiation as a threat because of its links with pre-Christian religious practices and circumcision, its invocations of Ruwa and the waruma, and its reinforcement of the wamasya's power. They encouraged people to give up the practice and adopt baptism in its place. Baptism was in many ways analogous to initiation, transforming the individual while bringing them into a new form of community. Since nearly all baptisms before 1940 involved adolescents or adults, those being baptized also received instruction.[52] Most notably, baptism used water as an agent for cleansing people and giving them new life. Based on church membership records, we can infer that people became increasingly receptive to baptism during the 1930s. The number of baptisms per year increased, while initiation became less and less prominent. With converts finally arriving en masse, the Catholics and Lutherans forbade their converts from participating in initiations. Over the next decade, these rites became increasingly uncommon, and by the 1950s they had more or less disappeared from public view.

The decline of initiation amid the rise of baptism can be attributed to several factors. Many people likely viewed the two ceremonies as analogous and, with increasing pressure from the missions to end initiation, abandoned one for the other. Lema notes that amid the changes in practice advocated by the missions, from ending polygamy to adopting hymns, baptism came the closest to the "spirit of expressing beliefs in ritual action."[53] Drawing on water in familiar terms, as a "symbol for cleansing and new life, [it was a] meaningful ceremony." Baptism also had the benefit of bringing membership in a community (the mission or parish) that was increasingly attractive. This membership opened access to the full fruits of the mission, such as coffee pulperies, hospitals, and schools. Another factor in the decline of initiation seems to have been the disappearance of age-sets.

In the nineteenth century, these social categories served both as a form of identity and community among the clans of each chiefdom and as units of organization that elders and the wamangi called on for corvée labor, warfare, raids of neighboring chiefdoms, and other tasks. Their role in warfare led the German colonial government to ban them. By the First World War, they had virtually disappeared.[54] Without the vital social institution that underpinned it, initiation died out because its significance and value had been drained. It also seems that membership in the churches became appealing as a route to new social and economic opportunities.

These changes involving the spiritual dimensions of water illustrate that the spread of Christianity was contingent on a range of social and economic factors. New beliefs and practices drew heavily on existing spiritual knowledge and frameworks. Water illustrates this vividly, as we see tremendous continuity in thinking about the origins, power, and significance of water despite the changes in how people framed these ideas. These changes empowered a new group of specialists—clergy and catechists—at the expense of older spiritual figures such as rain-makers and the wamasya. Over time, these social positions became less and less important and eventually died out.

ELEUSINE IS GONE

The third set of changes related to eleusine.[55] For centuries, the crop had been a staple of cultivation on Kilimanjaro and the premier male status crop. Nearly all the eleusine grown was used to produce mbege. The grain and the beer produced from it held great spiritual, cultural, and social significance. Mbege facilitated commercial and social transactions as well as relations with the waruma. For mountain peoples, eleusine was not merely a crop, but a vital part of community life. As noted in the last chapter, colonial agents discouraged farmers from growing eleusine under flood irrigation during the dry season. Yet their efforts bore little fruit. As late as 1945, the number of households growing the crop had increased to an estimated thirty thousand, or 80 percent of the whole mountain.[56] In the 1950s, however, the crop entered a swift decline. In 1968, English geographer P. J. M. Bailey remarked that in Marangu, "millet was once grown on every holding ... but is now rarely seen."[57] By the 1980s, it could be found only in marginal areas, and irrigated eleusine had vanished entirely. In 2005, the regional agricultural officer for Kilimanjaro summed up the plight of the crop, saying that "millet is gone."[58]

In the span of less than thirty years, the number of eleusine farmers plummeted from over thirty thousand to nearly zero. The decline in production took place at a time when the crop generated tremendous criticism. Colonial officials, scientists, missionaries, and settlers condemned eleusine as harmful to the mountain and inherently immoral. Criticizing its lack of market value, its potential to poison other crops, and its links to water wastage and soil erosion, they called on farmers to abandon the crop entirely. The relationship between the criticism and the death of the crop, however, was not causal. The decline of eleusine resulted from economic and social factors and was largely unrelated to government propaganda or the water-control efforts discussed in the last chapter.

One of the first government officials to condemn eleusine cultivation was A. J. Wakefield. As noted in the last chapter, he launched the first public criticism against the mifongo, calling them "a very primitive and wasteful system of irrigation."[59] His disdain for eleusine stemmed partly from the fact that most of it was grown with flood irrigation, a practice he considered destructive. Though Wakefield saw water wastage and soil erosion as serious problems, he felt that the greatest evil of eleusine was its effects on other crops. He claimed, though without any clear evidence, that it produced "toxic effects detrimental to all other crops," resulting in less land available for cash crops or foodstuffs.[60] His strongest argument focused on the burgeoning coffee industry. By growing eleusine, farmers were wasting time "at the expense of [their] coffee crop," in turn leaving little time for proper care of the coffee trees. This not only prevented the expansion of coffee cultivation in a time of favorable market conditions but also increased the likelihood of blight and other diseases. He further claimed that coffee trees were neglected because "the native is incapacitated by excessive beer drinking."[61] Wakefield felt that farmers would "have to choose between coffee and beer, or progress and what [they] may regard as the life of a gentleman at leisure." In this way, he framed the question of eleusine in moral terms. For the people of the mountain to progress, they needed to abandon a crop associated with waste, drunkenness, and laziness. His concluding recommendations for the director of agriculture included restricting eleusine cultivation to that needed for food use and limited beer production, preventing additional land from being claimed for it, and enforcing stricter beer-drinking regulations.

The war on eleusine intensified in the 1930s. At the front line were officers and assistants working for the Ministry of Agriculture. As stated in the previous chapter, the government had become extremely concerned with water use in agriculture. Initially it tried to discourage eleusine by asking the wamangi to restrict cultivation in high-risk areas, such as steep slopes and land near rivers. Such restrictions had little effect. In response, the ministry became involved in efforts to generate and disseminate information about the harms of flood irrigation, not just for eleusine but also for coffee and other crops. The newly opened research center at Lyamungu became a focal point for these efforts. Scientists working at Lyamungu ran a wide range of experiments, including ones proposed by Gillman to determine the "duty of water" for crops such as coffee and eleusine. The Ministry of Agriculture used their data to shape its agricultural policy on Kilimanjaro. In general, it discouraged eleusine while advocating the cultivation of crops that had high market values and did not require irrigation, such as coffee and maize, along with local foodstuffs such as bananas and yams. It disseminated these ideas through the work of the Moshi District agricultural officer's staff of African assistants. Throughout the 1930s and 1940s, agricultural assistants went to the chiefdoms, moving from one kihamba to the next, instructing farmers on various aspects of agricultural practice. People today remember these individuals coming around on motorcycles, providing sample seeds and instruction on cultivation techniques.[62] They discouraged the use of flood irrigation, pointing out how it was unnecessary and led to excessive soil wash. They called on farmers to give up eleusine entirely or shift it to the lower areas and grow it during the rains.

Another actor that promoted new agricultural change was the successor to the KNPA, the Kilimanjaro Native Cooperative Union (KNCU). The KNCU was founded in 1934 by a group of farmers in partnership with the government as a means of marketing their coffee overseas and bypassing European and Indian middlemen.[63] From the start, it was decentralized—a union of local affiliate offices with a central office in Moshi Town—and independent of chiefly control. It diversified its operations, marketing crops other than coffee and providing technical support to growers through its local affiliates.[64] By the late 1940s, the organization claimed nearly twenty-nine thousand members across the mountain and had become a powerful force in mountain politics.[65]

Like the agricultural assistants, KNCU staff taught farmers how to improve their cultivation techniques and management of land and water resources, focusing primarily on coffee. School-educated and trained by the KNCU, they went into the vihamba and provided hands-on training in the newest methods of growing trees and processing raw beans into export-quality parchment. They also circulated pamphlets and books written in Kiswahili and English that presented these concepts. Among the most popular was a book entitled *Habari zote za Kahawa ya "KNCU" (All about "KNCU" Coffee)*.[66] This text provided a brief history of coffee cultivation on the mountain and instruction on the proper means of growing and processing arabica coffee.

Habari zote demonstrates the knowledge and practice of water that the KNCU hoped to disseminate. It instructs the reader that irrigation is in most cases unnecessary and that flood irrigation of coffee fields (a practice adapted from the eleusine fields) is unnecessary and harmful:

> Some coffee growers irrigate their coffee in the dry season . . . other people do not irrigate their coffee because they say it is stronger if it does not become accustomed to water.
>
> Experiments have been carried out with irrigation at Lyamungu and it has been found that in months when there is not any appreciable rain one good irrigation increases the yields of coffee much more if the soil is covered with mulch of bananas or thatching grass. Irrigation by itself without mulching spoils and compacts the soil.
>
> Great care must be taken with irrigation not to wash the soil away. Water must be led into the soil slowly, and it is best to make ridges between the coffee trees and to fill these with water [by hand]. The water can then soak into the soil without washing the soil away. Do not let the water from the canal run through your shamba . . . or it will remove the soil and expose the roots of the coffee trees. In that case both the soil in your shamba and your coffee trees will be worse than without any irrigation at all.[67]

The first part of this passage implies that while farmers *could* irrigate, they would have stronger coffee if they did not. The last parts focus on better irrigation techniques, including the use of mulch, ridges, and hand irrigation instead of flooding. While the KNCU did not challenge eleusine directly, its teaching undermined the flood irrigation central to its cultivation.

Around the middle of the century, farmers started to abandon eleusine. Highland farmers in densely populated areas (such as Marangu) were the first to do so, while those in the southern foothills and Rombo were the last. In their study of Kilimanjaro farming systems, A. O'Kting'ati and J. F. Kessy shed some light on the process.[68] They found that by the 1960s, eleusine production had fallen well behind that of coffee, maize, and beans. Despite periodic spikes in production, the total acreage of eleusine declined sharply between 1964 and 1987, while per capita production fell from over 80 kilograms to just over 20.[69] By the late 1980s, the crop had virtually disappeared, a fact attested to by Bailey, François Devenne, and Sam Maghimbi.[70]

The disappearance of eleusine can be explained partly by increases in coffee and maize. Coffee cultivation, which took off in the 1930s, continued to grow steadily. In 1945 there were approximately 29,310 coffee growers on the mountain, by 1955 there were 36,200, and by 1960 the number was 45,130.[71] The total acreage used for coffee rose at an even faster rate, from around 16,980 in 1945, to 27,150 by 1955, and 34,000 by 1960. Favorable rainfall and high market value (£591 per ton in 1955) fueled this growth. Maize experienced growth because of export opportunities created by the war as well as the fact that it had become a part of local diets, second only to bananas. By the end of the war, maize had an estimated forty thousand growers, nearly equal to the total number of households.[72] By 1964, production per capita exceeded 1,000 kilograms.[73] Both crops possessed advantages over eleusine. Coffee's high market value made it particularly appealing. Though it required substantial labor in processing (like eleusine), the labor burden was shared by members of the whole family. Furthermore, as a kihamba crop, the trees could share space and some labor (tilling, weeding, mulching) with bananas, yams, and other vegetables. Coffee trees could last for decades with proper care, meaning less labor spent clearing land and planting. Maize, on the other hand, grew in separate plots like eleusine but required less labor and produced higher yields per hectare. The pattern that developed from the 1940s onward was the expansion of kihamba agriculture into former shamba in the lower slopes and the expansion of maize production into the more arid foothills.

Why did farmers not continue growing eleusine alongside these new crops? Part of the answer lies in the changing demographics of the mountain. The previous chapter showed the tremendous rise in population throughout the twentieth century. As striking was the rise in population density. Between 1967 and 1988, the average for the central chiefdoms (from Kibosho to Marangu) rose from 155.4 people per square kilometer to 219.9, while for the western chiefdoms it jumped from 77.3 to 135.5, and for Rombo, from 51.6 to 88.2.[74] In each chiefdom, the areas farthest uphill became the most densely populated. In some cases, local densities reached between 650 and 1,000 people per square kilometer, on par with that of cities.[75] These shifts resulted in widespread land scarcity. Most men aspired to have their own kihamba, the locus of community and family life, but this form of agriculture was not possible in the lowlands. Alienation of land to settlers and missionaries earlier in the century exacerbated these land-scarcity problems. With uphill expansion blocked by colder weather and the Kilimanjaro Forest Reserve, and downhill expansion blocked by aridity and settler farms, many families subdivided their kihamba to ensure that young men had access to land. This strategy resulted in a substantial decrease in the average size of vihamba, from over 10 acres in 1900 to around 2 by 1960.[76] Some had no choice but to abandon kihamba agriculture and settle permanently in the foothills, seek wage labor on settler farms or in Moshi Town, or migrate to cities such as Arusha, Dar es Salaam, and Nairobi.

The decline of eleusine took place at a time not only when rival crops offered much higher returns but also when the growing population made land increasingly scarce. With smaller amounts of land available, farmers shifted to crops that would reap higher yields per hectare with less labor input. These factors—new crop opportunities, population growth, and land scarcity—have been cited by other scholars who have worked on agrarian change on Kilimanjaro. Devenne, for example, argues that "population growth thus signed the death sentence for [eleusine] irrigation," because the rising number of people required more vihamba, which in turn pulled resources away from eleusine.[77] Indeed, most farmers on the mountain today, as well as district and regional agricultural officers, describe the demise of the crop as a direct result of shrinking farms and increasing coffee cultivation.[78]

Though many people abandoned eleusine for practical reasons, it should be noted that the crop's cultivation had never been pragmatic. Grown in a laborious manner on its own plots, it demanded time, land, and water that could have been spent on other crops. Its persistence owed much to its social and cultural significance. Eleusine embodied notions of masculinity and power. The mbege produced from it was crucial to virtually every local rite and ritual, and it also acted as a currency that facilitated numerous transactions between people. While new crops and land scarcity might have made the crop less appealing, they did not necessarily make it expendable. Given eleusine's centrality to culture and society, the decline of the crop cannot be explained without looking to sociocultural changes.

One of these changes was the emergence of coffee as the preeminent male status crop. Introduced mainly by male missionaries, coffee came to Kilimanjaro in the context of masculine power. As it became part of kihamba agriculture, men largely retained control over the trees themselves as well as the berries they produced. This occurred even though the coffee industry relied on the labor of families, especially women who were responsible for the overall maintenance of the vihamba. Marketing of the crop occurred through the KNPA and its successor, the KNCU. Both organizations were led by men, as opposed to local markets, which were managed by women. The rise of coffee as a prestige crop is revealed in the extent to which wamangi and clan heads adopted it, converting large amounts of eleusine land into vihamba. Over time, coffee cultivation denoted status, and only those of low standing, unable to finance coffee, continued to grow eleusine.[79]

Another factor was the transformation in the social importance of mbege. The collapse of eleusine led not to a decline in mbege, but rather to much the opposite. Beer production thrived on the mountain and is still today an important aspect of local life. Mbege shops can be found in every corner of the mountain, and they are very busy places most afternoons.[80] However, the nature of mbege's importance has changed dramatically. One way this can be seen is in production and distribution. Beer is now produced with eleusine sourced from other regions of Tanzania, such as Mpanda and Rukwa, that specialize in growing cereals.[81] While the use of eleusine purchased from someone else became common in the nineteenth and early twentieth centuries—the result of droughts, interchiefdom warfare, and trade—it was unheard of for any person of status not to grow and use their own, particularly those with a significant ritual role in the community. Also, mbege came to be produced by more women and fewer men, especially in the case of beer offered for sale at shops, which are largely run by women. It is a further indication both of the transition away from eleusine as a male crop and also of the increasing availability of beer as a commodity beverage.

Mbege also declined in importance as a unit of exchange. Throughout the nineteenth century, the brew had been used to facilitate numerous social transactions including tribute payments, fines for breaking laws or social norms, compensation for services performed, and, most notably, bridewealth. In the early decades of the twentieth century, people began to use currency to make these payments (German East African rupies from 1890 to 1920, East African shillings from 1921 to 1969, and Tanzanian shillings from 1969 to the present). Though brew in some cases accompanied these transactions, particularly bridewealth payments, cash emerged as the key mechanism for exchange on the mountain. In turn, it decreased the value of beer in creating and maintaining social connections.

Lastly, though mbege has remained an important part of local ceremonies, the ceremonies themselves have changed. For generations, mbege had been essential to almost every rite and ritual on the mountain. But the decline of old rites and the rise of Christian ones, the emergence of coffee as a status crop, and the brewing of mbege for sale severed the grain from its cultural significance and eroded much of the ritual aspects. Starting in the 1940s, it became less important how brew was produced, who produced it, and what ingredients were used. With cheap market prices for eleusine and the high value of coffee, farmers became comfortable with buying eleusine rather than growing it on their own.[82] Some have given up brewing altogether, buying their mbege from the local shops, though there is still a strong belief that people should brew for their own celebrations. Nonetheless, the changing nature of social life on the mountain has fundamentally altered perceptions of eleusine and mbege. Whereas one hundred years ago it was unthinkable not to use local eleusine to brew, today it is equally unthinkable to do so.

Thus, the decline of eleusine did not result from people relenting to pressures from colonial officials, settlers, and missionaries, nor was it simply a product of crop substitution. Rather, it stemmed from several interconnected factors. The opportunities posed by coffee and maize cultivation clearly appealed to many, and in the context of land scarcity and escalating population growth, it made sense for many to convert existing eleusine plots into vihamba or maize. Given the deep social and cultural significance of eleusine, demonstrated not only by its role in precolonial rituals but also by its resilience in the face of colonial opposition, its decline cannot be understood without looking to the changing significance of the grain itself and the brew manufactured from it. Changes in both the masculine traits of eleusine and the social and cultural importance of mbege made the shift away possible.

⤺

In the middle decades of the twentieth century, Kilimanjaro was a swiftly changing place. The consolidation of British colonial rule; the spread of Christianity; the development of schools, hospitals, and dispensaries; and the rise of coffee created new opportunities and obligations for everyday people. As people took advantage of these, the social fabric of the mountain began to change. Some gained access to new routes to wealth, power, and status that in turn challenged and redefined social networks and relationships. These three examples from Kilimanjaro—involving health, religion, and agriculture—illustrate how interventions related to one series of practices could affect many aspects of life. Knowledge of water formed a web that bound together the spiritual, the cultural, the social, and the political. When people were confronted with new ideas, concepts, and practices different from their own, they did not simply adopt the new in place of the old. Rather, they negotiated new knowledge as they saw fit.

Changes in community water management illustrate a dynamic process whereby people actively engaged with and shaped their experience as colonial subjects. These changes also indicate how certain social groups benefited from new knowledge at the expense of others. The biggest losers were those who held social roles linked to spiritual knowledge of water. Though spiritual knowledge remains central to how people envision the waterscape, spiritual figures have become less prominent in the management of water systems. This is especially true with new water systems, such as canals and water pipelines, that the government began developing in the 1950s and 1960s.

6 ◁ More and Better Water

*Emerging Nationalisms and High
Modernist Management, 1945–85*

ON NOVEMBER 10, 1952, people from across Kilimanjaro gathered in Moshi Town to celebrate the first annual Chagga Day. This event, organized by the district office and the Chagga Native Authority, commemorated the previous year's election of Thomas Marealle as the first paramount chief, or *mangi mkuu,* of the mountain's chiefdoms. The celebration started with prayer services held at local churches, followed by a ceremony attended by dignitaries including colonial governor Sir Edward Twining.[1] In their speeches, Twining and Marealle declared Chagga Day to be more than a celebration of an election; they praised it as a sign that the people had finally embraced their common identity as Chagga. Marealle proclaimed that it commemorated the day when "the Chagga tribe miraculously came together in a unity."[2] Since the dawn of European rule, colonial officers had referred to the mountain's residents as a single people—"the Chagga." This designation stemmed both from their perception of the mountain as a single, unified landscape and from the similarities of mountain communities in terms of agricultural and cultural practices. The people had eschewed this term, referring to themselves instead by the names of their respective clans and chiefdoms. The events of November 10 signaled a growing acceptance of this identity not only by political elites but also by the people themselves.

For Kilimanjaro, the 1950s were a high point of both Chagga nationalism and the coffee economy, and the mountain became known worldwide as a place of prosperity. Within a few years, a competing Tanzanian nationalism challenged the Chagga one, promoted by the newly formed Tanganyika African National Union (TANU) and its leader Julius Nyerere. By the late 1950s, the nationalistic overtones of Chagga identity began to fade. Promoting a shared Tanzanian identity became a government imperative with the emergence of the independent state in the 1960s. It also featured as a key element of Ujamaa, the program of socialist economic development that began in 1967. Water management figured prominently into the emergence of both nationalisms. Proponents of these new political identities encouraged people to think of themselves as part of larger communities, and promises to improve water access featured centrally into their strategies. A number of studies have examined the development of Tanzanian nationalist thinking from the founding of TANU to the 1980s.[3] Emma Hunter's *Political Thought and the Public Sphere in Tanzania* has taken this a step further, examining the rise of ethnic and national political thinking on Kilimanjaro in the postwar period. For those promoting new identities that transcended the boundaries of clans and chiefdoms, water proved to be an attractive tool for generating popular appeal. In the years after the Second World War, mountain communities faced increasing land and water scarcity because of population growth and the continued rise of coffee. Proponents of these new identities promised to provide more and better water in ways that traditional authority figures could not.

The new development projects they proposed bore little similarity to how water had been managed for centuries. They involved large-scale, government-managed projects using the latest technologies. Politicians extolled the power of these technologies to bring progress and improve lives, a good example of what James Scott refers to as high modernism.[4] In the 1950s, the Chagga Council and the mangi mkuu pursued "modern" canals and pipelines to address land scarcity while providing water to users free of charge. These projects—designed, built, and maintained by the government—made water available in new ways, to new users, in new areas. They challenged, and to an extent reshaped, how many envisioned the waterscape. The Tanzanian state likewise used water as a political tool. Under Ujamaa, the government considered water to be a national resource that would be provided to people for free. It invested in piped-water projects to provide tap water across the mountain. These projects, however, were designed in part to create dependency on the national government and weaken ethnic and clan-based power structures.

Water development posed opportunities and challenges for mountain communities. For those struggling to secure water, new canal and pipe systems were very appealing. Many embraced new identities as a means of securing access to these resources, just as people had for centuries. Yet these systems promoted fundamental changes to how people envisioned the waterscape. New technologies moved water in different ways, often out of sight, and to different locations, such as the lowlands and Rombo. This heightened tensions between communities over who held legitimate rights to water. Furthermore, these new technologies were developed by engineers, managed by paid staff, and controlled by government agencies. They disregarded local knowledge and discouraged local participation. This threatened the long-held belief that local communities actively managed the waterscape, and it threatened the authority and status of local actors, particularly the meni mifongo and the canal societies.[5]

THE POSTWAR ERA, WATER, AND THE EMERGENCE OF CHAGGA IDENTITY

Although the Second World War changed life on Kilimanjaro, it proved less disruptive than the first. The region remained outside the actual fighting, though thousands of men fought abroad in the King's African Rifles. The most pressing challenge that faced mountain communities was instability in the price of coffee. Between the 1938–39 and 1940–41 growing seasons, coffee prices fell from £45 to £31 per ton.[6] By 1943, demand had rebounded, but the government forced the KNCU to sell at below-market prices. Aside from creating financial hardships, this also left less money for infrastructure investment. Settlers and missionaries felt the impact of war even more acutely. At the onset of hostilities in 1939, the government rounded up all German and Italian nationals, around three thousand people in total, and placed them into internment camps. This constituted nearly 50 percent of the mountain's settler population as well as all the Leipzig missionaries, who were again replaced by the Augustana order. The government eventually deported the interned settlers and seized their lands. Those who remained suffered through unstable coffee prices and poor access to imported inputs, such as fertilizer and pesticides.

After the war, the British embarked on a number of administrative changes, partially because of a change in Tanganyika's legal status.

Since 1922, the territory had been a League of Nations mandate under British administration. When the United Nations (UN) assumed oversight in 1946, Tanganyika became a trust territory. The Trusteeship Council of the UN set guidelines requiring that trust territories be administered in a way that prepared them for eventual independence and majority rule. Another reason for the changes to administration was that Tanganyika assumed a more important role in the postwar British empire. Saddled by debt and economic stagnation, Britain looked to its colonies as tools for rebuilding the metropole. With its loss of India in 1947, Britain focused on Africa for these efforts. As part of this process, Parliament implemented the Colonial Development and Welfare Acts of 1940 and 1945. These provided grants for projects in the colonies that would improve social services and bring economic growth, in turn "raising the standards of health, education, social welfare and general well-being."[7] Colonial Development and Welfare grants aimed not only to improve conditions in the colonies but also to place the colonies in a better position to contribute to the empire as a whole.[8] The government also promoted changes in agriculture to benefit the metropole, such as wider cultivation of sisal and cereals such as maize and wheat.

On Kilimanjaro, several administrative reforms took place right after the war, the first of which were to Native Authority governance.[9] These stemmed from frustration that the mountain remained a politically decentralized place amid its economic success. In a 1931 report entitled "The Political Tendencies of the Wachagga," the district officer noted with frustration that "if a Chagga, about to give evidence in Court, is asked his tribe he invariably replies 'Mkibosho' or 'Mkilema' or whatsoever the name be by which the people in his particular area are called: if he adds 'Mchagga' it is as an afterthought."[10] Though the administration considered the chiefdoms to be a single Chagga society, people identified politically with their clans first and foremost, and with their chiefdoms second. The decentralized nature of the Native Authority, with dozens of individual wamangi, made it cumbersome and expensive to administer. In 1946, the administration attempted to create a more streamlined, hierarchical system of governance. It consolidated the chiefdoms to fourteen and organized them geographically into three divisions—Hai, Vunjo, and Rombo (see map 6.1)—that each received its own chief, or *mangi mwitori* (pl. *waitori*). The three waitori became the joint leaders of the Chagga Council and also served as the supervisors of the other chiefs in their respective divisions. In a nod to the coffee interests, the administration created a handful of elected seats on the newly constituted council, but these held little actual power.

Land reform also figured into the postwar strategy. Since the 1930s, land scarcity in the chiefdoms had been a growing concern. Though ample land lay in the foothills, and in the lowlands beyond the chiefdoms, this area lacked enough rainfall for kihamba agriculture and therefore was unappealing. Between 1937 and 1938, the government developed the Chagga Expansion Scheme to solve this dilemma. This proposed to develop land in the foothills near the Moshi-Himo Road, using a new canal constructed from the Rau River.[11] This project reflected Provincial Commissioner F. C. Hallier's belief that "advanced irrigation" could solve the land problem: "Instruction in advanced irrigation methods is important as the day must come, if it has not already

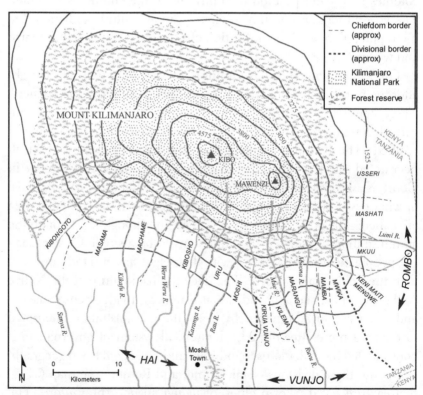

MAP 6.1. Kilimanjaro in 1945 (*Brian Edward Balsley, GISP*)

arrived, when most of the waters of Kilimanjaro will be harnessed in order to irrigate the adjacent arid plains which is the only possible outlet for a rapidly growing population."[12] Despite its seeming potential, the project remained on the drawing board because of cost and viability concerns as well as strong objections from TANESCO. During the war, the utility installed a third generating unit at Pangani Falls to supply the sisal factories that were deemed vital to the war effort. Per its agreement with the government, the utility had a right to a flow of 450 cusecs, a rate often not achieved during droughts. Therefore, the utility blocked the proposal and others that would have drawn more from the watershed.

The land question reemerged after the war's end. While the problem of providing water to the lowlands remained, more land became available because of the deportations. During the war, the administration seized 24,052 hectares and placed it under the authority of the Custodian of Enemy Property.[13] The availability of arable land with existing canals and water rights held the potential to solve the land problem. In 1946, the administration created the Arusha-Moshi Lands Commission, under the leadership of Judge Mark Wilson, to collect testimony and develop a proposal for how to redistribute enemy property and excess mission lands. Colonial officers from Kilimanjaro largely favored giving the land to the African population.[14] In a memo to Wilson, Assistant District Officer H. F. I. Elliott and Agricultural Officer R. J. M. Swynnerton remarked that the chiefdoms faced acute land scarcity and that vihamba were becoming too small to be viable.[15] They predicted that, with annual population growth of 2 percent, the mountain's African communities would require all alienated land in order to meet their needs over the next twenty to fifty years. They called for the Custodian of Enemy Property to hand over the property to the Chagga Native Authority as an immediate relief and for the government to develop the lowlands as a long-term solution. The memo estimated that without irrigation, lowland cultivation of bananas would be possible only in river valleys, while annual crops would fail three out of every five years.[16] To make these areas viable, the government needed to invest in irrigation.

The Chagga Council also submitted a memo to Wilson.[17] It stressed that the land situation had reached a critical point, with an estimated 11,000 men without vihamba. They predicted that this number would grow to 81,400 within ten years. The council asked the commission to "hand back to us all the alienated land . . . gratis" and also to assist with the water situation in the lowlands: "We beseech the Government to give us a help in developing permanent irrigation systems in the dry lowlands of the Chagga, so that we may be able to open them up more rapidly, and thus render it more and more habitably fertile."[18] The council's memo framed the problem as one that threatened the very fabric of mountain society. It noted that a kihamba "holds a peculiarly important position in the body of the Chagga tribal traditions and customs" and that "it confers upon its owner the overruling significance of belonging to the tribe." In this way, the council drew on the idea of a single Chagga people to argue that land scarcity posed cultural as well as economic challenges.

In 1947, the commission released its final recommendations. In the report, Wilson called for the government to transfer 9,093 hectares on the south side of the mountain, less than half of what the Custodian of Enemy Property held, to the Chagga Native Authority, with the rest set aside for European use.[19] The transferred lands were to be placed in the hands of the wamangi to distribute as they saw fit. The district and provincial offices, Swynnerton, and the Chagga Council criticized the report's findings and accused Wilson of ignoring the realities of the mountain and relying on bad data. The report especially angered the new generation of elites: the coffee growers and the school educated. They had long accused the wamangi of favoritism and failing to advocate for the common interest, and now they found themselves shut out of access to the newly available land. In early 1945, a group of farmers led by Joseph Merinyo and Petro Njau formed the Chagga Association. This organization arose from questions of governance and land and water rights. In a letter to the district commissioner, the association's leadership indicted the Chagga Council for what they saw as haphazard and inconsistent laws among the chiefdoms. They called for government to provide a "decent law to govern Wachagga," one that would foster unity and involve young, educated people to a greater extent.[20] They advocated the replacement of the appointed waitori with an elected mangi mkuu, a change that they felt would reduce the arbitrary nature of governance and lead to fairness in land and water issues.

In its attack against the waitori, the association employed the term "Chagga" in a way that challenged how it was used by the wamangi. In the political context, the term had come to denote colonial governance through "traditional" authorities: the wamangi and the Chagga Council. The association, however, used the term to describe the unity of the people and their struggle against the oppressive power of the wamangi. In a letter to the waitori, Merinyo stated:

> I would be glad if we could cooperate and look into the deep distress the Wachagga are expressing at this very moment: and we should reflect objectively irrespective of the flattery that the Wachagga have progressed and are in good condition.
>
> You, our leaders—the Waitori and the Wamangi—it is obvious that you are interested only in strengthening your positions, and that you are not interested in the welfare of your people.[21]

In using the term this way, Merinyo transformed it from one of exploitation into one of liberation. The key to freedom from the oppression of chiefly power lay in the unity of the people. To build this unified front, Merinyo and the association leveraged a term long used by the administration but eschewed by the people.

After the Arusha-Moshi Lands Commission debacle, local activism intensified. In 1949, Merinyo and Njau organized a new political organization, the Kilimanjaro Chagga Citizens Union (KCCU).[22] It shared many of the Chagga Association's objectives but aimed for broader membership. Iliffe notes that the organization became popular among a wide range of politically alienated people, including "dispossessed chiefs, ambitious traders and farmers, old KNPA activists, unprivileged Muslims, [headmen] who resented chiefly authority, and young educated men impatient with the old order."[23] It grew quickly, sporting twelve thousand members in 1951, and established itself as a thorn in the side of the Chagga Council.[24]

The British administration viewed the KCCU with anxiety, as it feared that popular resistance could undermine its reforms. Still, it shared the desire to bring central leadership to the mountain. In 1951, it struck a deal with the Chagga Council and the KCCU to hold an election for a paramount chieftaincy. By the summer, four candidates had emerged to run in the October 8 election, three of whom were the sitting waitori: Petro Itosi Marealle of Vunjo, Abdiel Shangali of Hai, and John Maruma of Rombo.[25] The fourth, Thomas Marealle, was a relative outsider. The son of a former mangi, he held the required chiefly blood to stand for election, but unlike his opponents, he had not spent his life in local politics. After completing his secondary education in Tabora, he studied at the London School of Economics and at Trinity College, Cambridge, before returning to Tanganyika to work in the colonial bureaucracy.[26] His chiefly heritage, combined with his education and disconnection from local politics, made him attractive to the KCCU. Marealle campaigned as representing all the mountain's people, not just a single chiefdom. Rogers notes that the KCCU devised powerful propaganda for Marealle. It claimed that as mangi mkuu, he would "abolish the *Waitori* system, do away with the coffee cess [tax], and lead the Chagga to greatness as an independent sovereign."[27] Further, "he would restore respect to the clans and clan leaders and abolish corruption in the administration, and speak authoritatively to Government, and they would be forced to listen." Most importantly, he promised that "Chagga vihamba would be safe forever, and more land provided."

Voters responded favorably to his message. Marealle swept to victory with 15,661 out of 24,002 votes, winning every chiefdom except Machame.[28] People's ongoing struggle to secure access to land and water, and their belief that Marealle would champion their interests, contributed first and foremost to his victory. As John Tawney, a writer for *Corona*, noted in a 1952 article summarizing the election, "land is life to the Chagga and their feeling for it was a main cause of the election."[29] Marealle took office as mangi mkuu on January 17, 1952. The installation ceremony, led by Governor Twining, featured a blend of "traditional" rites and rituals alongside modern ones. Marealle himself dressed in a white Western-style suit with a black tie. After a speech by Twining, members of the Chagga Council came forward, dressed him in a ceremonial robe and hat made with the skins of a leopard and a colobus monkey, and declared him Mshumbue, "the anointed one." The ceremony ended with speeches by Marealle and the waitori and an evening of dancing and sundowners. Among the people, hopes ran high that the election marked a turning point, a start to solving the region's resource problems.

NATIVE AUTHORITY WATER DEVELOPMENT IN THE 1950S

As mangi mkuu, Marealle worked through the Chagga Council to address the issues of land scarcity and water provision. A potential stumbling block was that the body had no authority over water. The 1948 Water Ordinance, as mentioned in chapter 4, stipulated a dual legal system for water management in which Native Authorities dealt with issues related to customary rights, while the District Water Board and Water Court managed all new rights. As of 1954, the Moshi Water Court had three seats held by wamangi. This gave the council some voice in water matters but not the means to develop projects on its own. Seeking to build modern, large-scale water projects, the council looked beyond local specialists and partnered with the colonial government's Water Development Department (WDD). Created in 1945 to provide technical assistance in the development of rural water systems, the WDD acted as a contractor, designing and building projects on the behalf of the council.[30] It funded projects on a cost-sharing model, the council paying one-third of the total cost and the WDD paying the rest.[31] On completion, the council assumed ownership of the system and responsibility for repairs and maintenance. Local communities contributed manual labor for projects, and in return they were allowed to use water at no charge. In terms of scale, expertise, financing, and maintenance, these projects broke with the long-standing conventions of water management on the mountain.

In the 1950s, the Chagga Council and the WDD partnered on dozens of projects. Many were large water canals designed to open up lowland areas for settlement. Locals referred to these as the government canals.[32] One example was the Kimashuku canal, constructed in 1952 to provide water to the foothills of Hai and to the Weru Weru grazing reserve. Originating high up the slopes in Machame, it flowed for several kilometers to its end near the Moshi-Arusha Road. Though similar to the mangi-led canal projects of the 1930s, Kimashuku differed from existing canals in that it had been designed by WDD engineers and funded by the WDD and the council. The only local contribution was manual labor, fifty men per day, organized by Mangi Mwitori Shangali. Once the canal opened, the Native Authority hired a fundi to manage and maintain it. Furthermore, since the canal had been designed to provide water to lower areas, individuals living next to it were banned from digging their own connecting canals and running water to their vihamba.[33] These canals soon proved to be problematic. Their length, combined with their running through arid areas with high temperatures and little shade, meant that they were prone to seepage and evaporation. They frequently lacked water in dry seasons, leading to complaints that the "government canals [were] useless."[34] Furthermore, the people who lived alongside them had little incentive to care for them, and thus they were subject to pollution and water theft. The construction of illegal branch canals became a major problem, as attested to by the livestock superintendent who oversaw the Weru Weru grazing reserve: "Since the opening of [Kimashuku], the local Natives living in the vicinity of the canal have constituted themselves a permanent nuisance i.e. blocking up the canal, irrigating maize, etc., etc."[35] Further opposition came from TANESCO. The scale of these canals threatened to reduce further the water flows from the mountain, creating greater challenges for power generation at Pangani Falls.

An alternative solution emerged in the form of gravity-flow water pipelines. Pipes had been used in limited capacity since the late 1930s, mostly by the missions and government offices in Moshi Town. Piped water followed the same general premise as the canals, using gravity to channel water from upper areas to lower ones. Pipelines began with an intake, constructed of concrete, that diverted water from a river or stream (fig. 6.1). The intake channeled water into a galvanized steel pipe, between 5 and 30 centimeters in diameter and buried around 15 centimeters underground. The pipe then carried the water downhill. En route, the water passed through a series of break-pressure tanks and storage tanks, constructed of concrete and covered with steel lids. Finally, the water reached public taps (fig. 6.2), from which users could access the water for free. These systems became increasingly popular in this period because of their potential to solve the problems of evaporation, seepage, pollution, and water stealing that afflicted the government canals. Furthermore, they enabled storage, which promised to make water more available in dry periods. By the mid-1950s, the WDD's work focused exclusively on pipelines. Most were single-line systems intended to serve dispensaries, hospitals, and missions in water-scarce areas such as Kirua Rombo, Mkuu Rombo, Kirua Vunjo, Msaranga, Mwika, Lumi, Olele, Mashati, and Keni Mriti.[36] Costs averaged between £2,000 and £7,000 per project. The largest and most notable project of the 1950s was Operation Dammit, which aimed to provide water to lowland areas of Kirua Vunjo.[37] It called for the development of earthen dams (fig. 6.3) to capture rainy-season flood flows, which would then be sent via pipeline to settlements near the

Moshi-Himo Road. By 1959, the WDD had identified five viable dam projects and constructed four of them.

The colonial administration also made some legal and administrative changes to water management in the 1950s. Though pipes promised to solve persistent technical problems, there remained the issue of conflicting rights and claims to them, exacerbated by the dual

FIGURE 6.1. Water pipeline intake, Kilema (*Matthew V. Bender*)

legal system in place since 1923. In response to this, the government implemented a new water ordinance in 1959, which disbanded the water courts and replaced them with twenty water districts across the colony. A water officer administered each district and could adjudicate disputes. This reflected the government's belief that "experts" could best manage water resources. It also called for the registration

FIGURE 6.2. Public tap, Kilema (*Matthew V. Bender*)

FIGURE 6.3. Cholo Dam, Kirua Vunjo (*Matthew V. Bender*)

of all "native" water rights and imposed penalties for individuals who violated another person's right to water. The law represented a shift to technocratic water management by putting the power to adjudicate water disputes in the hands of trained officers rather than appointed officials. Despite these changes, the 1959 ordinance kept in place many previous policies, particularly the dual legal system for water.

Despite the money being spent on water projects in the 1950s, Marealle and the council made little headway in addressing the problems of the mountain. The office of mangi mkuu offered Marealle little power with which to make change. As noted by Rogers, "he was to be, in fact, a Chief in Council—more than a simple executive officer, but far less than the independent ruler [that KCCU] leaders and followers had envisioned and hoped for."[38] He could suggest projects and offer financing, but he had little power to shape the development agenda. Furthermore, many of the projects were inherently flawed. For example, although Operation Dammit was designed to promote new settlements, it instead fueled resentment between the highland populations of Kirua Vunjo and new lowland residents. Many in Kirua despised the dams because they occupied prime land, sent precious water to the lowlands, and provided nothing in return. Even worse was that piped water could only be used for domestic purposes and livestock, not irrigation. This miscalculation proved damning. Without access to water for bananas and coffee, the new settlements proved unpopular. Furthermore, nearly all the council money going toward projects came from the coffee cess, a despised tax that Marealle had promised to eliminate. Since the council collected the bulk of the tax in the highlands, these areas essentially subsidized new lowland settlements. Most of all, these projects were socially disconnected, not really part of the waterscape in the eyes of locals. These systems had been conceived and developed by outsiders without any local expertise or input. They therefore lacked any sense of local buy-in, ownership, or responsibility. As the Chagga Council proved incapable of funding maintenance, most systems of this period quickly deteriorated.

Marealle, for his part, seemed focused on other issues. In the 1950s he became a public figure, arguably Tanganyika's most famous chief (fig. 6.4). He spent much of his time promoting a shared Chagga identity. He organized annual Chagga Day celebrations, funneled money into the creation of a cultural heritage organization called the Chagga Trust, and hired Cambridge historian Kathleen Stahl to write a "history" of the Chagga people.[39] He traveled the country, bragging about the progress being made in providing water to Chagga communities and in opening new lands for settlement. In 1957, he traveled to New York City and testified in front of the Trusteeship Council. He explained that the Chagga Council was "making Herculean efforts to provide the necessary water supplies for domestic or irrigation purposes in order to make settlement in these dry areas possible," noting that they had spent £40,000 on water schemes in the past three years alone.[40] He presented the image of a prosperous Chagga society grounded in tradition but embracing modern knowledge and opportunities. During his tenure, the mountain was even featured in *Time*. The 1958 article, "Tanganyika: Look What We Can Do!," claimed that the mountain "brims with more promise and progress than almost any land in Africa."[41]

Despite some successes, Marealle began to lose support. Clan heads and coffee farmers criticized him for failing to deliver on land reform. He alienated educated youth, who questioned his dedication to land reform and his reliance on traditional imagery. Marealle's political views also created conflict with the burgeoning nationalist movement. Formed in July 1954, TANU emerged as the colony's preeminent nationalist political movement. Julius Nyerere (also called Mwalimu, Kiswahili for "teacher") became the face of the movement and a vocal

FIGURE 6.4. Mangi Mkuu Marealle with the secretary of state for the colonies (*The National Archives of the UK, ref. Co1069/157 (27)*)

advocate for the end of colonial rule. He envisioned an independent Tanganyika with a strong sense of shared national identity, and he viewed with skepticism ethnic nationalism and the role of traditional authorities. Nyerere's vision conflicted with that of Marealle, who was both a chief and a confidant of Governor Twining. Their differences came to a head in 1957, when they both testified at the Trusteeship Council and gave contradictory opinions on the process and timeline for independence. On Nyerere's return to Tanganyika, he helped establish the Chagga Democratic Party, an affiliate of TANU on Kilimanjaro meant to undermine Marealle. By 1959, criticism of the mangi mkuu reigned across the mountain. Amid falling coffee prices and accusations of corruption, Marealle resigned his position in 1959 and largely sat on the sidelines as Tanganyika moved toward independence. Persona non grata in the new nation, he took a position with the World Food Program and lived in Rome for fifteen years before retiring on Kilimanjaro.

UHURU, UJAMAA, AND WATER

On December 9, 1961, Brigadier General Alexander Nyirenda of the King's African Rifles successfully reached the summit of Kibo (fig. 6.5). Though nearly seventy years after Hans Meyer's trek, Nyirenda's expedition held deep symbolic importance. Taking place on the day of Tanganyika's independence, it marked the end of British rule and the emergence of the sovereign state. Nyirenda reached the peak just after midnight, after which he planted the flag of the new nation and a kerosene torch. In doing so, he fulfilled the words of Prime Minister Julius Nyerere in a speech he made to the Tanganyika Legislative Assembly more than two years earlier: "We the people of Tanganyika, would like to light a candle and put it on top of Mount Kilimanjaro which would shine beyond our borders giving hope where there was despair, love where there was hate, and dignity where there was before only humiliation."[42] From that moment, the summit became known as Uhuru Peak. *Uhuru*, meaning freedom in Kiswahili, marked the mountain as a symbol of the state and an embodiment of its hopes to bring freedom, dignity, and development to its peoples. Furthermore, it intended to shine light on those still in the shadows of colonial rule. It came as little surprise that the leadership of the new nation would begin its era on Kilimanjaro. For a hundred years, the mountain had served as a symbol of colonial rule in all its economic, political, and religious manifestations. By planting a flag, a torch, and a new name, the new government appropriated the mountain for its own ends. Kilimanjaro would be a symbol of the nation rather than one of the colonial state or any one ethnicity (see fig. 6.6).

Independence brought with it a period of swift transformations. Tanganyika shed more vestiges of colonial rule by becoming a republic in 1962, and within another two years it entered a union with Zanzibar, becoming the United Republic of Tanzania. Nyerere became its first president, and he focused on the challenges facing the fledgling nation. One of the greatest lay in building allegiance to the new

FIGURE 6.5. Nyirenda at Kibo Peak (*United Republic of Tanzania*, The Executive Summary of the Report on the Fifty Years of Independence of Tanzania Mainland, 1961–2011 (*Dar es Salaam: Government of Tanzania, 2011*))

FIGURE 6.6. Postage stamps featuring Kilimanjaro from the early 1960s

government and a shared sense of national identity. The split between nationalist rhetoric and the reality on the ground was most obvious in the country's bifurcated political apparatus, featuring elected officials in national, regional, and district offices, and hereditary chiefs at the local level.[43] TANU feared that the persistence of chiefly authority would result in "national factions" and "tribalism" rather than national unity.[44] In 1963, the government issued the African Chiefs Ordinance (Repeal) Act, which dissolved hereditary chieftaincy and implemented a new system of local governance based on wards (mitaa), villages (vijiji), and units of ten houses (ten-cells).[45] Two years later, the government enacted a constitution that mandated a democratic single-party state and banned political parties other than TANU.[46]

The fledgling nation also faced economic problems. Poverty and underdevelopment persisted in the early years of independence, and the quality of public services such as education and healthcare remained poor. Nyerere chose to take the country's development efforts in a new direction. On February 5, 1967, he delivered the Arusha Declaration, in which he outlined his vision for a Tanzanian socialist state.[47] Calling his program Ujamaa ("brotherhood" in Kiswahili), he proposed a shift in national development priorities, from emphasis on urban industry and large-scale plantation agriculture to small-scale rural cooperative agriculture. Nyerere felt that rural life inherently held the socialist values of hard work, cooperation, common purpose, and self-reliance, values on which the whole nation could thrive. A "communitarian ethic" would not only give rise to economic and social development but would also help build the sense of common purpose the nation needed as a whole.[48] Starting in mid-1967, the government implemented reforms to make Ujamaa a reality, including nationalizing select corporations and commercial farms and developing Ujamaa vijijini (villages) across the country.[49] Two years later, it embraced "villagization" of rural populations as a key element of this policy, Nyerere ordering that rural services be situated in the new villages and that rural-development funding be withdrawn from those not living in, or intending to move to, Ujamaa villages.[50] In 1973, the government nationalized settler farms and opened these lands for cultivation by Africans. Settler society, which had for decades been a strong presence on Kilimanjaro, came to a rather unceremonious end.

The political and economic transformations of the 1960s had tremendous implications for rural water development. A major obstacle to nation building was the fact that Tanzania was largely semiarid—more than 33 percent of arable land received less than 800 millimeters of rain per year—and featured few surface water resources.[51] This contributed to a host of problems, most notably life-expectancy rates that were low even by African standards (forty years in 1967).[52] The village-based development model promised to exacerbate the problem by creating high population densities in areas without much water. In his writings, Nyerere cites the need for water in order to reach his goals for rural development. "One of the major problems of rural development in most parts of Tanzania," he writes, "is the dearth or irregularity of water supplies. Although a water point does not have a spectacular appearance, it can often be more important for the progress of the people in an area than an imposing building, or a factory, put somewhere else; progress in this matter is thus an indication of the seriousness of Tanzania's development efforts."[53]

In the early years of Ujamaa, water development emerged as a national priority. Nyerere expanded the mandate of the Water Development Department to include urban and town supplies. In 1970, his government replaced the WDD with the Water Development and Irrigation Department (WD&ID), under a new Ministry of Water and Power.[54] This agency embarked on projects across the country including irrigation, pipelines, boreholes, and cattle dips, covering the costs of construction, operation, and maintenance. It also commissioned regional water studies in partnership with international development agencies. The next year, the WD&ID declared a twenty-year Water Supply Program, with the goal of providing all Tanzanians with a clean, adequate water supply within 400 meters of their homes.[55] This plan involved the development of regional water master plans as well as a master plan for the whole nation. The government increased spending on rural water supplies from 2.4 million East Africa shillings in 1961 to 25 million by 1971.[56] Most importantly, it committed to providing water to all Tanzanians in rural areas free of charge. By developing water systems and providing free access, the government hoped to foster Ujamaa values while providing a catalyst for economic growth.

Water—more than just an instrument of development—emerged as a benchmark of economic and social progress and the success of nation building.[57] The government extolled water projects for their social benefits, such as improving public health and relieving women and children of the rigors of gathering water.[58] Water development also served the strategic interests of the state. As noted by White, Bradley, and White in their study of rural water in East Africa published in 1972, the Tanzanian government realized the value of water as "a conspicuous public service cementing public support for the central government."[59] In other words, the presence of a system that provided a needed service, running through the heart of a community, emphasized the government's role in local life and reinforced the relationship between the locality and the nation.

In this period of development and nation building, Kilimanjaro presented an obstacle as well as an opportunity for TANU. Economically, the region exemplified the nation Nyerere wished to build. It featured a thriving economy, fueled by coffee prices that had boomed from £128 per ton in 1948 to £582 by 1954.[60] Coffee revenue had developed roads, hospitals, schools, and irrigation systems, and it had given the region the nation's highest numbers of primary schools and medical facilities per capita.[61] Yet the mountain had a lukewarm attitude toward TANU's nationalist agenda. In 1958, the party's regional branch had only 7,710 members out of a total population of 365,000.[62] Though membership grew in the 1960s, the Kilimanjaro branch of TANU became dominated by clan interests. Party members at the national level expressed frustration at the mountain's refusal to put aside its "provincial" concerns and become involved in nation building. After the restructuring of local governance and the banning of chieftaincy in 1963, clan-based authority remained strong. Local leaders layered new structures, like the ten-cell units, on top of clan structures, a process that Sally Falk Moore refers to as pyramiding.[63] Though the chiefs were gone, clan elders remained important players in local political life.

Water is perhaps the best example of the persistence of local political actors. In the early 1960s, local communities exercised a tremendous amount of agency in water management. Though the development of new management knowledge had led to the decline of some social positions, such as rainmakers and diviners, people still considered water to be a resource that should be managed by community members with expertise. Meni mifongo and user societies still managed canals much as they had for generations, despite attempts by the British and the wamangi to undermine their position. In fact, the system continued to grow. By the 1960s, the mountain was home to one thousand canals, consisting of 1,800 kilometers of main channels and carrying 200 million cubic meters of water annually.[64] The volume and proximity of water afforded by the mifongo contributed to the fact that households were using nearly 75 liters per capita daily for domestic tasks, more than double that of other rural areas.[65] Thus, people on the mountain relied on a water system built on the kinds of traditional leadership structures that TANU despised. Furthermore, local control of water was antithetical to TANU's vision of a strong central government that planned resources at a national level. In other words, the mifongo posed an obstacle to the nation as envisioned by TANU.

Fortunately for the ruling party, the water situation was becoming critical. In 1960, a severe drought afflicted Tanzania, and it had tremendous implications for Kilimanjaro. Hundreds of canals dried up, as did thousands of hectares of coffee and bananas. In Rombo, conditions became especially desperate, with women walking up to a dozen kilometers a day in search of water.[66] The devastating effects provided an opening for TANU. Local leaders called on the government for assistance in developing new systems that would provide more water in the highlands and allow for settlement in the foothills and lowlands. The government's newfound desire to provide water, combined with new problems facing the mountain, presented a means of challenging the existing water order.

NYUMBA YA MUNGU AND THE RURAL WATER SUPPLY PROGRAMME

In the 1960s, the Tanzanian government embarked on several major water projects in the region. Of these, the most ambitious were the Nyumba ya Mungu Dam and the Rural Water Supply Programme. Both adopted the same strategy that had been employed by the British in the 1950s. The national government, through the WD&ID, led the design and construction phases of the projects, and it sought funding from local and national governments and the Colonial Development and Welfare Fund. The Nyumba ya Mungu project (Kiswahili for "House of God") called for the construction of a dam and reservoir where the Ruvu and Kikuletwa Rivers formed the Pangani, 50 kilometers south of Moshi Town.[67] The reservoir would be East Africa's largest man-made lake, with an area of 180 square kilometers. Capable of storing 920,000 acre-feet of water, it promised to solve a host of problems that had hindered development in the region. By storing water and releasing it downstream in a controlled manner, the dam would solve TANESCO's problem of inadequate flow rates. This would in turn enable more lowland irrigation projects to be developed. D. N. M. Bryceson, the minister of agriculture, noted in a letter to the regional commissioners for Arusha, Kilimanjaro, and Tanga on December 28, 1963, that "construction of the Nyumba ya Mungu Dam will automatically enable virtually unlimited quantities of water to be released for development in the Pangani Valley."[68] He anticipated that 1,000 acre-feet of new water, enough for 8,000 hectares of irrigation, would be available above the reservoir, and a similar amount beneath it. A third benefit of the project was that it would add 8 kilowatts of hydroelectric capacity to the national grid.

Design work on Nyumba ya Mungu began in 1961. Construction on the dam began two years later and concluded in December 1965. Power generation did not start until 1969. Though the project promised to transform the water situation in lowland Kilimanjaro, it failed to live up to its billing. Located in an arid region, the reservoir suffered high rates of evaporation, with as much as one-fourth of the incoming water flow lost.[69] Combined with lower than average rainfall, the reservoir rarely filled to capacity. While the water available helped the flows at Pangani Falls and Hale, it did not prove sufficient to enable more irrigation. The reservoir did become home to a thriving fishing industry, with Nyumba ya Mungu tilapia sold as far afield as Arusha and Dar es Salaam. In general, lowland irrigation schemes below the Himo-Arusha Road were unsuccessful in the period. Most never left the drawing board, because of a lack of sufficient water to make them viable. Those that did failed to entice mountain peoples to resettle.

The Rural Water Supply Programme for Kilimanjaro Region was a much more expansive set of projects, aimed at modernizing access in the agroforest zone and making water available in the foothills above the Himo-Arusha Road.[70] Devised by the WD&ID, the district and regional water officers, and the recently established Kilimanjaro Region Water Advisory Board, it outlined a ten-year program to tackle the mountain's water problems by constructing an entirely new distribution system. Rather than modifying or extending the existing mifongo, it called for a network of gravity-driven water pipelines: "This area . . . can only be served by a close network of gravity piped supplies, obtained from the major streams. A series of main feeder pipe lines are proposed which will provide adequate water to the whole rural population whether they be living in the few villages or on farm homesteads."[71] The pipelines promised to provide the people with a clean, abundant, and modern water supply that would replace the mifongo, rivers, streams, and springs. At a cost of nearly £1.6 million, the system would serve the mountain and its 476,000 residents with 34 million liters of water per day, at no charge.[72]

Like many proposals during Ujamaa, the program did not lack ambition. It called for the construction of eighteen pipe systems, seventeen on the mountain's south side and one on its east. The south pipelines were all of similar design, running from the rainforest region to the edge of the plains within the boundaries of former chiefdoms. Each began with a concrete intake, extracting water from a river or stream within the rainforest (uphill of settlement and grazing areas, where in theory there would be no risk of pollution). The water would then flow downhill in 20- to 30-centimeter steel piping buried 15 centimeters underground. After passing through a series of storage and break-pressure tanks, the pipes would run into areas of settlement and be available through public taps. The project on the east side, the East Kilimanjaro Trunk Main, called for a reticulated design, with multiple intakes feeding a 30-centimeter main pipeline. The WD&ID chose this design to compensate for the lack of year-round surface water in Rombo. In fact, it called for the largest of the intakes to be located above Mwika, and not actually in Rombo. From the trunk main, sixteen branch lines would lead the water into local communities.[73] Despite the ambition, the £1.6 million price tag was actually cheaper per capita than most systems in the country because of reliance on gravity and the lack of need for filtering or chemical treatment. The primary source of funding for the project was the Kilimanjaro District Council treasury, along with some Colonial Development and Welfare grants.

According to its proponents, the purpose of the Rural Water Supply Programme was to bring "more and better water" to the people of Kilimanjaro.[74] Making free tap water available would alleviate the problems of supply and quality. Piped water would also serve a higher purpose, as a facilitator of the values of Ujamaa. It would bring self-reliance by alleviating chronic water shortages that bred dependency, by mobilizing national money rather than dependence on donors, and by encouraging community participation as people provided labor through self-help initiatives. Piped water would also bring social equality to the region. Pipes were a more egalitarian form of distribution than the mifongo and would put water in the hands of hardworking farmers rather than elites. For women and children, pipes offered a panacea that could save "time spent by many . . . in walking long distances to collect water."[75] Lastly, proponents claimed that piped water would lead to "community development," by improving health and sanitation. Flowing through enclosed pipes rather than open canals would protect water from contamination and evaporation. Citing drought and outbreaks of diarrhea and cholera, the government claimed that the pipes would improve the living standards of the mountain.[76] These social benefits, in turn, would be crucial to the overall development of the nation.

Though promoted as an instrument of rural empowerment, the program had underlying political objectives. First, it proposed a fundamentally different way of managing the waters of Kilimanjaro. The existing mifongo system embodied decentralized control by local specialists. The program, however, envisioned a centralized system of pipelines and taps over which the government would have complete control. Decisions concerning management would be made not by local elites, but by the District Water Office. Local mafundi would be responsible for ensuring that the pipes delivered water as promised and that everyone had their share. This new model essentially transferred jurisdiction of water from the locality to national bodies, and it actively discouraged local participation beyond the construction process. While the program extolled the rural-empowerment aspects of Ujamaa, it threatened to reduce local control and cooperative attitudes toward water resources.

Second, the program promoted piped water as a direct competitor to other sources. In many cases, new pipelines ran alongside existing mifongo and even tapped into the same rivers at the same point. In practical terms, this permitted the designers of the pipes to utilize an already proven grade, thus alleviating the expense of surveying. This close proximity was also a strategic choice. By running pipes alongside canals, the government could extend its presence directly into the heart of mountain communities. Side by side, people could choose between canal water and the supposedly cleaner, more reliable piped water, which also had the advantage of being free of charge and requiring no input of labor. This strategy played into the government's long-term goal, to render the mifongo obsolete.[77]

Finally, the program made no provision for irrigation. In fact, it expressly forbade people from irrigating in any form, even watering plants by hand. This prohibition reflected the government's belief that highland irrigation was unnecessary and that the nation would be best served by diverting water to the lowlands. Government officers believed that farmers would abandon irrigation on their own accord and in turn give up the mifongo.[78] From this perspective, the development of piped water would bring an end to irrigation and the canal societies, which would give government agencies greater control over the waters of the mountain and the whole Pangani Basin. The government would then have more power to manage the hydrology of Northeast Tanzania with the needs of upstream *and* downstream users in mind.

Beginning in 1967, the government implemented the program through a series of projects, the first of which was the East Kilimanjaro Trunk Main. The WD&ID started with this project, the most complex in terms of design, because Rombo had been so devastated by the recent drought. Personnel from the WD&ID and the Moshi District Water Office supervised the project from start to finish, eliciting no input from locals as to the location of the pipes, tanks, and taps. WD&ID staff also managed all technical aspects of construction. The local contribution consisted of hard labor: men excavating pipe trenches, constructing tank foundations, and carrying steel piping and bags of concrete.[79] The trunk main opened in 1970, providing approximately 11.4 million liters to around 150,000 people.[80]

After completion of the East Kilimanjaro system, the WD&ID turned its attention to the seventeen pipeline systems on the south side, but the agency soon encountered financial roadblocks. A steep decline in the price of coffee in the early 1970s, combined with a dramatic rise in fuel prices in 1973, took a heavy toll on the region's economy. At the same time, turbulent relations between Britain and Tanzania led to a suspension of Colonial Development and Welfare grants.[81] The lack of funding threatened many Ujamaa projects, including those for water development. International development agencies, including UNICEF, Oxfam, the Japan International Cooperation Agency (JICA), and the Swedish International Development Authority (SIDA), began to make up for the shortfall. Like TANU, these external agencies extolled the social benefits of water development. Oxfam, for example, noted that many women across the country had to walk "as much as [eight kilometers] each way for water," arduous work that left them with little time for bettering themselves or taking care of their families.[82] "Holding back" women, in turn, stunted "improvement" in their families and "development" in their villages. Money from these agencies and the World Bank financed most of the remaining Kilimanjaro pipelines. By the early 1980s, all the planned projects had been completed, and the slopes of Kilimanjaro were home to Tanzania's most extensive rural water system.

MORE AND BETTER WATER?

The primary goal of the Rural Water Supply Programme was to raise the standard of living by bringing "more and better water" to the people. On paper, the results were mixed. The completion of the eighteen pipe systems succeeded in providing 60 percent of the mountain's population with taps within 400 meters of their homes by 1986.[83] This figure, though impressive, was not the "total coverage" envisioned in the program's proposal. The inability to reach more people stemmed from financial and technical difficulties as well as population growth. The original plans had estimated a total population of 467,000. By 1978 the actual population had risen beyond 600,000. The rest of the country experienced a similar phenomenon. Between 1967 and 1978, more than 7.7 million people across the country had become beneficiaries of rural water supply projects.[84] This paled in comparison to the country's population, which had risen from 12.3 million to 23.3 million in the same period.[85]

These figures provide telling information about the spread of piped water, but they only consider proximity, rather than utilization. The experiences of those who lived through this period tell a different story. In Mkuu Rombo, piped water had an immediate impact on daily life, in many cases becoming the water of choice. Elders recall that the taps provided water at much closer proximity than existing sources, and making use of them dramatically reduced the amount of time spent collecting water.[86] Edita Hendry recalled that before the pipes, she walked several kilometers each day to the nearest stream, Shokoni.[87] The completion of the nearby tap brought water to within a thirty-minute walk. She soon abandoned Shokoni and used the tap exclusively. She remembered that the pipes gave her more time for cultivating crops and selling them at market, while her children were more alert in school. Leoni Motesha told a similar story.[88] As a young woman she had lived considerably closer to a water source than Hendry. The Nana spring emerged about 1.5 kilometers from her kihamba, a trip that took her between thirty and forty minutes each way. Around 1970, the government installed a tap within a ten-minute walk. She recalled the added convenience of the new source, noting that it allowed her to do her clothes washing at home. Both women extolled piped water: Hendry explained that it was "better than water from the canals and streams because the latter is dirty and full of disease-carrying organisms. Water from pipes, on the contrary, is safe."

The first pipeline in Kilema arrived around 1970, and in areas where coverage was good, it was utilized readily. Again, many people cited the appeal of piped water in terms of proximity and cleanliness. Liberati Mbando remarked that women of the area "used to ferry water from long distances, but now water is nearby and much cleaner than the canals water."[89] Further uphill, Michael Safari praised the pipes in similar fashion. He asserted that the water was "of better quality," and that "piped water has made it easier to get water by reducing the distance covered for fetching water from other sources."[90] Though people in Kilema remember the advent of pipes in positive terms, most in the highlands did not abandon other sources of water as those in Rombo had done. Because of the closer location of springs and rivers and the greater abundance of mifongo, most continued to enjoy a multiple-source water economy, simply adding piped water to their list of choices. Gustave Gerard recalled that before the pipes, his family relied primarily upon two sources of water: Ndishini spring for domestic water and brewing and the Kyou mfongo for other tasks. The former lay a short thirty-minute walk away, while the canal ran directly through it. When the government completed the nearby tap, Gerard's wife chose it as her source for domestic water, but they continued to use the mfongo for irrigation and high-volume tasks such as washing clothes, cleaning their house, and pulping coffee. Gerard explained that "piped water cannot cater for all the needs. There was still a need to have the canals." For tasks that required large volumes of water, public taps could not surpass the convenience of mifongo.

Pipeline development proved to be the most problematic in Machame. This region boasted the largest concentration of surface water resources, and though it had piped water by the mid-1970s, it remained underserved relative to its population. While those with nearby taps utilized them, many felt that pipes did not live up to their promise. Efraim Muro recalled that the nearest pipeline was of little use to him.[91] He had assisted with digging trenches as the government had asked, but the taps ended up being further away than springs. Rather than trek the extra distance, he continued to use nearby springs and his mfongo. Efraim's preference for closer proximity sources was to some extent about distance and labor burden, but it also indicated a belief among many that piped water was no better than other sources. There was much truth to this, especially as time passed and people began to settle around pipe intakes. Without a treatment system, piped water was only as good as the water flowing into the intake. Within a few years of construction, pipe systems became prone to contamination, and some provided water of poorer quality than the springs and mifongo. In many cases, pipes failed to live up to their promise of providing water that was actually better.

Across the mountain, different usage patterns arose from the development of piped water. In arid areas with unreliable surface water and in newly settled areas of the lowlands, pipes became the source of choice. For communities in water-rich areas with close-proximity taps, a multiple-source water economy remained the norm. For people who found taps to be farther away than existing reliable sources, pipelines had little impact on their lives. Piped water was, in and of itself, rarely enticing enough to change successful usage patterns. It did, however, begin to attract some people to the lowlands. Maro notes that by the 1970s, population pressure had forced a "limited and gradual movement of people down slope toward the dry lowlands."[92] The first areas to be settled were in the foothills, former shamba lands closest to the existing vihamba. These areas became appealing because of water as well as new varietals of bananas, such as *mkojosi*, that thrived in the drier conditions.[93] This allowed people to develop vihamba further downhill than previously possible. Lowland areas beneath the Himo-Arusha Road, however, remained largely unappealing.

DYING A NATURAL DEATH?

The government hoped that pipelines would help strengthen its control over water on the mountain. By using taps, people would come to accept government jurisdiction over water. Mifongo would fall out of use, canal societies would collapse, and the government would gain greater control over management of the resource. In most areas, these goals did not materialize as planned. While people accepted the government's jurisdiction over pipes and taps, they did not cede claim to the mountain's waters. The mifongo, for example, remained an important part of life across much of the mountain, especially for the more than 40 percent of the population without any access to taps. They continued to be managed as they had been for generations alongside the government-controlled pipeline system. Unsuccessful in eroding these local power structures, the government implemented the Village and Ujamaa Village Act in 1975, which removed control of mifongo from local societies and placed them in the hands of government officials.[94] Despite this change, most mifongo continued to be run by the same people.[95]

By the 1970s, the number of canals in the highlands of the agroforest belt began to decline. Numbering over one thousand in 1960, they declined to around five hundred by 1986.[96] This was most pronounced in areas near pipelines, and throughout East Kilimanjaro. At the same time, there appears to have been an intensification of irrigation in the lowlands. Mattias Tagseth has argued that changes in irrigation in this period can best be understood as a "restructuring, where declines in irrigation in the densely settled highland areas were offset by increases in irrigation in the foothills and lowlands, and some increase in scale."[97] In areas where mifongo began to decrease in number, people explain the phenomenon as sad but inevitable. Hubert Mbuya, from Kilema, simply sighed and said, "The canals are dying a natural death."[98] The decline of canals in some highland areas raises the question of whether the government's thinking regarding the pipelines was indeed correct. While it might seem that the increasing use of piped water would render mifongo irrelevant, or that government intervention would finally undermine them, upon further study it is clear that piped water did not directly cause the mifongo system's decline, nor did the decline result from people consciously choosing piped water over other sources. Canals did not die a "natural," inevitable death. Rather, their decline resulted from shifting demographics and labor patterns.

Maro discovered that from the 1960s onward, increasing numbers of young men, from ages twenty to forty, began to seek employment outside the mountain. In the 1930s, most men worked full-time in agriculture, on their own kihamba or on settler or mission farms. By the late 1960s, only 65 percent of men worked full-time in farming, the remainder supplementing or replacing farming with wage labor.[99] New opportunities in Moshi Town and beyond, in occupations such as teaching, truck driving, and carpentry, allowed people to make a living independent of the mountain's agrarian economy. Many continued to live on the mountain, adopting a commuter lifestyle that endures today, but they were less willing to participate in the canal societies or contribute to community labor. Vitalis Mosha from Kilema explained: "When the canals started to break down we asked local people to contribute to have it repaired. They did nothing. But later when the damage was too big we could not get enough funds to make repairs. This resulted in the complete breakage of the canal at its intake. We used to get water from both the pipes and canals at the same time. When water from the canals became unavailable we had to use only the piped water."[100] The decline of young working men in agriculture likewise contributed to the weakening of canal societies. As elders passed away, many societies died out as few younger men chose to join them or assume the role of meni mfongo, and thus they lacked the manpower or expertise to maintain the mifongo properly. Hence, frustration over the canals' decline is often expressed in terms of laziness. Martin Mosha, for example, emphatically declared that "people became lazy and forgot the canals."[101]

The last goal of pipeline development related to further integrating the mountain into the nation. Pipelines were one of many instruments TANU used to integrate the periphery into the nation-state. By providing services directly to rural communities, it could steer economic and social development, solidify loyalty to the party, and erode customary forms of authority. The Rural Water Supply Programme gave the national government a new presence in communities along Kilimanjaro, and it contributed to changes in local authority structures. Yet as we see with other Ujamaa projects, piped water failed to bring about the broader transformation envisioned. This is clear when looking at the nature of political change between 1967 and 1986. As Grove notes, this period was marked by the decline of many clan-based political units, with many hereditary positions replaced by elected offices.[102] The clan-based, hereditary authority of the water-canal societies gradually gave way, especially after 1975, as canal societies began to elect their leaders. Ethnic nationalism also became more muted. Commemoration of Chagga Day ended, and icons of Chagga nationalism, such as the flag, have largely been forgotten. Yet a strong sense of being Chagga remains, an identity that arose in defending the mountain against outside interests. Despite the decline of clan-based units, local politics and political actors remained important. Sally Falk Moore observed that local political discourses remained important despite the changes brought by Ujamaa.[103] Local chapters of TANU remained forums for political contestation, and after the end of single-party politics, opposition parties gained a strong foothold in the region.

↜

In the decades following the introduction of piped water, Kilimanjaro became a more integral part of the nation while retaining a tremendous sense of autonomy. This coexistence is exemplified by the simultaneous presence of water canals and pipelines. The introduction of new piped-water systems signified a new form of government presence in the heart of mountain communities, one that thousands chose to take advantage of. The mere presence of this system did not force the demise of the mifongo, nor did it alter how people conceptualized water. Similarly, a sustained government presence in the heart of the mountain did not result in the nationalist transformation envisioned by TANU. Rather than becoming a bastion of national identity, Kilimanjaro has remained a place with a strong sense of self and skepticism toward the agendas of those from beyond its boundaries.

Still, pipelines helped dramatically reshape the waterscape. They represented a new way of moving water as well as a fundamentally different notion of how water should be managed. Though pipes did not kill off the mifongo entirely, they contributed to growing dependency on the government and the erosion of local knowledge. Communities in the upper areas were the most resistant to this, because of the availability of alternate water sources and the greater ease of maintaining smaller, shorter mifongo. In Rombo and the lower areas, people very quickly became dependent on pipes. Local knowledge of water became less important, and local specialists held less of an esteemed role. It is safe to say that over time, uphill and downhill communities came to see the waterscape differently. Though both shared the same fundamental view of the mountain as the source of water and of life, they possessed different ideas about what constituted relevant management knowledge and who could exercise it. The erosion of local management knowledge, particularly in lower areas, became increasingly problematic as the government proved unable to adequately maintain these new systems.

7 ◦ Water Is Our Gift from God!
Devolution and Cost Recovery in the Neoliberal Era

ON NOVEMBER 4, 1985, Julius Nyerere delivered his final speech as president of Tanzania at the Diamond Jubilee Hall in Dar es Salaam.[1] After serving for nearly twenty-five years, Mwalimu's term ended with the election of his successor, Ali Hassan Mwinyi, and a peaceful transition of power. On this solemn occasion, he recalled many of the successes and failures of his time in office. He noted with pride that Tanzanians had "built a nation—together," and that "the angel Gabriel could not have built Tanzania alone, still less a fallible man." In his eyes, creating a strong sense of Tanzanian identity and unity by overcoming religious differences and tribalism stood as his crowning achievement. Tanzania had become a "proud, united, and self-confident nation." However, Nyerere did acknowledge the severe economic troubles facing the country. He noted that "over the last six or seven years our country has been hit by many events over which neither Government nor people had any control. Our standard of living has consequently gone down instead of going up." Nyerere cited drought, the fall in export prices, and international recession as causes of the troubles, factors he considered beyond the reach of his policies. He thanked his fellow countrymen for facing "the sacrifices" and fighting "the difficulties together." Throughout the speech, Nyerere describes a Tanzania that was fighting the good fight. Despite economic problems, the people had made tremendous strides in coming together as a nation.

A notable aspect of Nyerere's speech is that he never once mentioned the defining policy of his time in office, Ujamaa. While his government's policy of social and economic development did achieve some successes, notably a pervasive sense of Tanzanian national identity, it proved to be an economic failure. By the mid-1980s, the country faced widespread shortages, hyperinflation, falling agricultural production, declining exports, rising corruption, a stalling manufacturing sector, balance-of-payments deficits, and skyrocketing debt. Villagization, the "ideological backbone" of Ujamaa, had proved unpopular and ineffective in raising agricultural production.[2] For Kilimanjaro, the period was especially devastating. Long an economic powerhouse, the mountain's coffee industry faced falling prices and disastrous government interventions such as enforcing price controls and disbanding the KNCU. By 1985, Tanzania stood at the edge of a precipice: it had become one of the poorest countries in the world. At the beginning of Mwinyi's term, the government and the International Monetary Fund (IMF) initiated a comprehensive economic-recovery program designed to restore economic stability and accelerate reforms.[3] The next decade saw a series of structural adjustments that were painful for many Tanzanians.

Water management exemplifies the dramatic nature of policy change in the neoliberal period. During Ujamaa, the government considered water to be a national resource, a basic human need that it should provide for free. It invested heavily in large-scale development projects meant to provide more and better water to people. In the process, it undermined local forms of water management that reinforced notions of authority and belonging, forms that it deemed harmful to the nation. The government's attempts to manage water centrally and provide it free of charge proved unsustainable. As the economy faltered, new projects depended on donor money, and insufficient funds were available for maintenance and cleaning, leading to the decay of recently built systems. The adoption of neoliberal reforms after 1985 led to a push for what development agencies call Integrated Water Resources Management (IWRM). This refers to a holistic and coordinated approach to water management that accounts for the need of users as well as environmental sustainability. The shift to IWRM brought about two notable changes in policy: devolution and cost recovery. Control over water shifted from the central government to regional water basin authorities, such as the Pangani Basin Water Office, which then devolved some control to local water user associations (WUAs). These new agencies expected users to pay for water not only from pipes but from mifongo as well. Those who promoted IWRM justified charging tariffs and fees by citing the need to generate revenue for maintenance, revitalization, and new systems, as well as the concern with water conservation. Both policy changes, in theory, would promote local partnership in management and greater resource sustainability. Yet they also promoted the notion that water is a commodity, an economic good rather than a human right.

These reforms have proved controversial on Kilimanjaro. For centuries, the peoples of the mountain have considered the waterscape to be their divine right, a gift from God. Throughout Ujamaa, they resisted attempts to centralize control of their resources. Yet over time, local water-management knowledge declined in many areas, as did the social networks that made mfongo irrigation possible. The shift to more local management might seem to be a positive development, but in practice little real power has made its way back to communities. The Pangani Basin Water Office, which retains policy-making authority and control over allocation, considers mifongo to be primitive and wasteful and considers clan-based canal societies to be inefficient and insufficiently participatory. The new WUAs provide some role for local communities in water management, but they are divisive and seen as illegitimate and overly political. The shift to cost recovery has been even less popular. Though there is a long history of contributing labor and mbege for water, the notion of cash payment violates cultural norms. The shift to a model in which people pay for water that was previously free has generated responses ranging from outright disregard and grudging acceptance to sabotage and water theft. The response is most vehement regarding the mifongo, for which the government charges fees even though it contributes nothing to maintenance. Overall, water policy reforms over the past thirty years have disregarded local management knowledge. While in some cases they have improved access to water, they have frequently alienated the mountain's population.

THE DECLINE OF UJAMAA AND RISE OF THE NEOLIBERAL STATE

Ujamaa was an ambitious program aimed at nation building, economic growth, social development, and self-reliance. It sought to raise living standards and reduce poverty for all Tanzanians. Nyerere laid out specific policies for the program in the *Second Five-Year Plan for Economic and Social Development* in 1969.[4] Rural agricultural development lay at the core of the government's strategy. It aimed to modernize agriculture through technological advancement and central planning, such as using price controls and agglomerating peasant farmers into planned villages. These collective communities, called Ujamaa villages, would increase production while eliminating class distinctions and inequality. The surplus generated would in turn provide resources for developing services such as health care, education, and water provision as well as industry. Expanding access to water became crucial to the government's rural-development strategy. The government also nationalized key industries and cooperative societies and managed them as parastatals. This gave it the ability to plan the economy centrally with minimal wastage of resources. In 1973, Nyerere announced the government's intention to move the capital from Dar es Salaam to the more centrally located town of Dodoma. The creation of an entirely new capital, at the heart of the country, symbolized the massive program of transformation being undertaken.

Nyerere sold Ujamaa as a program that would foster self-reliance. By building a socialist state, he would bring economic growth and create a society with a shared identity, unmarred by class distinctions. Initially, many shared in his enthusiasm. As Edwards notes, aid agencies—particularly from the Nordic countries—praised the strategy, especially the villagization component.[5] Money flooded in from donor countries and the World Bank, foreign aid flows rising from $22.6 per capita in 1967 to $65.3 in 1974 and reaching $82 in 1982. Swedish academic Goran Hyden referred to Tanzania as the "shining star" of Africa in 1967, a sentiment echoed by prominent Swedish politicians such as Prime Minister Olaf Palme and State Secretary for Development Cooperation Lennart Klackenberg.[6] In 1973, the World Bank's Country Program Note remarked that "from a donor's point of view Tanzania comes close to being a model development country" and that "development policies and priorities are generally well thought and well-conceived."[7] Much of this money flooded into the rural water development sector, enabling the development of piped systems, boreholes, and taps across the country. For its first few years, Ujamaa was viewed by development specialists as an exemplar strategy for African development, and it achieved some notable successes. Primary school enrollments soared from 25 percent at independence to 93 percent in 1980.[8] Adult illiteracy fell markedly, from 80 percent in 1961 to 5 percent in 1985. Access to health-care facilities and medical personnel likewise improved. Availability of piped water—the standard for "more and better water"—improved from 750,000 Tanzanians served in 1961 to at least 10 million by 1980.

By the early 1970s, however, the Tanzanian economy began to struggle. Agricultural production stagnated amid depressed prices and people's reluctance to move into Ujamaa villages. Only 15.5 percent of rural Tanzanians, and only 2 percent of rural peoples of Kilimanjaro, had settled in Ujamaa villages as of 1973.[9] The onset of severe drought in 1972 and the oil crisis of 1973 exacerbated these problems. Displaced from lands they knew and forced to cultivate crops designated by the government, people were less able to adjust to reduced precipitation. Many water systems, such as those in Ujamaa villages and in the lowlands of Kilimanjaro, had been designed to provide only for domestic needs and livestock. Without irrigation, people had no way to counter the effects of drought. Furthermore, the oil crisis caused prices for agricultural inputs such as fertilizer and pesticide to skyrocket. The combination of drought and increased prices for key goods contributed to more than two years of famine. In 1973, the government took several steps to address these issues. It created the National Price Commission to control the price of goods and curb inflation. It also embarked on Operation Vijiji, a plan to relocate people into communal villages, by force if necessary. By 1975, more than 5 million people had been moved into six thousand villages, one of the largest resettlement efforts in African history.[10] In response to food shortages, the government purchased large quantities of maize from overseas for the first time in its history.

The economic troubles had deep implications for Kilimanjaro. For the most part, villagization had little effect in the agroforest belt. Because of the mountain's dense population, the government merely reorganized mitaa into a series of "cooperative villages" that were mostly administrative.[11] Some Ujamaa villages were developed in lowland areas south of the main road, such as Chekereni, located along the Ruvu River between Moshi Town and the Nyumba ya Mungu Dam.[12] Relatively few people from the mountain ended up settling in these communities. Though villagization had little impact, the drought, the oil crisis, and new government policies proved devastating to mountain communities. Coffee yields suffered because of insufficient water for irrigation and reduced use of fertilizers and pesticides, and government policy prohibited people from pulling up coffee trees and planting foodstuffs. This left many people with insufficient funds to buy food. Mary Howard and Ann Millard note that the conditions of 1972–74 exacerbated inequalities and led to a rise in child malnutrition across the mountain.[13] In 1976 the government abolished the KNCU and replaced it with a state-managed marketing board.[14] The decision, motivated by both economics and politics, dealt another blow to the coffee industry. The board proved inefficient, corrupt, and unable to adjust to the market realities of coffee. Despite a temporary spike in global coffee prices from 1975 to 1977, domestic-producer prices for coffee declined significantly as a fraction of export prices in the late 1970s, from 57 percent to 28 percent.[15] By the end of the decade, the mountain was a poorer place than it had been a decade before, and a far cry from the heyday of the 1950s.

Between 1969 and 1974, GDP growth per capita averaged only 0.66 percent, well beneath the expected growth rate of 3.7 percent.[16] By 1976, Tanzania had become the twenty-fifth-poorest country on Earth. Furthermore, declining performance in the agricultural sector contributed to a lack of foreign-exchange earnings. This stalled the manufacturing sector, which was dependent on imports, and also precipitated a balance-of-payment crisis. As the decade went on, conditions worsened. Profits from parastatals and the agricultural sector declined, and the government printed money and ran deficits to maintain services. It continued to borrow large sums from donors, so much that by 1977, foreign aid financed almost 60 percent of its development budget.[17] Another blow in 1977 was the dissolution of the East African Community, the economic partnership with Kenya and Uganda. In October 1978, Ugandan forces invaded Tanzania's northwest Kagera region. Nyerere mobilized the army, fought back the invasion, and sent his troops into Uganda after dictator Idi Amin. By 1979, Amin had fled and Tanzanian troops had taken control of Kampala. The Organization of African Unity saw the invasion as an act of aggression and offered no financial backing. Tanzania took on debt to finance the war and subsequent peacekeeping operation. Furthermore, the oil crisis of 1979 resulted in another set of price spikes for fuel and agricultural inputs, and another major drought in 1980 created more setbacks for agricultural production.

Facing bankruptcy, Nyerere and the ruling party, Chama Cha Mapinduzi (which succeeded TANU in 1977), sought assistance from the

IMF. In 1979 the IMF developed a recovery program that included a package of loans in exchange for reforms. These included liberalizing interest rates and imports, removing price controls, reforming parastatals, reducing government expenditures, and devaluing the currency. Nyerere, however, found the conditions unacceptable and rejected the call for currency devaluation.[18] Unable to come to terms, he rebuked the proposal and expelled the IMF team. Nyerere defended his actions as necessary to protect his people from being bullied by wealthy foreign interests. Yet the calls for reform became only more fervent. In 1980, Elliot Berg at the World Bank published a report entitled *Accelerated Development in Sub-Saharan Africa: An Agenda for Action*.[19] Known more commonly as the Berg report, it calls on African states to implement free-market liberalization policies including "correction of overvalued exchange rates . . . improved price incentives for exports and for agriculture; lower and more uniform protection for industry; and reduced use of direct controls."[20] It also suggests streamlining government and parastatals and allowing the private sector to take on a bigger share of public services, such as water development. Most notably, it calls for "policy action and foreign assistance that are mutually reinforcing," or making donor money conditional on political reform.[21] In Berg's opinion, donors needed to leverage loan and aid money to encourage states such as Tanzania to adopt economic liberalization.

Reluctant to abandon African socialism or embrace reform, Tanzania continued to experience economic decline. Staunch supporters such as Norway, Finland, Sweden, and the Netherlands began to withdraw financial support. In 1985, with his country facing imminent economic collapse, Nyerere announced his intention not to seek another term as Tanzania's president. Ali Hassan Mwinyi, Nyerere's handpicked successor, came to power on November 5, 1985. Mwinyi opened dialogue with the IMF and worked to repair the country's relationship with the international development community. In the fall of 1986, Tanzania and the IMF agreed to terms on an economic-recovery program, the first in a series of structural-adjustment programs that marked the end of Ujamaa and the rise of neoliberal reform. In exchange for a series of financial disbursements, the government agreed to a package of reforms that included devaluing currency, reducing price controls, raising interest rates, liberalizing exports, and reducing the number of parastatals. The first few years of reform saw progress:

between 1986 and 1990, per capita GDP grew at an average of 2.2 percent.[22] Yet in 1991, Tanzania was the second-poorest country on earth, next to war-torn Mozambique. The early 1990s saw stagnation and negative growth rates, along with high inflation and mismanagement of parastatals. Frustration grew between the IMF and the World Bank, the Tanzanian government, and international donors.

The situation began to stabilize in the mid-1990s with the implementation of a new round of reforms. In 1995, Benjamin Mkapa succeeded Mwinyi as president of Tanzania. Two years later, his government laid out a plan called the *Tanzania National Development Vision, 2025.*[23] The document set forth the goal of transforming Tanzania into a middle-income country by 2025. This would involve transitioning the economy away from low-productivity agriculture and toward industry and modern, high-productivity agriculture. Though similar to the Arusha Declaration, the *Vision* is a neoliberal product and clearly expresses the desire of the government to embrace reform and the global economy. Furthermore, it explicitly criticizes the policies of Ujamaa, noting that "the strategy of the Arusha Declaration did not sufficiently address the complexity and dynamic character of policies and incentive structures which were necessary to effectively drive the development process." Mkapa's government accelerated the pace of reform, working to privatize parastatals and implement fiscal reform. By 2000, the economy began to show signs of sustained growth, although the country remained poor and lacked resources to invest in infrastructure and social services.

THE HARM OF FREE WATER

For Tanzanians, the shift from Ujamaa to neoliberalism had a tremendous impact on everyday life. Reforms such as currency devaluation created hardships for families struggling to purchase food and agricultural inputs. Critics of structural-adjustment policies have noted how the poorest populations often bear the deepest burden of reforms. Less often discussed is how some neoliberal policies are diametric opposites of those that preceded them. For example, the development of water resources was a centerpiece of rural development initiatives under Ujamaa, crucial to both economic- and social-development goals. Two key premises defined rural water policy: that water should be a national resource provided by the government to its people, and that it should be provided for free. These policies were reversed as part of neoliberal reform in the 1980s and 1990s.

The policy of providing water for free, though popular among the people, had many critics. In a presentation during a workshop on rural water supply at the University of Dar es Salaam in 1969, G. L. Cunningham expressed concern that the provision of free water was contrary to the values of Ujamaa.[24] By providing water free of charge, the government actually lost an opportunity to teach self-help and self-reliance. The policy made users dependent on systems managed by the government, and thus dependent on outside management knowledge. Gerhard Tschannerl, senior research fellow at the university's Bureau of Resource Assessment and Land Use Planning, criticized the free-water model for promoting neocolonial dependency. He observed that "although the aims of water supply had undergone a change with independence, the means of planning and building them [had] not."[25] Foreign donors funded most water projects, which relied on foreign expertise and involved minimal input from local users. Tschannerl criticized foreign technocrats for chastising locals with phrases such as "they don't know" and "they don't understand."[26] He concluded by saying that the government had created a "client relationship between government staff and peasants . . . that is the ideology of the bureaucratic bourgeoisie as opposed to proletarian ideology." Others criticized the policy for being financially unsustainable. In 1971, the University of Dar es Salaam held a conference on rural water supply in East Africa. Experts in the field debated the pros and cons of the free-water policy, eventually concluding that water needed to be an economic good rather than a social good.[27] Donor agencies also became concerned at the rising costs and lack of provision for maintenance funds. Referring to a water project in Mtwara funded by the Finnish International Development Agency, Matti Viitasaari, professor of engineering at the Tampere University of Technology, concluded that it was not possible to sustain water development and provide for maintenance without a cost-recovery mechanism.[28] By the time the regional water master plans were completed, Tanzania was in economic turmoil and unable to fund the recommended projects. Nonetheless, water projects in the period provided free water to nearly ten million people by 1980.

Though many specialists within and outside Tanzania had growing concerns about the free-water strategy, Nyerere's government remained steadfast. Throughout the 1970s it worked to expand government control over the water sector. In 1974, it passed the Water Utilization (Control and Regulation) Act, which finally ended the separate legal spheres of water control that had existed since 1923. It called upon all those who "divert, dam, store, abstract, and use" water to register a water right with the government, including those claiming a customary right.[29] The law also created a top-down hierarchical structure for water control, with a national Ministry of Water (nicknamed MAJI), a Central Water Advisory Board, regional water boards, and local water officers. The government further monopolized control of water by promoting large-scale projects and mandating that the Water Development and Irrigation Department, an office of MAJI, manage most of them. Lastly, Nyerere continued to solicit donor money for projects. While in West Germany in 1976, he extolled the value of such projects in making people's lives better, noting, "For a woman who now has to walk miles for water, a village tap might mean life itself." Selling water projects in humanitarian terms proved effective, and money flooded into the sector.

The flaws of the government's approach soon became too evident to ignore. Even with donor support, MAJI lacked the financial resources to meet the needs of its projects. Between 1972 and 1984, the government only paid out the full budgeted amount for rural water development once, in 1982. In 1978 it paid out only 62 percent of the funds budgeted. In 1984, it was 73 percent.[30] With the economy near collapse and the government at a stalemate with the IMF, donors pushed the government to implement cost recovery. In November 1980, the United States Agency for International Development completed a study entitled *Rural Water Projects in Tanzania: Technical, Social, and Administrative Issues*.[31] It focused on the problem of inadequate funds for staff training and maintenance, noting that in 1976 the government provided only 10 percent of the funds required for maintenance. The study presented three arguments supporting why users should pay for water. It argued that funds were inadequate to ensure the continued operation of rural systems, that users were able and willing to pay for water, and that when users help decide on a payment system, it becomes a community agreement supported by the pressure of community residents.[32] The study made a number of overgeneralizations about Tanzania, such as assuming that the views of people in arid areas like

Shinyanga would translate to places like Kilimanjaro, and assuming that the experiences of Latin America were directly applicable. Yet it indicates how the development community had turned against free water. The Berg report also criticized free-water programs by noting, "It is clear that the only hope of broadly based provision of services in a self-reliant Africa is through greater emphasis on charging beneficiaries for the services they receive."[33]

By 1980, the country faced a backlog of unfinished water projects and an escalating problem of maintenance and upkeep. Although Kilimanjaro had fared better than other regions in building piped systems because of strong coffee revenues from the 1960s, many of these systems began failing within two decades. The piped supply projects built in the 1960s and 1970s had been designed with a forty-year life span.[34] This did not, however, account for the high mineral content of the water, which corroded the metal pipes, nor did it account for breakage. Buried only 15 centimeters deep, the pipes were frequently struck by farmers while tilling the soil, resulting in breaks that often went ignored or unreported. By the 1980s, many pipelines were corroded or broken and provided insufficient water for the population. Mafundi, the employees charged with maintaining the pipes, lacked the training to address serious problems, and parts for repairs were not easy to find. Furthermore, they often went long periods without receiving paychecks, making them more susceptible to bribery. The lack of local buy-in for pipe maintenance became a liability. Nyerere admitted as much in a 1982 speech at the Second Ordinary Party Conference: "Whatever the technique used, for building water supplies, it must be adopted in consultation with the local people, and from the beginning the responsibility for looking after the facilities must clearly be theirs. The government cannot finance the maintenance and repair work of basic village equipment if new developments are to go ahead."[35]

Nyerere's statement was too late; the government had already invested millions into inadequate and failing systems that had been designed purposefully to exclude local participation. Furthermore, water management at the national level tended to be by fiat, and numerous aspects of water law were partially enacted or not enacted at all. One example was a 1981 amendment to the 1974 water law to create water basin authorities. As of 1985, no steps had been taken to designate any of these, and management still rested largely in the hands of MAJI. As a result, only 40 percent of Tanzanians, and 57 percent of people from Kilimanjaro, had access to sufficient drinking water.[36] The Ujamaa strategy for providing more and better water ultimately failed to provide either.

WATER REFORM IN THE POST-UJAMAA ERA

In the early years of Mwinyi's presidency, the Tanzanian government began investigating potential reforms to address the problems of the water sector. This reflected the broader movement toward liberalization of the economy and structural adjustment, as well as the increasing influence of international actors in national decision-making. In March 1986, MAJI cohosted a seminar in Arusha with the Norwegian National Committee for Hydrology. The seminar, entitled Implementation of Rural Water Supply and Sanitation in Tanzania, focused on how to develop an immediate and long-term plan for water resource development. One of the earliest presenters, S. J. Makundi, emphasized community participation.[37] He noted that despite the national ideology of socialism and self-reliance, involvement of beneficiaries had been very minimal. He attributed this to several things, including water's being a "free service, poor mobilization of the people, use of paid labor, and non-involvement of women." The government and donors had to meet the full costs of projects, and as resources became more restricted, the approach proved too costly. To move forward, users needed to contribute to the financial costs of water provision. Makundi remarked that "both the Government and the donors have come to realize that drinking water is not a 'God Given' free service. The cost involved is enormous and should be borne or at least shared by beneficiaries." The seminar reached consensus that the future of water development should be driven by less central management, by more regional and community engagement, and with users contributing to maintenance costs.

In 1991, these concepts became part of the government's new National Water Policy (NWP).[38] Prepared by MAJI, the NWP was a set of principles to guide water development and bring aspects of existing law into practice. It set the goal of providing clean and safe water to the whole population of the country, within 400 meters of each homestead, by the end of 2020.[39] Under the NWP, the state retained control over water, but planning and management shifted to the nine basin-level authorities. The first basin-level authority, the Pangani Basin Water Office, opened in July 1991. The basin created an administrative unit that included Kilimanjaro, Meru, the Pare and Usambara Mountains, and the entirety of the Pangani River and its tributaries to the Indian Ocean (see map 7.1). This included 2.6 million people and 43,650 square kilometers of territory.[40] Oversight of the office lay with the Pangani Basin Water Board. Composed of individuals appointed by MAJI, the board set policy for the basin and managed the activities of the office. The creation of basin offices and boards represented the first step in

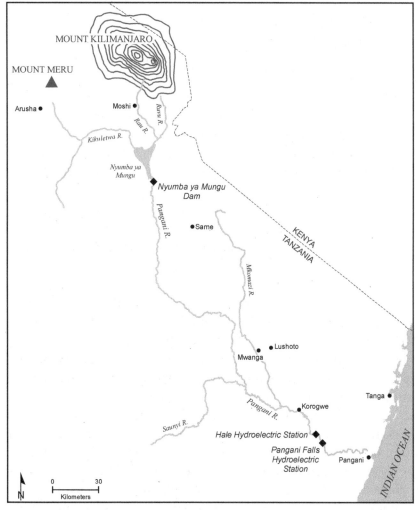

MAP 7.1. The Pangani Basin (*Brian Edward Balsley, GISP*)

Devolution and Cost Recovery in the Neoliberal Era ⇐ 211

devolving water control to regional actors. The NWP also was the first government policy to treat water as an economic good, a commodity for which people should pay. It called for the implementation of cost recovery by charging users to file for water rights, as well as charging them for usage by volume (volumetric pricing).

The NWP laid out two substantial changes in water management: a devolution of central authority and the start of cost recovery. Meanwhile, development agencies called for deeper changes that would bring about more community involvement. Consensus began to take form at the International Conference on Water and the Environment, held in Dublin, Ireland, on January 31, 1992. At this meeting, delegates released a statement entitled the Dublin Statement on Water and Sustainable Development.[41] Citing the threats facing water supplies worldwide, the statement laid out guiding principles to shape the management of these resources.

1. Fresh water is a finite and vulnerable resource, essential to sustain life, development, and the environment.
2. Water development and management should be based on a participatory approach, involving users, planners, and policymakers at all levels.
3. Women play a central part in the provision, management, and safeguarding of water.
4. Water has an economic value in all its competing uses and should be recognized as an economic good.

These principles align with the trend toward devolution and cost recovery, but what makes them notable is how they define a "participatory approach." They specifically identify women as having a key role in water management, and they indicate that management should involve users as well as planners and policymakers. The document advances this point by saying that decisions should be made at "the lowest appropriate level, with full public consultation and involvement of users in the planning and implementation of water projects." Under this model, basin authorities would become planning and allocation bodies, while community-based agencies would handle daily management and conflict resolution. The principles reaffirm a "basic right of all human beings to have access to clean water and sanitation at an affordable price" but note that "past failure to recognize the economic value of water has led to wasteful and environmentally damaging uses of the resource." Thinking of water as an economic good would allow for "efficient and equitable use, and of encouraging conservation and protection."

The Dublin Principles emerged as the gold standard for neoliberal water development, and in 2002 they became part of a new NWP. This new policy established the goal of providing universal access to drinking water by 2025. It also embraced an IWRM approach to water development. In short, this involved planning the resource in a way that involved policymakers, donors, engineers, and users across sectors while considering environmental sustainability. The new policy outlined three major shifts in national policy toward water management:[42]

1. Comprehensiveness: A holistic basin approach for integrating multi-sector and multi-objective planning and management that minimizes the effects of externalities, and ensures sustainability and protection of the resource.

2. Subsidiarity: Decentralizing decision-making and devolving to the lowest practicable level, with stakeholders participating in the planning, design, implementation of the management actions and decision-making.

3. Economic: Decision-making in the public sector, in the private sector, and in civil society on the use of water should reflect the scarcity and value of water as well as water pricing, cost sharing, and other incentives for promoting the rational use of water.

Several aspects of the policy are notable. It considers water users to be stakeholders and partners who should have a voice. The policy outlines four levels of decision-making: national, basin, district, and community or user level. The basin retains its role as the main planning body, but community-level participation is considered crucial to the implementation of management programs. It calls for the creation of community-level WUAs to handle local allocation of water and mediation of disputes and to promote efficient and effective use of water as well as respect for the law and the conditions of water rights. These communities would serve as "the primary users, guardians, and managers of water sources."[43] Furthermore, the emphasis on community involvement represents a departure from more than two decades of water policy that had created no space for the views and opinions of users.

Another aspect of the policy is how it speaks of water as an economic good: "Recognizing the extent to which the water source contributes to economic productivity on the one hand, and the financial investments required for water development on the other, development of water for productive purposes will, therefore, be treated as an economic undertaking requiring efficient management of the resource and financed by water users themselves."[44] While it identifies that "water is a basic need and right" for all Tanzanians, it emphasizes the importance of payment. The power to determine the level of tariffs and fees rests with the basin and community authorities. Furthermore, the policy shows a further shift toward thinking of water as a commodity. It defines the basic level of service for domestic water in rural areas in terms of quantity: 25 liters per capita per day year-round, within 400 meters, and with no more than 250 persons per outlet.[45] It also calls on water systems to be "owned" by communities, as a means of promoting active participation and sustainable use of water. Lastly, the document is the first to describe women as partners in water management and the first to have provisions for environmental sustainability. It calls for "fair representation" of women in local water committees and for programs to "raise awareness, train, and empower women to actively participate at all levels in water programs, including decision making."[46] Toward sustainability, it calls not only for conserving water resources, but also for ensuring the health of ecosystems and biological diversity.[47] To this end, it requires new water projects to complete environmental-impact assessments.

The 2002 NWP represented the culmination of more than a decade of changing views toward water. It also set the framework for a new irrigation master plan and a new water law, the Water Resources Management Act of 2009, that replaced the outdated 1974 law and its amendments. The new policy, master plan, and water law were decidedly neoliberal, focusing on private sector investment, devolution, and cost recovery. They also indicate the extent to which the IMF, the World Bank, and governmental development agencies had shaped policy. Despite the rhetoric of local engagement, water management was now more in the hands of outsiders than ever before. Furthermore, new policies remained laden with contradictions, such as which sectors had priority (e.g., hydroelectric or irrigation) or which group had certain powers, local communities vis-à-vis the basin authorities. Most importantly, the presence of policies did not mean that they were applied fairly and effectively. Often, the lofty ideals extolled in documents remained but ideals. This is evident in the Pangani Basin, the most economically important of the basin regions and the one most plagued by conflicts.

STRUGGLES OVER WATER IN THE PANGANI BASIN

In 1991, the Pangani Basin Water Office (PBWO) became Tanzania's first basin-level planning authority. As such, it pioneered the government's new approach to management. The basin grouped together more than 2.4 million users across tens of thousands of kilometers. It included mountains and steppe, highland farmers and pastoralists, urban users and rural, and industrial agriculture and hydropower interests. The two key principles of basin management were equality and fairness, values extolled in the 2002 NWP and the 2009 water law. Yet it took little time for the basin to become an arena for struggle between competing interests. The basin authority, a product of neoliberal policymaking and scientific management, has tended to side with downstream users while criticizing mountain irrigators in language reminiscent of that of the British in the 1930s. While mountain communities describe water as a gift from God that is rightfully theirs and should be free, basin planners and development agencies have co-opted this expression to explain away the deeper cultural significance of water.

The PBWO opened for business with a main office in Moshi Town and branches in Arusha and Tanga. It featured a water officer who served as a director, as well as other staff including a hydrologist, a hydrogeologist, an environmental engineer, a chemist, community-development officers, technicians, accountants, supplies officers, secretaries, and drivers. A board, consisting of ten members, handled the policy- and decision-making tasks of the office. The minister of water appointed these board members from public institutions and the private sector. The board held the power to set policy for the basin and manage all water rights and abstractions. The office staff, meanwhile, functioned as a science and research body and oversaw day-to-day operations.

The PBWO's mission statement called for it to "ensure that water resources are managed sustainably, through water governance and integrated water resources management principles." Its ultimate vision was to "achieve a sustainable management and development of water resources, providing equitable opportunities and benefits to the basin population and Tanzania as a whole."[48]

Conditions on the ground challenged these lofty ideals. The basin faced increasing demand for water from all sectors, as well as the continued problem of poor data. Furthermore, the government had recently committed to two major projects in the basin. The first of these was the Lower Moshi Irrigation Scheme. Developed by the Japan International Cooperation Agency (JICA), the plan called for redeveloping four Ujamaa villages 17 kilometers southeast of Moshi Town into a massive 2,300-hectare estate, of which 1,100 hectares would be reserved for rice paddy cultivation.[49] The scheme relied on the development of a massive irrigation system that would draw water from two rivers and a series of boreholes. It came online in 1986 but was plagued from the start by insufficient water. It did not help that precipitation at the site averaged 590 millimeters per year.[50] The government, which inherited ownership of the scheme from JICA, placed pressure on the PBWO to provide more water downstream. A second project, redeveloping the Pangani Falls Power Station, likewise placed pressure on the PBWO. In 1989, the Norwegian, Finnish, and Swedish governments agreed to finance jointly the Pangani Falls Redevelopment Project.[51] Their plan called for an entirely new power station to replace the original built in the 1930s, providing 66 megawatts of power at a cost of $127 million. Combined with Nyumba ya Mungu and Hale, the Pangani System would contribute 17 percent of the country's total electrical output. As the opening date for the project approached, concerns arose that there would be insufficient water in the Pangani to run it at capacity.

In its first year of operation, the PBWO gathered data on the watershed to get a sense of the water available and how it was being used. It also sought to identify registered and nonregistered water abstractions.[52] The idea behind this research was to measure the amount of available water in comparison to how much had been allocated through water rights. They counted a total of 1,015 abstractions with registered water rights.[53] These users had been allocated a total of 33.4 cubic meters of water per second.[54] They also estimated at least 1,881 unregistered abstractions, most of which were mifongo. This meant that the actual water draw on the basin approached 48 cubic meters per second. Given that between 30 and 40 percent of the annual runoff from Kilimanjaro went to mifongo, mountain farmers were consuming water that had legally been allocated to downstream users.[55] Simply put, there was not enough water to meet the demands of all users.

The PBWO viewed mifongo as the culprit in this crisis of overallocation. As of the early 1990s, more than five hundred canals remained in use, and though fewer than in previous decades, they were still the primary water source for thousands of people. The PBWO considered most mifongo to be illegal because they lacked a registered water right. Furthermore, the office held that such systems were a "waste of water."[56] It decided against banning mifongo outright, and instead it instituted measures to control them and encourage more conscientious use of water.[57] In 1991, it introduced a new system of statutory water rights for all "customary" canals, and it sent officials into communities to force people to register them. It also raised the cost for registering a water right from TSh100 to TSh40,000 to cover expenses. As part of these rights, it introduced volumetric fees. In addition to a one-time registration fee, mfongo users were charged TSh15 per 1,000 cubic meters of water consumed. Using a grant from the Norwegian Agency for Development Cooperation, it constructed concrete sluice gates on more than three hundred canals. These structures, built just beneath the intakes, featured movable metal gates designed to limit the flow of water (see fig. 7.1). The office intended for these structures to prevent wastage by channeling more water into rivers, making more available for storage in Nyumba ya Mungu. To improve communication with communities, it organized a so-called Awareness Committee to go around to villages and inform local officials about the basin authority and its plans for managing water. Lastly, the PBWO set out to reform canal societies into registered, standardized WUAs.[58] This action was intended to make managers of canals more accountable and responsive to government initiatives.

Rather than stimulating cooperation, these actions provoked widespread anger and resistance, particularly regarding the issue of payment. As they had for centuries, mountain peoples considered water to be their divine inheritance. Martin Mosha recalled this period with frustration, noting that "water is owned by God."[59] Epifania Mbando, a

FIGURE 7.1. Sluice gate, Machame (*Matthew V. Bender*)

housewife living nearby, concurred by saying that "it is God who brings water."[60] While gifts of tribute had long been a part of the social world of the mifongo, cash payments struck a nerve as a violation of cultural norms. Mattias Tagseth, in his research in Marangu, received similar responses. One of his interviewees remarked that "all water is a gift from God. It is a sin to pay for water. A sin against God."[61] What most infuriated users was that their ancestors had given them the mifongo as an inheritance, and the mifongo persisted because of their labor. The government contributed nothing to them, yet now it expected payment. Canal committees resisted the increasing government influence over their canals, and as of 1995, less than 5 percent had applied for water rights.[62] The sluice gates became a target of people's anger. Irrigators circumvented them by constructing bypasses, and some even engaged in vandalism that rendered them unusable. By 2009, only 20 percent of sluice gates still functioned.

The conflict that arose between the PBWO and mountain irrigators has been described by geographer Haakon Lein as a "conflict between indigenous water management practices and a technocratic water management system promoted through the PBWO."[63] The office viewed mifongo as harmful because they were unregulated, haphazard, and seemingly unnecessary. Rather than stop people from irrigating, the office sought to impose order on the system through instruments such as tariffs, rights, and sluice gates. The PBWO spoke of resistance by noting that mountain people considered water to be a "gift from God."[64] By invoking this phrase, however, the office was not recognizing a legitimate grievance, but rather reducing it to a superstitious belief. Office staff spoke of their work in communities as informative, a mission to change "attitudes and perceptions."[65] They spent little effort to understand the deeper cultural meanings of water or to engage local farmers in meaningful dialogue. This lack of empathy was evident in the process for applying for water rights. The application required the applicant to submit data such as the volume of water being abstracted, a foreign thought for people accustomed to measuring water in time, not volume. Furthermore, the PBWO discouraged applications for water rights that came from clans.[66] Since clan-based societies controlled nearly all mifongo, especially in the highlands, this precluded most people from applying. As a result, the PBWO granted almost no water rights for mifongo between 1995 and 2000. As of 2005, there were more than 1,000 users in the basin with registered water rights and still an estimated 1,800 abstractions without.[67] Also, very few people actually paid for water. In 2003 and 2004, only 150 users paid fees to the PBWO, most of whom were large-scale farmers and TANESCO.

The government created the PBWO as a tool for allocating and managing water, thus ideally promoting development and alleviating conflict. Instead, it became the focal point of "fierce competition over available water resources between, among others, upstream versus downstream users, large estates versus local farmers, and agriculture versus hydropower."[68] The basin office conglomerated a diverse array of interests, but it showed preference toward large-scale projects, downstream users, and those with political clout or support from the development community. Mountainside irrigators were dismissed as people who refused to embrace change, and therefore they lacked any voice in decision-making. The office's staff included individuals trained in technocratic water management who were ill-equipped to see the social and economic significance of the mifongo. Furthermore, the Pangani Basin Water Board consisted of appointees drawn from the policy sector and large-scale interests. Not a single smallholder from Kilimanjaro or elsewhere in the basin has ever held a seat.

To address the continuing conflict between upstream and downstream users, the PBWO initiated the Pangani Basin Water Management Project in 2002. A partnership with the International Union for the Conservation of Nature, the Netherlands Development Organization, and a local NGO called PAMOJA, it initiated a series of programs meant to promote water conservation and reduce conflict in the basin. One of these programs involved developing a dialogue process between community representatives, local and national government officials, and technical experts.[69] In a set of five test communities, they held stakeholder workshops to discuss the water situation, the activities of the PBWO, and conflicts that had arisen. Based on these, they made recommendations for improving relations with stakeholders. These included recognizing and accommodating traditional water governance, giving people a stake in resources as an incentive to use them sustainably, strengthening forums for dialogue (particularly WUAs), developing better dialogue processes, creating more inclusive processes to accommodate both legal and illegal users, building more local capacity, and considering the local context of history and politics.[70]

Despite these efforts, conflict is still rife in the basin, especially during dry periods. Between 2011 and 2014, a protracted drought afflicted the region. Water flows in the Pangani dropped so much that Hale and Pangani Falls generated at only a fraction of their capacity (9 megawatts and 32 megawatts, compared to 21 megawatts and 68 megawatts).[71] This resulted in nationwide rolling blackouts and TANESCO's firing threats at the PBWO and upstream irrigators. Naomi Lupimo, director of water resources protection at the Ministry of Water, said in an interview with a reporter that "the traditional canal irrigation schemes used by small-scale farmers in the upper Pangani basin were the major source of the dispute. These people have probably forgotten their traditional ways of conserving water sources, that's why they use it haphazardly as if there is no tomorrow. They must be reminded that the water belongs to the state and everybody has the right to it."[72] Her response indicates that despite attempts to promote dialogue, MAJI and the basin authority still consider mifongo to be the problem rather than a solution to region's water supply challenges. Though mountain farmers may be at the top of the watershed, they are at the bottom of the PBWO's concerns.

LOCAL INITIATIVES? REDEVELOPING PIPED WATER ON THE MOUNTAIN

Despite the tensions that have arisen from irrigation, there have been more successful attempts at community-engaged water development through efforts to revitalize pipes. In 1990, the Tanzanian government partnered with three German development agencies—DED, KfW, and GTZ—to address issues of water service.[73] Since then, they have developed four projects for revitalizing and expanding piped water to mountain communities and Moshi Town. In addition to new infrastructure, these projects included new management structures aimed at building local buy-in, increasing participation, and minimizing resistance to payment. The results have been mixed, some communities receptive and others resistant. Overall, the partnership reflects the recent trend toward community-based development and a move away from the large-scale projects of earlier decades.

The first partnership involved the redevelopment of water pipelines in Hai. In 1990, the government and the German agencies created the Hai District Water Supply Project, with the goal of rebuilding and extending the systems that had been built as part of the Rural Water Supply Programme. The first phase aimed to serve 140,000 people with clean drinking water.[74] From the start, it involved much more collaboration than previous projects. Technical experts from Germany consulted with officials from the Ministry of Water, the district water office, and the PBWO, and they solicited input from local communities. Once construction began, communities provided self-help (unpaid) manual labor such as trench excavation. Technical experts trained paid local staff to handle higher-skilled tasks such as masonry and carpentry. These laborers handled nearly all the project work including rehabilitation and construction of intakes, gravity pipes, reservoirs, break-pressure tanks, air valves, washouts, public taps, house connections, and meters.[75] As the first phase neared completion in 2013, the Germans and the government agreed to partner on three additional phases. As of 2015, the completed portions of the Hai District Water Supply carry 21,212 cubic meters of water per day to an estimated 426,000 people in the agroforest belt and near the Moshi-Arusha Road. The length of the pipe network is 1,028 kilometers, and it includes thirty-five intakes, 12,620 house connections, and 1,527 public taps. A total of €32 million has been spent, most contributed by Germany.

A novel aspect of the Hai Project is its institutional structure. The completed parts of the project have been handed over to four water supply trusts. These are "owned by the communities and operate independently of the district administration."[76] Managed by a board of trustees, they are responsible for setting rates and supervising management staff. Each community within a trust's area of coverage elects its own village water committee, which manages and maintains the system within its boundaries, discusses water-related problems raised by users, organizes self-help labor, allocates public taps, and elects representatives to the board. All users pay fees based on the volume of water consumed. The institutional structure of the system is designed to encourage participation and maximize the influence of end users, and for the most part it has been received positively. Communities have contributed more than €935,000 worth of self-help labor. According to the German Embassy, collection efficiency (the percentage of bills paid) exceeds 90 percent. Furthermore, the presence of village water committees has discouraged sabotage and water stealing.

The second partnership undertaken by the government and the German agencies was the redevelopment of the East Kilimanjaro system. As the oldest of the Rural Water Supply Programme pipe systems, it had fallen into decay by the early 1990s. Given the reticulated design of this system and Rombo's lower population density, the German agencies chose to organize a private nonprofit company rather than a trust to manage its redevelopment. This company, called Kiliwater Ltd., became Tanzania's first private water company in 1995. In 2001, Kiliwater began to redevelop the main intakes, trunk main, and storage tanks, with the goal of providing water for more than 300,000 users. Unlike in Hai, paid labor was used for all aspects of the work. By 2003, the supply network consisted of 900 kilometers of pipeline, 112 storage tanks, a 3.78-million-liter reservoir, eight thousand house connections, and more than one thousand public taps.[77] It also featured a water treatment facility, a rarity for rural water systems. Though Kiliwater succeeded in revitalizing the intakes, storage, and the trunk main and installed more than 2,600 water meters, many of the distribution lines and taps functioned poorly. In 2005, it embarked on a second phase of revitalization that focused on branch lines and extending the system to the north. As of 2007, it had spent more than €10.4 million on the system, mostly financed by Germany. By 2014, the system had the capacity to produce 40,000 cubic meters of water per day, serving more than 330,000 inhabitants.[78] An estimated 80 percent of residents in Rombo now depend on pipes as their main source of water.

Administratively, the private nonprofit Kiliwater is very different from the model used in Hai. As organized in 1995, it is a shareholder company governed by a board of directors, which includes the district water engineers of Rombo and Moshi Rural Districts and representatives from six supply zones and one subzone.[79] The board of directors appoints the management of the company, which takes care of technical services, customer relations, finance, and administration. The seven elected board members are chosen annually by the seventy-eight local water committees in the service area. Each committee has six elected members (three men and three women) and two standing members: the village chairperson and the village executive officer. These committees are responsible for acting as intermediaries between users and the company. Furthermore, all registered water users are eligible to become shareholders, and as of 2007, Kiliwater had more than fifteen thousand.[80]

On the whole, Kiliwater is more corporate and less participatory than Hai. Therefore, there has been less community buy-in and more resistance, which has included sabotage of pipes and taps, illegal connections, water theft, diverting water for irrigation, and refusal to pay bills. These problems have been most noticeable in Mwika, the only area of Moshi Rural District served by the system and also the home of the primary water intake. Leaders in Mwika have long complained that they should not pay a company in Rombo for water that rightfully belongs to them. Kiliwater's 2003 *Annual Progress Report* notes that in Mwika, "some few leaders and trouble fomenters induce/mobilize some people to act against the company by vandalizing structures and refusing to pay their water bills." Two years later, payment for water emerged as an issue in local elections, with candidates for Parliament and local council seats calling for a return to "free water."[81] Across the Kiliwater service region, people have appreciated the rising availability of water while resisting paying for it. In 2003, the company achieved a collection efficiency of 75 percent, quite a bit less than that of Hai. Moreover, the rate of illegal connections is alarmingly high. At the 2014 meeting of the Kiliwater board, Chairman Theodory Silayo admitted to shareholders that about 70 percent of the water produced was lost before it reached consumers, most through illegal connections.[82] In response to these problems, Kiliwater has dedicated resources to "sensitize" users to the importance of respecting the system and paying for water. Resistance to payment is higher in Rombo than in other areas partly because of the administrative structure of Kiliwater, which discourages buy-in, and also because of the greater poverty in the region. Many people do not have the resources to pay for water, which can cost as much as a single month's income for a year's worth of use.

In addition to the Kiliwater and Hai projects, the German agencies have also funded a redevelopment of the Moshi Urban Water Supply as well as a smaller project in Uchira, a small village on the Moshi-Himo Road. Each of these have different governing structures from those of Hai and Rombo. The most recently proposed project is the Moshi Rural District Water Supply. It calls for the revitalization of 800 kilometers of pipes, along with reservoirs, break-pressure tanks, house connections, and public taps. Water use will be metered, as in other rehabilitated systems. The estimated cost is €15 million, and it is estimated to serve four hundred thousand people, 90 percent of those in the service area. The proposed administrative structure is even more decentralized than that of Hai. It calls for a series of "independent legal registered community-based water supply organizations" under guidance from the regional and district water offices.[83]

ASSESSING INTEGRATED WATER RESOURCES MANAGEMENT ON KILIMANJARO

For the past twenty years, the Tanzanian government and international development agencies have worked to reform the water sector using the concept of IWRM as a key premise. The stated goal of this approach is to manage resources in a way that ensures equity, economic efficiency, and environmental sustainability.[84] Devolution and cost recovery are essential aspects. Furthermore, IWRM extols the importance of participation and dialogue among users to ensure equitable distribution and fairness. To what extent has this approach succeeded for Kilimanjaro? Responses from local communities as well as some scholars indicate that it has fallen short. In a paper entitled "Winner and Losers of IWRM in Tanzania," Barbara van Koppen and her coauthors argue that smallholder farmers have been the losers in this approach, while large-scale water users have been the winners. For smallholders, the reform process has stifled their access to water (by defining water as a zero-sum game), excluded them from basin-level planning, and criminalized traditional irrigation.[85] Though cloaked in a language of local control and participation, these reforms left people with less effective control over water management.

The experiences of Kilimanjaro echo these critiques. As part of IWRM, the PBWO has created more than five hundred WUAs, ostensibly to provide local communities with a voice in management. Most are village-level bodies with elected memberships. Though the WUAs were conceived as a modern version of the canal societies, scholars such as Tagseth, Frances Vavrus, and Donald Mosgrove have questioned their effectiveness. Vavrus, who conducted ethnographic work in Old Moshi in 2001, noted the following exchange in a focus group session:

> Woman: I know the water committee exists, but I don't know what it does.
>
> Man: They are new committees, and they are committees in theory but not in practice.
>
> Woman: They are more active in private than in public.
>
> Man: They are only to be shown to any NGOs—sponsors—who might come around, but they are very inactive.

Woman: They don't do anything.

Man: They just pretend to do work, but they're cheating about work. No one knows them. It's a government effort, but they're just shadows.[86]

She found that people view the new committees with suspicion and skepticism. They are seen as foreign impositions rather than representative bodies, neither participatory nor effective, mere "shadows" of the canal societies. Furthermore, they are directly associated with the burden of paying for water. Vavrus noted that people felt they had "participated in the development of water services through their labor: they had dug the trenches and laid the pipes themselves."[87] Notably, she found desire among people to revive canal societies as a means of reducing dependency on piped water.[88]

The negative perception of WUAs reflects several factors. Created by outsiders, they are viewed as foreign entities imposed to suit the needs of MAJI, the PBWO, or donors. WUAs are also composed of elected officials, a decision made by MAJI to provide for equal and fair representation. In the eyes of communities, this had made them inherently political. Unlike canal societies, which were composed of users and led by someone with knowledge of irrigation or with a hereditary link to the founder, the WUAs feature individuals without any expertise. They also have no social meaning or cultural connectivity. People view WUAs as a tool with which the government enforces the notion of water as a commodity, a good for sale, rather than as their rightful heritage. While some express this by saying that water is God's gift to mountain peoples, others express it by saying that water is earned by the collective labor that they and their ancestors have contributed for generations. Lastly, the WUAs provide people with no input into the larger issues related to management. Designed for each to administer a single source, the WUAs have little influence over the PBWO, which holds power over broader allocation and planning. While the local committees may allow for some community participation, there is little opportunity for ideas to radiate upward.

The main goal of water reform has been to provide people with more and better water, and on this the results have been mixed as well. The mifongo persist despite their illegality and resistance from the PBWO. Canal societies in the agroforest belt have few resources with which to revitalize or modernize canals, and there is little trust between them and the basin office. The government has asked them to apply for water rights, using the carrot of donor money for canal improvements, but local communities fear that this would only make them pay for water and abandon the local institutions and social relationships that have made the mifongo sustainable. Pipe redevelopment in the past decade has brought more water to hundreds of thousands of users, but projects have lagged in Moshi Rural District. In Kibosho, for example, residents of Kati Ward have lacked access to reliable tap water for more than eight years.[89] While overall availability has improved in many areas, cost recovery has introduced a class dimension to water access. People with means have the luxury of paying for private connections to their homes. In Hai and Rombo alone, there are more than twenty thousand of these connections, serving homes, schools, dispensaries, and public offices. Those who cannot afford private connections but can pay fees rely on public taps. In the early mornings, many taps have a line of people waiting with their debes or plastic jerry cans in hand.[90] Those who cannot afford tap water at all make do with canals, streams, and springs (fig. 7.2), indicating a direct relationship between financial means and proximity to safe water. People who struggle the most are likewise the ones who dedicate the most time to procuring water, which leaves less time for economically productive activities.

⮌

The rise of neoliberal water management has precipitated new struggles over water on Kilimanjaro. This is the product of the deep disconnections that exist between how different stakeholders envision the waterscape. Government agencies and the development community see the mountain's waters as part of a bigger region, the Pangani, and their attempts to plan these resources center on making them more widely available. They dismiss the claims of mountain farmers, consider mifongo to be primitive and wasteful, and deny the validity or usefulness of local management knowledge. In the process, they have criminalized tens of thousands of users. Mountain communities, on the contrary, view the mountain's waters as their divine right and see outside attempts to assert control—especially by charging for water—as deeply offensive. In the highlands, where local management

FIGURE 7.2. Woman procuring water from a canal (*Matthew V. Bender*)

knowledge remains strongest, these new reforms have been greeted with much resistance. People resist the work of the PBWO, which they see as an outsider, and the WUAs, which they view as illegitimate. In the foothills, lowlands, and Rombo, where water is most scarce, pragmatism has ruled. People appreciate attempts to revitalize the pipes, even if they loathe the idea of paying for water. Despite the differences in opinion between uphill and downhill communities, and between those who have private connections and those who use canals, people have a shared belief that the waters of the mountain are rightfully theirs, as well as a common frustration that water is becoming harder to come by.

The most looming challenge is that water is only becoming scarcer. According to the PBWO, surface runoff from Kilimanjaro that feeds rivers and streams is expected to decline by 5–11 percent in the next few decades because of global climate change. On the whole, the region is becoming more arid. Populations on the mountain and across the basin continue to rise, as does demand for water from all sectors. As the next chapter will show, the supply of water has been decreasing as well. This trend has been linked, both scientifically and symbolically, to the shrinking size of the glaciers on the mountain. While the glaciers have garnered the lion's share of attention, becoming a symbol of debates over climate change, the future of the mountain's water supply has received less attention. With the available supply of water dwindling amid steadily rising demand, the conflicts that have plagued the region are likely only to intensify.

8 ᓭ It Is God's Will, and Also Deforestation

Global versus Local in the Disappearance of the Glaciers

IN MAY 2006, former US vice president Al Gore leaped from the political podium to the big screen, starring in his documentary film *An Inconvenient Truth*.[1] The film paints an ominous portrait of global climate change, and it offers a scathing critique of fossil fuels and the lack of action to control greenhouse gas emissions. One of the examples he presents is the shrinking glaciers atop Africa's tallest peak. In the past century, Kilimanjaro's eleven-thousand-year-old white cap has shrunk in size by nearly 80 percent.[2] Gore makes the bold claim that the glaciers' retreat is the direct result of human-induced global warming. He predicts, "Within the decade, there will be no more snows of Kilimanjaro." In his eyes, the mountain is a symbol of impending global catastrophe, one that politicians have been reticent to acknowledge, much less address.

Climate change has been a contentious issue in global politics for more than twenty years. The topic has stimulated the production of new scientific knowledge and generated vigorous debate involving scientists as well as politicians, business interests, the media, and the public. *An Inconvenient Truth* shifted Kilimanjaro to the forefront of this debate, making it a symbol of the struggle between those who assert the existence of human-induced climate change and those who are skeptical. In the past decade, scholars have studied the shrinking glaciers, generating new knowledge about why they are receding and the likely impacts that their disappearance will have. This production of globally oriented knowledge about Kilimanjaro's glaciers has been almost wholly disconnected from the experiences of the mountain's peoples, whose local knowledge and viewpoints have been largely overlooked. Indeed, a cursory look at the literature might lead one to believe that nobody actually lives on the mountain.

This final chapter examines the competing global and local discourses on Kilimanjaro's receding snows. As this book has shown, Kibo's white cap has long been considered the heart of the waterscape, and as such it holds deep religious, cultural, and practical importance. For the peoples of the mountain, the nature of its importance has shifted over time in response to the broader changes that accompanied colonial rule and the emergence of the independent state. Nonetheless, the white peak remains the home of God and the heart of the mountain's water supply, which rivers, streams, mifongo, and pipes carry down the mountain like arteries through the human body. Given that glacial recession is a visible phenomenon, most people are aware that the glaciers are getting smaller, and they link this with reduced rainfall and flow in streams. What is notable is how people across the mountain describe the cause of the phenomenon and their ability to influence it. They cite a host of factors that are part of the global discourse, such as carbon emissions, as well as local factors such as deforestation and even spiritual factors such as the will of God. For example, when asked about the glaciers, Martin Mosha expressed without hesitation that "it is God's will, and also deforestation."[3] This understanding of glacial recession fuses local knowledge with outside ideas, enabling people to make sense of it using their own experiences. It has also fueled action, the best example being successful tree-planting campaigns. The peoples' actions to create locally grounded knowledge about glacial recession illustrate the broader pattern inherent in this book: local people express agency in the face of external pressures by producing knowledge they find relevant and using it to reinforce locally oriented viewpoints.

For the peoples of Kilimanjaro, the stakes could not be greater. The prospect of a future in which the mountain has no white cap is daunting. This is due to the perceived link between the glaciers and the whole of the waterscape as well as the deep symbolism of the mountain and its place in local identity. This chapter shows how people make sense of glacial recession in ways that are meaningful to them. They acknowledge the potential global influences but retain their belief that the mountain and its resources are rightfully theirs, and they refuse to cede control over its fate. The West's discussion of the glaciers has largely ignored the human impacts of glacial recession for the people who call the mountain home. By introducing questions arising from local perspectives, I encourage more research into what glacial recession means to the region and its people, not only in terms of physical survival but also in terms of culture and identity.

THE EVOLVING SYMBOLISM OF THE WHITE CAP

As mentioned in chapter 1, Kilimanjaro's white cap has long been its defining feature. For the peoples of the mountain, it represented the hub of the spiritual world and the heart of the waterscape. Rivers, streams, and mifongo carried these life-giving waters directly into their vihamba. The white cap not only gave life and sustenance, but it also symbolized the deep connection of societies to the physical space of the mountain. For Maasai, Kamba, and Swahili, viewing the sight from farther afield, the white cap represented a beacon for navigation and a source of trade goods and supplies. European explorers, the first to identify the cap as ice, considered it a sign of providence. The mountain emerged as a symbol of outside objectives, particularly evangelization and colonization. To this day, the glaciers carry the names of German mountaineers and scientists given to them in the period. In the 1950s, proponents of shared Chagga identity appropriated the glaciers as a symbol of ethnic nationalism. For the first time, the white cap was illustrated, appearing on invented elements of shared culture such as the Chagga flag. A decade later, the Tanzanian government appropriated the peak for itself, giving it a new name—Uhuru—and placing symbols of the independent state on it. Indeed, the glaciers' history of appropriation mirrors the broader history of the region.

Kilimanjaro and its venerable ice emerged as a symbol beyond the region as well. In the Western imagination, it became the dominant physical symbol of Africa. It embodied mystery and intrigue, as exemplified by Hemingway's "The Snows of Kilimanjaro." The main character Harry, on safari in Africa, develops an infected wound and lies awaiting a slow, agonizing death. As he contemplates his life and his primary regret of selling out his talent, the mountain towers above him. Kilimanjaro becomes the primary symbol of his passage from life into death. Harry mentions how the locals refer to it as "the House of God," and he describes it as "wide as all the world, great, high, and unbelievably white in the sun."[4] The white snows allude to his impending passage to the afterlife. As Harry recounts the follies of his life, the reader is left with a mysterious ambiguity; what kind of afterlife does the mountain represent? "The Snows of Kilimanjaro," both as a short story and in its 1952 film adaptation, popularized the symbol of the ice-capped mountain and linked it with a sense of mystery, even romance.

Most Western encounters with the mountain now come in the form of tourism. Long the purview of German and British mountaineers, the climbing of Kilimanjaro emerged as a focal point of attempts to develop tourism in the 1970s. In 1973, the government reclassified the Kilimanjaro Forest Reserve as a national park, and four years later the park was opened to the public with designated climbing routes, campgrounds, and other facilities. Today, the park is a crucial part of the tourist infrastructure and a major earner of foreign exchange. A 2009 study by the Overseas Development Institute (ODI) and the Netherlands Development Organization (SNV) found that the park receives thirty-nine thousand nonresident visitors per year, generating revenue just shy of $50 million.[5] The Tanzania National Parks Authority and the Tanzania Tourist Board market Kilimanjaro as a place of mystery and adventure that, unlike other high peaks, is accessible to climbers without technical training. Further attention to Kilimanjaro as a symbol came in 1989, when the UN Educational, Scientific, and Cultural Organization classified it as a World Heritage Site.

Local communities have greeted this outside appropriation with ambivalence. On the one hand, people believe that the mountain is first and foremost their heritage, not a mere symbol of livelihood but its actual source. This is still understood in terms of the waterscape. The glaciers are the mountain's heart and the source of the water that fills rivers and streams. As outsiders have latched on to the image of the glacier, locals have likewise transformed it into a prominent symbol. Though the images created by the mangi mkuu in the 1950s are no longer in use, pictures and paintings of Kibo are present all over Moshi Town. Locals still think of Kibo as their inheritance, and they vehemently defend their right to it. One need only mention photographs of the mountain taken from the other side of the border to spark a rant about Kenyans attempting to claim Kilimanjaro as their own.

On the other hand, people have come to rely on the symbolic appeal of the mountain to outsiders. The influx of tourists has been a lifesaver to a local economy devastated by the decline of coffee. Though government agencies, NGOs, and the KNCU (which was revived in 1984) have worked to revitalize coffee production, the industry remains a shadow of its former self. The ODI-SNV study indicates that tourism on Kilimanjaro, unlike that in other areas of Tanzania, has proven lucrative for the locality. The study estimates that the climbing industry creates jobs for around four hundred guides, ten thousand porters, and five hundred cooks.[6] Furthermore, 28 percent (around $13 million) of in-country revenue from mountain climbing is "pro-poor," meaning that it is spent locally and benefits working people rather than businesses, tour operators, or the government. This includes salaries and tips for climbing personnel, food and beverages, and souvenirs. The study indicates that the economic benefits of tourism are felt widely. Indeed, most people on the mountain recognize that tourism is now the most vibrant local industry, though they speak nostalgically of the heyday of coffee or the promise of new crops such as sunflowers. This duality reflects the attachment of local identity to agriculture amid the fact that most people have family and friends who work in tourism. People are also proud of the international reputation of their homeland. They see tourists from all over the world flocking to the mountain, and they take pride in the mystique that it holds to these outsiders.

The symbolic appropriation of Kilimanjaro by both local people and outsiders, though manifesting in different ways, remains deeply tied to the white cap. But what happens if the mountain no longer has ice? In the past decade, the retreating "snows of Kilimanjaro" have generated attention in the media and have emerged as a focal point of scientific research and political debate. Speculation that the glaciers are retreating, however, is by no means a new phenomenon. Since the late nineteenth century, observers have noted that the mountain's white cap has been getting smaller.

GLACIAL RECESSION IN HISTORICAL CONTEXT

The peoples of Kilimanjaro have long understood the mountain's peak to be dynamic. The white cap grows during the rains because of snowfall, and it shrinks in the dry seasons as the snows dissipate. This seasonal change in the cap coincides with variations in water flow in rivers and streams. When the white cap is large, water is abundant, and when it is smaller, water is less prevalent. This perceived connection between the white cap and the water supply reinforced the metaphor of the mountain as a heart and watercourses as arteries. Mountain communities did not distinguish between permanent ice and seasonal snow, as they did not know the composition of the white cap until the twentieth century. The notion of the white cap's growing and shrinking over time, though, was widely accepted.

Hans Meyer, the first European to summit the mountain, was also the first to notice glacial recession. During his successful 1891 ascent, he measured several glaciers. In 1898, he returned to complete his mapping of them. He found that in only seven years, they had decreased in size, as much as 100 meters on some sides.[7] Furthermore, the glacial pass he used in his initial ascent had become twice as wide. Given these observations, he concluded that within three decades all the ice would be gone. Many mountaineers who followed in Meyer's footsteps shared similar observations. In 1912, German geographer Fritz Klute spent five months on the mountain, producing the first complete photogrammetric survey of the massif and its ice coverage.[8] Like Meyer, he concluded that the glaciers were receding. He attributed the recession to "direct radiation" from the sun, which caused ice melt that quickly evaporated. Others who visited the mountain in the first half of the century, including Clement Gillman, Fritz Jaeger, Eric Nilsson, and Walter Mittelholzer, corroborated these findings. In 1936, Walter Geilinger assembled these observations into the first published work on the topic, entitled "The Retreat of Kilimanjaro's Glaciers." [9] He developed a longitudinal perspective by comparing his personal observations with those of his predecessors, concluding: "Since the time of their first discovery the glaciers have been in a constant regression which small and passing advances [seasonal growth due to snowfall] have not been able to stop. . . . Should the climatic conditions which have existed for the last fifty years continue, one might be justified in concluding that the ice within the crater may disappear entirely in decades to come, followed later on by the disappearance of the glaciers on the outer slopes."[10]

The geology of Kilimanjaro and its glaciers continued to be a point of scientific interest in the later years of colonial rule and into independence. In 1953 and 1957, the Department of Geology of the University of Sheffield and the Geological Survey of Tanganyika undertook two exhaustive geological surveys. The final published study, by C. Downie and P. Wilkinson in 1972, contained the most detailed description and history of glacial activity on Kilimanjaro to that point.[11] It found that the glaciers were a "relic of . . . colder and wetter climatic conditions." Not only were they receding, but their recession was also "no modern phenomenon."[12] Two sets of data supported this conclusion: accumulated debris (moraine) that showed the glaciers had previously been much larger, and documentary evidence gathered by previous visitors to the glaciers. Downie and Wilkinson concluded that the "recession of the ice is now so rapid that it seems likely that within a few decades the shining cap of Kibo will have ceased to exist."[13]

THE GLACIERS AND THE CLIMATE CHANGE DEBATE

The first person to propose a link between the recession of Kilimanjaro's glaciers and a broader global warming phenomenon was English engineer Guy Callendar. In 1938, he published an article in the *Quarterly Journal of the Royal Meteorological Society* entitled "The Artificial Production of Carbon Dioxide and its Influence on Temperature."[14] This is recognized as the first scientific paper to link human activities with rising global temperatures. Callendar compared measurements of global temperature over a period of fifty years alongside atmospheric CO_2. He concluded that rising consumption of fossil fuels was causing global temperatures to rise. As an example of the impacts, he referred to the recession of tropical glaciers like those on Kilimanjaro. Callendar's peers largely rebuked his conclusions. In the April 15, 1944, issue of *Nature*, British geologist Percy Edward Kent claimed that glacial recession on Kilimanjaro was the result of increased volcanic activity.[15] The next week, Callendar wrote a letter to the editor, challenging Kent's claim. He noted that neighboring Mount Kenya and Mount Rwenzori had shown no signs of volcanic activity, yet their glaciers were also receding. In his opinion, "there is one fact . . . which gives a pointer to the immediate cause of this recession, for it has been observed at meteorological stations where very accurate records of temperature have been kept over a long series of years, that the annual means tend to be slightly higher than they were half a century ago."[16] Despite Callendar's findings, the scientific community dismissed the notion of human-induced climate change.

Scientists began warming to the notion of human-induced climate change in the 1970s. By the late 1980s, scientists working on climate issues had reached consensus that the human production of greenhouse gases, particularly carbon dioxide, was responsible for a steady rise of atmospheric and water temperatures since the nineteenth century. A key year in the history of climate science is 1988, when James Hansen, director of the NASA Goddard Institute for Space Studies, testified before the United States Senate that human activity had caused measurable change in climate. Also in 1988, the UN Environment Programme and World Meteorological Organization jointly established the Intergovernmental Panel on Climate Change, a scientific intergovernmental body charged with supporting scientific inquiry into climate change; its potential consequences for the environment, economy, and living conditions; and the options for mitigating or adapting to its effects.[17]

In the decades since, climate change has been a focal point of research in numerous scientific disciplines, particularly climatology, geology, and glaciology. It has also generated a tremendous amount of debate, some from skeptical scientists, but most from industrial interests and politicians concerned with the economic impacts of mitigation measures. In these debates, glaciers have emerged as a potent symbol for both proponents of climate change science and denialists. They are considered the most sensitive indicators of climate change, as they reflect a delicate balance of two climatic processes: accumulation through snowfall, and ablation (erosion) through melting or sublimation (evaporating without transitioning to liquid). As many of the world's glaciers and ice sheets have receded dramatically in the past thirty years, scientists have considered them a "warming beacon" of more destructive changes to come.

The most prominent research linking global warming with Kilimanjaro's receding glaciers has come from a team led by paleoclimatologist Lonnie Thompson. In early 2000, they traveled to Kilimanjaro to extract ice cores from the Northern and Southern Ice Fields and the Furtwängler Glacier inside the crater. Two years later they published an article entitled "Kilimanjaro Ice Core Records: Evidence of Holocene Climate Change in Tropical Africa."[18] The team argued that the cores provide a "nearly continuous, high-resolution record of Holocene climate conditions" over the past 11,000 years.[19] Through chemical and physical analysis, they identified three historical climate events in which the glaciers receded because of rising temperatures and lower precipitation: at around 8,300 years ago, around 5,200 years ago, and around 4,000 years ago. They also discovered that present climate conditions are unprecedented in the Holocene, more extreme now than at any of these times. Using the cores as well as temperature data, aerial photography, and comparison with previous glacier surveys, they concluded that the glaciers have receded around 80 percent over the course of the twentieth century (see map 8.1) and will disappear completely between 2015 and 2020. The article thus argued for a direct connection between rising temperatures and the

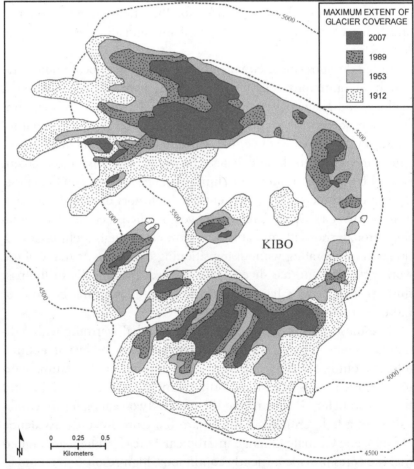

MAP 8.1. Maximum glacier extents on Kilimanjaro (*Brian Edward Balsley, GISP. Based on data from Hastenrath and Greischar (1997) and Thompson et al. (2002)*)

shrinking of the glaciers. Lastly, Thompson predicted that "the loss of Kilimanjaro's permanent ice fields will have both climatological and hydrological implications for local populations, who depend on the water generated from the ice fields during the dry seasons and monsoon failures."[20]

The 2002 paper and subsequent work by Thompson's team effectively made Kilimanjaro the icon of the climate change debate.[21] Thompson's work on tropical glaciers has earned him numerous honors in the scientific community and popular press. He served as an advisor to Al Gore in the filming of *An Inconvenient Truth*. He was even the subject of Mark Bowen's 2005 book *Thin Ice*, an adventure-science book aimed at a popular audience that documented his expeditions and findings.[22] Thompson's conclusions, however, have not gone without criticism. In the past decade, numerous scientists have challenged his findings, questioning neither global warming nor glacial recession, but whether the former is the proximate cause of the latter.

One of the first studies to challenge Thompson's conclusion came in 2004, from a team led by glaciologist Georg Kaser.[23] In a paper entitled "Modern Glacier Retreat on Kilimanjaro as Evidence of Climate Change: Observations and Facts," Kaser accepted Thompson's assertion that the glaciers are receding and will disappear in the next few decades. He disagreed, however, with the conclusion that recession was solely the product of increasing temperature, calling this view unsubstantiated and "overly simplistic."[24] Rather, he asserted that recession should be attributed to "reduced precipitation" unrelated to temperature change and "increased availability of shortwave radiation due to decreases in cloudiness" that began in the late nineteenth century. In other words, the glaciers were receding because East Africa was drying out, not because it was getting warmer. Kaser also questioned the conclusion that glacial recession would affect the local water supply, noting that "meltwater has been of little importance to the lowlands in modern times" and that surface water came instead from rainforest precipitation.[25] Thus, while increasing aridity across the region might affect water supply, there is no direct correlation between smaller glaciers and less downhill surface water. Kaser pointed out that his findings in no way challenged the general premise of anthropogenic climate science or the possibility that climate change could be a factor in the region's declining precipitation.

In the past decade, numerous scientists have chimed in.[26] What has emerged in the scholarly discourse is a back and forth between Thompson and his team, who support the conclusion that glacial recession is a product of increasing temperature, and those who support Kaser's position that it results from decreasing precipitation and increasing sun exposure. Thompson has largely stood by his position, though he has revised his estimates for the timing of the glaciers' demise. In 2009, he and his team published a paper acknowledging that the glaciers will persist beyond his initial estimate of 2015–20, but the paper also provided additional evidence to support temperature as a causative factor while rejecting the notion that drier conditions alone could account for glacial loss.[27] In 2011, he published another paper that used new temperature measurements on the Northern Ice Field to show sustained surface temperatures of 0°C, enough to cause surface melting of the glacier.[28] Citing ice core samples from his work in 2000, he asserted that sublimation could not be a major driver for ice loss, thus challenging a core premise of Kaser's work.

The trend in the scholarship, however, has been in support of the aridity hypothesis. In 2007, Kaser copublished an article with climatologist Philip Mote, in which they noted that a rise in global temperature "fails spectacularly" to explain glacial recession and that the phenomenon bears "only indirect connections, if any, to recent trends in global climate."[29] Rather, glacial recession stems from "a drying of the surrounding air that reduced [ice] accumulation and increased ablation." In backing the aridity claim, they cite evidence from Lake Victoria showing a "substantial decline in regional precipitation at the end of the nineteenth century after some considerably wetter decades." This indicates that the large white cap noted by explorers may have been an anomaly, the product of an unusually wet period. Several other papers have since followed that support Kaser's conclusion.[30] In 2012, geographer Nicolas Cullen and his collaborators published a longitudinal study of the glaciers, comparing current satellite data with the maps and surveys of Hans Meyer and several twentieth-century mountaineers.[31] He notes that the glaciers have retreated from their former extent of 11.40 square kilometers in 1912 to 1.76 square kilometers in 2011, a loss of about 85 percent of the total ice coverage. By the middle of the twenty-first century, virtually all the ice will have disappeared. Cullen further concurs with Kaser on the issue of downstream water, noting that "the loss of ice will have no hydrological significance to lowland areas."[32]

For the most part, the scholarly literature has focused on what factors are causing the glaciers to recede, a question inspired by the current debates over global climate change. Yet there are other ways in which climate change is affecting Kilimanjaro. Andreas Hemp, a plant physiologist, has explored how climate change is affecting the mountain's forests and downstream water supplies. In a 2005 article, he noted that over the previous seventy years, Kilimanjaro had lost nearly one-third of its forest cover, or about 600 square kilometers.[33] The bulk of this loss, around 450 square kilometers, came from clear-cutting of forests. The rest came from increased incidences of fire in the upper areas. These fires had become more frequent and aggressive because of climatic changes that had rendered the region more arid.[34] He predicted that if the trend persisted, the mountain would lose its high-altitude forests within the next few years. Though engaged with the literature on glaciers, Hemp is concerned with the impact of deforestation on the mountain's water supply. In his opinion, the demise of the glaciers would rid the mountain of "a part of its beauty and an important archive of paleoclimatic records," but "with its forests, it loses its major ecosystem service to a water-demanding society."[35] In the past decade, other scholars have followed Hemp in examining more local questions of climate change impact, such as how rising temperatures will affect precipitation and crop cultivation. For example, in 2014 a team of scholars working with the Intergovernmental Panel on Climate Change completed an expansive study on the effects of climate change on precipitation levels across Africa, concluding that "climate change will amplify existing stress on water availability."[36]

Despite this recent trend in the literature, most work on climate change and Kilimanjaro focuses on global implications rather than local ones, and the works that do consider the local implications rarely discuss people's opinions or perspectives. In interviews, some scientists have mentioned likely impacts for mountain communities, but in passing. For example, Stefan Hastenrath, professor of atmospheric sciences, remarked that "if the ice disappears, it'll be an aesthetic disaster. There's hardly anything more beautiful than the glaciers on Kilimanjaro."[37] Climatologist Douglas Hardy noted that "the sad reality is that the loss of Kilimanjaro's glaciers probably has to affect the local economy."[38] These answers indicate another pattern in the literature: a lack of engagement with local knowledge. Few scientists consider local knowledge to have scientific merit, and thus few have engaged with communities to understand their views regarding the glaciers or broader patterns of climate change. As a result, communities have no voice in the scholarship and no ability to steer the scholarly discourse to issues of local concern. This distance from the local context is exemplified by a 2008 book chapter "Tropical Glaciers, Climate Change, and Society: Focus on Kilimanjaro," written by Mölg, Hardy, Cullen, and Kaser.[39] While most of the fourteen-page chapter discusses the science behind glacial recession, it dedicates three pages to local issues such as the impact of the glaciers on hydrology and water supply, impacts on tourism, and changing land-use patterns. The chapter does not delve into cultural meanings of water or the broader social impact that glacial recession may have for the mountain's populations. Besides one casual reference to the ice cap as a "place in the myths of African tribes living at the base . . . viewed as the shining 'house of god,' " there is no discussion of locally produced knowledge about the glaciers.[40]

KILIMANJARO AS CARICATURE

This pattern of detaching the glaciers from the social context is even more apparent in the media and political discourse that has arisen in the past decade. As Kilimanjaro emerged as a focus of scientific inquiry, it became a poster child for environmental advocacy groups and politicians eager to draw attention to climate change and gain public support for action. It also became a lightning rod for climate change denialists, who have used the disagreement between Kaser and Thompson to challenge the whole premise of human-induced climate change. These individuals oversimplify the mountain and glacial recession, often to promote agendas well beyond its boundaries. Their work has, in the words of Andrew Revkin, transformed Kilimanjaro "from a complicated scientific puzzle into a simplistic caricature."[41]

Since the publication of Thompson's paper, the snows of Kilimanjaro have emerged as a potent symbol for supporters of action against global warming. Climate action groups have faced a distinct challenge in galvanizing public support for policy action. Unlike other environmental catastrophes, it has been difficult to point to tangible examples of harm. The receding glaciers seemed to present a solution: a highly recognizable place that is being physically altered by changes in climate. One of the first groups to leverage Kilimanjaro in this way was Greenpeace, which in late 2001 sent a climbing expedition to the mountain to "bear witness" to the effects of climate change. Joris Thijssen, a Greenpeace climate campaigner, noted his reasons for joining the climb: "You read about all the dramatic impacts that climate change has and will have on the environment and the lives of people all around the world. I wanted to see it for myself, I wanted to witness climate change and make other people a witness to it. So when Greenpeace decided to go to Mount Kilimanjaro, I was more than happy to join the expedition. Mount Kilimanjaro's fast-melting glaciers symbolise the fact that climate change may be felt first and hardest by the environment and people of Africa."[42] Even as scientists have become skeptical of the influence of temperature on Kilimanjaro's glaciers, Greenpeace has continued to leverage the mountain in this way, and it is not alone. The World Wildlife Fund, known for transforming the panda into a global symbol of conservation, has linked the Kilimanjaro glaciers to global climate change, and in 2009 it organized a fundraiser involving a mountain climb and the Kilimanjaro Marathon.[43]

The symbol of Kilimanjaro also appealed to politicians eager to galvanize public support for climate change legislation, as seen in Vice President Gore's use of Kilimanjaro in *An Inconvenient Truth*. Another example is the testimony given on the floor of the United States Senate during deliberation over Senate Bill 139 in 2003. Entitled the Climate Stewardship Act of 2003, it called for increases in government-funded research on climate change and the establishment of a mandatory cap-and-trade system to limit greenhouse emissions. The ensuing debate featured members of Congress citing examples of global warming including the glaciers. Senator Hillary Clinton noted in her testimony that the "snows of Kilimanjaro will be gone by 2015."[44] She showed a photo of a 20-foot high glacier taken by one of her staff while on a mountain climb in 1970. She then mentioned that when his daughter climbed to the same point in 1999, there was only a trace of ice left. Other senators, including Olympia Snowe and bill cosponsor John McCain, also linked Kilimanjaro's glaciers with global warming. Since the publication of Kaser's 2004 paper, however, many politicians have shied away from using Kilimanjaro as an example of climate change.

Politicians and officials in Tanzania have likewise latched on to the image of Kilimanjaro. Despite the shift in the literature, they have continued to support Thompson's argument for a direct connection between glacial recession and rising temperatures, while acknowledging the possibility that deforestation is a contributing factor. President Jakaya Kikwete, who served from 2005 to 2015, leveraged the mountain to point out how Africa is feeling the impacts of climate change first, though it contributes less CO_2 than other continents. In a panel at the World Economic Forum in 2010, he remarked, "It is a threat for us . . . on Kilimanjaro the snow is fast disappearing."[45] Two years later, at the African Ministerial Conference on Environment, he again attributed the fast decline of snow on the mountain to temperature. He critiqued the West by saying that countries in sub-Saharan Africa "contribute the least to the serious environmental challenges threatening our planet" and that "those who pollute more should shoulder a bigger burden [and] also have a responsibility to those who suffer because of their actions and inaction."[46] Another Tanzanian to contribute to the public discourse of the mountain was Erasto Lufungulo, chief warden of Kilimanjaro National Park. In a 2015 speech marking the seventieth anniversary of the UN, he remarked that "ice has been decreasing at a fast rate during the last 100 years since records began. It's all due to global warming."[47] Both Kikwete and Lufungulo used glacial recession to speak to audiences beyond national borders, both to link the experience of Tanzania with a broader global phenomenon and to request financial and technical assistance. The significance of Kilimanjaro in Tanzania's climate change outreach is best exemplified by the choice of Father Adian Msafiri as the country's UN climate change ambassador in 2017. Msafiri is a Catholic priest who holds a PhD in environmental ethics. He is also from Kilema and has long been involved in grassroots activism in development and the environment on the mountain. Since his appointment, he has become a public voice for the impact of climate change on local communities.

As politicians and advocacy groups have latched on to the symbol of the glaciers, so have climate change skeptics. For these individuals, the scientific disagreement about the glaciers has served as a tool for denying climate science more generally. In 2002, Patrick Michaels, senior fellow in environmental studies at the Cato Institute and a self-described global warming skeptic, wrote an article entitled "The Snow Jobs of Kilimanjaro," in which he criticized the conclusions in Thompson's 2002 paper and referred to it as the latest "spasm of 'envirodoom.'"[48] In 2004, an essay appeared in the newsletter *World Climate Report*, published by the now defunct Greening Earth Society, a nonprofit financed by the coal industry. Entitled "Snow Fooling! Mount Kilimanjaro's Glacier Retreat Is Not Related to Global Warming," the paper uses Kaser's argument to make a broader case against climate science.[49] Conservative think tanks such as the Heartland Institute—considered by the *Economist* to be the "most prominent think tank promoting skepticism about man-made climate change"[50]—and the Cato Institute have also leveraged Kilimanjaro to further their skepticism of climate science.

The use of Kilimanjaro by climate change denialists has generated strong rebuke from the scientific community. On May 7, 2010, *Science* published a letter signed by 255 members of the National Academy of Sciences, including Thompson, criticizing the assault on climate change science, the harassment of scientists, and the outright lying by skeptics and denialists. They note that "recent assaults on climate science and, more disturbingly, on climate scientists by climate change deniers, are typically driven by special interests or dogma, not by an honest effort to provide an alternative theory that credibly satisfies the evidence."[51] In a paper reaffirming his findings about Kilimanjaro, Thompson remarked that "climatologists, like other scientists, tend to be a stolid group." He added: "We are not given to theatrical rantings about falling skies. Most of us are far more comfortable in our laboratories or gathering data in the field than we are giving interviews to journalists or speaking before Congressional committees. Why then are climatologists speaking out about the dangers of global warming? The answer is that virtually all of us are now convinced that global warming poses a clear and present danger to civilization."[52]

For scientists supporting Kaser's argument about aridity, the clash with skeptics has hit closer to home. They see the use of their contention about Kilimanjaro to support climate change denial not merely as politically motivated, but as a flagrant misuse of their science. Douglas Hardy, for example, remarked in a 2004 interview that "climate skeptics are making generalizations not only to the rest of the tropics but the rest of the world."[53] By oversimplifying the science, skeptics aimed to transform the mountain into an icon they could use to pursue their own political agendas.

In the past fifteen years, politicians, activists, and skeptics have used Kilimanjaro as an icon in the broader debates about human-induced global climate change. Their work largely follows that of scientists and organizations that are working to more deeply understand the causes of climate change and to develop strategies for combating it or mitigating its effects. While many are working to understand the broader phenomenon of climate change and its relationship to Kilimanjaro, a smaller number seek to understand its local impacts, and virtually none have engaged with the people of the mountain to ascertain their views and opinions. In discussions of Kilimanjaro's glaciers, these outside actors have considered local knowledge and local voices to be insignificant and inconsequential. Yet as this book indicates, mountain people have long generated management knowledge about the glaciers and the water supply. For them, Kilimanjaro is a lived space as well as a symbolic one, and not merely a "warming beacon."

PERSPECTIVES FROM THE MOUNTAIN

The lack of attention to the local communities in these scholarly and political discourses raises the question of how the peoples of the mountain are producing knowledge about glacial recession. Who recognizes the phenomenon? How do they understand its causation and potential impacts? How do they understand it in relation to their views of the waterscape and their understandings of history? Most importantly, what place is there for local cultural and scientific knowledge in a discussion that is so inherently global? These questions are timely for two reasons. First, scientists agree that the glaciers will disappear within the lifetime of people on the mountain. Second, local communities have some understanding of climate change from what they have heard through the media, from politicians, and in schools. This makes it possible to get a sense of how people are integrating new ideas with their existing knowledge about the glaciers.

My personal curiosity in these questions was piqued by the conversation I had in 2004 with Martin Mosha, who remarked that glacial recession is "God's will, and also deforestation."[54] The comment inspired me to conduct follow-up interviews in Kilema in 2008. Most people I spoke with have strong—and varied—opinions about the glaciers. The diversity of responses I received reflects several factors: age, occupation, gender, level of education, and access to news media. Nonetheless, a common pattern emerged: people recognize that the glaciers are getting smaller. They tend to describe its causation in terms of both global factors, such as pollution, warfare, or God's will, and local factors, particularly mountain slope deforestation. They are generally more concerned with impacts than with causation, yet many retain hope that recession can be stopped. They describe a Kilimanjaro without glaciers as a global catastrophe *by virtue* of its being a local one. Compared with the scholarly and political discourse that is disconnected from the local, the discourse on Kilimanjaro claims that an impending local tragedy should inspire global concern.

Of the more than forty people interviewed, nearly all agreed that the glaciers are getting smaller.[55] The near unanimity is not surprising. The Southern Ice Field is visible from Kilema, and the recession measured by scientists is evident to the naked eye. Most who are middle-aged or elderly cite their own visual observations as evidence. They note that the glaciers look much smaller than they used to, and that there is less water in rivers, streams, and canals. This reflects the perseverance of belief in the white cap as the heart of the mountain's waters. Younger people, particularly those in school, explain that they have learned this from teachers or other adults. Only a handful of people, among the oldest I interviewed, claim that the glaciers are not getting smaller.[56]

A more diverse set of answers came from the question of what is causing them to recede. Most people answered by referring to multiple causative factors, often striking in their juxtaposition. Martin Mosha, a man who had never heard of global climate change, responded that the glaciers are receding because of God's will and deforestation. I encountered a similar response from Ewald Kessy, a village chairman. He said that the glaciers are shrinking because "the snow is decreasing, more than before."[57] When asked why, he first replied, "Deforestation! People are misusing the forests." I asked him if he thought there were other reasons, to which he said, "Some other countries are polluting the air, so it's becoming worse." When asked who is most responsible, he revealed, "You want me to be honest? America is number one."

The pattern of referring to multiple causative factors is just as pronounced among younger people. Sabiano Temba, who teaches secondary school history and geography, first cited global warming.[58] He said, "Global warming is an increase of temperature in the world. Take for example our mountain there, as you can see the ice of Mount Kilimanjaro. Due to the increase of heat it can cause a lot of problems to the ice there." When asked to elaborate, he linked global warming not only with global issues such as air pollution but also with local ones. He said, "Ice on our mountain is decreased due to people who destruct our environment, who are cutting trees, burning the forest in the mountain. So the ice begins to decrease." A teacher at another secondary school, Mathias Mosha, spoke similarly.[59] He noted, "The ice at the cap of Mount Kilimanjaro is really affected by global warming." Yet he also mentioned industrial activity in other countries as well as deforestation and a lack of tree planting.

In the tourism industry, there is likewise a tendency to explain glacial recession in terms of multiple factors. Timba Kileo has been working as a climbing guide since 2000.[60] Unlike most people on the mountain, he has seen the glaciers firsthand, and he is frequently asked about them by the climbers he escorts. When asked why they are receding, he replied, "The primary cause would be global warming. It's impossible to avoid the fact that global warming is taking its toll on Kilimanjaro." However, he also said that there are other factors as well. He stated, "It's a global problem, and there are the secondary problems, which are deforestation or habitat destruction and war and all those things. They add up to what is causing these problems."

The range of factors that people cite is striking, from global warming and God's will to deforestation and excessive burning. Several even mentioned that the glaciers were melting because of the bombs detonated during the world wars. The most common replies, however, were global warming, God's will, and mountainside deforestation. Most people who described global warming had learned of the concept from school lessons or working in tourism, though some had heard about it through radio, television, or newspapers. Deforestation is the most interesting response, as it crosses age and education lines and is the most common response I received. This reflects the historical experience of the mountain. Since the early twentieth century, colonial administrations and the independent state worked to limit activity in the forests as a means of safeguarding the water supply. Yet for more than seventy years, forests have been shrinking as local communities have sought timber and more space for vihamba. As Hemp has noted, the forest zone remains under threat from excessive logging, illegal logging, and burning.[61] The shrinking of the forests, like that of the glaciers, is plainly visible from the agroforest belt. This reduction in forest cover has occurred alongside both glacial recession and reduced surface water flow. In people's minds, deforestation is a direct cause of both shrinking glaciers and less available water in rivers, streams, and canals. This shows that the plight of the glaciers is understood in terms of not only the waterscape, but also the historical experience of the people.

Recent scientific data confirms the link between climate change, deforestation, and surface water. In October 2016, the UN Environment Programme produced a report entitled *Sustainable Mountain Development in East Africa in a Changing Climate*. It notes that higher temperatures due to climate change have increased the number of wildfires, destroying 13,000 hectares of forest since 1976.[62] With fewer trees, the mountain is less able to capture water, in effect losing the equivalent of enough drinking water to supply one million people per year. The report urges Tanzania to protect the catchment area by reforesting the mountain, which will both generate more water and protect mountain ecosystems. The report mentions the recession of the glaciers, but it is careful not to link them to deforestation. This reflects recent scientific work indicating that deforestation, though a factor in downhill water supply, has had little effect on the glaciers.[63] The scientific opinion on the relationship between climate change, trees, and water, interestingly, seems to be trailing that of the people on the mountain. In 2004, when I first conducted interviews, few scholars or politicians had connected the three, yet people such as Vitalis Mosha clearly had.

The prevalence of multiple causative factors is revealing in and of itself. Most respondents mentioned a globally oriented factor (global warming, pollution) alongside a locally oriented one (deforestation, burning) and a spiritual one (God's will). This was particularly true among those with some knowledge of climate science. This tendency to link global and local factors reflects the broader pattern seen throughout this book. The peoples of the mountain have long fused outside knowledge with their own as a means of preserving local agency and their long-standing claims to the mountain's resources. Someone who cites climate change and deforestation acknowledges both the global dimension of the problem, over which they have little control, as well as a local dimension, over which they could effect change. In citing God's will, they bridge the two by leaving open the possibility of prayer to bring about broader change. In other words, by citing multiple causative factors, people admit the greater scope of the problem while retaining hope that it can be alleviated through local action.

And there has been local action in recent years, notably through the proliferation of tree-planting partnerships. The Tanzanian government, the UN Environment Programme, and local groups including NGOs, churches, schools, and clubs have embarked on programs to encourage tree planting. Local Rotary clubs, for example, have been partnering with schools since 2013. In only four years, schools in Mkuu Rombo planted more than 8,500 trees, with a further 4,200 seedlings sent home with the children.[64] Other organizations, such as Trees 4 Kilimanjaro, Carbon Covenant, and the Catholic Diocese of Moshi, have announced expansive programs aimed at planting millions of trees over the next several years.[65] In response to these successful efforts, the Tanzanian government has adopted tree planting as part of its climate change response. Terezya Luoga Huvisa, the minister of state for the environment, noted in 2013 that "climate change is a national and global threat. We can only deal with it through planting more trees, preserving water sources and wetlands. We should urge the people to rally behind these efforts."[66] In stark contrast to the water-development interventions discussed in the last chapter, residents seem invested in these programs and eager to participate. Modeling the success of these campaigns, other organizations have formed in recent years, one of which is the Kilimanjaro Center for Development and Environment. Created by Father Msafiri in 2017, it aims to foster sustainable development solutions through dialogue between science and praxis. It envisions that the solution to climate change lies in partnerships between the global and the local.

The most pressing question is what will happen if the glaciers vanish entirely. When asked, people primarily focused on local impacts. They expressed concern that losing the cap would make the waterscape dry up. Eleuther Assey, a village executive officer, feared that the mountain would become hotter and drier, like the steppe. She explained, "If it's all gone, the temperature in this area will be hot, compared to when the ice is there. It's going to be a disaster if it melts."[67] Christina

Lyimo expressed similar concerns.[68] She feared that if the ice vanished, there would be insufficient water for people, and "that will be the end of the Chagga people." Ewald Kessy likewise feared that if the glaciers vanish "it is the end of our life. Everything will perish."[69] Some even speculated that the end of the ice would make Kibo an active volcano again. Ebes Lyimo pointed out that the "mountain is a dormant volcano. If the snow disappears there, it means it will erupt again."[70] Mathias Mosha was the most emphatic. He exclaimed, "Can you imagine if maybe the eruption of the volcano can be caused because of the disappearing of the glacier? You find no life. No Chagga at all. Chagga will vanish. Kilimanjaro will perish. Tanzania will no longer be known to the world."[71]

Responses like these indicate how people interpret glacial recession based on historical understandings of the waterscape. Without an ice cap, the mountain will lose its heart. The peak will no longer provide life-giving water, and in turn the slopes will become lifeless like the plains. Mountain society, defined by water and vihamba, would cease to exist. These fears represent the local point of view and the linkages between water and society discussed throughout this book. What is also interesting is how people described these local impacts as having global importance. As Mathias Mosha explained, "It will be everyone's problem. I can say that Mount Kilimanjaro is not only for Tanzanians or for Chagga people. It is a worldwide precious thing. It should be preserved." This sentiment came across in numerous interviews; glacial recession would have global implications through local impact. Aside from their concerns about water and the environment, some also expressed concern about tourism. They feared that if the ice-capped mountain in the heart of Africa no longer has ice, it will not draw tourists. This would seriously impact the economy of an already struggling region. Not everyone is certain, though. Timba Kileo noted "the funny thing is, when the ice caps were bigger, Tanzania had very few tourists coming to it. Now the ice caps are getting smaller, we're about to hit the million marker. So maybe when they disappear, we'll get to two million."[72]

To what extent are these fears legitimate? Outside observers have echoed concerns about the potential decline of the mountain-climbing industry, though this is difficult to project. The question of water supply is more complicated. In many areas of the world, glaciers are crucial sources of water to surrounding areas. For Kilimanjaro, climate scientists maintain that nearly all surface water is derived from forest precipitation, not glacial melt. The disappearance of the glaciers will therefore not cause the mountain to dry up. However, there are larger, unsettled questions concerning the impact of climate change on precipitation and crop cultivation in the region.[73] Temperatures across sub-Saharan Africa are likely to rise by 2°C by midcentury and 4°C by the end of the century, and floods and droughts are likely to increase in frequency and intensity.[74] Reforestation efforts could increase the available water in the intermediate future, yet many questions remain as to the long-term prospects for Kilimanjaro.

From the perspective of a historian, one of the most important impacts is to local identity. This book has shown that the peoples of Kilimanjaro have long identified with the mountain as a physical space. The white cap of Kibo, the home of God and the source of life, has long held spiritual significance. My analysis has also shown that this significance has been highly dynamic, shifting in response to social and cultural changes and the availability of new knowledge over the past 150 years. Kibo is now known to be covered in ice, and Ruwa is no longer considered a supreme deity. It is unclear how local culture and identity will change because of the loss of the glaciers. What is clear is that people will adapt. It seems likely that if the ice cap vanishes yet the water supply remains intact, Kibo will remain a place of significance despite its altered form. The waterscape will still have a heart.

⌐

The experience of Kilimanjaro shows how communities are producing knowledge about the causes of climate change, its impacts, and how it will affect their futures. This knowledge reflects their deep historical attachment to the mountain as both a lived and a symbolic space. It is deeply meaningful and capable of inspiring action. People attribute glacier loss to several causes, some of which—including God's will and deforestation—are amenable to local action such as praying and tree planting. Scientists, politicians, and activists have largely ignored local knowledge of climate change. The way they speak about community engagement mirrors that of the development community over the past twenty years, too often a one-way dissemination of information rather than an exchange of ideas. The example of forestation has shown that a locally embraced idea, drawing on local knowledge and connected to local thinking, can lead to positive action in a way that externally imposed ideas and structures cannot. The peoples of Kilimanjaro possess a deep understanding of their local waterscapes and a powerful desire and incentive to steward them. The mountain can serve as an example of how embracing local knowledge can aid in the development of successful climate change–mitigation programs. Though local people may not be able to save the snows of Kilimanjaro, they may be able to save its waters.

Conclusion

Tanzania faces an acute water crisis. As of 2017, nearly twenty-three million people in the country lack consistent access to safe drinking water, nearly 44 percent of the whole population.[1] This is an astonishing figure considering the attention that the national government and foreign donors have paid to the water sector for decades. Since 1971, universal access to clean water has been a priority of five Tanzanian administrations and nearly a dozen international agencies, and millions of dollars have been spent on wells, pumps, concrete, and pipelines. Yet there is little to show for it. Kilimanjaro exemplifies this crisis. In a region known for its waterscapes — a region with a long history of water-management knowledge — universal access to clean water remains where it has been for nearly forty years: a distant dream. In many areas, both on the mountain and nationwide, access to water has actually become worse rather than better. The failure of water initiatives raises deep questions about approaches to the development and management of vital yet scarce natural resources.

This book has addressed underlying questions of community water management from a historical perspective, aiming to help resolve these present-day problems. It has shown that on the slopes of Kilimanjaro, water has been and remains a defining aspect of local culture and identity. For hundreds of years, the peoples of the mountain have considered water to be a blessing bestowed on them, one that gives life to their farms and distinguishes them from outsiders. It has shaped and continues to shape cultural practices, social relationships, and notions of belonging. It has inspired deep debates between knowledge holders and raised questions about whose knowledge is salient. Though many individual beliefs and practices have changed over the 150 years covered by this book, the overall framework for how people think about the waterscape remains largely consistent. People see the mountain and its waters as rightfully theirs, and they resist attempts by outsiders to exert influence over them. The cultural aspects of water management are as dynamic as the resource itself. Today, one need not look far to see reminders of the mountain and its waters, or adages such as *maji ni uhai*, "water is life" (fig. C.1).

FIGURE C.1. Maji ni Uhai, Moshi Town (*Matthew V. Bender*)

This book has also shown how water emerged as a key point of struggle between mountain peoples and outsiders. The term struggle, as opposed to conflict, rightfully indicates the long-term nature and multiple forms that water conflict has taken. Initially, it involved competing perceptions of the waterscape. Whereas mountain people envisioned a waterscape in which water could be readily available or in short supply, necessitating careful management—spiritual, social, and practical— European explorers saw Kilimanjaro as otherworldly, a place of abundance. As time passed, the focal point of struggle shifted to resisting the attempts by outside actors—colonial officers, scientists, missionaries, and settlers—to reshape local water-management practices. These attempts involved the public as well as the private, not just the control of canals and irrigation practices but also the control of hygiene practices and the management of domestic water. In the 1950s and 1960s, the mountain's people struggled to resist attempts by Chagga and Tanzanian nationalists to seize control of their waters through development projects and place it in the hands of government agencies. The 1980s brought struggle against neoliberal policies set on charging users for something they had used for generations for free. Most recently, people have struggled against glacial recession and climate change, which hold the potential to radically change the waterscape.

Despite these struggles, mountain peoples proved adept at negotiating new water-management knowledge and practice. This process of negotiation has taken numerous forms. In the early decades of the colonial encounter, mountain peoples used European dependence on their water technology as a tool for managing other areas of the colonial encounter. Starting in the 1930s, mountain peoples selectively incorporated new ideas and practices as they saw fit, in ways that were meaningful to them. The concept of harm is a revealing example of how this played out. Colonial actors criticized numerous local practices, from irrigation to spirit worship, as harmful to people and the waterscape. Mountain people chose to incorporate some new ideas to broaden their notion of harm and make it compatible with new realities such as waterborne disease. Changes in popular adages, such as "water brings no harm," indicate the deep cultural implications of this. In the face of unpopular measures such as registering canals or filing permits to build new ones, noncompliance became the most effective weapon. People negotiated new technologies, such as government canals and pipelines, by using them as they saw fit rather than in the manner prescribed by politicians or technocrats.

By the 1970s, however, many people had become dependent on government-managed water systems. This effectively limited their ability to negotiate these systems or maintain many forms of local water knowledge. In the highlands, demographic and economic changes made mifongo harder to maintain amid alternative systems that did not require any labor input. In the foothills and lowlands, people often lacked alternative sources of water. The growing divide between uphill and downhill interests is reflected in how people view older forms of water management and the role of specialists such as meni mifongo. Highland populations express dismay at the decline of these bodies of knowledge and their corresponding social institutions, while those in the lower areas express enthusiasm for new management models. Nonetheless, all these groups express a shared skepticism of government agencies, particularly the PBWO, and fear that these agencies will continue to erode their claims to the mountain's waters. In the past two decades, they have struggled to negotiate unpopular policies that have accompanied neoliberal reform and the shift to IWRM. While some people choose to pay for water, others refuse. Still others engage in sabotage or water stealing. Though people struggle to negotiate these new policies, as they have for decades, it has become much more difficult.

Lastly, this book has shown that attempts by the independent Tanzanian state to improve water management have resulted in conflicting and ineffective strategies that have, more times than not, actually harmed people's access to water. Perhaps no aspect of policy in the country—or across the Global South—has been subject to more change and inconsistency than water development. In 1900, the German administration considered local water management to be ingenious. By 1930, the British administration had called it harmful and advocated for more scientifically based management. In the 1950s, Chagga nationalist politicians shunned local management in favor of projects designed and managed by government agencies. The independent Tanzanian state largely adopted this position to bolster its authority and undermine traditional authority figures. In 1980, water was a human right and the government committed to providing it for free. A decade later, water was an economic good for which people had to pay. Furthermore, the national government and international donors decided to shift water management back to the locality by devolving control from Dar es Salaam to the PBWO and creating hundreds of WUAs. In short, government attempts to develop water on Kilimanjaro have been hindered by conflicting policies and strategies as well as disregard for the views, needs, and knowledge of local users.

Today, many people on Kilimanjaro have effectively poorer access to water than previous generations. Some of this can be attributed to the fact that the mountain is a different place. There are nearly eight times more people on the mountain than a century ago, leaving less land and water available for users. Climate change and increasing aridity have reduced the available water supply, and demand continues to rise from users on the mountain as well as interests in the Pangani Basin and (through hydropower) the rest of Tanzania. Population growth and resource scarcity are certainly significant issues. Yet a more significant issue, as this book has shown, is that the peoples of Kilimanjaro see the waterscape differently from how outsiders do. This gap in perspective is exacerbated by the fact that outsiders express little interest in understanding local ways of thinking. For decades, government administrations dismissed local knowledge while extolling scientific planning and high-modernist development. In recent years, the government and donors have claimed a participatory ethos, but community engagement tends to consist of surveys, focus groups, or other instruments that are better at relaying information than engaging people. These outsiders speak of cultural knowledge with dismissive expressions, such as "they think water is a gift from God," while not seeing the broader cultural context in which people think about water management.

This book indicates that the problem with water development on Kilimanjaro and beyond lies in a failure to grasp the dynamism of water as a resource, the extent to which that dynamism is cultural as well as physical, and the vital role that locally generated knowledge must play in developing sustainable solutions to the water crisis. Too often, government agencies and the development community have focused on the technical, financial, and legal aspects of water provision while giving minimal thought to how people will make sense of a new project or whether it will meet their needs. For example, the primary focus of community water development on Kilimanjaro today is domestic water. Yet if you ask people in the agroforest belt or the foothills, they express an urgent need for irrigation. Outsiders reduce the problem to one of needing to sensitize people and teach them that irrigation is unnecessary. This ignores not only the historical experience of the mountain but also the perceived needs of the people. This gap between those who are "developing" water and those who will use it contributes to a lack of buy-in and a host of other issues such as nonpayment, sabotage, and water stealing.

A solution lies in embracing local knowledge to make water-development initiatives more effective and relevant. Though the technology behind the mifongo may be antiquated, the social system that supported them empowered local expertise and encouraged a sense of ownership and obligation. It provides a model for building local capacity. Governments and development agencies need to deliberately attempt to understand local ways of thinking and develop solutions with that knowledge in mind. The concept of community-based WUAs is fundamentally sound, and it could potentially engage across gender and generational divides in ways that canal societies never could. Yet on Kilimanjaro, the WUAs have not generated much enthusiasm because they are political, imposed from the outside, and possess little power. These communities could be reformed in a way that gives them legitimacy, like the canal societies, yet adapts to the changing times. They should also have a means of influencing the broader policymaking of the basin. Lastly, mountain people and outsiders need to agree on the future of the mifongo. As long as water supplies dwindle and demand increases, mifongo will be a focal point of conflict. Working with communities to accommodate their irrigation needs, rather than criminalize them, seems like a smart way to move forward.

The past and future struggles over water on Kilimanjaro have implications well beyond its boundaries. Though Kilimanjaro is a unique waterscape with a unique history, it is hardly an outlier regarding local communities' developing knowledge of water or struggling to secure adequate supplies for their needs. Worldwide, much progress has been made in providing drinking water over the past twenty years, as part of the UN's Millennium Development Goals and other programs. Yet between 783 million and 1.1 billion people still lack access to drinking water, and as many as 2.7 billion experience water scarcity at least one month per year.[2] Global demand is estimated to rise by 55 percent by 2050, and 1.7 billion people live in river basins where water draw exceeds the recharge rate, meaning that the source is unsustainable in the long term.[3] Climate change, population growth, and migration promise to make water even less available in many areas, particularly the countries of sub-Saharan Africa. Much of the pattern of global water development mirrors that of Tanzania, where projects to provide safe water have proven inadequate to meet local needs in the long term. The historical experience of Kilimanjaro indicates the pitfalls of past and present water-development strategies but also the promise of embracing local knowledge, practice, and perspective.

Glossary

Italicized terms are in the Vunjo dialect of Kichagga unless otherwise noted; plurals are noted if different from singular or if a word is conventionally used in plural form.

askari	African soldier (Kiswahili)
chemchem	stream
debe	18-liter tin can, originally used to ship gasoline and kerosene but adapted for collecting and carrying domestic water (nickname used widely across East Africa)
fuli	short rains (October and November)
fundi (pl. *mafundi*)	maintenance person; pipe attendant (Kiswahili)
Hai	western administrative district of Kilimanjaro
ilumbo	division within an age-set
Kibo	highest peak of Kilimanjaro
kihamba (pl. *vihamba*)	homestead
kishari (pl. *vishari*)	localized patrilineal kin group
kisiye	long rains (March–May)
kiwamaenyi	canal intake
maji	water (Kiswahili)
mangi (pl. *wamangi*)	chief
mangi mkuu	paramount chief

mangi mwitori (pl. *waitori*) divisional chief

masale — dracaena plants

Mawenzi — second peak of Kilimanjaro

mbege — alcoholic brew; eleusine

mchili (pl. *wachili*) — mtaa leader/headman

meni mfongo — water canal specialist

mfo — river

mfereji (pl. *mifereji*) — water canal (Kiswahili)

mfongo (pl. *mifongo*) — water canal

mmasya (pl. *wamasya*) — spirit diviner

mringa — water

mruma (pl. *waruma*) — spirit (usually a deceased ancestor)

msesewe — a variety of tree (*Rauvolfia caffra*) whose bark is used to flavor mbege

mtaa (pl. *mitaa*) — administrative district

nduwa — a pooling of water in a river

njamaa — councils composed of lineage heads

nyika — bush or hinterland (Kiswahili)

rika — age-set

Rombo — eastern administrative district of Kilimanjaro

Ruwa — creator god of Kilimanjaro

shamba — farmland in the foothills

uhuru — freedom (Kiswahili), name for Kibo after 1961

Ujamaa — familyhood (Kiswahili), program of African socialism

Vunjo — central administrative district of Kilimanjaro (later part of Moshi Rural District)

Notes

INTRODUCTION

1. "Memorandum from the Chiefs of Kilimanjaro to the Governor of the Tanganyika Territory," July 1937, Tanzania National Archives 24674 I.

2. British colonial officers described mifongo as "furrows," a term that is also found throughout the literature. However, recent work by Mats Widgren indicates that the term "furrow" is misleading in terms of international comparisons and is at odds with the engineering and archeological literature. Widgren's work suggests that the term "canal" better describes the nature of these systems. Mats Widgren, "Furrows in Africa—Canals in the Americas?," *Azania* 49, no. 4 (2014): 524–29.

3. Examples include Marq de Villiers, *Water: The Fate of Our Most Precious Resource* (Boston: Houghton Mifflin, 2001); Fred Pearce, *When the Rivers Run Dry: Water—The Defining Crisis of the Twenty-First Century* (Boston: Beacon, 2007); Alex Prud'homme, *The Ripple Effect: The Fate of Freshwater in the Twenty-First Century* (New York: Scribner, 2012).

4. Vandana Shiva, *Water Wars: Privatization, Pollution, and Profit* (Cambridge, MA: South End, 2009).

5. Karl Wittfogel, *Oriental Despotism: A Comparative Study of Total Power* (New Haven: Yale University Press, 1957).

6. Donald Worster, *Rivers of Empire: Water, Aridity, and the Growth of the American West* (New York: Pantheon Books, 1985).

7. Richard White, *The Organic Machine: The Remaking of the Columbia River* (New York: Hill and Wang, 1996).

8. Paul Gelles, *Water and Power in Highland Peru: The Cultural Politics of Irrigation and Development* (New Brunswick: Rutgers University Press, 2000); Stephen Lansing, *Priests and Programmers: Technologies of Power in the Engineered Landscape of Bali* (Princeton: Princeton University Press, 2007);

David Mosse, *The Rule of Water: Statecraft, Ecology, and Collective Action in South India* (Oxford: Oxford University Press, 2003).

9. James McCann, *People of the Plow: An Agricultural History of Ethiopia, 1800–1990* (Madison: University of Wisconsin Press, 1995).

10. Christopher Conte, *Highland Sanctuary: Environmental History in Tanzania's Usambara Mountains* (Athens: Ohio University Press, 2004); Gregory Maddox, James Giblin, and Isaria Kimambo, *Custodians of the Land: Ecology and Culture in the History of Tanzania* (Athens: Ohio University Press, 1996); Helge Kjekshus, *Ecology Control and Economic Development in East African History: The Case of Tanganyika, 1850–1950* (Athens: Ohio University Press, 1996).

11. Richard Grove, *Green Imperialism: Colonial Expansion, Tropical Island Edens, and the Origins of Environmentalism, 1600–1860* (Cambridge: Cambridge University Press, 1995).

12. Robert Harms, *Games against Nature: An Eco-Cultural History of the Nunu of Equatorial Africa* (Cambridge: Cambridge University Press, 1999).

13. Steven Feierman, *Peasant Intellectuals: Anthropology and History in Tanzania* (Madison: University of Wisconsin Press, 1990).

14. Examples include David Anderson, *Eroding the Commons: The Politics of Ecology in Kenya* (Athens: Ohio University Press, 2002); Kate Showers, *Imperial Gullies: Soil Erosion and Conservation in Lesotho* (Athens: Ohio University Press, 1995); Pauline Peters, *Dividing the Commons: Politics, Policy and Culture in Botswana* (Charlottesville: University of Virginia Press, 1994).

15. Heather Hoag, *Developing the Rivers of East and West Africa* (London: Bloomsbury, 2013).

16. Allen Isaacman and Barbara Isaacman, *Dams, Displacement, and the Delusion of Development: Cahora Bassa and Its Legacies in Mozambique, 1965–2007* (Athens: Ohio University Press, 2013).

17. These include J. E. G. Sutton, "Engaruka and Its Waters," *Azania*, no. 13 (1978): 37–38; John E. G. Sutton, "Engaruka," in *Islands of Intensive Agriculture in Eastern Africa*, ed. Mats Widgren and John E. G. Sutton (Athens: Ohio University Press, 2004), 114–32.

18. Monica van Beusekom, *Negotiating Development: African Farmers and Colonial Experts at the Office du Niger, 1920–1960* (Portsmouth: Heinemann, 2002).

19. Maurits Ertsen, *Improvising Planned Development on the Gezira Plain, Sudan, 1900–1980* (London: Palgrave Macmillan, 2016).

20. James McCann, *Green Land, Brown Land, Black Land: An Environmental History of Africa, 1800–1990* (Portsmouth: Heinemann, 1999), 1–2.

21. One scholar who has embraced the term in describing Kilimanjaro is Mattias Tagseth, who wrote a dissertation on hillside irrigation. See Tagseth, "Studies of the Waterscape of Kilimanjaro, Tanzania: Water Management in Hill Furrow Irrigation" (PhD thesis, Norwegian University of Science and Technology, 2010).

22. Hoag, *Developing the Rivers*, 4.

23. Erik Swyngedouw, "Modernity and Hybridity: Nature, Regeneracionismo, and the Production of the Spanish Waterscape, 1890–1930," *Annals of the Association of American Geographers* 89, no. 3 (1999): 443–65.

24. Erik Swyngedouw, "The City as a Hybrid: On Nature, Society and Cyborg Urbanisation," *Capitalism, Nature, Socialism* 7, no. 1 (1996): 65–80.

25. Sara Berry, *No Condition Is Permanent: The Social Dynamics of Agrarian Change in Sub-Saharan Africa* (Madison: University of Wisconsin Press, 1993), 6.

26. Paul Richards, *Indigenous Agricultural Revolution: Ecology and Food Production in West Africa* (London: Hutchinson, 1985).

27. Timothy Mitchell, *Rule of Experts: Egypt, Techno-Politics, Modernity* (Berkeley: University of California Press, 2002).

28. Helen Tilley, *Africa as a Living Laboratory: Empire, Development, and the Problem of Scientific Knowledge, 1870–1950* (Chicago: University of Chicago Press, 2011), 25.

29. James Ferguson, *The Anti-Politics Machine: "Development," Depoliticization, and Bureaucratic Power in Lesotho* (Cambridge: Cambridge University Press, 1990), 257–58.

30. James Scott, *Seeing Like a State: How Certain Schemes to Improve the Human Condition Have Failed* (New Haven: Yale University Press, 1998), 7.

31. Van Beusekom, *Negotiating Development*.

32. Tanzania National Parks / African Wildlife Foundation, *Kilimanjaro National Park* (Arusha: Tanzania National Parks, July 1987); United Nations Environment Programme, "Africa without Ice and Snow," *Environmental Development*, no. 5 (2013): 146–55.

33. *Sky island* refers to mountains surrounded by lands that are drastically different in terms of climate. This creates distinct, biologically isolated habitats. The term derives from the field of island biogeography and relates to the work of ecologists such as Robert MacArthur and E. O. Wilson.

34. Knut Odner, "A Preliminary Report on an Archeological Survey on the Slopes of Kilimanjaro," *Azania*, no. 6 (1971): 131–49.

35. Examples include Emma Hunter, *Political Thought and the Public Sphere in Tanzania: Freedom, Democracy, and Citizenship in the Era of Decolonization* (Cambridge: Cambridge University Press, 2015); Sally Falk Moore, *Social Facts and Fabrications: "Customary" Law on Kilimanjaro, 1880–1980* (Cambridge: Cambridge University Press, 1986); Robert Munson, *The Nature of Christianity in Northern Tanzania: Environmental and Social Change, 1890–1916* (Lanham: Lexington Books, 2013); Ludger Wimmelbücker, *Kilimanjaro: A Regional History* (Münster: Lit Verlag, 2002).

36. Alison Grove, "Water Use by the Chagga on Kilimanjaro," *African Affairs*, no. 92 (1993): 431–48; Donald Mosgrove, "Watering African Moons: Culture and History of Irrigation Design on Kilimanjaro and Beyond" (PhD diss., Cornell University, 1998); Tagseth, "Studies of the Waterscape of Kilimanjaro."

37. Charles Dundas, *Kilimanjaro and Its People* (London: Frank Cass, 1924); Bruno Gutmann, *The Tribal Teachings of the Chagga*, trans. Ward Goodenough and Dorothy Crawford (New Haven: Human Relations Area Files, 1958); Alexandre Le Roy, *Au Kilima-Ndjaro* (Paris: L. de Soye, 1893).

38. See, for example, Gutmann, *The Tribal Teachings of the Chagga*; Gutmann, *Dichten und Denken der Dschagganeger* (Leipzig: Verlag der Evang.-Luth. Mission, 1909); Gutmann, *Chagga Law*, trans. A. M. Nagler (New Haven: Human Relations Area Files, 1963). See also the extensive bibliography in Sally Falk Moore and Paul Puritt, *The Chagga and Meru of Tanzania* (London: International African Institute, 1977).

39. Marcia Wright, *Strategies of Slaves and Women: Life Stories from East/Central Africa* (New York: Lilian Barber, 1993), 180.

40. Jan Vansina, *Oral Tradition: A Study in Historical Methodology* (London: Routledge, 1961).

41. Luise White, Stephan Miescher, and David William Cohen, *African Words, African Voices: Critical Practices in Oral History* (Bloomington: Indiana University Press, 2002).

42. Emily Osborn, *Our New Husbands Are Here: Households, Gender, and Politics in a West African State from the Slave Trade to Colonial Rule* (Athens: Ohio University Press, 2011).

CHAPTER 1: THE GIVER OF
ABUNDANCE AND PEACE

1. "A Chagga Legend: Why Mawenzi Is So Jagged," recalled by Aristarck Nguma, Kilema, 2004. From the field notes of the author.

2. Versions of this story can also be found in the writings of Charles Dundas and Bruno Gutmann. They share the same general plot but with some differences in detail. For example, Dundas and Gutmann describe Kibo and Mawenzi as male. See Dundas, *Kilimanjaro and Its People*, 36; Gutmann, *Dichten und Denken der Dschagganeger*.

3. Dundas, *Kilimanjaro and Its People*, 38.

4. Ibid., 39.

5. Wittfogel, *Oriental Despotism*.

6. These are the terms used in Kilema, Marangu, and Mwika, adjacent communities in southeast Kilimanjaro. Another name for the long rains was *masika*. See Moore and Puritt, *The Chagga and Meru*, 71.

7. Nicolas J. Cullen et al., "Kilimanjaro Glaciers: Recent Areal Extent from Satellite Data and New Interpretation of Observed 20th Century Retreat Rates," *Geophysical Research Letters* 33, no. 16 (2006): 2.

8. Ibid., 1.

9. These include Georg Kaser et al., "Modern Glacial Retreat on Kilimanjaro as Evidence of Climate Change: Observations and Facts," *International Journal of Climatology* 24, no. 3 (2004): 329–39; Thomas Mölg et al., "Tropical Glaciers, Climate Change, and Society: Focus on Kilimanjaro," in *The Darkening Peaks: Glacier Retreat, Science, and Society*, ed. Benjamin S. Orlove, Ellen Wiegandt, and Brian H. Luckman (Berkeley: University of California Press, 2008), 168–82; Douglas R. Hardy, "Kilimanjaro," in *Encyclopedia of Snow, Ice, and Glaciers*, ed. Vijay P. Singh, Pratap Singh, and Umesh K. Haritashya (New York: Springer, 2011), 672–79.

10. Jeff McKenzie et al., "A Hydrochemical Survey of Kilimanjaro (Tanzania): Implications for Water Sources and Ages," *Hydrological Journal* 18, no. 4 (2010): 985–95.

11. Christian Lambrechts et al., *Aerial Survey of the Threats to Mt. Kilimanjaro Forests* (New York: United Nations Development Programme, 2002), 7.

12. Dundas, *Kilimanjaro and Its People*, 39.

13. The Hai region, as it came to be defined in the nineteenth and twentieth centuries, does not share the same boundaries as the current Hai District. The current Hai District is smaller, as several of its chiefdoms were placed in a new district called Siha (to the west) and an enlarged Vunjo, which was renamed Moshi Rural District.

14. These figures are from Paul Maro, *Population Growth and Agricultural Change in Kilimanjaro, 1920–1970*, research paper no. 40 (Dar

es Salaam: University of Dar es Salaam Bureau of Resource Assessment and Land Use Planning, December 1975), 4-7.

15. Wimmelbücker, *Kilimanjaro: A Regional History*, 228.

16. The adage and interpretation are from Petro Itosi Marealle, "Chagga Customs, Beliefs, and Traditions," *Tanganyika Notes and Records*, no. 64 (1965): 56.

17. For more on descent, see Moore and Puritt, *The Chagga and Meru*; Kathleen Stahl, *History of the Chagga People of Kilimanjaro* (London: Mouton, 1964).

18. See Derek Nurse, *Classification of the Chaga Dialects: Language and History on Kilimanjaro, the Taita Hills, and the Pare Mountains* (Hamburg: Helmut Buske Verlag, 1979); Gérard Philippson, *"Gens des bananeraies"*: *Contribution linguistique a l'histoire culturelle des Chaga du Kilimanjaro* (Paris: Editions Recherche sur les Civilisations, 1984); J. Christoph Winter, "Internal Classifications of Kilimanjaro Bantu Compared: Towards an East African Dialectometry," in *Dialectologie et comparatisme en Afrique Noire*, ed. Gladys Guarisma and Suzy Platiel (Paris: Société d'Études Linguistiques et Anthropologiques de France, 1980), 101–32.

19. J. E. Goldthorpe, "The African Population of East Africa: A Summary of Its Past and Present Trends," app. 7 in *Report of the East African Royal Commission, 1953–1955* (London: Her Majesty's Stationery Office, 1955), 100.

20. This estimate of the size of vihamba applies to the time before 1940, after which population growth and intensification of agriculture led to swiftly decreasing farm sizes. See Paul Maro, "Agricultural Land Management under Population Pressure: The Kilimanjaro Experience, Tanzania," *Mountain Research and Development* 8, no. 4 (1988): 280.

21. Wimmelbücker, *Kilimanjaro: A Regional History*, 51.

22. Dundas, *Kilimanjaro and Its People*, 258.

23. William Louis Abbott, *Descriptive Catalogue of the Abbott Collection of Ethnological Objects from Kilima-njaro, East Africa* (Washington, DC: US Government Publishing Office, 1891), 394.

24. For more on this see Wimmelbücker, *Kilimanjaro: A Regional History*, 54–58.

25. Dundas, *Kilimanjaro and Its People*, 55.

26. Moore and Puritt, *The Chagga and Meru*, 6, 29; Moore, *Social Facts and Fabrications*, 17.

27. Moore and Puritt, *The Chagga and Meru*, 6.

28. For more about age-sets, see ibid., 29–30.

29. Dundas, *Kilimanjaro and Its People*, 287.

30. Moore, *Social Facts and Fabrications*, 19.

31. Mashina is one of the only examples we have of a female mangi. It appears that women could assume these roles in times of transition. Wimmelbücker, *Kilimanjaro: A Regional History*, 90–91.

32. Ibid., 292–93.

33. Anza A. Lema, "Chaga Religion and Missionary Christianity on Kilimanjaro: The Initial Phase, 1893–1916," in *East African Expressions of Christianity*, ed. Thomas Spear and Isaria Kimambo (Athens: Ohio University Press, 1999), 45–47.

34. Tagseth, "Studies of the Waterscape of Kilimanjaro," 155.

35. Lema, "Chaga Religion," 41.

36. Ibid., 42.

37. John Mbiti, *African Religions and Philosophy* (New York: Praeger, 1969), 2–3.

38. Tagseth, "Studies of the Waterscape of Kilimanjaro," 148.

39. The term *mifongo* is from the Vunjo dialect spoken in the southeast. They were also known by other names including the Kiswahili word *mifereji*. Studies on the Kilimanjaro canals include Matthew V. Bender, "Do Not Imagine That Every Cloud Will Bring Rain: A History of Irrigation on Kilimanjaro, Tanzania," in *Water and Food*, ed. Terje Tvedt and Terje Oestigaard, A History of Water, series 3, vol. 3 (New York: I. B. Tauris, 2016), 185–209; Grove, "Water Use by the Chagga"; Fidelis Masao, "The Irrigation System in Uchagga: An Ethno-historical Approach," *Tanzania Notes and Records*, no. 75 (1974): 1–8; Mosgrove, "Watering African Moons"; A. G. Pike, "Kilimanjaro and the Furrow System," *Tanganyika Notes and Records*, no. 64 (1965): 95–96; and papers by Mattias Tagseth including "The Expansion of Traditional Irrigation in Kilimanjaro, Tanzania," *International Journal of African Historical Studies* 41, no. 3 (2008): 461–90.

40. Neighboring regions such as Engaruka and the Kamba areas of central Kenya had canal systems much earlier than Kilimanjaro. It is likely that the technology behind the mountain's canals originated there or elsewhere. See Sutton, "Engaruka," in *Islands of Intensive Agriculture*.

41. Gutmann, *Chagga Law*.

42. Mathieu Fréon, "L'irrigation traditionnelle à Uru Mashariki, versant sud du volcan Kilimandjaro: Un témoin de l'identité Chagga," *IFRA Les cahiers d'Afrique de l'Est*, no. 26 (2004): 49–73; see also Mattias Tagseth, "Social and Cultural Dimensions of Irrigation Management in Kilimanjaro,"

in *Culture, History, and Identity: Landscapes of Inhabitation in the Mount Kilimanjaro Area, Tanzania,* ed. Timothy A. R. Clack, British Archaeological Reports International Series, no. 1966 (Oxford: Archaeopress, 2009), 89–105.

43. This account is from an interview with Joshua Maina, Machame, 2003.

44. It was believed that these ants had been sent by the spirits to provide guidance to the water specialist. Interview with Remi Siara, Kilema, 2004.

45. These names were mentioned in several interviews in Kilema, in particular during my interviews with Piuce Kiwali, Kilema, 2004; Atanas Simba, Kilema, 2004; and Sebastian Lyimo, Kilema, 2004.

46. H. H. Johnston, *The Kilima-Njaro Expedition: A Record of Scientific Exploration in Eastern Equatorial Africa* (London: Kegan, Paul, Trench, 1886).

47. Abbott, *Descriptive Catalogue of the Abbott Collection,* 387.

48. Otto Raum, *Chagga Childhood: A Description of Indigenous Education in an East African Tribe* (Oxford: International African Institute, 1940), 133.

49. This is based on data I compiled from interviews and surveys in Kilema. Unfortunately, little data exist until the 1960s as to how much water individuals consumed daily. People recall water use from this period in terms of numbers of pots rather than the volume of water consumed. Chagga did not manufacture pottery and instead procured it via trade from neighboring areas. Abbott notes that pottery used on the mountain for brewing averaged between 5 and 20 gallons (19–75 liters) in capacity. See Abbott, *Descriptive Catalogue of the Abbott Collection,* 415. Given the weight and size of these vessels, it is likely that the smaller ones were used more frequently for collecting water.

50. Interview with Edita Hendry, Kelamfua, Mkuu Rombo, 2004.

51. Dundas, *Kilimanjaro and Its People,* 255–57.

52. Ibid., 256.

53. Raum, *Chagga Childhood,* 71–72, 354.

54. Ibid., 194; Moore, *Social Facts and Fabrications,* 349.

55. This estimate is from informal discussions at mbege shops in Kilema in 2005, also an interview with Mary Mushi, Kibosho, 2005.

56. Tagseth, "Studies of the Waterscape of Kilimanjaro, Tanzania," 148.

57. This invocation was recorded during an interview with Martin Mosha, Kilema, 2004.

58. Interview with Liberati Mbando, Kilema, 2004.

59. Gutmann, *Chagga Law,* 372.

60. Ibid., 372.

61. Ibid., 376–77.

62. Ibid., 377.

63. Ibid., 377.

64. These bylaws are compiled from several interviews in Kilema in 2004.

65. From Interviews Martin Mosha, Kilema, 2004; and Atanas Simba, Kilema, 2004.

66. Fréon, "L'irrigation traditionnelle à Uru Mashariki," 49–73.

67. There were several cases in which brutal warfare ensued because canal rights were impaired. See Dundas, *Kilimanjaro and Its People*, 264.

68. Ibid., 38.

69. Lema, "Chaga Religion," 41–45.

70. Dundas's account was recorded sometime before publication of his text in 1924. He claims that the story was taken from elders and that it was not influenced by Christianity or Islam, despite the similarities. See Dundas, *Kilimanjaro and Its People*, 120.

71. Ibid., 117–20.

72. Ibid., 155–56.

73. Ibid., 156.

74. Ibid., 156–57.

75. Ibid., 157.

76. Raum, *Chaga Childhood*, 62–63. Other studies of education on Kilimanjaro include R. Sambuli Mosha, *The Heartbeat of Indigenous Africa: A Study of the Chagga Educational System* (London: Routledge, 2000); Amy Stambach, *Lessons from Mount Kilimanjaro: Schooling, Community, and Gender in East Africa* (New York: Routledge, 2000).

77. Raum, *Chaga Childhood*, chapter 1.

78. Paraphrased from an interview with Leoni Motesha, Mkuu Rombo, 2004.

79. Interview with Wilhelm Maunga, Mkuu Rombo, 2004.

80. Interview with Father Aidan Msafiri, Kilema, 2004.

81. Raum, *Chaga Childhood*, 206–7.

82. Mosha, *The Heartbeat of Indigenous Africa*, 61.

83. Raum, *Chaga Childhood*, 208. See also Gutmann, *The Tribal Teachings of the Chagga*, 283.

84. See Gutmann, *Chagga Law*, 283–87; Raum, *Chaga Childhood*, 285–367.

85. The following example is based on the observations of Gutmann, *The Tribal Teachings of the Chagga*, 341–42.

86. Ibid., 342.

87. Dundas, *Kilimanjaro and Its People*, 212–14.

CHAPTER 2: THE MOUNTAINS OF JAGGA

1. Johannes Rebmann, "First Journey to Jagga," in *Travels, Researches, and Missionary Labours during an Eighteen Years' Residence in Eastern Africa*, ed. J. L. Krapf (London: Trübner, 1860), 235–37.

2. See ibid. and also Johannes Rebmann, "Narrative of a Journey to Jagga, the Snow Country of Eastern Africa," *Church Missionary Intelligencer*, no. 1 (1849–50): 12–23; Rebmann, "Narrative of a Journey to Madjame," *Church Missionary Intelligencer*, no. 1 (1849–50): 327–30, 376–81; Rebmann, "Narrative of a Journey to Madjame, in Jagga," *Church Missionary Intelligencer*, no. 1 (1849–50): 272–76, 307–12.

3. Edward Said, *Orientalism* (New York: Pantheon Books, 1978); Benedict Anderson, *Imagined Communities* (New York: Verso, 1991).

4. Nurse, *Classification of the Chaga Dialects*, 28–31.

5. For more on irrigation in these communities see Patrick Fleuret, "The Social Organization of Water Control in the Taita Hills, Kenya," *American Ethnologist* 12, no. 1 (February 1985): 103–18; Michael Sheridan, "An Irrigation Intake Is Like a Uterus: Culture and Agriculture in Precolonial North Pare, Tanzania," *American Anthropologist* 104, no. 1 (March 2002): 79–92; Thomas Spear, *Mountain Farmers: Moral Economies of Land and Agricultural Development in Arusha and Meru* (Oxford: James Currey, 1997), 126.

6. John Iliffe, *A Modern History of Tanganyika* (Cambridge: Cambridge University Press, 1979), 19.

7. Sheridan, "An Irrigation Intake Is Like a Uterus," 79.

8. See Christopher Ehret, *The Civilizations of Africa: A History to 1800* (Charlottesville: University of Virginia Press, 2002), 119–23, 275–78.

9. Wimmelbücker, *Kilimanjaro: A Regional History*, 153.

10. Nurse, *Classification of the Chaga Dialects*, 28.

11. J. L. Krapf, *Travels, Researches, and Missionary Labours, during an Eighteen Years' Residence in Eastern Africa* [. . .] (London: Trübner, 1860), 544.

12. Le Roy, *Au Kilima-Ndjaro*, 5.

13. Iliffe, *A Modern History of Tanganyika*, 42.

14. For more see Wimmelbücker, *Kilimanjaro: A Regional History*, 114–17; Edward A. Alpers, *Ivory and Slaves: Changing Pattern of International*

Trade in East Central Africa to the Later Nineteenth Century (Berkeley: University of California Press, 1975); John Lamphear, "The Kamba and the Northern Mrima Coast," in Pre-Colonial African Trade, ed. Richard Gray and David Birmingham (London: Oxford University Press, 1970), 75–102; Isaria Kimambo, Penetration and Protest in Tanzania: The Impact of the World Economy on the Pare, 1860–1960 (Athens: Ohio University Press, 1991), 2–4.

15. Krapf, Travels, Researches, and Missionary Labours, 544.

16. Wimmelbücker, Kilimanjaro: A Regional History, 125.

17. For more on this topic see Abdul Sheriff, Slaves, Spices, and Ivory in Zanzibar: Integration of an East African Commercial Empire into the World Economy, 1770–1873 (Athens: Ohio University Press, 1987).

18. Moore and Puritt, The Chagga and Meru, 12.

19. Cited in Stahl, History of the Chagga People, 38.

20. Rebmann, "Narrative of a Journey to Jagga."

21. Krapf, Travels, Researches, and Missionary Labours, 192.

22. Georg Wilhelm Friedrich Hegel, Lectures on the Philosophy of World History: Introduction, Reason in History, trans. H. B. Nisbet (Cambridge: Cambridge University Press, 1975).

23. Hans Meyer, Across East African Glaciers: An Account of the First Ascent of Kilimanjaro (London: Longmans, Green, 1891), 20.

24. Rebmann, "First Journey to Jagga," 230–35.

25. Ibid., 236.

26. Ibid., 237–38.

27. Ibid., 241.

28. Ibid., 241.

29. Charles New, Life, Wanderings and Labours in Eastern Africa [. . .] (London: Hodder and Stoughton, 1873), 132–35.

30. Ibid., 129.

31. Ibid., 283–84.

32. Ibid., 309.

33. Ibid., 313.

34. Ibid., 378–81.

35. Ibid., 392.

36. Ibid., 370.

37. Ibid., 430.

38. Johnston, The Kilima-Njaro Expedition, 3.

39. Ibid., 43.

40. Ibid., 55–56.

41. Ibid., 68.

42. Ibid., 71–72, 152, 136.

43. Ibid., 322, 396.

44. Ibid., 325–26.

45. Ibid., 120.

46. Ibid., 322.

47. Ibid., 122–23.

48. Ibid., 96, 91.

49. Alex Johnston, *The Life and Letters of Sir Harry Johnston* (London: J. Cape, 1929), 93.

50. Johnston, *The Kilima-Njaro Expedition*, 555; 306.

51. Meyer, *Across East African Glaciers*, xii, vi.

52. Ibid., 65.

53. Ibid., 81–82.

54. Ibid., 103.

55. Ibid., 326.

56. Ibid., 318–19.

57. Ibid., 319–20.

58. Ibid., 146.

59. William Desborough Cooley, *Inner Africa Laid Open, in an Attempt to Trace the Chief Lines of Communication Across That Continent South of the Equator* (London: Longman, Brown, Green, and Longmans, 1852), 90–92.

60. Krapf, *Travels, Researches, and Missionary Labours*, 545–46.

61. For more on this expedition see Karl Klaus von der Decken, *Reisen in Ost-Afrika in den Jahren 1859 bis 1865* (Leipzig: C. F. Winter, 1869).

62. A full copy of the poem is reprinted in Johnston, *The Kilima-Njaro Expedition*, v.

CHAPTER 3: DO NOT BELIEVE THAT EVERY CLOUD WILL BRING RAIN

1. Richard Baker, *Africa Drums* (London: Lindsay Drummond, 1945), 28–29.

2. Karen Blixen, *Out of Africa* (London: Penguin, 2001).

3. Juhani Koponen, *Development for Exploitation: German Colonial Policies in Mainland Tanzania, 1884–1914* (Helsinki: Tiedekirja, 1994), 169–76; Philippa Söldenwagner, *Spaces of Negotiation: European Settlement and Settlers in German East Africa, 1900–1914* (München: Martin Meidenbauer,

2006); Thaddeus Sunseri, *Vilimani: Labor Migration and Rural Change in Early Colonial Tanzania* (Portsmouth: Heinemann, 2001).

4. Kirk to Salisbury, November 19, 1885, as quoted in Norman Bennett, *Arab versus European: Diplomacy and War in Nineteenth-Century East Central Africa* (New York: Africana, 1986), 130.

5. Iliffe, *A Modern History of Tanganyika*, 91.

6. Ibid., 100.

7. Moore and Puritt, *The Chagga and Meru*, 15.

8. Stahl, *History of the Chagga People*, 185.

9. For a detailed discussion see Michelle Moyd, *Violent Intermediaries: African Soldiers, Conquest, and Everyday Colonialism in German East Africa* (Athens: Ohio University Press, 2014).

10. Iliffe, *A Modern History of Tanganyika*, 101.

11. Moore and Puritt, *The Chagga and Meru*, 17; Moore, Social Facts and Fabrications, 99.

12. Iliffe, *A Modern History of Tanganyika*, 275.

13. Wimmelbücker, *Kilimanjaro: A Regional History*, 272–74.

14. Moore and Puritt, *The Chagga and Meru*, 16.

15. Koponen, *Development for Exploitation*, 169–76.

16. Ibid., 258–80.

17. Wimmelbücker, *Kilimanjaro: A Regional History*, 294.

18. Ibid., 295.

19. Ibid., 321.

20. Gutmann, *Chagga Law*, 392.

21. "Ullerhöchte Verordnung, betreffend Kronland in Ostafrika, 26 November 1895," in *Die Deutsche Kolonial-Gesetzgebung* (Berlin: E. S. Mittler, 1898), 200–202.

22. For a broader history of German Forestry see Robert Munson, Forest Reserves and Local Rights: German East Africa's Mount Kilimanjaro, Program for the Study of the African Environment Research Series 5 (Boston: Boston University, 2009); Thaddeus Sunseri, Wielding the Ax: State Forestry and Social Conflict in Tanzania, 1820–2000 (Athens: Ohio University Press, 2009).

23. Munson, Forest Reserves, 9.

24. Ibid., 5.

25. E. Gilg, "Die Nutzhölzer Ostafrikas und ihre Verwertung," in *Die Pflanzenwelt Ost-Afrikas und der Nachbargebiete*, ed. Adolf Engler (Berlin: Geographische Verlagshandlung Dietrich Reimer, 1895), 286.

26. "Jahresbericht 1907/1908, FV Mos (Rohrbeck)," 21 July 1908, pp. 3–4, Tanzania National Archives (hereafter TNA) G 8/514; "Brief von Forstbezirk Moschi, Arusha (Rohrbeck) an Dar," 25 November 1907, TNA G 8/548. As cited in Munson, *Forest Reserves*, 9.

27. Siebenlist was based in Wilhelmstal (now Lushoto), in the Usambara Mountains, but his jurisdiction included Kilimanjaro. See Theodor Siebenlist, *Forstwirtschaft in Deutsch-Ostafrika* (Berlin: Verlagsbuchhandlung Paul Parey, 1914), iii.

28. Norman Bennett, "The British on Kilimanjaro, 1884–1892," *Tanzania Notes and Records*, no. 63 (1964), 229–44; also E. A. Fitch and J. A. Wray, "The First Year of the Chagga Mission," *Church Missionary Intelligencer*, no. 2 (1886), 555–62.

29. Meyer, *Across East African Glaciers*, 98.

30. Bennett, "The British on Kilimanjaro," 241.

31. The Holy Ghost Fathers, now known as the Spiritans, were founded in 1709 by Father Poullart des Places. They began work in Africa in 1800 and had a presence in Senegal, Sierra Leone, Nigeria, French Congo, Gabon, Zanzibar, Kenya, German East Africa, and elsewhere. See Henry J. Koren, *The Spiritans: A History of the Congregation of the Holy Ghost* (Pittsburgh: Duquesne University Press, 1958); Reginald Walker, *The Holy Ghost Fathers in Africa: A Century of Missionary Effort* (Dublin: Blackrock College, 1933).

32. Father Le Roy kept a detailed account of this journey and his subsequent time of residence on the mountain. These memoirs were published in 1914. See Le Roy, *Au Kilima-Ndjaro*.

33. Journal entries from the mission indicate that in 1892, soldiers from Moshi frequently launched raids on Kilema, seeking weapons, livestock, and humans. See *Journal de la communauté de Kilema*, yrs. 1892–93, Congrégation du Saint-Esprit Archives (hereafter CSEA) 2K2.7.

34. "Documents divers au l'Afrique Orientale, 1910–1922," CSEA 2K1.11B3.

35. For more on the Lutheran missions, see Marcia Wright, *German Missions in Tanganyika, 1891–1941: Lutherans and Moravians in the Southern Highlands* (Oxford: Clarendon, 1971); Anza Lema, "The Impact of the Leipzig Lutheran Mission on the People of Kilimanjaro, 1893–1920" (PhD diss., University of Dar es Salaam, 1972).

36. G. N. Shann, "The Early Development of Education among the Chagga," *Tanganyika Notes and Records*, no. 45 (1945): 25.

37. "Érection du Vicariat du Kilimandjaro, 1910–1922," CSEA 2K2.11a1.

38. Moore and Puritt, *The Chagga and Meru*, 74. For information on the violence in Buganda, see D. A. Low, *Religion and Society in Buganda, 1875–1900*, East African Studies 8 (Kampala: East African Institute of Social Research, 1956); Michael Twaddle, *Kakungulu and the Creation of Uganda* (Athens: Ohio University Press, 1993).

39. John Comaroff and Jean Comaroff, *Of Revelation and Revolution*, vol. 2, *The Dialectics of Modernity on a South African Frontier* (Chicago: University of Chicago Press, 1997).

40. J. A. Kieran, "Christian Villages in North-Eastern Tanzania," *Transafrican Journal of History* 1, no. 1 (1971): 24–38.

41. Wimmelbücker, *Kilimanjaro: A Regional History*, 308. The elevation difference is based on GPS measurements I made in the summer of 2005.

42. These events are pieced together from entries in the *Journal de la communauté de Kilema*, yrs. 1908–9, CSEA 2K2.7; as well as an interview with Gustave Gerard, Kilema, 2004.

43. Gustave Gerard recalls Matonga being from Rosho village. Interview with Gustave Gerard, Kilema, 2004.

44. *Journal de la communauté de Kilema*, 5 February 1909, CSEA 2K2.7.

45. Locals attribute this name to an incident involving a missionary. They say that while taking communion to a sick person, he fell and dropped a host into the canal. From that point on, people believed that the water carried the presence of the Holy Spirit, and thus it received the name. Interview with Father Aidan Msafiri, Kilema Parish, 2004.

46. Interview with Father Aidan Msafiri, Kilema Parish, 2004.

47. From field notes, Kilema, 2004.

48. *Journal de la communauté de Kibosho*, 8 January 1894, CSEA 2K2.5.

49. *Journal de la communauté de Kibosho*, 9 February 1894, CSEA 2K2.5

50. Specifications are from a letter sent to the District Officer regarding mission canals. See *Journal de la communauté de Rombo*, 30 November 1921, CSEA 2K2.18. Entries concerning the construction of the canal can be found from January to September of 1899.

51. *Journal de la communauté de Rombo*, yrs. 1908–9, CSEA 2K2.18.

52. J. A. Kieran, "The Origins of Commercial Arabica Coffee Production in East Africa," *African Historical Studies* 2, no. 1 (1969): 52.

53. The origin of the seeds is uncertain, likely Aden or Réunion. See Kieran, "The Origins of Commercial Arabica," 61.

54. "Etat des recettes et dépenses pour l'année 1912," *Propagation de la foi sur Kilimandjaro*, 1911–21, CSEA 2K1.11a3.

55. Though the mission balanced its books with money sent from Paris, it preached an ethos of financial self-sufficiency generated through the labors of their clergy and converts. See Kieran, "The Origins of Commercial Arabica," 51.

56. *Journal de la communauté de Kilema*, 1901, CSEA 2K2.7.

57. Kieran, "The Origins of Commercial Arabica," 52.

58. *Journal de la communauté de Kilema*, 25 July 1902, CSEA 2K2.7

59. Hermann Paasche, *Deutsch-Ostafrika: Wirtschaftliche Studien* (Berlin: Schwetschke, 1906), 413. See also Söldenwagner, *Spaces of Negotiation*, 24–25.

60. Söldenwagner, *Spaces of Negotiation*, 26.

61. "Ullerhöchte Verordnung, betreffend Kronland in Ostafrika, 26 November 1895," in *Die Deutsche Kolonial-Gesetzgebung* (Berlin: E. S. Mittler, 1898), 200–202.

62. Söldenwagner, *Spaces of Negotiation*, 84.

63. These figures, generated by the German administration, were republished in 1923 by the British government. See Geographical Section of the Naval Intelligence Division, *A Handbook of German East Africa* (London: His Majesty's Stationary Office, 1923), 424–25.

64. Johannes Tesch, *Kolonial-Handels-Adressbuch* (Berlin: W. Süsserott, 1914), 76–78.

65. Wimmelbücker, *Kilimanjaro: A Regional History*, 324.

66. Iliffe, *A Modern History of Tanganyika*, 144.

67. Wimmelbücker, *Kilimanjaro: A Regional History*, 312.

68. The term "iron ring" was coined by Thomas Spear, who used it to describe the similar situation on nearby Mount Meru. See Spear, *Mountain Farmers*.

69. Paul Maro, "Population and Land Resources in Northern Tanzania, the Dynamics of Change, 1920–1970" (PhD diss., University of Minnesota, 1974).

70. "Northern Province Native Agriculture," TNA 9/6/5.

71. Dundas noted in 1921 that Europeans had acquired benefits outside their farms, such as water and timber, by "arrangement with the local chiefs and without reference to the Government." See "Circular of Dundas," 17

October 1921, Moshi, Moshi Catholic Diocese Archives. Also cited in Wimmelbücker, *Kilimanjaro: A Regional History*, 314.

72. Interview with Mzee Mwasha, Machame, 2004.

73. "Mr. Vincent Humplick to the Moshi Water Board," 25 February 1925, TNA 5/69/C, vol. 1.

74. Ibid.

75. "Agreement between Mr. Vincent Humplick and Marai Shangali, Mangi of Machame," 7 January 1925, TNA 5/69/C, vol.1.

76. Interview with Mzee Mwasha, Machame, 2004

77. Söldenwagner, *Spaces of Negotiation*, 24–25.

78. *Journal de la communauté de Rombo*, yr. 1908, CSEA 2K2.18.

79. Wimmelbücker, *Kilimanjaro: A Regional History*, 388.

80. *Journal de la communauté de Rombo*, 12 July 1908, CSEA 2K2.18.

81. *Mtsimbii* is a derogatory term for people from the eastern slopes of the mountain. See Wimmelbücker, Kilimanjaro: A Regional History, 388–92.

82. Discussion of this meeting is summarized in "Memo from the Moshi District Officer to the Colonial Office, Dar es Salaam," 11 September 1907, TNA G 4/115.

83. "Memo from the Moshi District Officer to the Colonial Office, Dar es Salaam," 16 December 1907, TNA G 4/115.

84. Oscar Bongard, *Wie wandere ich nach Deutschen Kolonien aus?*, trans. in *The German Colonial Experience: Select Documents on German Rule in Africa, China, and the Pacific, 1884–1914*, ed. Arthur Knoll and Hermann Hiery (Lanham, MD: University Press of America, 2010), 14.

85. Wimmelbücker, *Kilimanjaro: A Regional History*, 347.

86. These regulations were published in the *Amtlicher Anzeiger für den Bezirk Moschi* (Official gazette for the Moshi District). From Wimmelbücker, *Kilimanjaro: A Regional History*, 348.

87. "Wasserecht," TNA G 4/115.

88. Moyd, *Violent Intermediaries*, 143.

89. Iliffe, *A Modern History of Tanganyika*, 243.

90. Ibid., 262.

91. Ibid., 247.

92. League of Nations, Mandate Agreement for Tanganyika, July 1922, art. 7.

93. Government of Tanganyika, Native Authority Ordinance, 1921.

CHAPTER 4: FROM ABUNDANCE TO SCARCITY

1. Dundas, *Kilimanjaro and Its People*, 6.

2. Ibid., 13.

3. Richards, *Indigenous Agricultural Revolution*; Tilley, *Africa as a Living Laboratory*, van Beusekom, *Negotiating Development*.

4. "Memorandum on the Control of Water Supplies in Arusha and Moshi," January 1928, TNA 472/A-232/1.

5. Wimmelbücker, *Kilimanjaro: A Regional History*, 323–24.

6. Government of Tanganyika, *Blue Book, 1921.*

7. See R. R. Kuczynski, *Demographic Survey of the British Colonial Empire* (Oxford: Institute of International Affairs, 1949) and J. E. Goldthorpe, "The African Population of East Africa."

8. Maro, *Population Growth and Agricultural Change*, 9–10.

9. Government of Tanzania, Central Bureau of Statistics, volumes for 1968 and 1988.

10. Moore, *Social Facts and Fabrications*, 110.

11. This figure included 182 Greeks, 175 Germans, 98 British, and 33 Afrikaners. See Government of Tanganyika, "Northern Province Annual Report, 1927," TNA 11681.

12. This is difficult to quantify, as the Germans never gathered statistics on water use and the British did not until the 1950s. Based upon my field notes, it seems that domestic consumption doubled. Irrigation is more difficult to estimate, as flow rates varied between canals, across seasons, and year-to-year.

13. Interview with Augustina August, Kilema, 2004; Interview with Dauseni Massawe, Mkuu Rombo, 2004.

14. Applications for water rights required applicants to calculate water use per capita based upon the race of the prospective users. They estimated that African users consumed water at one-third the rate of Europeans. See TNA 474/1022.

15. J. A. Kieran, "The Origins of Commercial Arabica," 51–67.

16. M. A. Ogutu, "The Cultivation of Coffee among the Chagga of Tanzania, 1919–1939," *Agricultural History* 46, no. 2 (1972): 283.

17. Iliffe, *A Modern History of Tanganyika*, 276.

18. Ibid., 276.

19. "D. Ghikas to the District Commissioner, Moshi," 7 September 1922, in *Moshi Water Board, 1922–1923*, TNA 5/1017, vol. 1.

20. "Edgar R. Beech to the President, Moshi Water Board," 15 November 1923, in *Moshi Water Board, 1922–1923*, TNA 5/1017, vol. 1.

21. Didas Kimaro et al, "Review of Sisal Production and Research in Tanzania," *African Study Monographs* 15, no. 4 (1994): 230.

22. Claude Guillebaud, *An Economic Survey of the Sisal Industry of Tanganyika* (Welwyn, UK: James Nisbet, 1958), 82.

23. Government of Tanganyika, *Blue Book 1940*; Government of Tanganyika, *Blue Book 1945*.

24. B. A. Datoo, "The Generation of Hydro-Electric Power on the Lower Pangani River," *East African Record* 3, no. 51 (1965): 47–49.

25. "Tanganyika Electric Supply Company to the Hon. Chief Secretary to the Government, the Secretariat," 27 February 1935, in *Water Problems in Tanganyika, 1929–1953*, TNA 69/246/1.

26. Richard Grove, *Green Imperialism*.

27. David Anderson, "Depression, Dust Bowl, Demography, and Drought: The Colonial State and Soil Conservation in East Africa during the 1930s," *African Affairs* 83, no. 332 (July 1984): 327.

28. G. V. Jacks and R. O. Whyte, *The Rape of the Earth: A World Survey of Soil Erosion* (London: Faber and Faber, 1939).

29. "Memorandum on the Control of Water Supplies in Arusha and Moshi, 1928," TNA 472/A-232/1; see also E. Harrison, *A Memorandum on Soil Erosion* (Dar es Salaam: Government of Tanganyika, 1937).

30. "Memo from A. J. Wakefield, Senior Agricultural Officer, North-Eastern Circle, Tanganyika, to the Director of Agriculture, Tanganyika," 26 January 1931, TNA 19542. Wakefield also sent the memo to the commissioner of the Northern Province at Arusha, the Moshi District commissioner, and the Moshi District entomologist.

31. "Monthly Report of the Topo-Hydrographic Survey, Moshi, for the Month of October 1941," TNA 69/481.

32. "Senior Collector of Customs, Dar es Salam, to the Hon. Chief Secretary, Dar es Salaam," 1 March 1939, in *Anti-Erosion Measures by Native Authorities*, TNA 25754.

33. Government of Tanganyika, Natural Water Supply Regulation Ordinance of 1923, no. 4 of 1923, *Annotated Ordinances, Tanganyika Territory, 1923*.

34. Ellen Hillbom, "The Right to Water: An Inquiry into Legal Empowerment and Property Rights Formation in Tanzania," in *The Legal*

Empowerment Agenda: Poverty, Labour and the Informal Economy in Africa, ed. Dan Banik (London: Ashgate, 2011), 199.

35. Government of Tanganyika, Natural Water Supply Ordinance, para. 9, sec. 1–8.

36. Moshi District Office, "Moshi Water Board, 1923," TNA 5/177 D.

37. "Meimarides (The Mweka Coffee Estates) to the District Officer, Moshi," 13 September 1927, in *Water Disputes, 1925–1928,* TNA 5/69D.

38. "Mangi Ngilisho to the District Officer, Moshi," 19 September 1927, in *Water Disputes, 1925–1928,* TNA 5/69D.

39. "District Officer, Moshi, to Mr. E. Meimarides, Esq.," 18 October 1927, in *Water Disputes, 1925–1928,* TNA 5/69D.

40. "Harold MacMichael, Governor of the Tanganyika Territory, to the Secretary of State for the Colonies, London," 15 May 1936, TNA 22962.

41. E. O. Teale and C. Gillman, *Report on the Investigation of the Proper Control of Water and the Reorganization of Water Boards in the Northern Province of Tanganyika Territory, November–December 1934* (Dar es Salaam: Government Printer of Tanganyika, 1935).

42. Ibid., para. 71.

43. Ibid., paras. 174–75.

44. Ibid., para. 89.

45. Clement Gillman, *The Clement Gillman Diaries,* vols. 13–14, Rhodes House Library (hereafter RHL) MSS Afr. S 1175/13-14.

46. Teale and Gillman, *Report,* para. 169.

47. Ibid., para. 119.

48. Francis Kanthack, *Report on the Control of the Natural Waters of Tanganyika and the Framework of a Water Law on Which Such Control Should Be Based* (Dar es Salaam: Government of Tanganyika, 1936), 6.

49. Ibid., 6.

50. Ibid., 11–12.

51. Government of Tanganyika, "Water Ordinance of 1948," no. 23 of 1948, *Annotated Ordinances, Tanganyika Territory, 1948,* para. 3. The ordinance did not apply to any water right conferred by agreement or license before its implementation or to the use of water in the mining sector.

52. The rising wealth of the people is discussed in "Memorandum on the Development of the Chagga Tribe, 1937," TNA 24898.

53. "Memorandum on the Expansion of the Chagga Tribe into the Rau-Himo Plains," 20 July 1939, TNA 26045.

54. "Native Authority Orders, 1931," in Government of Tanganyika, *Northern Province Annual Report, 1931*, TNA 11681.

55. A Native Authority rule prohibiting the pollution of rivers, springs, and canals was originally passed in the 1940s and revised in 1958. See "Copies of NA Orders," TNA 5/23/33/2. Revised rules on issues related to soil erosion were passed in 1937, and a more comprehensive version came to light in 1957. An order requiring people to remain outside the borders of the forest reserve was passed in 1942. See "Native Authority Rules," TNA 5/23/33.

56. Government of Tanganyika, *Northern Province Annual Report, 1931*, TNA 11681.

57. Because of several difficulties, including a lack of staff and the dynamic nature of the mifongo, this quickly turned into a long-term project that was not completed until the 1960s. See TNA 471/w.2/8, vol.2.

58. Other chiefs also limited eleusine cultivation in areas of their chiefdoms. See TNA 19415.

59. Interview with Michael Safari, Kilema, 2004. The practice of wamangi's leading canal projects started on a limited scale at the turn of the century. Gutmann mentions them briefly but sees them as insignificant. See Gutmann, *Chagga Law*, 413–21.

60. Africans applying for a new water right were required to utilize the same paperwork as settlers, missionaries, and other prospective users. See TNA 5/45/30.

61. "M. T. Avery, Hydrographic Surveyor, Water Development Department, Arusha, to the Provincial Commissioner, Northern Province, Arusha," 10 December 1947, TNA 26045.

62. See TNA 471/w.2/8, vol.2.

63. Government of Tanganyika, "The Water Office, Annual Report, 1960–1961," 3, RHL 754.14 r.5.

64. "Northern Province Annual Report, 1928," TNA 20378.

65. Extract from a speech by the governor of Tanganyika, 30 July 1937, TNA 24674 I.

CHAPTER 5: WATER BRINGS HARM

1. Petro Itosi Marealle, *Maisha ya Mchagga hapa Duniani na Ahera* (Dar es Salaam: Mkuki na Nyota, 2002).

2. This was the observation of Reverend R. Reusch, superintendent of the Chagga Lutheran Church, in his introductory note to Marealle's book. See ibid., p. xiv.

3. Comaroff and Comaroff, *Of Revelation and Revolution*; Timothy Burke, *Lifebuoy Men, Lux Women: Commodification, Consumption, and Cleanliness in Modern Zimbabwe* (Durham, NC: Duke University Press, 1996); Berry, *No Condition Is Permanent*.

4. Derek Peterson, *Creative Writing: Translation, Bookkeeping, and the Work of Imagination in Colonial Kenya* (Portsmouth: Heinemann, 2004).

5. "Application for a Water Right, Moshi District Water Board," November 1947, TNA 474/w.1/8.

6. This figure is from a personal communication from the Tanzanian Ministry of Works in 1965, published in Gilbert White, David Bradley, and Anne White, *Drawers of Water: Domestic Water Use in East Africa* (Chicago: University of Chicago Press, 1972), 112.

7. From Field Notes, Kilema, 2004.

8. Burke, *Lifebuoy Men*, 43.

9. Interview with Leoni Motesha, Mkuu Rombo, 2004.

10. Interview with James Mbuya, Kilema, 2004.

11. Interview with Augustina August, Kilema, 2004.

12. Interview with Liberati Mbando, Kilema, 2004.

13. Interview with Martin Mosha, Kilema, 2004.

14. "Memorandum written by the chiefs of Kilimanjaro to the Governor of Tanganyika Territory," July 1937, TNA 24674 I.

15. These institutions had largely been established and run by the Catholic and Lutheran missions since the beginning of the century. Most schools and educational centers remained under the control of the religious orders until the 1960s, when the central government took control of most schools. See G. N. Shann, "The Early Development"; A. A. Lema, "The Lutheran Church's Contribution to Education in Kilimanjaro," *Tanzania Notes and Records*, no. 68 (1966): 87–94.

16. Of the 14,740 students enrolled, 8,987 were male and 5,753 female. See "Returns of Schools, Vicariate of Kilimanjaro," in Centenary Book Committee, *The Catholic Church in Moshi: A Centenary Memorial, 1890–1990* (Ndanda, Tanzania: Ndanda Mission Press, 1990), 79.

17. For more on the health aspects of school curricula on Kilimanjaro, see A. A. Lema, "The Lutheran Church's Contribution"; G. N. Shann, "The Early Development."

18. Interview with Liberati Mbando, Kilema, 2004.

19. A number of other teachers I interviewed confirmed these details as well. Interview with Clara Mathias, Kilema, 2004; also informal discussions with Aristarck Stanley, Kilema, and Efraim Muro, Machame.

20. Lema, "The Impact of the Leipzig Lutheran Mission," v.

21. An excellent example is Nancy Rose Hunt, A *Colonial Lexicon of Birth Ritual, Medicalization, and Mobility in the Congo* (Durham, NC: Duke University Press, 1999).

22. Rural Midwifery, Health, and Child Welfare Service, "Training Guidelines, 1948," TNA 10409.

23. Interview with Hedwigha Mosha, Kilema, 2005.

24. Rural Midwifery, Health, and Child Welfare Service, "Syllabus, 1948," TNA 10409.

25. Gutmann notes in 1926 that while the government required people to construct pit latrines, most continued to defecate in their vihamba, as had been the established practice for years. Gutmann, *Chagga Law*, 292.

26. At the Catholic mission in Kilema, for example, priests announced outbreaks of diseases such as typhoid, dysentery, and smallpox during masses on several occasions. Some of the first incidences to appear in the missionary journals were an outbreak of dysentery in 1932 and an outbreak of diarrhea in 1933. See *Journal de la communauté de Kilema*, yrs. 1908–50, CSEA 2K2.7. In Kibosho, there were recorded cases of dysentery as early as 1901. See *Journal de la communauté de Kibosho*, June 1901, CSEA 2K2.5. See also Interview with Augustina August, Kilema, 2004.

27. *Debe* were tin cans originally used to import gasoline and kerosene. By the 1960s, they had become a preferred tool for carrying water, because of their caps and lighter weight. They also established 18 liters as a standard unit of measure for domestic water. See White, Bradley, and White, *Drawers of Water*, 64.

28. Interview with James Mbuya, Kilema, 2004; Interview with Augustina August, Kilema, 2004; Interview with Clara Mathias, Kilema, 2004. Also Field Notes, Kilema and Mkuu Rombo, 2004.

29. See *Journal de la communauté de Kilema* and *Journal de la communauté de Rombo*, yrs. 1930–40, CSEA 2K2.7; CSEA 2K2.18.

30. Two individuals from Rombo, who wished not to be identified by name, told me in 2004 that they knew of people who would make offerings of chickens or mbege near the Lumi River during droughts. From Field Notes, Mkuu Rombo, 2004.

31. From "Bulletin des oeuvres, 1933–1953," CSEA 2K1.12.6; and "Kilimanjaro District: Correspondence, 1960–1968," CSEA 2K1.16A3.

32. Michael von Clemm, "Agricultural Productivity and Sentiment on Kilimanjaro," *Economic Botany* 18, no. 2 (1964): 99.

33. Paul Landau, for example, argues in his study of missions in the Ngwato Kingdom of southern Africa that Christianity cannot be understood apart from the "reorganization of politics, gender, and status" that were taking place. These changes all together allowed Christians to create a new "political realm of power." See Paul Landau, *The Realm of the Word: Language, Gender, and Christianity in a Southern African Kingdom* (Portsmouth: Heinemann, 1995), xvi–xvii.

34. While there were exceptions, notably Bruno Gutmann and Otto Raum, most Catholic and Lutheran missionaries considered Chagga religious practices to be nothing short of superstition. Lema, "Chaga Religion," 54.

35. Examples include Interview with Dauseni Massawe, Mkuu Rombo, 2004; Interview with Mzee Mwasha, Machame, 2004; Interview with Martin Mosha, Kilema, 2004; Interview with Clara Mathias, Kilema, 2004.

36. Interview with Herbert Mbuya, Kilema, 2004.

37. Field Notes, Rombo, 2004.

38. Lema, "Chaga Religion," 48.

39. Gen. 1:1–23.

40. I made this observation while conducting my first interview in Mkuu Rombo in 2004. Field Notes, Mkuu Rombo, 2004.

41. Field Notes, 2004 and 2005.

42. Interview with Mzee Mwasha, Machame, 2004.

43. Wimmelbücker, *Kilimanjaro: A Regional History*, 292.

44. Ibid., 387–96.

45. "Documents divers au l'Afrique Orientale, 1910–1922," CSEA 2K1.11B3.

46. *Journal de la communauté de Rombo*, 10 August 1908, CSEA 2K2.18.

47. *Journal de la communauté de Rombo*, yrs. 1907–8, CSEA 2K2.18.

48. *Journal de la communauté de Kilema*, 29–30 October 1907 and 11 October 1908, CSEA 2K2.7.

49. "Documents divers au l'Afrique Orientale, 1910–1922," CSEA 2K1.11B3.

50. Ibid.

51. Anza Lema, Paul Landau, and others have made this argument regarding African belief systems. See Lema, "Chaga Religion," 40.

52. The Catholic missions kept a policy against baptizing infants (except those in danger of death) for several decades. This made sense, as there were relatively few Christian families to bring up children in the church. This policy loosened gradually as more and more married couples became members of the church. Centenary Book Committee, *The Catholic Church in Moshi*, 60.

53. Lema, "Chaga Religion," 57.

54. Moore and Puritt, *The Chagga and Meru*, 74.

55. Parts of this section are drawn from Matthew V. Bender, "Millet Is Gone! Considering the Demise of Eleusine Agriculture on Kilimanjaro," *International Journal of African Historical Studies* 44, no. 2 (2011): 191–214.

56. In 1945, the average size of a family's millet plot ranged from one-half to three-quarters of an acre. See Government of Tanganyika, "Northern Province Native Agriculture, 1945," TNA 9/6/5.

57. P. J. M. Bailey, "The Changing Economy of the Chagga Cultivators of Marangu, Kilimanjaro," *Geography* 53, no. 2 (1968), 168.

58. Interview with Rogasian Kimaro, Moshi, 2005.

59. "Memo from A. J. Wakefield to the Director of Agriculture," 26 January 1931, TNA 19542.

60. Ibid.

61. Ibid.

62. Interview with Philip Tesha, Uru, 2005; Field Notes, Kilema, 2005.

63. For more on the history of the KNCU, see R. J. M. Swynnerton and A. L. B. Bennett, *Habari zote za Kahawa ya "KNCU"* (Moshi, Tanzania: Moshi Native Coffee Board, 1948).

64. In 1948, there were twenty-six co-ops affiliated with the KNCU. See "Kilimanjaro Native Cooperative Union, 1938–1950," TNA 5/237.

65. Swynnerton and Bennett, *Habari zote*, 14.

66. Ibid.

67. Ibid, 52–53.

68. A. O'Kting'ati and J. F. Kessy, "The Farming Systems on Mount Kilimanjaro," in *The Conservation of Mount Kilimanjaro*, ed. William Newmark (Cambridge: International Union for Conservation of Nature, 1991), 71–80.

69. Ibid., 75–76.

70. Bailey, "The Changing Economy"; François Devenne, "On 'the Mountain of Waters,' the Furrows Are Running Dry: Rethinking Mount Kilimanjaro's Irrigation System," in *Kilimanjaro: Mountain, Memory, Modernity*, ed. François Bart, Milline Jethro Mbonile, and François Devenne

(Dar es Salaam: Mkuki na Nyota, 2006), 201–14; Sam Maghimbi, "Recent Changes in Crop Patterns in the Kilimanjaro Region of Tanzania: The Decline of Coffee and the Rise of Maize and Rice," *African Study Monographs*, suppl. 35 (March 2007): 73–83.

71. Von Clemm, "Agricultural Productivity," 112.

72. Government of Tanganyika, "Northern Province Native Agriculture, 1945," TNA 9/6/5.

73. O'Kting'ati and Kessy, "The Farming Systems on Mount Kilimanjaro," 74.

74. Government of Tanzania, Central Bureau of Statistics, volumes for 1968 and 1988.

75. Food and Agriculture Organization of the United Nations (FAO), *Rehabilitation of Traditional Schemes (Phase I), Tanzania*, AG: TCP/URT/4522, Mission Report, Rome, 1986.

76. Maro, *Population Growth and Agricultural Change*, 19.

77. Devenne, "On 'the Mountain of Waters.'"

78. Interview with Rogasian Kimaro, Moshi Town, 2004; Field Notes, Kilimanjaro, 2003–2005.

79. Field Notes, 2004.

80. For example, in Kilema one can find four beer shops on the road between the main Catholic church and the nearest bus stop, a distance of less than a kilometer. Field Notes, Kilimanjaro, 2004.

81. O'Kting'ati and Kessy, "The Farming Systems on Mount Kilimanjaro," 76. As John Iliffe has noted, Tanganyika experienced regional differentiation in agriculture starting in the 1930s, some regions specializing in cash crops for export, others providing labor to cash-cropping areas, and the rest producing food for cash-cropping areas. This meant that Kilimanjaro, an area specializing in export coffee production, could rely on other areas of the colony for purchasing foodstuffs like eleusine. Iliffe, *A Modern History of Tanganyika*, 311–14.

82. Interview with Philip Tesha, Uru, 2005.

CHAPTER 6: MORE AND BETTER WATER

1. A schedule of the events and copies of the speeches can be found in G. K. Whitlamsmith, *Recent Trends in Chagga Political Development* (Moshi: KNCU, 1955). Memories of the first Chagga Day celebration come from my field notes (2004, 2005, and 2008) and Heckton Chuwa, "Interview with Thomas Marealle, OBE," *Express* (Dar es Salaam), November 25, 2004, 365.

2. Thomas Marealle, "Chagga Day Speech at the Sundowner, November 10, 1952 by Mangi Mkuu of the Wachagga Marealle II," in Whitlamsmith, *Recent Trends*, ii.

3. Recent examples include Priya Lal, *African Socialism in Postcolonial Tanzania: Between the Village and the World* (Cambridge: Cambridge University Press, 2015); Leander Schneider, *Government of Development: Peasants and Politicians in Postcolonial Tanzania* (Bloomington: Indiana University Press, 2014).

4. James Scott, *Seeing Like a State*, 4.

5. Sections of this chapter are drawn from Matthew V. Bender, "Being 'Chagga': Natural Resources, Political Activism, and Identity on Kilimanjaro," *Journal of African History* 54, no. 2 (2013): 199–220; and Bender, "'For More and Better Water, Choose Pipes!': Building Water and the Nation on Kilimanjaro, 1961–1985." *Journal of Southern African Studies* 34, no. 4 (2008): 841–59.

6. Iliffe, *A Modern History of Tanganyika*, 344.

7. Overseas Development Institute, *Colonial Development: A Factual Survey of the Origins and History of British Aid to Developing Countries*, British Aid 5 (London: Overseas Development Institute, 1964), 33.

8. For more on the Colonial Development and Welfare Acts, see Iliffe, *A Modern History of Tanganyika*, 437–39.

9. These are summarized in P. H. Johnston, "Chagga Constitutional Development," *Journal of African Administration*, no. 5 (1953), 134–40; as well as Susan Geiger Rogers, "The Search for Political Focus on Kilimanjaro: A History of Chagga Politics 1916–1952 with Special Reference to the Cooperative Movement and Indirect Rule" (PhD diss., University of Dar es Salaam, 1972), 793–98.

10. Moshi District Office, "The Political Tendencies of the Wachagga, 1931," TNA 19475.

11. "Assistant District Officer, Moshi, to the Provincial Commissioner, Northern Province, Arusha," 17 January 1938, in *Expansion of the Chagga Tribe and Their Settlement on Lands below Kilimanjaro*, TNA 69/45/1/2, vol. 1.

12. "Memo by F .C. Hallier," 20 February 1937, in *Expansion of the Chagga Tribe and Their Settlement on Lands below Kilimanjaro*, TNA 69/45/1/2, vol. 1.

13. H. F. I Elliott and R. J. M. Swynnerton, "Memorandum on Land Distribution in Moshi District," 20 August 1946, p. 5, TNA 69/9/3.

14. This is different from Meru, where testimony favored the settlers. See Spear, *Mountain Farmers*, 213–14.

15. Elliott and Swynnerton, "Memorandum," TNA 69/9/3.

16. Ibid., 13.

17. "Memorandum to the Commissioner, the Moshi-Arusha Land Commission by a Committee Appointed by the Chagga Chiefs Council, Moshi," August 1946, TNA 69/9/3.

18. Ibid.

19. Iliffe, *A Modern History of Tanganyika*, 451.

20. "Chagga Association, Moshi, to the District Commissioner, Moshi," 31 May 1945, TNA 5/25/16.

21. "Merinyo to the Honorable Excellencies, the Wamangi Waitori, Hai, Vunjo, and Rombo," 29 September 1947, as cited in Rogers, "Search for Political Focus," 819.

22. For more on the KCCU, see Emma Hunter, "In Pursuit of the 'Higher Medievalism': Local History and Politics in Kilimanjaro," in *Recasting the Past: History Writing and Political Work in Modern Africa*, ed. D. R. Peterson and G. Macola (Athens: Ohio University Press, 2009), 149–70.

23. Iliffe, *A Modern History of Tanganyika*, 493.

24. Michael von Clemm, "People of the White Mountain: The Interdependence of Political and Economic Activity amongst the Chagga in Tanganyika with Special Reference to Recent Changes" (PhD thesis, Oxford University, 1962), 222.

25. Chuwa, "Interview with Thomas Marealle."

26. Iliffe, *A Modern History of Tanganyika*, 491; Chuwa, "Interview with Thomas Marealle."

27. Rogers, "Search for Political Focus," 891.

28. "Election Results, 1951," TNA 23/49.

29. J. Tawney, "Election in Tanganyika," *Corona* 4, no. 5 (1952): 181–83.

30. For more on the WDD, see Ministry of Lands, Settlement, and Water Development, *This Land Is Ours! The Story of the Ministry of Lands, Settlement, and Water Development* (Dar es Salaam: Government of Tanzania, 1968).

31. Government of Tanganyika, *Department of Water Development Annual Report, 1951* (Dar es Salaam: Government Printer of Tanganyika, 1952).

32. "Native Furrows, Hai, 1950," TNA 5/45/23.

33. "Livestock Superintendent, Moshi, to the District Commissioner, Moshi," 24 February 1954, TNA 5/45/23.

34. "Mangi of Machame to the District Commissioner, Moshi," 20 October 1950, TNA 5/45/23.

35. "Livestock Superintendent, Moshi, to the District Commissioner, Moshi," 24 February 1954, TNA 5/45/23.

36. Several projects are described in "Water Development Policy and Instructions, 1948–1956," TNA 471/w.2/1, vol. 1.

37. "Moshi District, Northern Province, Operation Dammit," TNA 69/250/23.

38. Rogers, "Search for Political Focus," 891.

39. Stahl, *History of the Chagga People*.

40. Thomas Marealle, speech to UN Trusteeship Council, 20th session, 817th meeting, document no. T/PV.817, New York (June 17, 1957).

41. "Tanganyika: Look What We Can Do!" *Time*, August 25, 1958.

42. Julius Nyerere, speech to the Tanganyika Legislative Assembly, Dar es Salaam, October 22, 1959, in Godfrey Mwakikagile, *Life under Nyerere* (Dar es Salaam: New Africa Press, 2006), 28.

43. Iliffe, *A Modern History of Tanganyika*, 318–34.

44. This is discussed in greater detail by Cranford Pratt in his book *The Critical Phase in Tanzania, 1945–1968: Nyerere and the Emergence of a Socialist Strategy* (Cambridge: Cambridge University Press, 1976), 108–14, 194–201.

45. Government of Tanganyika, African Chiefs Ordinance (Repeal) Act, 1963.

46. Pratt, *The Critical Phase*, 201–8.

47. Tanzania African National Union, *The Arusha Declaration and TANU's Policy on Socialism and Self-Reliance* (Dar es Salaam: Government of Tanzania, 1967).

48. Paul Nugent, *Africa since Independence: A Comparative History* (London, Palgrave Macmillan, 2004), 141.

49. Before Ujamaa, villages were the exception rather than the rule in Tanzania, with more than 80 percent of rural peoples living in dispersed homesteads. J. E. Moore, "Traditional Rural Settlement," in *Tanzania in Maps*, ed. L. Berry (London: University of London Press, 1971), 124–27.

50. Michael Jennings, "Ujamaa," in *Oxford Research Encyclopedia of African History*, article published September 2017, http://doi.org/cwtr.

51. "Water," United Republic of Tanzania, accessed July 25, 2007, http://www.tanzania.go.tz/waterf.html.

52. Rodger Yeager, *Tanzania: An African Experiment* (Boulder: Westview, 1982), 28.

53. Julius Nyerere, *Freedom and Development: A Selection from Writings and Speeches, 1968–1973* (Oxford: Oxford University Press, 1973), 320.

54. Jannik Boesen, *Aiming Too High, Planning Too Much and Achieving Too Little* (Copenhagen: Center for Development Research, 1986), 2.

55. Allison Smith, "Rural Water Supply Development in Tanzania: A Case Study of Foreign Donor Policies," (MA thesis, Brown University, 1994), 15.

56. "Water Supply—Service to the Nation to Speed Development," *Tanzania Notes and Records*, no. 76 (1975): 191.

57. For more on this topic see W. Edmund Clark, *Socialist Development and Public Investment in Tanzania, 1964–1973* (Toronto: University of Toronto Press, 1978).

58. "Water Supply," 191.

59. White, Bradley, and White, *Drawers of Water*, 81.

60. Kilimanjaro Native Cooperative Union, *Annual Report, 1960–1961* (Moshi: KNCU, 1961).

61. Iliffe, *A Modern History*, 445.

62. Of the 7,710, nearly 5,000 lived in Moshi Town, not on the mountain. See ibid., 513.

63. Moore, *Social Facts and Fabrications*, 213–16.

64. Japan International Cooperation Agency, *Water Master Plan Kilimanjaro Region*, vol. 4 (Dar es Salaam: Ministry of Water, Energy and Minerals, 1977), cited in Grove, "Water Use," 431.

65. "Application for a Water Permit," TNA 474/1022; also Water Development and Irrigation Division, Ministry of Lands, Settlement, and Water Development, "A Rural Water Supply Programme for Kilimanjaro Region, 1967," TNA 558/RCD/167/A.

66. Field Notes, Mkuu Rombo, 2004.

67. Provincial Commissioner, Tanga, "Pangani River—Hale Hydroelectric Scheme and Investigations, 1961–1965," TNA 562/w.2/16.

68. "Minister for Agriculture, D. N. M. Bryceson, to the Regional Commissioners for Arusha, Kilimanjaro, and Tanga Regions," 28 December 1963, TNA 562/w.2/16.

69. Patrick Denny, "Nyumba ya Mungu Reservoir, Tanzania: The General Features," *Biological Journal of the Linnean Society* 10, no. 1 (1978): 5–28.

70. Water Development and Irrigation Division, Ministry of Lands, Settlement, and Water Development, "A Rural Water Supply Programme for Kilimanjaro Region, 1967," TNA 558/RCD/167/A.

71. Ibid, 5.

72. The report calculated the demand for water to be 26.5 million liters per day, based upon estimated need of 75 liters of water per capita. The remaining 7.5 million liters were set aside to handle population growth and rural industries such as coffee pulping. Ibid, 5–6.

73. Ibid, 5–6.

74. The phrase "more and better water" appears in numerous documents of this period. See "Water Development Policy and Instructions," TNA 474/w.2/1, vol. 2.

75. "Rural Water Supply Programme," TNA 558/RCD/167/A.

76. "Water Development Policy and Instructions, 1956–1965," TNA 474/w.2/1, vol. 2.

77. The Kilimanjaro Region Water Advisory Board and the district and regional water officers for Kilimanjaro declared that over time, pipes would take the place of all canals in the upper areas of settlement. See "Kilimanjaro Region Water Advisory Board, Ministry of Lands, Settlement, and Water Development, 1963," TNA 518/c.50/3.

78. For more on this topic see A. H. Pike, *Water Resources, Moshi District* (Moshi: Water Development and Irrigation Division, 1959).

79. Field Notes, Mkuu Rombo, 2004.

80. Ministry of Lands, Settlement, and Water Development, *This Land Is Ours*, 12–13.

81. Relations between Britain and Tanzania became turbulent in the late 1960s and early 1970s. Britain and much of the West disapproved of Nyerere's socialist reforms and his friendship with China, while Tanzania criticized Britain's tolerance of the white minority regimes in Rhodesia and South Africa.

82. Village Clean Water Wells and Small Piped Water Supplies, 1972, Oxfam Archives (hereafter OXF) Project File 2307.

83. Grove, "Water Use," 434.

84. Yeager, *Tanzania: An African Experiment*, 71.

85. Tanzania National Bureau of Statistics, *Census 1978* (Dar es Salaam: National Bureau of Statistics, 1979).

86. Field Notes, Mkuu Rombo, 2003–2004.

87. Interview with Edita Hendry, Mkuu Rombo, 2004.

88. Interview with Leoni Motesha, Mkuu Rombo, 2004.

89. Interview with Liberati Mbando, Mkuu Rombo, 2004.

90. Interview with Michael Safari, Kilema, 2004.

91. From field notes and discussions with Efraim Muro, Machame, 2003.

92. Maro, "Agricultural Land Management," 281.

93. Spear, *Mountain Farmers*, 149.

94. Grove, "Water Use," 434.

95. Ibid., 438.

96. R. Burra and K. Van den Heuvel, *Traditional Irrigation in Tanzania*, (Dar es Salaam: SNV, 1987).

97. Tagseth, "The Expansion of Traditional Irrigation," 489.

98. Interview with Herbert Mbuya, Kilema, 2004.

99. Maro, *Population Growth and Agricultural Change*, 34.

100. Interview with Vitalis Mosha, Kilema, 2004.

101. Interview with Martin Mosha, Kilema, 2004.

102. Grove, "Water Use," 434.

103. Sally Falk Moore, *Social Facts and Fabrications*; also Moore, "Post-Socialist Micro-Politics: Kilimanjaro," *Africa* 66, no. 4 (1996): 587–606.

CHAPTER 7: WATER IS OUR GIFT FROM GOD!

1. Julius Nyerere, *Farewell Speech by the President, Mwalimu Julius K. Nyerere, at the Diamond Jubilee Hall* (Dar es Salaam, 1985).

2. Sebastian Edwards, *Is Tanzania a Success Story? A Long-Term Analysis*, National Bureau of Economic Research working paper no. 17764, Africa Project, January 11, 2012.

3. Roger Nord, *Tanzania: The Story of an African Transition* (Washington, DC: International Monetary Fund, 2009), 8.

4. United Republic of Tanzania, *Second Five-Year Plan for Economic and Social Development* (Dar es Salaam: Government of Tanzania, 1969).

5. Edwards, *Is Tanzania a Success Story?*, 18–20.

6. Jarle Simensen, "The Norwegian-Tanzanian Aid Relationship—A Historical Perspective," in *Tanzania in Transition: From Nyerere to Mkapa*, ed. Havnevik Kjell and Isinika Aids (Dar es Salaam: Mkuki na Nyota, 2010), 68; also cited in Edwards, *Is Tanzania a Success Story?*, 20.

7. Edwards, *Is Tanzania a Success Story?*, 20.

8. World Bank, *Tanzania at the Turn of the Century: From Reforms to Sustained Growth and Poverty Reduction* (Washington, DC: World Bank, 2001), 32.

9. P. Abraham and F. Robinson, *Rural Development in Tanzania: A Review of Ujamaa*, Studies in Employment and Rural Development 14 (Washington, DC: World Bank, 1974), 41 and app. B.

10. Goran Hyden, *Beyond Ujamaa in Tanzania: Underdevelopment and an Uncaptured Peasantry* (Berkeley: University of California Press, 1980), 130; Scott, *Seeing Like a State*, 223.

11. Moore, *Social Facts and Fabrications*, 139.

12. For more on this village, see Fred S. Lerise, *Politics in Land and Water Management: Study in Kilimanjaro, Tanzania* (Dar es Salaam: Mkuki na Nyota, 2005), 27–34.

13. Mary Howard and Ann Millard, *Hunger and Shame: Child Malnutrition and Poverty on Mount Kilimanjaro* (New York: Routledge, 1997), 32.

14. Moore, *Social Facts and Fabrications*, 127.

15. Edwards, *Is Tanzania a Success Story?*, 19.

16. Ibid., 19.

17. Ibid., 22.

18. Ibid., 23.

19. Elliot Berg, *Accelerated Development in Sub-Saharan Africa: An Agenda for Action* (Washington, DC: World Bank, 1981), 43.

20. Ibid., 30.

21. Ibid., 133.

22. Edwards, *Is Tanzania a Success Story?*, 35.

23. United Republic of Tanzania, *Tanzania National Development Vision, 2025* (Dar es Salaam: Government of Tanzania, 1997).

24. G. L. Cunningham, "Summary of Presentations by Panel Members," in D. Warner, ed., *Rural Water Supply in East Africa: Proceedings of a Workshop Held at the University College, Dar es Salaam, September 17–19, 1969*. Cited in D. A. Mashauri and T. S. Katko, "Water Supply Development and Tariffs in Tanzania: From Free Water Policy towards Cost Recovery," *Environmental Management* 17, no. 1 (1993): 32.

25. Gerhard Tschannerl, "Rural Water-Supply in Tanzania: Is 'Politics' or 'Technique' in Command?" (paper no. 52, Annual Social Science Conference of the East African Universities, University of Dar es Salaam, Tanzania, June 6–9, 1973), 174.

26. Ibid., 178.

27. Mashauri and Katko, "Water Supply Development," 32.

28. Ibid., 32.

29. United Republic of Tanzania, Water Utilization (Control and Regulation) Act, no. 42 of 1974, part 3, secs. 8 and 14.

30. S. Makundi, "Funding of Water Supply Projects" (presentation, 8th AWEC, Dodoma, Tanzania, September 1–5, 1986), A3–A7.

31. Daniel M. Dworkin, *Rural Water Projects in Tanzania: Technical, Social and Administrative Issues*, US AID Evaluation Special Study 3 (Washington, DC: US Agency for International Development, 1980).

32. Ibid., 10–12.

33. Berg, *Accelerated Development in Sub-Saharan Africa*, 43.

34. "Director of Water Development, Arusha, to the Divisional Engineer, Water Development Department, Arusha," 27 February 1953, TNA 471/W.2/1, vol. 1.

35. Julius Nyerere, "Speech to the Second Ordinary Party Conference," *Daily News*, October 21, 1982.

36. R. M. A. Swere, "Implementation Experience" (presentation, Arusha Seminar on the Implementation of Rural Water Supply and Sanitation in Tanzania, Arusha, Tanzania, March 3–7, 1986).

37. S. Makundi, "Donors Participation: A Review" (presentation, Arusha Seminar on the Implementation of Rural Water Supply and Sanitation in Tanzania, Arusha, Tanzania, March 3–7, 1986).

38. United Republic of Tanzania, Sera ya Maji (National Water Policy), 1991.

39. United Republic of Tanzania, *National Water Policy, July 2002* (Dodoma: Government of Tanzania Ministry of Water and Livestock Development, 2002), available at http://www.tawasanet.or.tz/files/Tanzania%20water%20policy%20-%202002.pdf.

40. Katharine Cross and Maria Hannah Bass, "Integrated Water Resources Management in the Pangani River Basin," accessed June 27, 2016, http://www.panganibasin.com/index.php/resources/more/integrated_water _resources_management_in_the_pangani_river_basin.

41. International Conference on Water and the Environment, "The Dublin Statement on Water and Sustainable Development," January 31, 1992, accessed February 23, 2010, http://www.wmo.int/pages/prog/hwrp /documents/english/icwedece.html.

42. United Republic of Tanzania, *National Water Policy, July 2002*, 14.

43. Ibid., 28.

44. Ibid., 31.

45. Ibid., 34.

46. Ibid., 36.

47. Ibid., 20.

48. "Pangani Basin Water Board," accessed February 21, 2017, http://www.panganibasin.com.

49. For a detailed discussion of the Lower Moshi Irrigation Scheme, see Lerise, *Politics in Land and Water Management*.

50. Ibid., 65.

51. Roger Andersson et al., *Pangani Falls Re-development Project in Tanzania* (Stockholm: Swedish International Development Cooperation Agency, 2005).

52. Haakon Lein, "Managing the Water of Kilimanjaro: Irrigation, Peasants, and Hydropower Development," *GeoJournal* 61, no. 2 (2004): 155–62.

53. Mattias Tagseth and Haakon Lein, "Competing Models of Water Resource Management and Their Implications Using the Example of Pangani River Basin in Tanzania," in *Shared Waters, Shared Opportunities: Hydropolitics in East Africa*, ed. Bernard Calas and Mumma Martinon (Dar es Salaam: Mkuki na Nyota, 2010), 27.

54. Pangani Basin Water Office, *Pangani Basin Authority Annual Report* (Tanga, Tanzania: Pangani Basin Water Office, 1997).

55. Polly Gillingham, *Indigenous Irrigation on Mount Kilimanjaro, Tanzania*, report to Kilimanjaro Zonal Irrigation Office and Kilimanjaro Regional Water Office, September 1997, 61.

56. International Union for the Conservation of Nature, *Pangani Basin: A Situation Analysis*, 2009, 27.

57. Gillingham, *Indigenous Irrigation*, 60.

58. Tagseth and Lein, "Competing Models," 27.

59. Interview with Martin Mosha, Kilema, April 20, 2004.

60. Interview with Epifania Mbando, Kilema, April 28, 2004.

61. Tagseth, "Irrigation among the Chagga in Kilimanjaro, Tanzania: The Organisation of Mfongo Irrigation," in Calas and Martinon, *Shared Waters*, 250.

62. Gillingham, *Indigenous Irrigation*, 61.

63. Lein, "Managing the Waters," 160.

64. Andrew Ngereza, "Water and Environment in Tanzania: A Case of Pangani River Basin," in *FWU Water Resource Publication Proceedings* (Siegen, 2006), 111.

65. Ibrahim Juma, Sikitiko Kapile, and Omari Wahure, *Managing Conflicts over Land and Water Resources in Pangani River Basin: A Study of Conflict Management in Plural Legal Settings*, Eastern and Central Africa Programme for Agricultural Policy Analysis, May 18, 2014, 7.

66. Ibid., 6.

67. Pangani Basin Water Office, unpublished data, 2005. Cited in Ngereza, "Water and Environment," 109.

68. M. R. Mujwahuzi. "Water Use Conflicts in the Pangani Basin: An Overview," in *Water Resources Management in the Pangani River Basin: Challenges and Opportunities*, ed. J. O. Ngana (Dar es Salaam: Dar es Salaam University Press, 2001), 128–37.

69. Julius Sarmett et al., "Managing Water Conflicts through Dialogue in Pangani Basin, Tanzania" (paper presentation, Conference on Water for Food and Ecosystems, The Hague, Netherlands, January 2005).

70. Ibid., 3.

71. Kizito Makoye, "Power Struggle Rises over Tanzania's Pangani River," Inter Press Service, October 24, 2013.

72. Ibid.

73. At the time, the German development community consisted of three agencies. The German Development Service (DED) focused on local capacity building. German Financial Cooperation (KfW) provided loans and grants to finance investment and advisory services. German Technical Cooperation (GTZ) offered technical assistance in development projects. In 2011 they joined together to form the German Cooperation for International Cooperation (GIZ).

74. *Water for Life: Lessons Learnt from 15 Years of German Development Cooperation in the Kilimanjaro Region* (Dar es Salaam: Embassy of the Federal Republic of Germany, 2007).

75. Consulting Engineers Salzgitter, "Hai District Water Supply, Phase I to IV-1 and IV-2," accessed February 21, 2017, http://cms.ces-info.com/CES/_pdf/74-HAI_1-4-cc_04-2015.pdf.

76. *Water for Life*, 10.

77. Kiliwater, Ltd., *Annual Progress Report, 2003*.

78. Rehema Matowo, "70 Per Cent of Tap Water in Moshi Lost," *Citizen*, December 29, 2014.

79. *Water for Life*, 19.

80. Ibid., 20.

81. Ibid., 21.

82. Matowo, "70 Per Cent of Tap Water in Moshi Lost."

83. District Water Engineer, Moshi Rural, "Project Proposal, Moshi Rural District Water Supply Project, Extension/Rehabilitation of Existing Water Supply System," April 2001.

84. Barbara van Koppen et al., "Winners and Losers of IWRM in Tanzania," *Water Alternatives* 9, no. 3 (2016): 596, 600.

85. Ibid., 599–602.

86. Frances K. Vavrus, "'A Shadow of the Real Thing': Furrow Societies, Water User Associations, and Democratic Practices in the Kilimanjaro Region of Tanzania," *The Journal of African American History* 88, no. 4 (2003): 405.

87. Ibid., 405.

88. Ibid., 406.

89. Fina Lyimo, "Tanzania: Kibosho Lacks Tap Water for Over 8 Years Running," *Citizen*, February 6, 2017.

90. Since the 1980s, the plastic jerry can has largely replaced the debe as the water-carrying tool of choice. See John Thompson, *Drawers of Water II: 30 Years of Change in Domestic Water Use and Environmental Health in East Africa* (London: International Institute for Environment and Development, 2001), viii.

CHAPTER 8: IT IS GOD'S WILL, AND ALSO DEFORESTATION

1. *An Inconvenient Truth*, directed by Davis Guggenheim (Hollywood, CA: Paramount, 2006), DVD.

2. L. G. Thompson et al., "Glacier Loss on Kilimanjaro Continues Unabated," *Proceedings of the National Academy of Sciences of the United States of America* 106, no. 47 (2009): 19770–75.

3. Interview with Martin Mosha, Kilema, Kilimanjaro, 2004.

4. Ernest Hemingway, "The Snows of Kilimanjaro," *Esquire*, August 1, 1936; later republished in Ernest Hemingway, *The Snows of Kilimanjaro and Other Stories* (New York: Scribners, 1961).

5. Jonathan Mitchell, Jodie Keane, and Jenny Laidlaw, *Making Success Work for the Poor: Package Tourism in Northern Tanzania*, report of the Overseas Development Institute and SNV Netherlands Development Organization, January 16, 2009.

6. Ibid., 5.

7. Hans Meyer, *Der Kilimandscharo* (Berlin: Reimer-Vohsen, 1900).

8. Fritz Klute, *Ergebnisse der Forschungen am Kilimandscharo 1912* (Berlin: Reimer-Vohsen, 1920).

9. Walter Geilinger, "The Retreat of the Kilimanjaro Glaciers," *Tanganyika Notes and Records*, no. 2 (1936): 7–20.

10. Ibid., 20.

11. C. Downie and P. Wilkinson, *The Geology of Kilimanjaro* (Sheffield: Department of Geology, the University of Sheffield, 1972).

12. Ibid., 34.

13. Ibid., 31.

14. G. S. Callendar, "The Artificial Production of Carbon Dioxide and its Influence on Temperature," *Quarterly Journal of the Royal Meteorological Society* 64, no. 275 (1938): 223–40.

15. P. E. Kent, "Kilimanjaro: An Active Volcano," *Nature*, no. 153 (April 1994): 454.

16. G. S. Callendar, "Volcanism or Climate Change?" Unpublished letter to *Nature*, April 24, 1944, G. S. Callendar Collection Box 1, University of East Anglia.

17. Intergovernmental Panel on Climate Change, *Principles Governing IPCC Work*, 2006.

18. L. G. Thompson et al, "Kilimanjaro Ice Core Records: Evidence of Holocene Climate Change in Tropical Africa," *Science* 298, no. 5593 (2002): 589–93.

19. Ibid., 591.

20. Ibid., 593.

21. Andrew C. Revkin, "Climate Debate Gets Its Icon: Mt. Kilimanjaro," *New York Times*, March 23, 2004.

22. Mark Bowen, *Thin Ice: Unlocking the Secrets of Climate in the World's Highest Mountains* (New York: Henry Holt, 2005).

23. Kaser et al., "Modern Glacier Retreat."

24. Ibid., 330–31.

25. Ibid., 336.

26. Examples include Thomas Mölg and Douglas Hardy, "Ablation and Associated Energy Balance of a Horizontal Glacier Surface on Kilimanjaro," *Journal of Geophysical Research* 109, no. D16 (2004): 1–13; Thomas Mölg et al., "Mass Balance of a Slope Glacier on Kilimanjaro and Its Sensitivity to Climate," *International Journal of Climatology* 28, no. 7 (2008): 881–92; Thomas Mölg et al., "Limited Forcing of Glacier Loss through Land Cover Change on Kilimanjaro," *Nature Climate Change* 2, no. 4 (2012): 254–58; Stefan Hastenrath, "Diagnosing the Decaying Glaciers of Equatorial East Africa," *Meteorologische Zeitschrift*, no. 15 (2006): 265–72.

27. Thompson et al., "Glacier Loss on Kilimanjaro."

28. L. G. Thompson et al., "A Paleoclimatic Perspective on the 21st Century Glacier Loss on Kilimanjaro, Tanzania," *Annals of Glaciology* 52, no. 59 (2011): 60–68.

29. Philip Mote and Georg Kaser, "The Shrinking Glaciers of Kilimanjaro: Can Global Warming Be Blamed?," *American Scientist* 95, no. 4 (2007): 318.

30. Thomas Mölg et al., "Quantifying Climate Change in the Tropical Midtroposphere over East Africa from Glacier Shrinkage on Kilimanjaro," *Journal of Climate* 22, no. 15 (2009): 4162–81; Georg Kaser et al., "Is the Decline of Ice on Kilimanjaro unprecedented in the Holocene?," *The Holocene* 20, no. 7 (2010): 1079–91.

31. N. J. Cullen et al., "A Century of Ice Retreat on Kilimanjaro: The Mapping Reloaded," *The Cryosphere Discussions* 6 (2012): 4233–65.

32. Ibid., 4252

33. Andreas Hemp, "Climate Change-Driven Forest Fires Marginalize the Impact of Ice Cap Wasting on Kilimanjaro," *Global Change Biology* 11, no. 7 (July 2005), 1022.

34. Ibid., 1021–22.

35. Ibid., 1022.

36. I. Niang et al., "Africa," in *Climate Change 2014—Impacts, Adaptation, and Vulnerability: Part B; Regional Aspects; Contribution of Working Group II to the Fifth Assessment Report of the Intergovernmental Panel on Climate Change,* ed. V. R. Barros et al. (Cambridge: Cambridge University Press, 2014), 1199–265.

37. Andrea Minarcek, "Mount Kilimanjaro's Glacier Is Crumbling," *National Geographic Adventure,* September 23, 2003.

38. Ibid.

39. Mölg et al., "Tropical Glaciers."

40. Ibid., 179.

41. Revkin, "Climate Debate Gets Its Icon."

42. "Mount Kilimanjaro Expedition," Greenpeace, accessed October 25, 2012, http://archive.greenpeace.org/climate/climatecountdown/kilimanjaro.htm#.

43. Paul Desanker, *Impact of Climate Change on Life in Africa* (Washington, DC: World Wildlife Fund, 2002).

44. 149 Cong. Rec. S13500 (daily ed. October 29, 2003).

45. Ben Hirschler, "Africa Feels the Heat on Climate Change," Reuters, January 28, 2010.

46. David Muwanga, "Tanzania: Mt. Kilimanjaro Declining Snow Worries the President," *East African Business Week*, September 23, 2012.

47. Zephania Ubwani, "80 Percent of Kilimanjaro Snow Lost, Expert Says," *Citizen*, August 24, 2015.

48. Patrick Michaels, "The Snow Jobs of Kilimanjaro," *Human Events*, November 4, 2002.

49. Greening Earth Society, "Snow Fooling! Mount Kilimanjaro's Glacier Retreat Is Not Related to Global Warming," *World Climate Report*, March 7, 2004, http://www.worldclimatereport.com/index.php/2004/03/07/snow-fooling/.

50. "Toxic Shock: A Climate-Change Skeptic Is Melting," *Economist*, May 26, 2012.

51. "Climate Change and the Integrity of Science," lead letter published in *Science*, May 7, 2010.

52. L. G. Thompson, "Climate Change: The Evidence and Our Options," *The Behavior Analyst* 33, no. 2 (2010): 153.

53. Revkin, "Climate Debate Gets Its Icon."

54. Interview with Martin Mosha, Kilema, 2004.

55. Field notes, Kilema, 2004, 2005, and 2008.

56. Interview with Francis Minja, Kilema, 2008.

57. Interview with Ewald Kessy, Kilema, 2008.

58. Interview with Sabiano Temba, Kilema, 2008.

59. Interview with Mathias Mosha, Kilema, 2008.

60. Interview with Timba Kileo, Moshi Town, 2008.

61. Hemp, "Climate Change-Driven Forest Fires," 1022.

62. United Nations Environment Programme, *Sustainable Mountain Development in East Africa in a Changing Climate* (2016).

63. Mölg et al., "Limited Forcing of Glacier Loss."

64. Rotary Great Britain and Ireland, *Community-Environmental Sustainability Newsletter*, February 2017.

65. Deus Ngowi, "Clerics Lead Tree Planting Campaign in Kilimanjaro," *Tanzania Daily News*, November 21, 2016. See also http://trees4kili.org/index.html; http://www.co2covenant.org/programs/plant-trees-on-kilimanjaro/.

66. "Minister Calls for Unity in Mitigating Climate Change," *Tanzania Daily News*, June 13, 2013.

67. Interview with Eleuther Assey, Kilema, 2008.

68. Interview with Christina Lyimo, Kilema, 2008.

69. Interview with Ewald Kessy, Kilema, 2008.

70. Interview with Ebes Lyimo, Kilema, 2008.

71. Interview with Mathias Mosha, Kilema, 2008.

72. Interview with Timba Kileo, Moshi Town, 2008.

73. One study that has examined some of these issues is Umesh Adhikari, A. Pouyan Nejadhashemi, and Sean Wozniki, "Climate Change and Eastern Africa: A Review of Impact on Major Crops," *Food and Energy Security* 4, no. 2 (July 2015): 110–32.

74. Niang, "Africa"; also L. Bernstein et al., *Climate Change 2007: Synthesis Report; An Assessment of the Intergovernmental Panel on Climate Change* (Geneva: Intergovernmental Panel on Climate Change, 2008).

CONCLUSION

1. "Tanzania," WaterAid, accessed March 30, 2017, http://www.wateraidamerica.org/tanzania.

2. "Water Scarcity: Overview," Word Wildlife Fund, accessed April 3, 2017, https://www.worldwildlife.org/threats/water-scarcity; "Water," Global Issues, United Nations, accessed April 3, 2017, http://www.un.org/en/sections/issues-depth/water/.

3. "Water," United Nations; Organization for Economic Co-operation and Development, *OECD Environmental Outlook to 2050: The Consequences of Inaction* (Paris: OECD, 2012).

Bibliography

INTERVIEWS

Interviews conducted by the author or an assistant.

Assey, Eleuther. Kilema. June 9, 2008.
August, Augustina. Kilema. May 5, 2004.
Eugen, Benedicta. Mkuu Rombo. March 2, 2004.
Gerard, Gustave. Kilema. May 18, 2004.
Hendry, Edita. Mkuu Rombo. February 19, 2004.
Ignas, Victoria. Kilema. May 12, 2004.
Kessy, Ewald. Kilema. June 9, 2008.
Kessy, Maria. Kilema. June 2, 2008.
Kileo, Timba. Moshi Town. June 13, 2008.
Kimaria, Mark. Mkuu Rombo. March 11, 2004.
Kimaro, Rogasian. Moshi Town. 2005.
Kisoli, Rosina. Kilema. June 9, 2008.
Kiwali, Piuce. Kilema. April 20, 2004.
Kundy, Veronica. Kilema. May 30, 2008.
Ladislaus, Fr. Kilema. May 19, 2004.
Laswai, Michael. Mkuu Rombo. February 17, 2004.
Leana, Clements. Mkuu Rombo. March 2, 2004.
Lyaruu, Mary. Kilema. June 9, 2008.
Lyimo, Christina. Kilema. June 3, 2008.
Lyimo, Ebes. Kilema. June 3, 2008.
Lyimo, Elias. Kilema. June 3, 2008.
Lyimo, Luka. Kilema. May 27, 2008.
Lyimo, Sebastian. Kilema. May 5, 2004.
Maina, Joshua. Machame. December 11, 2003.
Mandele, John. Moshi Town. June 10, 2008.
Masaki, Tobia. Moshi Town. June 14, 2008.
Massawe, Dauseni. Mkuu Rombo. March 4, 2004.
Matemu, William. Kilema. June 26, 2008.
Mathias, Clara. Kilema. April 21, 2004.

Maunga, Wilhelm. Mkuu Rombo. March 3, 2004.
Mbando, Epifania. Kilema. April 28, 2004.
Mbando, Liberati. Kilema. April 27, 2004.
Mbando, Nicolaus. Kilema. June 13, 2008.
Mbando, Regina. Kilema. June 2, 2008.
Mbuya, Herbert. Kilema. May 11, 2004.
Mbuya, James. Kilema. May 11, 2004.
Minja, Francis. Kilema. June 11, 2008.
Mlay, Hillary and Rumisha Mlinga. Moshi Town. June 11, 2008.
Modest, Anastacia. Kilema. May 12, 2004.
Mosha, Basil. Kilema. May 28, 2008.
Mosha, Boniface. Kilema. May 10, 2004.
Mosha, Dainece. Kilema. June 2, 2008.
Mosha, Exuper. Kilema. May 28, 2008.
Mosha, Hedwigha. Kilema. July 22, 2005.
Mosha, Joseph. Kilema. May 6, 2004.
Mosha, Jovita. Kilema. June 11, 2008.
Mosha, Martin. Kilema. April 20, 2004.
Mosha, Mathias. Kilema. May 30, 2008.
Mosha, Vitalis. Kilema. April 28, 2004.
Mosha, Wilbard. Kilema. June 26, 2008.
Moshi, Agripina. Kilema. June 10, 2008.
Moshi, Bazzi. Mkuu Rombo. February 23, 2004.
Motesha, Leoni. Mkuu Rombo. March 3, 2004.
Mremi, Bariki. Kilema. May 27, 2008.
Msafiri, Fr. Aidan. Kilema. June 28, 2004.
Mtaba, Robert. Moshi Town. June 10, 2008.
Mtaki, George. Moshi Town. June 10, 2008.
Mtey, Raphael. Mkuu Rombo. February 24, 2004.
Muro, Efraim. Machame. December 15, 2003.
Mushi, Mary. Kibosho. July 27, 2005.
Mwasha, Mzee. Machame. January 23, 2004.
Mweta, R.A. Moshi Town. February 11, 2004.
Ngowi, Joseph. Kibosho. July 27, 2005.
Ngowi, Severin. Mkuu Rombo. March 5, 2004.
Nguma, Aristarck. Kilema. June 10, 2008.
Nguma, Edward. Kilema. May 28, 2008.
Nolasco, Peter. Kilema. April 14, 2004.
Safari, Michael. Kilema. May 3, 2004.
Shayo, Francis. Kilema. July 20, 2005.
Shayo, Theresa. Kilema. May 30, 2008.
Shirama, Genesis and Joseph Mosha. Moshi Town. June 14, 2008.
Shirima, Charles. Mengwe Rombo. March 9, 2004.
Shirima, Pascal and Sauma Msuya. Moshi Town. June 13, 2008.
Siara, Remi. Kilema. May 18, 2004.

Silayo, Titus. Mashati Rombo. February 25, 2004.
Simba, Atanas. Kilema. May 5, 2004.
Simon, Anastacia. Mkuu Rombo. March 8, 2004.
Someke, Samson. Moshi Town. June 10, 2008.
Sway, Methley. Moshi Town. June 13, 2008.
Tairo, Prosper. Mkuu Rombo. February 24, 2004.
Temba, Sabiano. Kilema. May 30, 2008.
Temu, Fulgens. Kilema. May 27, 2008.
Tesha, Philip. Uru. July 28, 2005.
Village Committee. Mkuu Rombo. February 19, 2004.

ARCHIVES

British National Archives, Kew (BNA)
Congrégation du Saint-Esprit Archives, Chevilly-Larue (CSEA)
Deutsches Historisches Museum, Berlin
East Africana Collection, University of Dar es Salaam Library (EAC)
Oxfam Archives, Oxford (OXF)
Rhodes House Library, Oxford (RH)
Smithsonian Institution Archives, Washington
Spiritan Photographic Archive, Paris
Tanzania National Archives, Dar es Salaam (TNA)

NEWSPAPERS AND JOURNALS

Bulletin General (Congrégation du Saint-Esprit)
Church Missionary Intelligencer
The Citizen (Dar es Salaam)
East African Business Week
East African Record
Tanganyika Notes and Records
Tanzania Daily News (Dar es Salaam)

BOOKS, ARTICLES, AND THESES

Abbott, William Louis. *Descriptive Catalogue of the Abbott Collection of Ethnological Objects from Kilima-njaro, East Africa*. Washington, DC: US Government Publishing Office, 1891.
Abraham, P. and F. Robinson. *Rural Development in Tanzania: A Review of Ujamaa*. Studies in Employment and Rural Development 14. Washington, DC: Word Bank, 2001.
Adhikari, Umesh, A. Pouyan Nejadhashemi, and Sean Wozniki. "Climate Change and Eastern Africa: A Review of Impact on Major Crops." *Food and Energy Security* 4, no. 2 (July 2015): 110–32.
Alpers, Edward A. *Ivory and Slaves: Changing Pattern of International Trade in East Central Africa to the Later Nineteenth Century*. Berkeley: University of California Press, 1975.

Anderson, Benedict. *Imagined Communities*. New York: Verso, 1991.

Anderson, David. "Depression, Dust Bowl, Demography, and Drought: The Colonial State and Soil Conservation in East Africa during the 1930s." *African Affairs* 83, no. 332 (July 1984): 321–43.

———. *Eroding the Commons: The Politics of Ecology in Kenya*. Athens: Ohio University Press, 2002.

Andersson, Roger, Fritz Wanseth, Melinda Cuellar, and Ulrike von Mitzlaff. *Pangani Falls Re-development Project in Tanzania*. Stockholm: Swedish International Development Cooperation Agency, 2005.

Bailey, P. J. M. "The Changing Economy of the Chagga Cultivators of Marangu, Kilimanjaro." *Geography* 53, no. 2 (1968): 163–69.

Baker, Richard. *Africa Drums*. London: Lindsay Drummond, 1945.

Bender, Matthew V. "Being 'Chagga': Natural Resources, Political Activism, and Identity on Kilimanjaro." *Journal of African History* 54, no. 2 (2013): 199–220.

———. "Do Not Imagine That Every Cloud Will Bring Rain: A History of Irrigation on Kilimanjaro, Tanzania." In *Water and Food*, edited by Terje Tvedt and Terje Oestigaard, 185–209. A History of Water, series 3, vol. 3. New York: I. B. Tauris, 2016.

———. "'For More and Better Water, Choose Pipes!': Building Water and the Nation on Kilimanjaro, 1961–1985." *Journal of Southern African Studies* 34, no. 4 (2008): 841–59.

———. "Millet is Gone! Considering the Demise of Eleusine Agriculture on Kilimanjaro." *International Journal of African Historical Studies* 44, no. 2 (2011): 191–214.

———. "Water Brings No Harm: Knowledge, Power, and Practice on Kilimanjaro, Tanzania, 1880–1980." PhD diss., Johns Hopkins University, 2006.

Bennett, Norman. *Arab versus European: Diplomacy and War in Nineteenth-Century East Central Africa*. New York: Africana, 1986.

———. "The British on Kilimanjaro, 1884–1892." *Tanzania Notes and Records*, no. 63 (1964): 229–44.

Berg, Elliot. *Accelerated Development in Sub-Saharan Africa: An Agenda for Action*. Washington, DC: World Bank, 1981.

Bernstein, L., P. Bosch, O. Canziani, Z. Chen, R. Christ, O. Davidson, W. Hare, et al. *Climate Change 2007: Synthesis Report; An Assessment of the Intergovernmental Panel on Climate Change*. Geneva: Intergovernmental Panel on Climate Change, 2008.

Berry, Sara. *No Condition Is Permanent: The Social Dynamics of Agrarian Change in Sub-Saharan Africa*. Madison: University of Wisconsin Press, 1993.

Blixen, Karen. *Out of Africa*. London: Penguin, 2001.

Boesen, Jannik. *Aiming Too High, Planning Too Much and Achieving Too Little*. Copenhagen: Center for Development Research, 1986.

Boesen, Jannik, Kjell J. Havnevik, Juhani Koponen, and Rie Odgaard, eds. *Tanzania: Crisis and Struggle for Survival*. Uppsala: Scandinavian Institute of African Studies, 1986.

Bowen, Mark. *Thin Ice: Unlocking the Secrets of Climate in the World's Highest Mountains.* New York: Henry Holt, 2005.

Burke, Timothy. *Lifebuoy Men, Lux Women: Commodification, Consumption, and Cleanliness in Modern Zimbabwe.* Durham, NC: Duke University Press, 1996.

Burra, R. and K. van den Heuvel. *Traditional Irrigation in Tanzania.* Dar es Salaam: SNV, 1987.

Callendar, G.S. "The Artificial Production of Carbon Dioxide and Its Influence on Temperature." *Quarterly Journal of the Royal Meteorological Society* 64, no. 275 (1938): 223–40.

———. "Volcanism or Climate Change?" Unpublished letter to *Nature*, April 24, 1944. G. S. Callendar Collection Box 1, University of East Anglia.

Centenary Book Committee. *The Catholic Church in Moshi: A Centenary Memorial, 1890–1990.* Ndanda, Tanzania: Ndanda Mission Press, 1990.

Chuwa, Heckton. "Interview with Thomas Marealle, OBE." *Express* (Dar es Salaam), November 25, 2004.

Clark, W. Edmund. *Socialist Development and Public Investment in Tanzania, 1964–1973.* Toronto: University of Toronto Press, 1978.

"Climate Change and the Integrity of Science." Lead letter published in *Science*, May 7, 2010.

Comaroff, John and Jean Comaroff. *Of Revelation and Revolution*, vol. 2, *The Dialectics of Modernity on a South African Frontier.* Chicago: University of Chicago Press, 1997.

Conference Proceeding. Arusha Seminar on the Implementation of Rural Water Supply and Sanitation in Tanzania, location, March 3–7, 1986.

Consulting Engineers Salzgitter. "Hai District Water Supply, Phase I to IV-1 and IV-2." Accessed February 21, 2017. http://cms.ces-info.com/CES/_pdf/74-HAI_1-4-cc_04-2015.pdf.

Conte, Christopher. *Highland Sanctuary: Environmental History in Tanzania's Usambara Mountains.* Athens: Ohio University Press, 2004.

Cooley, William Desborough. *Inner Africa Laid Open, in an Attempt to Trace the Chief Lines of Communication Across That Continent South of the Equator.* London: Longman, Brown, Green, and Longmans, 1852.

Cross, Katharine and Maria Hanna Bass. "Integrated Water Resources Management in the Pangani River Basin." Accessed June 27, 2016. http://www.panganibasin.com/index.php/resources/more/integrated_water_resources_management_in_the_pangani_river_basin.

Cullen, Nicolas J., Thomas Mölg, Georg Kaser, Khalid Hussein, Konrad Steffen, and Douglas R. Hardy. "Kilimanjaro Glaciers: Recent Areal Extent from Satellite Data and New Interpretation of Observed 20th Century Retreat Rates." *Geophysical Research Letters* 33, no. 16 (2006): 1–6.

Cullen, N. J., P. Sirguey, T. Mölg, G. Kaser, M. Winkler, and S. J. Fitzsimons. "A Century of Ice Retreat on Kilimanjaro: The Mapping Reloaded." *The Cryosphere Discussions* 6 (2012): 4233–65.

Datoo, B. A. "The Generation of Hydro-Electric Power on the Lower Pangani River." *East African Geographical Review*, no. 3 (1965): 47–49.

Denny, Patrick. "Nyumba ya Mungu Reservoir, Tanzania: The General Features." *Biological Journal of the Linnean Society* 10, no. 1 (1978): 5–28.

Desanker, Paul. *Impact of Climate Change on Life in Africa.* Washington, DC: World Wildlife Fund, 2002.

Devenne, François. "On 'the Mountain of Waters,' the Furrows Are Running Dry: Rethinking Mount Kilimanjaro's Irrigation System." In *Kilimanjaro: Mountain, Memory, Modernity*, edited by François Bart, Milline Jethro Mbonile, and François Devenne, 201–14. Dar es Salaam: Mkuki na Nyota, 2006.

De Villiers, Marq. *Water: The Fate of Our Most Precious Resource.* Boston: Houghton Mifflin, 2001.

District Water Engineer, Moshi Rural. "Project Proposal, Moshi Rural District Water Supply Project, Extension/Rehabilitation of Existing Water Supply System." April 2001.

Downie, C., and P. Wilkinson. *The Geology of Kilimanjaro.* Sheffield: Department of Geology, the University of Sheffield, 1972.

Dundas, Charles. *Kilimanjaro and Its People.* London: Frank Cass, 1924.

Dworkin, Daniel M. *Rural Water Projects in Tanzania: Technical, Social and Administrative Issues.* US AID Evaluation Special Study 3. Washington, DC: US Agency for International Development, 1980.

Edwards, Sebastian. *Is Tanzania a Success Story? A Long Term Analysis.* National Bureau of Economic Research working paper no. 17764, Africa Project. January 11, 2012.

Ehret, Christopher. *The Civilizations of Africa: A History to 1800.* Charlottesville: University of Virginia Press, 2002.

Ertsen, Maurits. *Improvising Planned Development on the Gezira Plain, Sudan, 1900–1980.* London: Palgrave Macmillan, 2016.

Feierman, Steven. *Peasant Intellectuals: Anthropology and History in Tanzania.* Madison: University of Wisconsin Press, 1990.

Ferguson, James. *The Anti-Politics Machine: "Development," Depoliticization, and Bureaucratic Power in Lesotho.* Cambridge: Cambridge University Press, 1990.

Fernandes de Enciso, Martin. *Suma de geographia que trata de todas las partidas y provincias del mundo.* 1519.

Fitch, E. A., and J. A. Wray. "The First Year of the Chagga Mission." *Church Missionary Intelligencer*, no. 2 (1886): 555–62.

Fleuret, Patrick. "The Social Organization of Water Control in the Taita Hills." *American Ethnologist* 12, no. 1 (1985): 103–18.

Fréon, Mathieu. "L'irrigation traditionnelle à Uru Mashariki, versant sud du volcan Kilimandjaro: Un témoin de l'identité Chagga." *IFRA Les cahiers d'Afrique de l'Est*, no. 26 (2004): 49–73.

Geilinger, Walter. "The Retreat of the Kilimanjaro Glaciers." *Tanganyika Notes and Records*, no. 2 (1936): 7–20.

Gelles, Paul. *Water and Power in Highland Peru: The Cultural Politics of Irrigation and Development*. New Brunswick: Rutgers University Press, 2000.

Geographical Section of the Naval Intelligence Division. *A Handbook of German East Africa*. London: His Majesty's Stationary Office, 1923.

Gilg, E. "Die Nutzhölzer Ostafrikas und ihre Verwertung." In *Die Pflanzenwelt Ost-Afrikas und der Nachbargebiete*, edited by Adolf Engler. Berlin: Geographische Verlagshandlung Dietrich Reimer, 1895.

Gillingham, Mary E. "Gaining Access to Water: Formal and Informal Rules of Indigenous Irrigation Management on Mount Kilimanjaro, Tanzania." *Natural Resources Journal*, no. 39 (1999): 419–41.

Gillingham, Polly. *Indigenous Irrigation on Mount Kilimanjaro, Tanzania*. Report to Kilimanjaro Zonal Irrigation Office and Kilimanjaro Regional Water Office, September 1997.

Goldthorpe, J. E. "The African Population of East Africa: A Summary of Its Past and Present Trends." App. 7 in *Report of the East African Royal Commission, 1953–1955*. London: Her Majesty's Stationary Office, 1955.

Greening Earth Society. "Snow Fooling! Mount Kilimanjaro's Glacier Retreat Is Not Related to Global Warming." *World Climate Report*, March 7, 2004. http://www.worldclimatereport.com/index.php/2004/03/07/snow-fooling/.

Grove, Alison. "Water Use by the Chagga on Kilimanjaro." *African Affairs*, no. 92 (1993): 431–48.

Grove, Richard. *Green Imperialism: Colonialism Expansion, Tropical Island Edens, and the Origins of Environmentalism, 1600–1800*. Cambridge: Cambridge University Press, 1995.

Guggenheim, Davis, dir. An Inconvenient Truth. Hollywood, CA: Paramount, 2006. DVD.

Guillebaud, Claude. *An Economic Survey of the Sisal Industry of Tanganyika*. Welwyn, UK: James Nisbet, 1958.

Gutmann, Bruno. *Chagga Law*. Translated by A. M. Nagler. New Haven: Human Relations Area Files, 1963.

———. *Dichten und Denken der Dschagganeger*. Leipzig: Verlag der Evang.-Luth. Mission, 1909.

———. *The Tribal Teachings of the Chagga*. Translated by Ward Goodenough and Dorothy Crawford. New Haven: Human Relations Area Files, 1958.

Hardy, Douglas R. "Kilimanjaro." In *Encyclopedia of Snow, Ice, and Glaciers*, edited by Vijay P. Singh, Pratap Singh, and Umesh K. Haritashya, 672–79. New York: Springer, 2011.

Harms, Robert. *Games against Nature: An Eco-Cultural History of the Nunu of Equatorial Africa*. Cambridge: Cambridge University Press, 1999.

Harrison, E. *A Memorandum on Soil Erosion*. Dar es Salaam: Government of Tanganyika, 1937.

Hastenrath, Stefan. "Diagnosing the Decaying Glaciers of Equatorial East Africa." *Meteorologische Zeitschrift*, no. 15 (2006): 265–72.

Hegel, Georg Wilhelm Friedrich. *Lectures on the Philosophy of World History: Introduction, Reason in History.* Translated by H. B. Nisbet. Cambridge: Cambridge University Press, 1975.

Hemingway, Ernest. "The Snows of Kilimanjaro." *Esquire*, August 1, 1936.

Hemp, Andreas. "Climate Change-Driven Forest Fires Marginalize the Impact of Ice Cap Wasting on Kilimanjaro." *Global Change Biology* 11, no. 7 (July 2005): 1013–23.

Hillbom, Ellen. "The Right to Water: An Inquiry into Legal Empowerment and Property Rights Formation in Tanzania." In *The Legal Empowerment Agenda: Poverty, Labour and the Informal Economy in Africa*, edited by Dan Banik, 193–214. London: Ashgate, 2011.

Hirschler, Ben. "Africa Feels the Heat on Climate Change." Reuters, January 28, 2010.

Hoag, Heather. *Developing the Rivers of East and West Africa: An Environmental History.* London: Bloomsbury, 2013.

Howard, Mary and Ann Millard. *Hunger and Shame: Child Malnutrition and Poverty on Mount Kilimanjaro.* New York: Routledge, 1997.

Hunt, Nancy Rose. *A Colonial Lexicon of Birth Ritual, Medicalization, and Mobility in the Congo.* Durham, NC: Duke University Press, 1999.

Hunter, Emma. "In Pursuit of the 'Higher Medievalism': Local History and Politics in Kilimanjaro." In *Recasting the Past: History Writing and Political Work in Modern Africa*, edited by D. R. Peterson and G. Macola, 149–70. Athens: Ohio University Press, 2009.

———. *Political Thought and the Public Sphere in Tanzania: Freedom, Democracy, and Citizenship in the Era of Decolonization.* Cambridge: Cambridge University Press, 2015.

Hutchinson, J. A. "The Meaning of Kilimanjaro." *Tanganyika Notes and Records*, no. 64 (1965).

Hyden, Goran. *Beyond Ujamaa in Tanzania: Underdevelopment and an Uncaptured Peasantry.* Berkeley: University of California Press, 1980.

Iliffe, John. *A Modern History of Tanganyika.* Cambridge: Cambridge University Press, 1979.

Intergovernmental Panel on Climate Change. *Principles Governing IPCC Work.* 2006.

International Conference on Water and the Environment. "The Dublin Statement on Water and Sustainable Development." January 31, 1992. Accessed February 23, 2017. http://www.wmo.int/pages/prog/hwrp/documents/english/icwedece.html.

International Union for Conservation of Nature. Pangani Basin: A Situation Analysis. 2009.

Isaacman, Allen and Barbara Isaacman. *Dams, Displacement, and the Delusion of Development: Cahora Bassa and Its Legacies in Mozambique, 1965–2007.* Athens: Ohio University Press, 2013.

Jacks, G. V. and R. O. Whyte. *The Rape of the Earth: A World Survey of Soil Erosion.* London: Faber and Faber, 1939.

Japan International Cooperation Agency. *Water Master Plan Kilimanjaro Region*. Dar es Salaam: Ministry of Water, Energy, and Minerals, 1977.

Jennings, Michael. "Ujamaa." In *Oxford Research Encyclopedia of African History*. Article published September 2017. http://doi.org/cwtr.

Johnston, Alex. *The Life and Letters of Sir Harry Johnston*. London: J. Cape, 1929.

Johnston, H. H. *The Kilima-Njaro Expedition: A Record of Scientific Exploration in Eastern Equatorial Africa*. London: Kegan, Paul, Trench, and Co., 1886.

Johnston, P. H. "Chagga Constitutional Development." *Journal of African Administration*, no. 5 (1953): 134–40.

Juma, Ibrahim, Sikitiko Kapile, and Omari Wahure. *Managing Conflict over Land and Water Resources in Pangani River Basin: A Study of Conflict Management in Plural Legal Settings*. Eastern and Central Africa Programme for Agricultural Policy Analysis, May 18, 2014.

Kanthack, Francis. *Report on the Control of the Natural Waters of Tanganyika and the Framework of a Water Law on Which Such Control Should Be Based*. Dar es Salaam: Government of Tanganyika, 1936.

Kaser, Georg, Douglas R. Hardy, Thomas Mölg, Raymond S. Bradley, and Tharsis M. Hyera. "Modern Glacial Retreat on Kilimanjaro as Evidence of Climate Change: Observations and Facts." *International Journal of Climatology* 24, no. 3 (2004): 329–39.

Kaser, Georg, Thomas Mölg, Nicolas J. Cullen, Douglas R. Hardy, and Michael Winkler. "Is the Decline of Ice on Kilimanjaro Unprecedented in the Holocene?" *The Holocene* 20, no. 7 (2010): 1079–91.

Kent, P. E. "Kilimanjaro: An Active Volcano." *Nature*, no. 153 (1944): 454–55.

Kieran, J. A. "Christian Villages in North-Eastern Tanzania." *Transafrican Journal of History* 1, no. 1 (1971): 24–38.

———. "Congregation and the Coffee Industry in East Africa." *Cor Unum* 3, no. 3 (1966): 20–26.

———. "The Holy Ghost Fathers in East Africa, 1863 to 1914." PhD thesis, University of London, 1966.

———. "The Origins of Commercial Arabica Coffee Production in East Africa." *African Historical Studies* 2, no. 1 (1969): 51–67.

Kilimanjaro Native Cooperative Union. *Annual Report, 1960–1961*. Moshi: KNCU, 1961.

Kiliwater. *Annual Progress Report, 2003*.

Kimambo, Isaria. *Penetration and Protest in Tanzania: The Impact of the World Economy on the Pare, 1860–1960*. Athens: Ohio University Press, 1991.

Kimaro, Didas, Balthazar M. Msanya, and Yasuo Takamura. "Review of Sisal Production and Research in Tanzania." *African Study Monographs* 15, no. 4 (1994): 227–42.

Kjekshus, Helge. *Ecology Control and Economic Development in East African History: The Case of Tanganyika, 1850–1950*. Athens: Ohio University Press, 1977.

Klute, Fritz. *Ergebnisse der Forschungen am Kilimandscharo 1912*. Berlin: Reimer-Vohsen, 1920.

Knoll, Arthur, and Hermann Hiery, eds. *The German Colonial Experience: Select Documents on German Rule in Africa, China, and the Pacific, 1884–1914*. Lanham, MD: University Press of America, 2010.

Koponen, Juhani. *Development for Exploitation: German Colonial Policies in Mainland Tanzania, 1884–1914*. Helsinki: Tiedekirja, 1994.

Koren, Henry J. *The Spiritans: A History of the Congregation of the Holy Ghost*. Pittsburgh: Duquesne University Press, 1958.

———. *Spiritan East Africa Memorial, 1863–1993*. Bethel Park, PA: Spiritus Press, 1994.

Krapf, J. L. *Travels, Researches, and Missionary Labours, during an Eighteen Years' Residence in Eastern Africa* [. . .]. London: Trübner, 1860.

Kuczynski, R. R. *Demographic Survey of the British Colonial Empire*. Oxford: Institute of International Affairs, 1949.

Lal, Priya. *African Socialism in Postcolonial Tanzania: Between the Village and the World*. Cambridge: Cambridge University Press, 2015.

Lambrechts, Christian, Bongo Woodley, Andreas Hemp, Claudia Hemp, and Paul Nnyiti. *Aerial Survey of the Threats to Mt. Kilimanjaro Forests*. New York: United Nations Development Programme, 2002.

Lamphear, John. "The Kamba and the Northern Mrima Coast." In *Pre-Colonial African Trade*, edited by Richard Gray and David Birmingham, 75–102. London: Oxford University Press, 1970.

Landau, Paul. *The Realm of the Word: Language, Gender, and Christianity in a Southern African Kingdom*. Portsmouth: Heinemann, 1995.

Lansing, Stephen. *Priests and Programmers: Technologies of Power in the Engineered Landscape of Bali*. Princeton: Princeton University Press, 2007.

Lein, Haakon. "Managing the Water of Kilimanjaro: Irrigation, Peasants, and Hydropower Development." *GeoJournal* 61, no. 2 (2004): 155–62.

Lema, Anza A. "Chaga Religion and Missionary Christianity on Kilimanjaro: The Initial Phase, 1893–1916." In *East African Expressions of Christianity*, edited by Thomas Spear and Isaria Kimambo, 39–62. Athens: Ohio University Press, 1999.

———. "The Impact of the Leipzig Lutheran Mission on the People of Kilimanjaro, 1893–1920." PhD diss., University of Dar es Salaam, 1972.

———. "The Lutheran Church's Contribution to Education in Kilimanjaro." *Tanzania Notes and Records*, no. 68 (1966): 87–94.

Lerise, Fred S. *Politics in Land and Water Management: Study in Kilimanjaro, Tanzania*. Dar es Salaam: Mukuki na Nyota, 2005.

Le Roy, Alexandre. *Au Kilima-Ndjaro*. Paris: L. de Soye, 1893.

Low, D. A.. *Religion and Society in Buganda, 1875–1900*. East African Studies 8. Kampala: East African Institute of Social Research, 1956.

Lyimo, Fina. "Tanzania: Kibosho Lacks Tap Water for Over 8 Years Running." *Citizen*, February 6, 2017.

Maddox, Gregory, James Giblin, and Isaria Kimambo. *Custodians of the Land: Ecology and Culture in the History of Tanzania.* Athens: Ohio University Press, 1996.

Maghimbi, Sam. "Recent Changes in Crop Patterns in the Kilimanjaro Region of Tanzania: The Decline of Coffee and the Rise of Maize and Rice." *African Study Monographs*, suppl. 35 (March 2007): 73–83.

Makoye, Kizito. "Power Struggle Rises over Tanzania's Pangani River." Inter Press Service, October 24, 2013.

Makundi, S. "Donors Participation: A Review." Presented at the Arusha Seminar on the Implementation of Rural Water Supply and Sanitation in Tanzania, Arusha, Tanzania, March 3–7, 1986.

———. "Funding of Water Supply Projects." Presented at the 8th AWEC, Dodoma, Tanzania, September 1–5, 1986.

Marealle, Petro Itosi. "Chagga Customs, Beliefs and Traditions." *Tanganyika Notes and Records*, no. 64 (1965): 56–61.

———. *Maisha ya Mchagga hapa Duniani na Ahera.* Dar es Salaam: Mkuki na Nyota, 2002.

Marealle, Thomas. Speech to the United Nations Trusteeship Council. 20th Session, 817th Meeting, document no. T/PV.817. New York, June 17, 1957.

Maro, Paul. "Agricultural Land Management under Population Pressure: The Kilimanjaro Experience, Tanzania." *Mountain Research and Development* 8, no. 4 (1988): 273–82.

———. "Population and Land Resources in Northern Tanzania, the Dynamics of Change, 1920–1970." PhD diss., University of Minnesota, 1974.

———. *Population Growth and Agricultural Change in Kilimanjaro, 1920–1970.* Research paper no. 40. Dar es Salaam: University of Dar es Salaam Bureau of Resource Assessment and Land Use Planning, December 1975.

Masao, Fidelis. "The Irrigation System in Uchagga: An Ethno-historical Approach." *Tanzania Notes and Records*, no. 75 (1974): 1–8.

Mashauri, D. A. and T. S. Katko. "Water Supply Development and Tariffs in Tanzania: From Free Water Policy towards Cost Recovery." *Environmental Management* 17, no. 1 (1993): 31–39.

Matowo, Rehema. "70 Per Cent of Tap Water in Moshi Lost." *Citizen*, December 29, 2014.

Mbiti, John. *African Religions and Philosophy.* New York: Praeger, 1969.

McCann, James. *Green Land, Brown Land, Black Land: An Environmental History of Africa, 1800–1990.* Portsmouth: Heinemann, 1999.

———. *People of the Plow: An Agricultural History of Ethiopia, 1800–1900.* Madison: University of Wisconsin Press, 1995.

McKenzie, Jeff, Bryan G. Mark, Lonnie G. Thompson, Ulrich Schotterer, and Ping-Nan Lin. "A Hydrochemical Survey of Kilimanjaro (Tanzania): Implications for Water Sources and Ages." *Hydrological Journal* 18, no. 4 (2010): 985–95.

Meyer, Hans. *Across East African Glaciers: An Account of the First Ascent of Kilimanjaro.* London: Longmans, Green, 1891.

———. *Der Kilimandscharo.* Berlin: Reimer-Vohsen, 1900.

Michaels, Patrick. "The Snow Jobs of Kilimanjaro." *Human Events*, November 4, 2002.

Minarcek, Andrea. "Mount Kilimanjaro's Glacier Is Crumbling." *National Geographic Adventure*, September 23, 2003.

"Minister Calls for Unity in Mitigating Climate Change." *Tanzania Daily News*, June 13, 2013.

Ministry of Lands, Settlement, and Water Development. *This Land Is Ours! The Story of the Ministry of Lands, Settlement, and Water Development.* Dar es Salaam: Government of Tanzania, 1968.

Mitchell, Jonathan, Jodie Keane, and Jenny Laidlaw. *Making Success Work for the Poor: Package Tourism in Northern Tanzania.* Report of the Overseas Development Institute and SNV Netherlands Development Organization, January 16, 2009.

Mitchell, Timothy. *Rule of Experts: Egypt, Techno-Politics, Modernity.* Berkeley: University of California Press, 2002.

Mölg, Thomas, Nicolas J. Cullen, Douglas R. Hardy, G. Kaser, and L. Klok. "Mass Balance of a Slope Glacier on Kilimanjaro and Its Sensitivity to Climate." *International Journal of Climatology* 28, no. 27 (2008): 881–92.

Mölg, Thomas, Nicolas J. Cullen, Douglas R. Hardy, Michael Winkler, and Georg Kaser. "Quantifying Climate Change in the Tropical Midtroposphere over East Africa from Glacier Shrinkage on Kilimanjaro." *Journal of Climate* 22, no. 15 (2009): 4162–81.

Mölg, Thomas, Martin Großhauser, Andreas Hemp, Marlis Hofer, and Ben Marzeion. "Limited Forcing of Glacier Loss through Land Cover Change on Kilimanjaro." *Nature Climate Change* 2, no. 4 (2012): 254–58.

Mölg, Thomas and Douglas R. Hardy. "Ablation and Associated Energy Balance of a Horizontal Glacier Surface on Kilimanjaro." *Journal of Geophysical Research* 109, no. D16 (2004): 1–13.

Mölg, Thomas, Douglas R. Hardy, Nicolas J. Cullen, and Georg Kaser. "Tropical Glaciers, Climate Change, and Society: Focus on Kilimanjaro." In *The Darkening Peaks: Glacier Retreat, Science, and Society*, edited by Benjamin S. Orlove, Ellen Wiegandt, and Brian H. Luckman, 168–82. Berkeley: University of California Press, 2008.

Moore, J. E. "Traditional Rural Settlement," In *Tanzania in Maps*, edited by L. Berry, 124–27. London: University of London Press, 1971.

Moore, Sally Falk. *Social Facts and Fabrications: "Customary" Law on Kilimanjaro, 1880–1980.* Cambridge: Cambridge University Press, 1986.

———. "Post-Socialist Micro-Politics: Kilimanjaro." *Africa* 66, no. 4 (1996): 587–606.

Moore, Sally Falk and Paul Puritt. *The Chagga and Meru of Tanzania.* London: International African Institute, 1977.

Mosgrove, Donald. "Watering African Moons: Culture and History of Irrigation Design on Kilimanjaro and Beyond." PhD diss., Cornell University, 1998.

Mosha, R. Sambuli. *The Heartbeat of Indigenous Africa: A Study of the Chagga Educational System*. London: Routledge, 2000.

Mosse, David. *The Rule of Water: Statecraft, Ecology, and Collective Action in South India*. Oxford: Oxford University Press, 2003.

Mote, Phillip and Georg Kaser. "The Shrinking Glaciers of Kilimanjaro: Can Global Warming Be Blamed?" *American Scientist* 95, no. 4 (2007): 318–25.

Moyd, Michelle. *Violent Intermediaries: African Soldiers, Conquest, and Everyday Colonialism in German East Africa*. Athens: Ohio University Press, 2014.

Mujwahuzi, M. R. "Water Use Conflicts in the Pangani Basin: An Overview." In *Water Resources Management in the Pangani River Basin: Challenges and Opportunities*, edited by J. O. Ngana, 128–37. Dar es Salaam: Dar es Salaam University Press, 2001.

Munson, Robert. *Forest Reserves and Local Rights: German East Africa's Mount Kilimanjaro*. Program for the Study of the African Environment Research Series 5. Boston: Boston University, 2009.

———. *The Nature of Christianity in Northern Tanzania: Environmental and Social Change, 1890–1916*. Lanham: Lexington Books, 2013.

Muwanga, David. "Tanzania: Mt. Kilimanjaro Declining Snow Worries the President." *East African Business Week*, September 23, 2012.

Mwakikagile, Godfrey. *Life under Nyerere*. Dar es Salaam: New Africa Press, 2006.

New, Charles. *Life, Wanderings and Labours in Eastern Africa* [. . .]. London: Hodder and Stoughton, 1873.

Ngereza, Andrew. "Water and Environment in Tanzania: A Case of Pangani River Basin." FWU Water Resource Publication Proceedings. Siegen, 2006: 109-115.

Ngowi, Deus. "Clerics Lead Tree Planting Campaign in Kilimanjaro." *Tanzania Daily News*, November 21, 2016.

Niang, I., O.C. Ruppel, M.A. Abdrabo, A. Essel, C. Lennard, J. Padgham, and P. Urquhart. "Africa." In Climate Change 2014 — Impacts, Adaptation, and Vulnerability; Part B; Regional Aspects; Contribution of Working Group II to the Fifth Assessment Report of the Intergovernmental Panel on Climate Change, edited by V. R. Barros, C. B. Field, D. J. Dokken, M. D. Mastrandrea, K .J. Mach, T. E. Bilir, M. Chatterjee, et al., 1199–265. Cambridge: Cambridge University Press, 2014.

Nord, Roger. *Tanzania: The Story of an African Transition*. Washington, DC: International Monetary Fund, 2009.

Nugent, Paul. *Africa since Independence: A Comparative History*. London: Palgrave Macmillan, 2004.

Nurse, Derek. *Classification of the Chaga Dialects: Language and History on Kilimanjaro, the Taita Hills, and the Pare Mountains.* Hamburg: Helmut Buske Verlag, 1979.

Nyerere, Julius. *Farewell Speech by the President, Mwalimu Julius K. Nyerere, at the Diamond Jubilee Hall.* Dar es Salaam, 1985.

——. *Freedom and Development: A Selection from Writings and Speeches, 1968–1973.* Oxford: Oxford University Press, 1973.

——. "Speech to the Second Ordinary Party Conference." *Daily News,* October 21, 1982.

——. Speech to the Tanganyika Legislative Assembly. Dar es Salaam, October 22, 1959.

Odner, Knut. "A Preliminary Report on an Archeological Survey on the Slopes of Kilimanjaro." *Azania,* no. 6 (1971): 131–49.

Ogutu, M. A. "The Cultivation of Coffee among the Chagga of Tanzania, 1919–1939." *Agricultural History* 46, no. 2 (1972): 279–90.

O'Kting'ati, A. and J. F. Kessy. "The Farming Systems on Mount Kilimanjaro." In *The Conservation of Mount Kilimanjaro,* edited by William Newmark, 71–80. Cambridge: International Union for Conservation of Nature, 1991.

Organisation for Economic Co-operation and Development, *OECD Environmental Outlook to 2050: The Consequences of Inaction.* Paris: OECD, 2012.

Osborn, Emily. *Our New Husbands Are Here: Households, Gender, and Politics in a West African State from the Slave Trade to Colonial Rule.* Athens: Ohio University Press, 2011.

Overseas Development Institute. *Colonial Development: A Factual Survey of the Origins and History of British Aid to Developing Countries.* British Aid 5. London: Overseas Development Institute, 1964.

Paasche, Hermann. *Deutsch-Ostafrika: Wirtschaftliche Studien.* Berlin: Schwetschke, 1906.

Pangani Basin Water Office. Pangani Basin Authority Annual Report (Tanga, Tanzania: Pangani Basin Water Office, 1997).

Pearce, Fred. *When the Rivers Run Dry: Water—The Defining Crisis of the Twenty-First Century.* Boston: Beacon, 2007.

Peters, Pauline. *Dividing the Commons: Politics, Policy, and Culture in Botswana.* Charlottesville: University of Virginia Press, 1994.

Peterson, Derek. *Creative Writing: Translation, Bookkeeping, and the Work of Imagination in Colonial Kenya.* Portsmouth: Heinemann, 2004.

Philippson, Gérard. *"Gens des bananerais": Contribution linguistique à l'histoire culturelle des Chaga du Kilimanjaro.* Paris: Editions Recherche sur les Civilisations, 1984.

Pike, A. G. "Kilimanjaro and the Furrow System." *Tanganyika Notes and Records,* no. 64 (1965): 95–96.

Pike, A. H. *Water Resources, Moshi District.* Moshi: Water Development and Irrigation Division, 1959.

Pratt, Cranford. *The Critical Phase in Tanzania, 1945–1968: Nyerere and the Emergence of a Socialist Strategy*. Cambridge: Cambridge University Press, 1976.

Prud'homme, Alex. *The Ripple Effect: The Fate of Freshwater in the Twenty-First Century*. New York: Scribner, 2012.

Raum, Otto. *Chaga Childhood: A Description of Indigenous Education in an East African Tribe*. Oxford: International African Institute, 1940.

Rebmann, Johannes. "First Journey to Jagga." In *Travels, Researchers, and Missionary Labours, during an Eighteen Years' Residence in Eastern Africa* [. . .], edited by J. L. Krapf, 230–47. London: Trübner, 1860.

———. "Narrative of a Journey to Jagga, the Snow Country of Eastern Africa." *Church Missionary Intelligencer*, no. 1 (1849–50): 12–23.

———. "Narrative of a Journey to Madjame." *Church Missionary Intelligencer*, no. 1 (1849–50): 327–30; 376–81.

———. "Narrative of a Journey to Madjame in Jagga," *Church Missionary Intelligencer*, no. 1 (1849–50): 272–76; 307–12.

Revkin, Andrew C. "Climate Debate Gets Its Icon: Mt. Kilimanjaro." *New York Times*, March 23, 2004.

Richards, Paul. *Indigenous Agricultural Revolution: Ecology and Food Production in West Africa*. London: Hutchinson, 1985.

Rogers, Susan Geiger. "The Search for Political Focus on Kilimanjaro: A History of Chagga Politics 1916–1952 with Special Reference to the Cooperative Movement and Indirect Rule." PhD diss., University of Dar es Salaam, 1972.

Rotary Great Britain and Ireland. *Community-Environmental Sustainability Newsletter*, February 2017.

Said, Edward. *Orientalism*. New York: Pantheon Books, 1978.

Sanders, Todd. *Beyond Bodies: Rainmaking and Sense Making in Tanzania*. Toronto: University of Toronto Press, 2008.

Sarmett, Julius, Raphael Burra, Rinus van Klinken, and Kelly West. "Managing Water Conflicts through Dialogue in Pangani Basin, Tanzania." Presented at the Conference on Water for Food and Ecosystems, The Hague, Netherlands, January 2005.

Schneider, Leander. *Government of Development: Peasants and Politicians in Postcolonial Tanzania*. Bloomington: Indiana University Press, 2014.

Scott, James. *Seeing Like a State: How Certain Schemes to Improve the Human Condition Have Failed*. New Haven: Yale University Press, 1998.

Shann, G. N. "The Early Development of Education among the Chagga." *Tanganyika Notes and Records*, no. 45 (1945): 21–32.

Sheridan, Michael. "An Irrigation Intake Is Like a Uterus: Culture and Agriculture in Precolonial North Pare, Tanzania." *American Anthropologist* 104, no. 1 (March 2002): 79–92.

Sheriff, Abdul. *Slaves, Spices, and Ivory in Zanzibar: Integration of an East African Commercial Empire into the World Economy, 1770–1873*. Athens: Ohio University Press, 1987.

Shiva, Vandana. *Water Wars: Privatization, Pollution, and Profit*. Cambridge, MA: South End, 2009.

Showers, Kate. *Imperial Gullies: Soil Erosion and Conservation in Lesotho*. Athens: Ohio University Press, 1995.

Siebenlist, Theodor. *Forstwirtschaft in Deutsch-Ostafrika*. Berlin: Verlagsbuchhandlung Paul Parey, 1914.

Simensen, Jarle. "The Norwegian-Tanzanian Aid Relationship—A Historical Perspective." In *Tanzania in Transition: From Nyerere to Mkapa*, edited by Havnevik Kjell and Isinika Aids, 57–70. Dar es Salaam: Mkuki na Nyota, 2010.

Smith, Allison. "Rural Water Supply Development in Tanzania: A Case Study of Foreign Donor Policies." MA thesis, Brown University, 1994.

Söldenwagner, Philippa. *Spaces of Negotiation: European Settlement and Settlers in German East Africa, 1900–1914*. München: Martin Meidenbauer, 2006.

Spear, Thomas. *Mountain Farmers: Moral Economies of Land and Agricultural Development in Arusha and Meru*. Oxford: James Currey, 1997.

Stahl, Kathleen. *History of the Chagga People of Kilimanjaro*. London: Mouton, 1964.

———. "Outline of Chagga History." *Tanganyika Notes and Records*, no. 64 (1965): 35–49.

Stambach, Amy. *Lessons from Mount Kilimanjaro: Schooling, Community, and Gender in East Africa*. New York: Routledge, 2000.

Sunseri, Thaddeus. *Vilimani: Labor Migration and Rural Change in Early Colonial Tanzania*. Portsmouth: Heinemann, 2001.

———. *Wielding the Ax: State Forestry and Social Conflict in Tanzania, 1820–2000*. Athens: Ohio University Press, 2009.

Sutton, J. E. G. "Engaruka and Its Waters." *Azania*, no. 13 (1978): 37–70.

———. "Engaruka." In *Islands of Intensive Agriculture in Eastern Africa*, edited by Mats Widgren and John E. G Sutton, 114–32. Athens: Ohio University Press, 2004.

Swere, R. M. A. "Implementation Experience." Presented at the Arusa Seminar on the Implementation of Rural Water Supply and Sanitation in Tanzania, Arusha, Tanzania, March 3–7, 1986.

Swyngedouw, Erik. "The City as a Hybrid: On Nature, Society and Cyborg Urbanisation." *Capitalism, Nature, Socialism* 7, no. 1 (1996): 65–80.

———. "Modernity and Hybridity: Nature, Regeneracionismo, and the Production of the Spanish Waterscape, 1890–1930." *Annals of the Association of American Geographers* 89, no. 3 (1999): 443–65.

Swynnerton, R. J. M and A. L. B. Bennett. *Habari zote za Kahawa ya "KNCU."* Moshi, Tanzania: Moshi Native Coffee Board, 1948.

Tagseth, Mattias. "The Expansion of Traditional Irrigation in Kilimanjaro, Tanzania." *International Journal of African Historical Studies* 41, no. 3 (2008): 461–90.

———. "Irrigation among the Chagga in Kilimanjaro, Tanzania: The Organisation of Mfongo Irrigation." In *Shared Waters, Shared Opportunities*:

Hydropolitics in East Africa, edited by Bernard Calas and Mumma Martinon, 235–60. Dar es Salaam: Mkuki na Nyota, 2010.

——. "Social and Cultural Dimensions of Irrigation Management in Kilimanjaro." In *Culture, History, and Identity: Landscapes on Inhabitation in the Mount Kilimanjaro Area, Tanzania*, edited by Timothy A. R. Clack, 89–105. British Archaeological Reports International Series, no. 1966. Oxford: Archaeopress, 2009.

——. "Studies of the Waterscape of Kilimanjaro, Tanzania: Water Management in Hill Furrow Irrigation." PhD thesis, Norwegian University of Science and Technology, 2010.

Tagseth, Mattias and Haakon Lein. "Competing Models of Water Resource Management and Their Implications Using the Example of Pangani River Basin in Tanzania." In *Shared Waters, Shared Opportunities: Hydropolitics in East Africa*, edited by Bernard Calas and Mumma Martinon, 19–36. Dar es Salaam: Mkuki na Nyota, 2010.

"Tanganyika: Look What We Can Do!" *Time*, August 25, 1958.

Tanzania African National Union. *The Arusha Declaration and TANU's Policy on Socialism and Self-Reliance.* Dar es Salaam: Government of Tanzania, 1967.

Tanzania National Bureau of Statistics. *Census 1978.* Dar es Salaam: National Bureau of Statistics, 1979.

Tanzania National Parks / African Wildlife Foundation. *Kilimanjaro National Park.* Arusha: Tanzania National Parks, July 1987.

Tawney, J. "Election in Tanganyika." *Corona* 4, no. 5 (1952): 181–83.

Teale, E. O. and C. Gillman. *Report on the Investigation of the Proper Control of Water and the Reorganization of Water Boards in the Northern Province of Tanganyika Territory, November–December 1934.* Dar es Salaam: Government Printer of Tanganyika, 1935.

Tesch, Johannes. *Kolonial-Handels-Adressbuch.* Berlin: W. Süsserott, 1914.

Temu, A. *British Protestant Missions.* London: Longman, 1972.

Thompson, John. *Drawers of Water II: 30 Years of Change in Domestic Water Use and Environmental Health in East Africa.* London: International Institute for Environment and Development, 2001.

Thompson, L. G. "Climate Change: The Evidence and Our Options." *The Behavior Analyst* 33, no. 2 (2010): 153–70.

Thompson, L. G, H. H. Brecher, E. Mosley-Thompson, D. R. Hardy, and B. G. Mark. "Glacier Loss on Kilimanjaro Continues Unabated." *Proceedings of the National Academy of Sciences of the United States of America* 106, no. 47 (2009): 19770–75.

Thompson, L. G., E. Mosley-Thompson, M. E. Davis, K. A. Henderson, H. H. Brecher, V. S. Zagorodnov, T. A Mashiotta, et al. "Kilimanjaro Ice Records: Evidence of Holocene Climate Change in Tropical Africa." *Science* 298, no. 5593 (2002): 589–93.

Thompson, L. G., E. Mosley-Thompson, M.E. Davis, and K. Mountain. "A Paleoclimatic Perspective on the 21st Century Glacier Loss on Kilimanjaro." *Annals of Glaciology* 52, no. 59 (2011): 60–68.

Tilley, Helen. *Africa as a Living Laboratory: Empire, Development, and the Problem of Scientific Knowledge, 1870–1950*. Chicago: University of Chicago Press, 2011.

Tschannerl, Gerhard. "Rural Water-Supply in Tanzania: Is 'Politics' or 'Technique' in Command?" Paper no. 52, presented at the Annual Social Science Conference of the East African Universities, University of Dar es Salaam, Tanzania, June 6–9, 1973.

Twaddle, Michael. *Kakungulu and the Creation of Uganda*. Athens: Ohio University Press, 1993.

Ubwani, Zephania. "80 Percent of Kilimanjaro Snow Lost, Expert Says." *Citizen*, August 24, 2015.

United Nations Environment Programme. "Africa without Ice and Snow." *Environmental Development*, no. 5 (2013): 146–55.

——. *Sustainable Mountain Development in East Africa in a Changing Climate*, 2016.

United Republic of Tanzania. The Executive Summary of the Report on the Fifty Years of Independence of Tanzania Mainland, 1961–2011. Dar es Salaam: Government of Tanzania, 2011.

——. *National Water Policy, July 2002*. Dodoma: Government of Tanzania Ministry of Water and Livestock Development, 2002. Available at http://www.tawasanet.or.tz/files/Tanzania%20water%20policy%20-%202002.pdf.

——. *Second Five-Year Plan*. Dar es Salaam: Government of Tanzania, 1969.

——. *Tanzania National Development Vision, 2025*. Dar es Salaam: Government of Tanzania, 1997.

——. "Water." Accessed July 25, 2007. http://www.tanzania.go.tz/waterf.html.

Van Beusekom, Monica. *Negotiating Development: African Farmers and Colonial Experts at the Office du Niger, 1920–1960*. Portsmouth: Heinemann, 2002.

Van Koppen, Barbara, Andrew Tarimo, Emmanuel Manzungu, Aurelia van Eeden, and Philip Sumuni. "Winners and Losers of IWRM in Tanzania." *Water Alternatives* 9, no. 3 (2016): 588–607.

Vansina, Jan. *Oral Tradition: A Study in Historical Methodology*. London: Routledge, 1961.

Vavrus, Frances K. "'A Shadow of the Real Thing': Furrow Societies, Water User Associations, and Democratic Practices in the Kilimanjaro Region of Tanzania." *The Journal of African American History* 88, no. 4 (2003): 393–412.

Von Clemm, Michael. "Agricultural Productivity and Sentiment on Kilimanjaro." *Economic Botany* 18, no. 2 (1964): 99–121.

——. "People of the White Mountain: The Interdependence of Political and Economic Activity amongst the Chagga in Tanganyika with Special Reference to Recent Changes." PhD thesis, Oxford University, 1962.

Von der Decken, Karl Klaus. *Reisen in Ost-Afrika in den Jahren 1859 bis 1865.* Leipzig: C. F. Winter, 1869.

Walker, Reginald. *The Holy Ghost Fathers in Africa: A Century of Missionary Effort.* Dublin: Blackrock College, 1933.

Water for Life: Lessons Learnt from 15 Years of German Development Cooperation in the Kilimanjaro Region. Dar es Salaam: Embassy of the Federal Republic of Germany, 2007.

"Water Supply—Service to the Nation to Speed Development." *Tanzania Notes and Records,* no. 76 (1975): 191–92.

White, Gilbert, David Bradley, and Anne White. *Drawers of Water: Domestic Water Use in East Africa.* Chicago: University of Chicago Press, 1972.

White, Luise, Stephan Miescher, and David William Cohen. *African Words, African Voices: Critical Practices in Oral History.* Bloomington: Indiana University Press, 2002.

White, Richard. *The Organic Machine: The Remaking of the Columbia River.* New York: Hill and Wang, 1996.

Whitlamsmith, G. K. *Recent Trends in Chagga Political Development.* Moshi: KNCU, 1955.

Widgren, Mats. "Furrows in Africa—Canals in the Americas?" *Azania* 49, no. 4 (2014): 524–29.

Wimmelbücker, Ludger. *Kilimanjaro: A Regional History.* Münster: Lit Verlag, 2002.

Winter, J. Christoph. "Internal Classifications of Kilimanjaro Bantu Compared: Towards an East African Dialectometry." In *Dialectologiue en Afrique Noire,* edited by Gladys Guarisma and Suzanne Platiel, 101–32. Paris: Société d'Études Linguistiques et Anthropologiques de France, 1980.

Wittfogel, Karl. *Oriental Despotism: A Comparative Study of Total Power.* New Haven: Yale University Press, 1957.

World Bank. *Tanzania at the Turn of the Century: From Reforms to Sustained Growth and Poverty Reduction.* Washington, DC: World Bank, 2001.

Worster, Donald. *Rivers of Empire: Water, Aridity, and the Growth of the American West.* New York: Pantheon Books, 1985.

Wright, Marcia. *German Missions in Tanganyika, 1891–1941.* Oxford: Clarendon, 1971.

———. *Strategies of Slaves and Women: Life Stories from East/Central Africa.* New York: Lilian Barber, 1993.

Yeager, Rodger. *Tanzania: An African Experiment.* Boulder: Westview, 1982.

GOVERNMENT DOCUMENTS

Central Bureau of Statistics, United Republic of Tanzania. *Annual Reports,* vols. for 1968 and 1988.

League of Nations. *Mandate Agreement for Tanganyika.* July 1922.

Republic of Tanganyika. African Chiefs Ordinance (Repeal) Act, 1963.

Tanganyika Territory. *Annotated Ordinances.*

——. *Blue Books.* 1921–1948.
——. *Department of Water Development Annual Report, 1951.*
——. Native Authority Ordinance, 1921
——. Natural Water Supply Regulation Ordinance of 1923. No. 4 of 1923. *Annotated Ordinances, Tanganyika Territory, 1923.*
——. Natural Water Supply Ordinance.
——. Water Ordinance of 1948. No. 23 of 1948. *Annotated Ordinances, Tanganyika Territory, 1948.*
United Kingdom. Colonial Development and Welfare Act, 1940.
United Republic of Tanzania. Sera ya Maji (National Water Policy), 1991.
——. Water Utilization (Control and Regulation) Act. No. 42 of 1974.
United States. Climate Stewardship Act of 2003 (SB 139, 108th Cong., 1st sess.). 149 Congressional Record S13500 (daily ed. October 29, 2003).

Index

British administration (*cont'd*) independence of Tanganyika from, 182; laws and policies regarding water, 128–31, 175, 177–79; local water management and, 12, 28, 119–20; scientific knowledge of water, 131–34; wamangi and, 1–2, 135–38; water boards, establishment of, 128–29, 134–35

bureaucracy, 94–95, 225–26. *See also* Pangani Basin Water Office

canals. *See* mifongo
canal specialists. *See* meni mifongo
caravans, 73–74
cash crops: eleusine cultivation and, 157–60; German administration and, 95–96. *See also* coffee cultivation
ceremonies and rituals: cleansing, 58–59, 64; decline of, 151–52, 154–56; home construction, 51; initiation into adulthood, 62–64; mangi mkuu installation ceremony, 174; mbege and, 51–52; mifongo construction, 48, 101–2
cess on coffee, 174, 180
Chagga: Association, 172–73; Council, 116, 138; Day, 166, 180; Expansion Scheme, 170–71; nationalism, 166–67; Native Authority, 116, 135–36. *See also* peoples of Kilimanjaro
chiefs. *See* mangi mkuu (paramount chief); waitori (divisional chiefs); wamangi (chiefs)
chieftaincies: under British administration, 116; dissolution of hereditary, 184, 186, 197; structure of, 42, 184; trade and, 65–66
children: education of, 59–65, 148; malnutrition of, 204; water management and, 49–50, 60
Christianity, 151–56; baptism, 154–

55; God, 151–53. *See also* missions and missionaries
Church Missionary Society (CMS), 98. *See also* Holy Ghost Fathers; missions and missionaries
circumcision, 63–64
clans. *See* chieftaincies
climate change: aridity and deforestation, 241; glaciers of Kilimanjaro and, 236–42; global and local factors in, 248–51; Kilimanjaro as a symbol for, 230, 246; local knowledge about, 234–35, 242, 246–52; skeptics, 244–46; water scarcity and, 229
CMS (Church Missionary Society), 98. *See also* Holy Ghost Fathers; missions and missionaries
coffee cultivation, 103–4, 106, 159–60; eleusine cultivation and, 157–60; First World War and, 116; growth of, 122–24, 160; Lyamungu research station, 133, 158–59; prestige and, 162; Second World War and, 168; tax/cess on, 174, 180; Ujamaa and, 186, 203–4; water consumption for, 122–24
Colonial Development and Welfare Acts (1940 and 1945), 169; grants, 187, 189, 191–92
colonialism. *See* British administration; German administration; settlers
commodification of water, 4, 201; neoliberal reform and, 210, 214; water-right system and, 129
common law and water rights, 133
community engagement: in environmental conservation, 250; in mifongo maintenance, 48–49, 53–54; in modern water resource development, 210, 212–14, 222; under Ujamaa, 190–91. *See also* Integrated Water Resources Management (IWRM)

drinking water, 210, 254, 259. *See also* domestic water usage

droughts, 38, 111–12; British administration and, 120; irrigation and, 49, 52; spirituality and, 153–54; Tanganyika African National Union and, 187

dual legal system of water management, 129–30, 142, 175; end of, 208; water boards and, 129

Dublin Statement on Water and Sustainable Development, 212–13

Dundas, Charles, 20, 118

Dust Bowl, 126

duty of water, 132–33, 158

East Africa: aridity and climate change, 239–41; climate and geography, 2; German (*see* German administration); peoples of, 2, 70–75 (*see also* peoples of Kilimanjaro); population growth in twentieth century, 121; trade within, 73–75

East African Community, 204

economy of Tanzania, 186, 191, 199–00; decline of Ujamaa and, 203–6; tourism and, 234

Eden, Kilimanjaro as an, 67–69, 76

education: of children, 59–65, 148; primary schools, 146, 148, 202; Ujamaa and, 202; about water-related disease, 146

elections, 173–74

eleusine cultivation, 40–41; cash crops and, 157–60; decline of, 156–64; as harmful, 127, 157–58

elites, 172–73

Enciso, Martin Fernández de, 18

environmental conservation. *See* conservation, environmental

erosion, 126–27, 136–37

Europeans: settlers: adoption of local water management, 92–93, 108–10; explorers, 76–85; percep-

tions of Kilimanjaro's people, 118; perceptions of Kilimanjaro's waterscape, 4, 67–69, 76–78, 112–14; rethinking of Kilimanjaro's waterscape, 118–28. *See also* missions and missionaries

Evangelical Lutheran Mission of Leipzig. *See* Leipzig Mission

expeditions to Kilimanjaro, 76–85, 98–99. *See also* tourism

fables: Kibo and Mawenzi, 33–34; Ruwa's flood, 57–58; about watercourses, 60–61. *See also* adages

famines, 38, 111–12; under Ujamaa, 203

farming. *See* agriculture; coffee cultivation

finger millet. *See* eleusine cultivation

fire ants, 48, 270

fires, 241, 249

First World War, 114–16

fishing industry, 188

flood irrigation, 127, 157–59

floods, 57

foothills. *See* lowlands

foreign aid, 202, 207

Forstwissenschaft (German forestry science), 97–98

free water, policy of, 185–86, 189–90, 206–10

frostbite, 75

fuli and kisiye (rainy seasons); agriculture and, 40, 49; mifongo and, 53

Genesis, book of, 57, 153

German administration: laws and policies regarding water, 92–93, 96, 114; missionaries and, 99–00; resistance to, 94–95; wamangi and, 93–96

glaciers of Kilimanjaro, 16, 35–36;

aridity, global warming, and, 238–40; European explorers and, 86–87, 235–36; ice cores of, 237–38; local knowledge about, 234–35, 242, 246–52; shrinking of, 234–52; surveys of, 235–38; as a symbol for climate change, 230, 242–43; water supply and, 36, 231, 234–35, 239–41

global warming, 238–40, 252

God, 151–53; water as a gift from, 217–19

Gommenginger, Auguste, 98–99, 101, 154

Gore, Al, 230

government canals, 175–76

gravity-flow water pipelines. *See* pipelines

Greeks, 105–6

Greenpeace, 243

Gutmann, Bruno, 20

hail. *See* precipitation

Hai region, 169–70; infrastructure of, 221–22; waterscapes of, 37

harm, language of, 10–11, 145–51; eleusine cultivation and, 127, 157–58; as a political tool, 29, 157–58; spirituality and, 43–44, 147

Hegel, Georg Wilhelm Friedrich, 75–76

Hemingway, Ernest, 232–33

high modernism, 167. *See also* Ujamaa

Hoag, Heather, 7, 9

Holy Ghost Fathers, 98–00, 151; expulsion due to war, 115. *See also* missions and missionaries

homesteads. *See* vihamba

Humplick, Vincent, 108–10

hydraulic societies, 6, 35

hydroelectric power, 16–17, 125, 216; Nyumba ya Mungu Dam and, 188

hygiene, 122, 149–50; Western ideals of, 145

ice cores of glaciers, 237–38

illegal water abstractions, 138–40, 217, 223–24; wamangi and, 140

illiteracy, 202

imagined geographies, 69, 76–77. *See also* Europeans: perceptions of Kilimanjaro's waterscape

An Inconvenient Truth, 230, 239

independence of Tanganyika, 182

India, 6

indirect rule, 116, 133

infrastructure development: cost-sharing model of, 175; by German administration, 95–96; by missions, 100–102; rural, 185–86, 190–95, 202, 222–24, 227; under Ujamaa, 185–96

initiation practices, 62–64; decline of, 154–56

Integrated Water Resources Management (IWRM), 31, 200–201, 213–14, 221–27

international development agencies, 192, 202, 216, 221–24

International Monetary Fund (IMF), 200, 205

interviews, 23–25

iron ring of settlement, 107, 278

irrigation, 1–2, 52; canals (*see* mifongo); of coffee, 122–24, 159–60; droughts and, 49, 52; duty of water, 132–33; of Europeans' crops, 122; flood, 127, 157–59; of foothills and lowlands, 170–71, 175–76, 180; initiation and, 62; large-scale, 124–25; patterns, changes in, 195; pipelines and, 179–80; prohibition on, 191; timetables, 54

ivory trade, 72–73

IWRM (Integrated Water Resources Management), 31, 200–201, 213–14, 221–27

Jagga. *See* Kilimanjaro; peoples of
Kilimanjaro
Johnston, Harry, 82–85
journals of missionaries, 22

Kaser, Georg, 239–40
KCCU (Kilimanjaro Chagga Citizens
Union), 173–74
Kenya, 204, 233
Kibo, 16, 113; in fables, 33–34; ice
cap of (*see* glaciers of Kilimanjaro); spirituality and, 34; Tanganyika independence and, 182–83
Kikwete, Jakaya, 244
Kilimanjaro: Kibo: average rainfall
by region, 37, 46; climate and
geography, 15–17; expeditions
to, 76–85, 98–99; Forest Reserve,
97, 233; nationalism and, 182–83,
186–87, 232; origin of name,
71–72, 74; outsiders' perceptions
of, 67–69, 67–75, 90, 232; peoples
of (*see* peoples of Kilimanjaro); in
popular culture, 87–89, 182–83,
230, 232–33; rivers of, 16–17, 37;
as a trading hub, 73–74; Ujamaa
and, 187–95, 203–4; waterscapes
of, 15–18, 35–38. *See also* glaciers
of Kilimanjaro
Kilimanjaro and Its People, 118
Kilimanjaro Chagga Citizens Union
(KCCU), 173–74
Kilimanjaro Native Cooperative
Union (KNCU), 158–60, 204
Kilimanjaro Native Planters Association (KNPA), 122, 140
Kilimanjaro Planters Association,
124
"Kilima-Njaro" (Taylor), 88–89
Kiliwater Ltd., 223–24
Kimashuku canal, 175–76
kisiye. *See* fuli and kisiye (rainy

seasons)
KNCU (Kilimanjaro Native Cooperative Union), 158–60, 204
knowledge about water: adaptation of
new, 145–65; local politics and, 3;
modern/scientific vs. traditional/
local, 13–14, 195–98, 219–21;
scientific, 131–35, 138
KNPA (Kilimanjaro Native Planters
Association), 122, 140
Krapf, J. Ludwig, 77, 87–88

labor-card system, 96
lakes, 188
land: scarcity, 161, 170–72. *See
also* alienation of
languages, 39
laws and policies regarding water:
British administration, 128–31,
175, 177–79; free-water policy,
206–10; German administration,
92–93, 96, 114; neoliberal National Water Policy, 210–15; Ujamaa,
185–86, 189–90, 208. *See also* dual
legal system of water management
League of Nations, 116, 169
Leipzig Mission, 99–00, 151; expulsion due to war, 115, 168. *See
also* missions and missionaries
Le Roy, Alexandre, 20, 98
Les Pères du Saint-Esprit, 98–00, 151;
expulsion due to war, 115. *See
also* missions and missionaries
Lettow-Vorbeck, Paul von, 114–15
life-expectancy rates, 185
literacy, 202
livestock, 52, 70, 179
local engagement. *See* community
engagement; Integrated Water
Resources Management (IWRM)
local knowledge: of climate change,
234–35, 242, 246–52; of water
management, 44–56
lowlands: farmland (shamba), 40,

194; irrigation, 170–72, 175–76, 180, 188; mountain peoples' perceptions of, 43, 56–57. *See also* steppe

Lyamungu coffee research station, 133, 158–59

Maasai, 2, 56, 71–73
mafundi (skilled craftsmen), 109–10, 190, 209
maize, 160, 203
Maji Maji uprising, 96, 106
MAJI (Ministry of Water), 208
malaria, 79
malnutrition, 204
management of water, 3–5; British administration vs. local, 12, 28, 119–20; centralization of, 167–68, 175–79, 185–86, 190; decentralization of, 3, 18, 34–35, 66; European missionaries and settlers and, 92; in highlands vs. lowlands, 30–31; local, 44–56; modern/scientific vs. traditional/local, 4–5, 119, 190–92; spiritual, 56–59; Tanzanian government and, 4–5, 175–79; women's role in, 49–50, 149, 192, 212, 214
mangi mkuu (paramount chief), 172–74, 179
manufacturing, 204
Marealle (mangi of Marangu; grandfather of Thomas), 94–95
Marealle, Petro Itosi (mangi of Marangu), 143, 173
Marealle, Thomas (mangi mkuu), 29–30, 166, 179–82; as a celebrity, 180–81; election of, 173–74
Mawenzi, 16; in fables, 33–34. *See also* Kibo; Kilimanjaro
mbege (beer), 40; changing social importance of, 162–64; as currency, 51; morality and, 157–58; rituals and, 51–52; shops, 162–63

Meli (mangi of Moshi), 94–95, 98
meni mifongo (canal specialists), 11, 49, 147, 187; decline of, 138, 196; duties, 52–54; missionaries and, 105; wamangi and, 1–2, 138
Meyer, Hans, 76, 85–87, 235
midwives, 148–49
mifongo (irrigation canals), 187, 263; bylaws, 55; construction, 45, 48–49, 101–2; decline of, 195; Europeans' use of, 92–93, 100–102, 108–10; government, 175–76; history, 45; illegal, 138–40, 217; maintenance, 53–54, 63–64; pipelines vs., 190–91, 193–97; as prodigal, 126–27, 201; purpose, 49; rainy seasons and, 53; registration of, 139, 178–79, 217; scientific knowledge and, 132; societies, 35, 135, 196–97, 201, 217–19; spirituality and, 52–53, 147
millet. *See* eleusine cultivation
Ministry of Water (MAJI), 208
missions and missionaries; American Augustana Lutheran order, 115, 168; Church Missionary Society (CMS), 98; conversion attempts, 100; expeditions of, 77–80; First World War and, 115–16; German administration and, 99–00; Holy Ghost Fathers, 98–00, 115, 151; journals of, 22; Leipzig Mission, 99–00, 115, 151, 168; new knowledge, introduction of, 150–56; schools, 122, 150; Second World War and, 168; social status of, 104–5, 151; wamangi and, 100–102
Mkapa, Benjamin, 206
montane areas, 16, 36–38; Rombo region; Vunjo region. *See also* Hai region
morality, 57; mbege and, 157–58. *See also* fables
Moshi Water Board, 120, 129–30

scholarship about: integrating new knowledge, 13–15, 144; power and science, 13–14; water, 5–8

schools: mission, 122, 150; primary, 146, 148, 202

Schutztruppe (German colonial army), 94–95

scientists: climate change, glaciers, and, 236–42, 245; colonial, 120, 126, 131–34, 157; debate over snow on Kilimanjaro, 87–89; as explorers, 85–87

Scramble for Africa, 81–82, 85

scrubland (nyika), 73

Second World War, 168–72

settlers, 105–10; diversity of, 106; First World War and, 115; iron ring of, 107, 278; Second World War and, 168; Ujamaa and, 184

shamba (foothill farmlands), 40, 194

Sina (mangi of Kibosho), 94, 102

sisal cultivation, 124–25

sky islands, 16, 265

slavery, 73, 75

sluice gates, 217–19. See also theft of water

snow. See precipitation

"The Snows of Kilimanjaro" (Hemingway), 232–33

socialism. See Ujamaa

soil conservation, 1, 97, 126–27, 136–37

songs, 50, 63

specialists: agricultural officers, 137, 158; consolidation of state power and, 13–14, 29, 119; health officers, 147–49; mafundi (skilled craftsmen), 109–10, 190, 209; modern, 191, 215; wamasya (spirit diviners), 43–44, 58–59, 145. See also meni mifongo; rainmakers

spirits (waruma), 43–44, 58

spirituality, 43–44, 56–65; Christianity, transition to, 151–56; droughts and, 153–54; harm and, 43–44,

147; Kibo and, 34; management of water, 56–59; mifongo and, 52–53; new knowledge and, 145, 151, 156

stamps, 183

steppe, 80; Kilimanjaro in contrast to, 38, 56–57, 82–83, 86; mountain peoples' perceptions of, 43, 56–57; peoples of, 70–71

sugar cultivation, 124

surveys; German administration land, 105; of glaciers, 235–38; hydrologic, 132; mfongo construction and land, 48; of mifongo (British era), 139, 141

Swahili people, 73–75, 232

Swyngedouw, Erik, 9–10

Taita Hills, 16, 70–72

Tanganyika African National Union (TANU), 166–67, 180–82, 207–8; Kilimanjaro and, 186–87, 196–98; local chapters of, 186, 197

Tanganyika Electric Supply Company (TANESCO), 125, 176

Tanganyika Territory (1916–61); formation of, 116; independence from Britain, 182; as a trust territory, 169

Tanzania (1964–): formation of, 182; nationalism, 166–67; political system of, 184. See also economy of Tanzania; neoliberalism; Ujamaa

Tanzania National Development Vision, 2025, 206

taxes, 96, 214

Taylor, Bayard, 88–89

teachers, 147–48

Teale-Gillman report, 131–33

technocratic water management, 178–79, 219–20. See also Pangani Basin Water Office

theft of water, 176, 201, 222, 223

Thompson, Lonnie, 237–40, 245

Time, 180